# Towards Integration:
# Comprehensive Services for
# People with Mental Handicaps

*Editor*

**David Sines** BSC (HONS) RMN RNMH

Director of Nursing and Operational
Services (Mental Handicap), Winchester
Health Authority

**Harper & Row Publishers London**
Cambridge Mexico City New York
San Francisco São Paulo Singapore Sydney
Philadelphia

Copyright © 1988. Editorial and selection material © David Sines.
Individual chapters © as credited.

First published 1988

Harper & Row Ltd
Middlesex House
34–42 Cleveland Street
London W1P 5FB

British Library Cataloguing in Publication Data
Sines, David
Towards Integration.
    1. Great Britain. Mentally handicapped patients. Nursing
    I. Title
    610.73'68'0941

ISBN 0-06-318403-6

Typeset by Inforum Ltd, Portsmouth
Printed and bound by Butler & Tanner Ltd, Frome and London

# CONTENTS

# List of Contributors

**Roy Bailey**
Consultant Psychologist and Visiting Professor in Managerial Psychology, International Management Centre, Buckingham

**Joan Bicknell**
Head of Department of Psychiatry and Professor of the Psychiatry of Mental Handicap, St George's Hospital Medical School, London

**Marion Cornick**
Assistant Director (Education), Head of Further, Continuing and Adult Education, Ravenswood Foundation

**Owen Cooper**
Officer-in-Charge, Second Network, Bolton Neighbourhood Network Scheme

**Felicity Lefevre**
Staff Development Officer, Buckingham Social Services Department

**Connie Flight**
Senior Nurse Manager (Residential Services), Winchester Health Authority

**Rob Hancock**
Deputy Head of Education, Suhar David Centre of Continuing Education, Ravenswood Foundation

**Ken Moore**
Senior Nurse Community, Winchester Health Authority

**David Sines**
Director of Nursing and Operational Services (Mental Handicap), Winchester Health Authority

**Mike Snell**
Vice-Principal, Bracknell College of Further Education

**Paul Taylor**
Principal Officer (Mental Handicap Development Team) and Project Co-ordinator, Bolton Neighbourhood Network Scheme

**Peter Wilcock**
District Psychologist, Winchester Health Authority

**Diane Worsley**
Administrator/Social Worker at Kilmore House, The Ockenden Venture, Camberley, Surrey

# Foreword

This is an informative and very positive book. It starts from the premise not that comprehensive services have been achieved but that they are achievable. Why the optimism when so many people with a mental handicap and their families are still waiting for much heralded community care and, in particular, for the supports which would make it possible to enjoy a more ordinary life?

The reason is that the contributors themselves have had direct personal experience and involvement in establishing one or more key elements in a comprehensive service. It is therefore possible for them to have a vision of what such a service – that is flexible, that is based on individual needs, and that does include those with the most severe disabilities – should look like. It puts them in a good position to argue persuasively the benefits, and to describe how such a service might be implemented. It is an essentially practical book which could have been subtitled 'making it work'. It is written in a common sense manner, with useful listings of key points.

Its main themes are familiar but important ones. It is *we* who have to change rather than people with a mental handicap (Paul Williams has spoken eloquently about our 'mutual handicap'). We must become more conscious of the powerful negative images which serve to maintain our prejudices, and the low status of people with a mental handicap in our society. We must begin to take more seriously the issue of choice and personal relationships, and to offer both greater opportunities and better support. These central themes along with the need to invest in people –

both paid and informal carers rather than buildings – come through strongly in many chapters.

The book starts with an eloquent statement about the importance of self-advocacy and citizen advocacy, and ends with a plea for a clear understanding of our own values, and the need to build our service around consumers' wishes.

Derek Thomas
Director
National Development Team

# Acknowledgements

The contributors wish to thank the following people for permission to reproduce material:

To Mr Steve Dowson, Director of the Campaign for the Mentally Handicapped for kindly agreeing for a diagram to be reproduced as Figure 2.1.

To Dr M. Shackleton-Bailey and Hampshire Social Services for kind permission to reproduce their Core and Satellite Model as Figure 6.1.

To Dr Philip Seed and Costello Publishers for kind permission to reproduce material in Table 6.1.

To Mr David Towell, Mr Ritchart Brazil and the King's Fund Centre for kindly agreeing for a diagram to be reproduced as Figure 7.1.

# Introduction

## SETTING THE SCENE

A large number of policy documents have emerged from government departments since 1980. Overall, the concern is to break the traditional dependence on institutional care, to provide a range of services in the community and to support mentally handicapped people living at home. Individualised treatment and care plans, normalisation of daily life and support for carers are major themes – so too are respecting people's rights and choices, and keeping children in particular out of statutory care. The *All Wales Strategy*, one of the recent documents, is notable for its insistence on Social Services involvement, on mentally handicapped people making use of the same health and educational facilities as others, and on the reorientation of a wide range of staff. Community Mental Handicap Teams with community nurses and social workers as core members are envisaged in many regional plans. 'Core and Cluster' models of residential care are frequent. The continuance of special needs groups, e.g. people with multiple and profound handicaps, is stressed, but joint planning and collaboration with local authorities and voluntary associations in new community services is also emphasised. . . . Joint and shared training is very likely to be developed considerably and to make an important contribution to effective team working in the community.[1]

The opening quotation for this book summarizes many of the key factors to be considered by all people involved in the provision of comprehensive services for people with mental handicaps and their families. There is no doubt that the pace of change involved in the design and implementation of local services has required a radical and sometimes traumatic revision of personal attitudes and in many areas has involved the creation of new structures, processes and service systems.

This book considers some of the main questions to be addressed in the design and introduction of comprehensive services for people with mental handicaps and presents some of the experiences and theories that people have shared and learnt from local practice and implementation. In doing so there will be, inevitably, some overlap between individual contributions and certainly differences in the way in which people have approached local intitiatives and challenges.

It is suggested that there is no one answer to the pattern of service design for this or for any client group and wherever possible the authors have deliberately avoided the prescription of standard models. However, the book presents many ideas and suggestions for the introduction of sound infra-structures for all human-based services in the community.

The book is divided into four sections, each concerned with one of the following themes:

- Service design and service systems;
- The implementation of comprehensive services and their nature;
- The management of small houses and their maintenance to assure quality;
- Meeting the needs of carers.

In Chapter 1 Mike Snell introduces one of the main themes which appears throughout the book – the importance of consumer involvement in all aspects of service design and implementation. The importance of advocacy and consumerism is emphasized, the arrogance of professionalism challenged and the role of the voluntary sector explored. David Sines continues this theme in Chapter 2 through the presentation of a recurrent theme to which all contributors refer – the core principles involved in the maintenance of 'an ordinary lifestyle'. The importance of individual choice, opportunities, rights and responsibilities are discussed within the context of a person's life within the community.

In Chapter 3 Peter Wilcock recommends the introduction of life-planning systems and describes some of the ways in which traditional assessment techniques have been replaced by more purposeful and challenging methods of attempting to understand people's needs and responses in ordinary life settings. Ken Moore describes the role of community specialists as facilitating access to local support networks in the local neighbourhoods in Chapter 4.

The recognition that effective service delivery will depend, in part, on the successful co-ordination of manpower resources is provided in Chapter 5 by Professor Joan Bicknell, who discusses the importance of introducing teambuilding strategies in the community. The first section on service design and service systems is completed by·Rob Hancock in

Chapter 6 in his presentation on the core elements of providing meaning-ful daily activities in nontraditional settings. This chapter demonstrates the complexity of service design and the necessity for effective co-ordination with a variety of agencies, resources and skills in order to provide meaningful opportunities for people with mental handicaps.

Section Two commences with a general introduction to the compo-nents of comprehensive service design and describes the nature of local services. David Sines in Chapter 7 presents an overview of services and emphasizes the importance of inter-agency co-operation in partnership with consumers. In Chapter 8 Connie Flight relates her own experiences in Winchester and offers some practical guidance to others in respect of the processes involved in the establishment of small houses in the community for people with severe learning difficulties. A number of appendices are included as examples for use in local services.

It is acknowledged that children and older people with mental handi-caps may have additional needs which may not be realized easily in comprehensive services which are primarily designed for adults during the more active years of their lives. Diane Worsley describes the specific needs of children in Chapter 9 and suggests that a variety of options be made available to children and their families locally both in respect of residential services and family support facilities. In Chapter 10 Marion Cornick turns her attention to the needs of elderly people and considers their needs within comprehensive services and within the wider context of societal attitudes to ageing.

The management of small houses in the community is for many a new concept and presents consumers and their carers with opportunities to create and design new structures and processes to assure both effective service delivery and quality of life. In Chapter 11 Paul Taylor and Owen Cooper describe some of their experiences in Bolton with the Bolton Neighbourhood Network Scheme in respect of the commissioning and management of local services. This chapter provides an alternative approach to local service design to that provided by Connie Flight (see Chapter 8) and illustrates the importance and success that may be achieved by inter-agency co-operation in local project design.

In Chapter 12 David Sines challenges local services and their managers to ensure that opportunities are provided to monitor the effect of their services in respect of the impact they have on the lives of their consumers. Suggestions for monitoring the quality of service quality are presented and a description of several quality measurement initiatives are de-scribed.

In the final section emphasis turns to the needs of carers who provide

consumers with what many would regard as their most important resource. In Chapter 13 Roy Bailey describes the importance of providing
staff with opportunities to share their concerns and sucesses and thus
reduce their own frustrations and stress levels. Several causes of stress are
described and various suggestions presented for their alleviation in a
rapidly evolving and changing service which presents some staff with
difficulties in adapting to new demands and working conditions.

Felicity Lefevre and Roy Bailey consider the importance of staff –
preparation, skill acquisition and personal development – in Chapter 14.
They consider the importance of ensuring that staff are adequately
prepared to work in local services, and that each person receives adequate and relevant in-service training to develop them as individuals and
to provide them with the skills and confidence to enhance the quality of
life for people living in the house. The need to challenge traditional
approaches to intra-professional training is emphasized and opportunities for shared training presented.

The book ends with a summary of some of the more important
recommendations which should be considered in the design, implementation and realization of comprehensive services for people with mental
handicaps and their families in the community.

Within any attempt to describe the bases of comprehensive services
there will always exist a temptation to capitalize on the experiences of
others who have pioneered local services. It is as the result of many
requests for information regarding the way in which my own authority has
succeeded in closing its hospital and commenced on the long road
towards realizing the objectives of a consumer-related service that this
book was written. Contributors were selected for their own experiences,
personal backgrounds and for their own commitment to local service
design. Many who have realized the introduction of local services will
recognize common elements to their own experiences as they read this
book, and this is of course the intention.

It is our understanding that the true success of a consumer-led model of
comprehensive service design will depend on the individual contributions
of local people who have a 'stake' in the service – not least the consumers.
Some may challenge the 'realism' of our suggestions, hypotheses and
recommendations, but there is one statement which cannot be contested
– they are all feasible and are happening at the present time following the
commitment, inspiration and confidence of the main service providers. It
is our hope that readers will inspire confidence from our enthusiasm and

review their services and build on their own successes.

David Sines

# REFERENCES

1. UKCC (1986) *Facing the Future: UKCC Project 2000*, paper no. 6, p. 16 ('Care for Mentally Handicapped People'), United Kingdom Central Council for Nursing, Midwifery and Health Visiting, London.

# Section One: Designing Service Systems to Meet Individual Needs

# 1. Putting People First
*Mike Snell*

## INTRODUCTION

In April 1974 the second of our four daughters was born. The elation which rightly and naturally accompanies such an event was short-lived when the doctors told us that Jessica was mentally handicapped. Her condition was Down's syndrome; it meant, we were told, that she would not develop normally and would need constant care and attention. The prognosis was not particularly hopeful: such children often suffered from associated deficiencies which could be life-endangering. Later, our GP 'comforted' us by suggesting that survival rates beyond the age of eight were not high. A local, well-meaning and, as judged by the hospital authorities, appropriately intellectual couple with a similarly handicapped child, descended armed with sympathy and an array of articles, pamphlets and medical texts designed to feed our curiosity and overcome ignorance.

The first years were not difficult, although I have no clear recollection of the early months. We received much encouragement from friends and relations but no formal training. Jessica became very much a part of the family which at first instinctively rejected her. She attended playschool – but only as a favour – and there was never any question that she would ultimately attend any other school than a special school. This she did, collected each morning at first by taxi and eventually by mini-bus, and returned each day to the bosom of the family.

Thirteen years on and now in a different locality, little seems to have changed in this routine. Jessica continues to travel by mini-bus to a segregated school, returning each day to take her special place in family life. But things are not the same. Jessica has survived the initial medical prognosis – she is healthy and pleased with many aspects of her life. The plans which we began to make for her only five years ago are now the subject of tense re-examination. An early acceptance that she would at some time have to be taken into long-term care is now challenged by internal doubts and a society which declares that normalization as part of the community is every person's birth-right, including or perhaps especially for people with a mental handicap.

Our assumptions about what is good for Jessica are now reinterpreted as parental over-protection – the image of a quiet place in the country, tending the animals and tilling the soil has more perhaps to do with our perceptions of the 'right' kind of life than meeting the wants of the individual concerned. But, as this brief and almost caricatured cameo of a mentally handicapped child's first 13 years illustrates, how else are the individual's wants and needs to be explained other than through the eyes of parents, doctors, health and social workers and teachers? What stimulus exists to place self-determination at the centre of the stage? The medical model of handicap places emphasis on the diagnosis of condition, the attachment of an appropriate label and the identification of suitable treatment. This is a self-perpetuating model of scientific observation which provides a playground of opportunity for professional decision-making. The role adopted by most parents falls into two categories – the protective and the advocatory: protection from a cruel society and advocacy for a cause against the impersonal professional and the bureaucrat. The process conspires at every turn not simply to deny individual rights but to prevent them from appearing on the agenda.

Like many parents, I have in the past been actively involved in the affairs of a voluntary society. This activity has included representation on a wide variety of committees, including those which represent consumer interests in local government and the health and social services. In 1982 the local society in which I played a working part gave birth to a project designed to habilitate four people from a local hostel into a council house allocated by the local district council. In the course of preparing this contribution I have had occasion to look back over the notes of the numerous meetings which were necessary to bring the project to fruition. These notes date back to the earliest recorded mentions of the idea, at local society meetings which regularly staggered on into the night. Important contributions were made by the manager of the local adult training centre who perceived acute accommodation problems for a number of his clients whose parents were ageing and unlikely to be able to provide much longer for their offspring.

The germ of an idea was taken on by parent professionals and a season of intense lobbying and pressure group activity eventually won the great prize – acceptance on the part of the social services department of the project and the offer of a council house from the district council. Suitable candidates were chosen – there were many and intensive meetings to discuss the choice; the question of compatibility, the temperament of each prospective resident, the advisability of mixing sexes, the need for a period of relevant training and transition. (How well I remember the skill gap when they finally moved in, our failure to tailor the training to the environment in which they were going to live.)

The tenants moved in. The society decorated and furnished the house with funds especially raised for the purpose. I became what I now understand to be an advocate – as I then saw it, I was keeping an eye on cleanliness, ensuring the grass was cut, that the milkman had been paid and that there was sufficient rent money. We sat and talked; the residents particularly liked it when I brought my small children to the house. Adult evening classes were arranged with a local adult institute, but transport proved a problem. There were what we termed 'teething troubles'; some incompatibility which led to periods of resettlement in the hostel. But these were largely overcome. I moved from the locality, other helpers and befrienders took over, and the project passed out of my experience.

As I now look back, it is not without some sense of achievement – the people concerned are still settled in their home. But the project model was not dissimilar from that which describes my daughter's experience. The decisions were made for people in their best interests – often as a result of heated debates between different professional groups. Hardly at all were the residents themselves involved in the process. The question of self-determination, self-advocacy, did not arise. This does not surprise me. The volunteers were in no sense trained for the job – in many respects our experience was positively unhelpful, based as it was upon years of bringing up children with a mental handicap. Neither were we well-equipped to handle relationships with practising professionals. Again, our experience could be described as counterproductive – battle-scarred individuals who had all fought in the corridors of County Hall or the consultant's waiting room.

This contribution might therefore be considered important in at least two respects; first, it arises out of personal experience as a parent (and must be read with that knowledge); second, it is placed at the beginning of a text which gathers together the combined wisdom and experience of a range of professionals whose daily lives are involved with people with a mental handicap. Together, these two groups have been largely responsible for the definition and practical meaning of the term 'special', particularly as it relates to the concept of mental handicap. It might be said that the moral framework within which these groups have operated has been one of benevolent humanitarianism, a concept which has been examined by, among others, Tomlinson.[1] The extent to which this ideology can lead to a harsh, barren and rigid regime of professional dogma and, in many cases despair, has been movingly documented by Ryan and Thomas:[2]

> Many people in the state institutions are attracted to working with mentally handicapped people from some kind of moral conviction: a desire to help, sympathy with the oppressed, guilt at their own advantages; and from some perception that all is not right with the world. . . The professional and hierarchical world of the hospital does very little to encourage the ideas and enthusiasm that motivate many of its staff initially, and it often makes life very difficult for staff who do persist with their original perceptions
>
> (Ryan and Thomas, p.151)

There are many instances of personal statements by parents which show how instinctive protectiveness of a disabled child leads ultimately to over-dependence and stunted relationships.

The placing of a statement which focuses on the concept of advocacy, and specifically self-advocacy, at the beginning of such a text bears some testimony to the intention of putting people first. There can be no doubt that the major strides now being made in the development of techniques of self-advocacy are the only foundation for ultimate success of care in the community. Without it, the concept will inevitably become a poor replica of the institutional models of care with which we are all so familiar and dissatisfied.

The aim of this chapter is to explore briefly the concept of advocacy in its various forms and to give some practical indications of the contribution which it can make to genuine consumer participation in service planning and delivery. Advocacy is not an easy concept to assimilate and it is even more difficult to put into practice – it requires training for all participants, both for the necessary skills to be acquired and for necessary changes in attitude to be achieved. Working materials are now coming forward, produced by those who have pioneered in this field. Reference is made to these in the bibliography to which the reader is directed. The real test, however, for the practising professional will be his or her commitment, through the acquisition of knowledge and skills, to the full interpretation of the principles.

## ADVOCACY

In 1975 the General Assembly adopted the United Nations Declaration on the Rights of Disabled Persons.[3] This followed an earlier declaration in 1971 on the Rights of Mentally Retarded Persons.[4] The clauses of the later document, which the United Kingdom co-sponsored, include the following:

- Disabled persons have the inherent right to respect for their human dignity . . . (they) have the same fundamental rights as their fellow-citizens of the same age . . .
- (they) have the same civil and political rights as other human beings . . .
- (they) are entitled to the measures designed to enable them to become as self-reliant as possible.

Such statements, which are now beginning to be enshrined in statute by member states, give rise to the word 'advocate'. A definition provided by the *Oxford English Dictionary* is: 'one who pleads for another; one who speaks on behalf of . . .'

As has already been suggested, until recently advocacy has implied an exclusive role for parents and professionals. Advances, initially by people with physical and sensory handicaps, have required a clearer categorization of the term. Guidelines on the implementation of the United Nations Declaration have been published by the International League for Societies for Persons with Mental Handicap, whose declaration recognizes three forms of advocacy:[5]

- Lay advocacy (originally known in the USA as citizen advocacy) refers to the persuasive and supportive activities of trained, selected and co-ordinated people. Working on a one-to-one or group basis, they attempt to foster respect for human rights and dignity. This may involve giving voice to the individual's personal concerns and aspirations, seeing that everyday social, recreational, health and related services are provided and other practical and emotional support.
- Self-advocacy involves persons with handicaps asserting their own rights, expressing their needs and concerns and assuming the duties of

citizenship which assist members to acquire the necessary training and skills and experience to participate more fully in their communities.

- Legal advocacy is a term to describe the broad range of methods and activities by which lawyers and other skilled individuals help mentally handicapped and mentally ill people to defend their rights. This can include reform or creation of new laws, as well as formal representation (e.g. at mental health review tribunals or supplementary benefit tribunals) and information activities to publicise the cause. Casework, negotiation, education and training, individual representation, and studying the way laws and regulations are compiled with, may be involved.

(As this was being written, all three definitions were glaringly brought to the public eye by the case of a mentally handicapped woman whose sterilization was legally endorsed by the High Court, on the initial recommendation of the local authority in whose care she was.)

## Lay advocacy

'An ordinary citizen develops a relationship with another person who risks social exclusion or other unfair treatment because of a handicap. As the relationship develops, the advocate chooses ways to understand, respond to, and represent the other person's interests as if they were the advocate's own.'[6]

Before 1981 a number of advocacy services existed and remain today:

- The 1959 Mental Health Act included a section on guardianship, whereby a local authority or private individual is able to act as a guardian for mentally disordered patients. This clearly contains elements of 'speaking on behalf of' but the emphasis is one of control.
- Statutory and non-statutory bodies act in a variety of situations on behalf of mentally handicapped people. Community health councils (CHCs) may take up individual cases which could ultimately find their way to the offices of the Health Service Commissioner. Voluntary organizations, e.g. the Royal National Society for Mentally Handicapped Children and Adults (MENCAP), provide a range of advisory and befriending services both at national and local level; in addition, many hospitals have well-established voluntary service support systems.
- Professionals, from the health, social services, education and voluntary sectors (professionals employed by voluntary organizations as

opposed to the lay members) provide dedicated help, support and advice as part of their day-to-day commitment to the people in their care.

None of these makes a special place for advocacy and there are real obstacles to its implementation, not least conflict of interest and difficulty of access.

In 1981, as part of the International Year of Disabled People, a pilot project for resident advocacy in three mental handicap hospitals in England was established jointly by One-to-One, MENCAP, the Spastic's Society, MIND and the Leonard Cheshire Foundation. Advocacy Alliance, as the project was named, presents a good model of lay advocacy and its experiences so far are a useful starting point to examine both the potential and problems of such an initiative. The incentive for lay advocacy arose from dissatisfaction largely associated with longstay hospitals for mentally handicapped people. However, there is no reason to suggest that the model cannot be transferred to care in the community. Given the increasing trend towards relocation within the community in small units of even the most profoundly handicapped people, some would argue that it will have to be.

A detailed examination of the practical issues raised by Advocacy Alliance may be found in O'Brien and Sang.[6] What follows is a summary of the main points and it is worth stating the objectives of Advocacy Alliance (pp. 11–12):

- Sustaining viable agreements and working relationships with the appropriate authorities and with management and staff within the relevant institutions.
- Obtaining support and backing from influential local groups and voluntary organizations.
- Recruiting and selecting volunteers from the community to befriend individual residents on a one-to-one basis and to learn and represent their interests.
- Establishing a cohesive training programme for these volunteers which would enable them to develop: an independent orientation; an understanding of the circumstances and the legal position and rights of longstay institutions; a primary loyalty to the person they have befriended and whose interests they seek to uphold.
- Developing the role of the advocacy office.
- Providing an evaluation of the project to assist its wider development.
- Identifying those residents who would most benefit from the advocacy

programme and at the same time ensuring that their wishes and feelings are always respected and that their human rights and dignity are protected.

First, in terms of the experiences gained, definitions have become more complex. As Sang has said[6]

an advocate is not:
a befriender, an advocate is more than that;
a conventional volunteer, advocacy is much more than this;
a trustee or guardian, an advocacy relationship is not enshrined within legal arrangements;
a surrogate parent; an advocacy relationship does not demand parental ties;
a pressure group activist, the essense of the advocacy programme is the one-to-one relationship, the aim is not to 'fight the system';
an amateur lawyer, advocacy is not solely concerned with representation and protection (pp. 24–5).

Second, the objectives quoted above have in practice posed a number of problems which go to the heart of the concept. Sustaining viable agreements and working relationships with appropriate authorities and staff is a noble aim, yet inevitably it raises key problems in relation to actual working practice. Only shared understanding between people will ultimately succeed in reaching the goal, but this must be built out of mutual confidence. There are many hurdles to the building of such confidence. I have experienced the suspicion and distrust which exists among and between professionals, parents and lay helpers. Present policies in relation to mentally handicapped people are not accepted universally. There are many interests to be served. Only a period of collaboration can bring about the trust which is necessary. But relationships and working practices must be formal as well as informal and there is a need for roles and functions to be defined. Advocacy Alliance developed an 'Ethical Code for Advocates' which provided the basis for the project. The code was based on three general assumptions:

- that the rights of all residents must be protected;
- that the professional position of staff must be recognized;
- that the independence of the Advocacy Alliance co-ordinator and the advocates must be maintained.

It then sets out, in some detail, the nature of the code and the procedures to be adopted. Such a document is invaluable as a reminder of the essential thought and planning which must accompany any such arrangement. To proceed without such planning is to put at risk principal objectives.

## Volunteers

An advocacy programme requires the support and backing of influential local groups and voluntary organizations. Without this support the recruitment of volunteers will be almost impossible. Again, understanding of the aims and objectives has to be achieved if members of local societies, volunteer bureaux and CHCs are not to raise objections founded upon ignorance. Most importantly, without such support the life blood of any such scheme – the volunteers themselves – will not flow.

Recruiting and selecting volunteers who will then learn to represent the interests of residents is the central problem. This is nothing new to anyone who has had experience of work within voluntary organizations. The project to which I referred at the start of this chapter was starved of volunteer help. The only way in which it operated was with the help provided by parent members; parents who themselves often faced the most exhausting of personal family situations. It simply would not have been possible for us to have continued on the basis of using independent lay advocates and yet such people would in many respects have been more suitable. The experience of Advocacy Alliance has matched this picture and is also well documented in other countries, in particular the USA. Not only is the identification of potential advocates very difficult, the actual recruitment can only be made on the basis of a significant commitment which many are unable to give. Practice shows that growth is slow, but does occur once an initial group can be formed.

The best recruiting officer to any advocacy scheme is an advocate him – or herself. Possibly the prospect of becoming attached to a community house or any other similar residence will prove more attractive than a longstay hospital, but there can be little doubt that many of the problems will be the same. Essential to any plans devised to support lay advocacy within the community is the need to obtain a strong commitment from the participants, and motivation of such people must become one of the prime tasks of both statutory services and voluntary organizations.

Commitment on the part of the volunteer is reflected in the requirement of a training programme before any relationship is begun. Once again, this represents a substantial advance upon the model of the benevolent and caring volunteers who respond on the basis of their own instincts, unrelated knowledge and experience. A training programme provides the opportunity to inform the advocate about the special needs of mentally handicapped people and the ways in which they can be met; to advise them of the rights which they have and to begin the process of giving the necessary skills.

The training programme developed by Advocacy Alliance is structured in two parts; the induction period, which introduces volunteers into non-institutional ways of thinking, the principles of normalization, the human rights issues and the advocacy role; followed by a longer period during which relevant staff are introduced and a range of community care facilities are visited. It is difficult to envisage any such scheme operating other than through some organized agency which can serve the local area – the 'advocacy office'.

Developing relevant training programmes is not just skilled work, it is also expensive and this is not a resource which is going to be available to individual homes within the community. A clear risk is that the whole programme becomes itself a bureaucracy and loses touch with the individual and his or her home. Associated with this risk is a greater danger that the lay advocate becomes yet another 'professional' to join what often appear to be ever expanding ranks. The only safeguard will be informed anticipation on the part of professionals and volunteers and a commitment on their part to the fundamental needs and rights of the individual.

To some, any system of advocacy which is founded on fundamental rights must start from the individual. Suspicion of the immovable vested interests of the professional added to a belief in institutionalized under-estimation of the abilities of people with a mental handicap leads to a changed emphasis. That change of emphasis is reflected in the rapidly growing movement of self-advocacy.

## Self-advocacy

Self-advocacy has its roots in Sweden and the USA. Much of the literature on the subject is American which raises the question of cultural differences and the extent to which experiences and findings can be easily transplanted. However, it is instructive to note that in both cases, initial impetus was provided by central or state support.

As long ago as the 1960s Sweden proposed that consultative bodies of handicapped people should be established within the range of institutions in which such people were to be found. This policy soon led to adult training programmes and a series of conferences in the late 1960s and early 1970s began the process of broadcasting. The message soon travelled to the USA and found expression in the formation of 'People First International', a movement run by and for mentally handicapped people. The conventions which followed invariably attracted much larger audiences than expected and the movement is now firmly established across the continent under the title 'People First'. Its essence has been one of grass-roots development of small peer groups offering both support and opportunity to attain self-advocacy skills. Significantly, the movement has now been recognized by both professional groups and voluntary organizations.

In Britain the first steps were taken by the Campaign for the Mentally Handicapped (CMH) which organized a conference at Castle Priory College in 1972. Twenty-two handicapped people attended and the consequent publication of the outcomes is the first published report of the views of mentally handicapped people.[7] Since then, the British movement has grown steadily to the point at which there are now many hundreds of self-advocacy groups, many of them entirely self-controlled and directed. London has its own 'People First' organization, producing among other things its own newsletter. The Adult Education Training Unit of the City Lit in London provides training in self-advocacy and gives the students rights in respect of the curriculum. Again in London, students have won the right to representation on appointments boards at the Isledon Road Centre, Lewisham, London, and the South East London Self-Advocacy Group, which brings together representatives of day centres in Lewisham, is formally represented on the borough's day care planning teams. Under the auspices of MENCAP in London, a group of people visited America in 1984 bringing back with them the seeds of the expanded movement as it is known today.

However, as in the case of lay advocacy, experience has shown the idea not to be a simple one and that it is dependent upon an organized and supported introduction in order to flourish. Crawley has produced evidence to show that groups are not always successful in sustaining themselves and many do not develop to the point of becoming genuine self-advocacy groups.[8] For the movement to grow strongly it must attract the necessary commitment of staff and resources.

Self-advocacy is the act of demanding one's entitlements oneself, and endeavouring to ensure that these entitlements are met. It also refers to the actions of a group or population to secure its rights. A component of self-advocacy is self-determination, the act of deciding for oneself. Similarly, this may be viewed in group terms.[8]

It is almost a truism to state that human dignity arises from the individual's ability to make choices. Without the right to self-determination, none of us would consider ourselves free. Yet, for a significant proportion of the population, those who have popularly been labelled as 'mentally handicapped', such freedom is neither a simple truth nor easy to achieve. Progress on human rights and the translation of general declarations into specific statutes of law has been rapid in recent years. Parallel progress in putting those rights into practice has been slower. But there is now a growing body of both research and experience which shows beyond doubt that the long-held views about the 'inabilities' of people with learning difficulties are wrong. There is confidence that it is possible to apply advanced techniques in teaching to the transferring of social and interpersonal skills to mentally handicapped people in such a way that choices can be both made and articulated. There are also rapidly growing numbers of self-advocacy groups in training centres, colleges, hostels, clubs and residential homes which provide evidence of the potential which it is possible to realize:

- It's not all for ourselves, it's for others as well.
- It is all about going out and meeting other people, helping them with their problems. Also, it helps them to share our difficulties. We've got the same difficulties that other people have.
- Need to find out what they want to say. Ask them; give them a chance to do it.
- We talk in the microphone to an audience of people about what we do, living on your own, different topics of interest. You are gaining experience as a consumer, so you become more professional and can take self-advocacy groups on your own.
- The staff need to know the people they are working with, because this makes it easier for people to speak for themselves.
- The staff need to help students to let their voices come out. To teach people how to wash, feed and dress isn't enough.
- I don't let people tell me off now. I have my say. Don't let anybody put you down or threaten you. That's the thing that frightens people.[9]

For people to have arrived at the point of being able to make such comments, a range of skills and techniques must have been acquired. There has also been the need for attitudinal changes on the part of all participants. Certainly, if the skills required are complex, this reflects the fact that the concept of self-advocacy is not a simple one. Wolfensberger discriminates between general discussion and self-expression and those acts of self-determination which patently assist in clarifying 'important' issues.[10] Williams and Shoultz take this point further and develop it into a dynamic mode – that self-advocacy is also about action and the achieving of aims established through self-expression.[11] Other writers have stressed the central importance of self-advocates retaining their independence – particularly as the great majority of such groups rely heavily on the initial and in some cases ongoing support of professionals.

Whatever the complexity, the outcomes are both exciting and diverse. People begin to work in groups to identify and solve common problems and concerns. Specific actions are identified. A common requirement is that labels should be banned: 'We do not like being called "mentally handicapped". We think it is cruel and unkind. Please call us "creative education students".'

This deep-seated resentment of labels is universal among self-advocacy groups. It was the first major outcome of the American self-advocacy movement 'People First' and it represents a total rejection of the use of a term which has meaning only in describing what people cannot do rather than what they can or are capable of doing. Furthermore, the outcomes necessitate a change in both attitudes and structures within the ranks of professionals.

The views which self-advocacy groups articulate are no different from those which emerge from any other consumer representative groups – they are not homogeneous, they do not add up to a neat and single statement about the voice of mentally handicapped people. They require negotiation from a standpoint of equal worth and value – a situation which will confront head on the traditionalist model of the professional. The process of normalization as interpreted in the policy of 'community care' has, like all policies devised for mentally handicapped people, been the product of professional planning. Views have been taken from the customary pressure groups but counsel has come principally from the professionals (not without the clamour of significant minority views). Self-advocacy has come upon the scene midway during policy implementation. People are now beginning to demand a right to have their views both heard and acted upon.

The effect upon such activities as case reviews and selection panels for community homes is already being felt. The implications for the day-to-day running of both hospitals and the much more numerous smaller homes within the community are substantial. It may yet be that the establishment of a structure which will both enable and facilitate genuine self-advocacy will be the only way in which policy can be effected. This structure will require, of necessity, a staff trained differently and with new skills. It will require a staff with new and different attitudes towards those with whom they will be working.

The need for practical advice is paramount. A staff training manual which focuses on the skills required for successful self-advocacy has recently been published.[9] It is accompanied by a video which illustrates each of the modules and is cemented in the experiences and expressed views of self-advocates. This resource can provide the starting point for the essential staff training and development needed for advocacy to become an effective part of care in the community.

The best evidence for the implications and practice of self-advocacy comes from experience within adult training and social education centres, sometimes in concert with colleges of further education. The common practice is through use of committees, and what follows is a summary of the key points identified by Crawley in the Habilitation Technology Project undertaken at the Hester Adrian Research Centre.[8] Further comment is to be found in the literature and particularly in Williams and Shoultz.[11]

It is necessary to provide a structure within which any committee activity can take place – 'without it, the opportunity presented is over-whelming and almost doomed to failure'.[12] The process needs to be analysed into its constituent skills and these, in turn, need to be learned and represented in specific actions. The notion of a hierarchy of skills is central to this approach. People learn best when skills and experiences can be built up in related stages. Within a committee environment it is vital to specify the actions needed to achieve specific ends – actual methods of communicating decisions as opposed to a general instruction to 'tell the others'. Roles must be stated clearly and the related duties formally adhered to, e.g. chairmanship, minute-taking. Assertiveness requires skill and knowledge; this must be acquired gradually by example and through training before all members can begin effectively to express their views. All actions and discussion must be explained in order that equal participation can be guaranteed; openness is central to the acquisi-tion of self-advocacy skills.

At the outset and possibly for some considerable time, committees will require the help of an adviser. Here there is an obvious link with the concept of the lay advocate. But, as has already been made clear, the adviser's role is a complex one. Both professionals and parents will face conflicts of interest however strongly they recognize the danger. Ideally, an adviser should be an outsider with no other involvement in the field. It is essential that he or she be trained. Advising without leading, knowing when to direct and when to withdraw, sensing the moments to intervene and those to ignore – the use of open questions and the establishing of an environment of negotiation and exchange – these are all skills which any experienced committee member or guidance and counselling tutor will recognise as invaluable. Used with skill and intelligence they are the route to the development of effective self-advocacy.

Questions relating to the size and formation of the committee are equally important. The group must be sufficiently large to be representative (it may in many cases be the whole group within a residential setting), but not so big as to discourage equal participation of members. Between 7 and 11 may be regarded as ideal. Roles, rights and responsibilities must be explained clearly; in the case of more severely handicapped people, it should be remembered that they can often be better represented by others less handicapped than themselves rather than by staff or other outsiders. In such cases, both the skills and processes required are more complex, indicating the need for explanation and a continuing programme of training. Meetings must be held regularly, in comfort and relative peace, and not extend beyond the point at which attention will naturally fall away. An hour may be regarded as a marker, but circumstances will obviously vary. The underlying principles are those of any democratic process. Indeed, what is so remarkable about the process of self-advocacy is its usefulness to everyone in the way in which daily lives are conducted both at home or at work.

Perhaps most important of all is the question of involvement of professional staff. A self-advocacy group which meets in a vacuum and whose decisions are unknown will have no impact on the institution concerned. The point has been made that professionals should neither lead nor interfere; however, their involvement in the sense of recognizing and valuing the outcomes of committee decisions is essential. For this reason it is vital that the limits of power and responsibility of committees or groups are known, explained and understood. The aim must be to extend those limits to the point where individuals can move effectively towards the point of self-determination. It is important for professional staff to recognize that the success of self-advocacy must lead to an extension of the areas of discussion: what might begin as a complaint about food or noise may eventually lead to a claim for rehousing or request for dismissal of staff. Progress will of necessity be slow, but it shows every sign of being inexorable.

The implications of this movement in self-advocacy are worth summarizing at this point:

- Professional people will have to reconsider the role of handicapped people in planning their future. The only way in which this can be achieved is through a process of training and education and that process will need to involve, first hand, the people for whom provision is being planned.
- Self-advocacy groups will sever themselves from the parent organization in order to avoid conflicts of interest and to retain independence.
- Groups will merge to form a wider network of self-advocacy. For example, students attending college or training centre, hostel or Gateway club (recreational clubs sponsored by MENCAP), may belong to individual representative committees which then connect to form a larger group. Extension will not be limited by borders, as experience has shown with the international nature of the 'People First' movement.
- Attitudes towards and expectations of mentally handicapped people will have to change. Self-advocacy will eventually force into the open issues which have hitherto been the subject of inter-professional discussion and debate. As a parent I share, not without some apprehension, in the anticipation of what this will bring, but I recognize its inevitability. I have only to look within my own experience with my daughter to see that the balance has weighed heavily against her being able to fulfil either her potential or her immediate wishes. Provided with the skills which I know she can acquire, provided with the environment in which I know she could express her own intentions, I have no doubt that her quality of life would be greatly improved – principally because it would reflect her choices rather than those who presently govern her life.

## A PARTNERSHIP OF EQUALS?

The theme behind this chapter has been one of change – changing roles, changing expectations, changing methods. We live in a time of rapid change and our experiences tell us that it often leads to conflict and confusion. The very rapidity of change denies the time for consultation and discussion which can provide that shared understanding through which a new spirit of co-operation can emerge. As a parent I am particularly conscious of the difficulties which self-advocacy presents, its challenge to my authority, the fears it raises in relation to thoughts of possible exploitation; voluntary societies, hitherto regarded as custodians of the welfare of their members now face the question, 'Who are the members?' Is it parent or is it the child or adult? The professional is faced with the responsibility of considering the interests of the client in a new and potentially threatening way. What is the way forward if the danger of entrenched groups defending their territory to the detriment of a common aim is to be avoided?

Partnership is not a new term in relation to mental handicap. The Warnock report called for closer collaboration between parents and professionals in order to achieve implementation of its recommendations,[13] and many authors have subsequently examined the notion in more detail. Among these, Mittler noted that whereas there was an emerging consensus about the need for closer collaboration, 'there is still considerable uncertainty about what to do and how to start'.[14] Perhaps the starting point is a recognition of who the partners are: the client, the parent, the professional and the community (including the voluntary societies). Each has to find a way of communicating within a common forum, a forum which finds expression in a multitude of different forms at all levels, from government committee to local training centre. A language must be found which is intelligible to each party and which allows the issues to be both understood and debated. These are indeed daunting tasks, though few would disagree with the agenda. In a general and almost trite sense, we are all in need of education – the word which might be used to describe the process of acquiring both knowledge and skills in relation to ourselves and to others.

Recent developments within the field of further education have involved parents of students with learning difficulties coming together in a structured way to examine the issues surrounding the education and development of their children. This semi-formalized approach is producing interesting results in respect of the greatly increased understanding of mutual wants and needs. Given the careful guidance of a trained tutor, parents find it easier to place their own problems, prejudices and aspirations within a broader context which allows the interests of their children to have equal expression.

It is my own view that the educational environment offers the best opportunity of arriving at that partnership of equals which is so often referred to. Commercial life does not expect its workers to adapt naturally and automatically to rapid change – it trains and educates them to cope. Why should the highly complex issues surrounding 'care in the community' be treated any differently? A bringing together of the partners within an educational setting would facilitate the restatement of respective roles which is now urgently required, not least within the diffuse and often confusing networks of district handicap teams and community mental handicap teams.[15]

Throughout the chapter reference has been made to the need for education and training – for advocates and self-advocates, for social and voluntary workers, for all the professionals who combine to make the community mental handicap team, for parents, for the community at large. Perhaps it is this area which has remained, at some cost, somewhat neglected and underdeveloped. This would be my own experience: not at all lacking in self-help and self-taught skills in learning other people's jargon and working one's way around and within the system, but singularly lacking in any direct education and training concerning the system and the needs and wants of the main actors within it. I have little doubt that, had this been available to me in a form which I could both understand and relate to, many of the early prejudices and misunderstandings which are thereafter so difficult to remove, would never have taken root.

As with all new developments, therefore, it has to be through the process of education that a shared understanding and agreement of the common aims is arrived at. This process has to involve all the partners, not necessarily always jointly but certainly at crucial stages. A simple but central question which any group at any level can ask itself before taking action is, 'Have we consulted our partners?' In this way, the interests of all will be properly represented.

And what if the differences cannot be resolved? When we talk of partnership, is it really a partnership of equals? I prefer a political analogy with the British Cabinet in which all are said to be equals – except that the prime minister is *primus inter pares*, first among equals. Once the point is reached when parents, professionals and the community at large recognize and support the ultimate right of people with learning difficulties to determine their own lives, then can we begin to have real confidence in our policies.

# BIBLIOGRAPHY/REFERENCES

1.  Tomlinson, S. (1982) *A Sociology of Special Education*, Routledge and Kegan Paul, London.
2.  Ryan, J. and Thomas, F. (1980) *The Politics of Mental Handicap*, Penguin, London.
3.  United Nations (1975) *Declaration on the Rights of Disabled Persons*, General Assembly Resolution 3447(XXX), United Nations.
4.  United Nations (1971) *Declaration on the Rights of Mentally Retarded Persons*, General Assembly Resolution 2856(XXVI), United Nations.

5. Standing Conference of Voluntary Organizations (1985) 'Working with mentally handicapped people in Wales', *A Report of the Advocacy Working Group: A Working Document*, June, p. 5. (Address of SCoVO: Llys Ifor, Crescent Road, Caerphilly, Mid Glamorgan, CF8 1XL.)
6. O'Brien, J. and Sang, R. (1984) *Advocacy: the UK and American Experiences*, King's Fund Publishing Office, London.
7. Shearer, A. (1972) *Our Life*, CMH, London.
8. Crawley, B. (1983) *Self-Advocacy Manual*, paper no. 49, Habilitation Technology Project, Hester Adrian Research Centre, Manchester.
9. Cooper, D. and Hersov, J. (1987) *We Can Change the Future – A staff training resource on self-advocacy for people with learning difficulties*, National Bureau for Handicapped Students, London.
10. Wolfensberger, W. (1972) *The Principle of Normalisation in Human Services*, National Institute on Mental Retardation, Toronto.
11. Williams, P. and Shoultz, B. (1982) *We can speak for ourselves*, Souvenir Press, London.
12. Crawley, B. (1980) Report of a Survey of Trainee-Committee in Adult Training Centres in England and Wales, Paper 49, p. 49, The Hester Adrian Research Centre, Manchester.
13. Warnock (Report) (1978) *Report of the Committee of Enquiry into the Education of Handicapped Children and Young People*, HMSO, London.
14. Mittler, P. (1983) *Parents, Professionals and Handicapped People*, Croom Helm, London, p. 8.
15. Gilbert, P. (1985) *Mental Handicap – A practical guide for social workers*, Business Press International, Surrey, p. 59.

# 2. Maintaining an Ordinary Life

*David Sines*

## INTRODUCTION

This chapter considers the structures, systems and processes that are necessary to maintain a desirable and ordinary lifestyle for people in their homes, whether it be with their families or with other people of their choice. The basic elements of a needs-led and individualized service are presented and, where relevant, readers are referred to other areas in the text for further elaboration on specific issues.

## WHAT ARE WE AIMING TO ACHIEVE?

This fundamental question has been addressed by planners and service providers for decades as the design and introduction of services for people with mental handicaps are debated. The move from the more traditional model of hospital-based care to ordinary life provision requires not only a blueprint for change but also a charter based on an assumption that the values and attitudes that underpin the philosophy of community care will be shared and accepted by all those involved in the care process. Such changes in attitude cannot be assumed to occur naturally by default but require sensitive and deliberate programmes of preparation, coaching and support. Service users, their families, professionals and their managers all need to agree on the fundamental principles around which the service will be designed.

This is perhaps the most important phase of the planning and consultation process and represents the foundation upon which all future agreements will be reached. Key concepts will need to be identified and a framework constructed within which the aims and objectives of the service may be provided and evaluated.

The first stage is to consider who needs to be consulted. Obviously, the person for whom service is being designed is the first person who should be involved along with his/her representative. There then follows a host of potential people who may have a justifiable reason to stake their claim to be involved. In many cases where moves to new services are considered, negotiations have been limited to key personnel in the existing service without extending the network more imaginatively to representatives from other agencies or from the community where the new services are being planned.

As a rule of thumb, a sociogram of the people who have a 'stake' or interest in the lives of each person being considered for the new service should be constructed to determine those people to involve at various stages of the planning process. This process may be divided into two specific components:

- Detailed discussion on the individual needs of each person using or identified as a potential user of the service (see Chapter 3).
- Operational and strategic aspects of planning new services.

Different people will be involved in each of these processes. For the first stage, emphasis is placed on the individual and consultation should take place with:

- The person concerned.
- Their representative.
- Professionals involved in their care from all agencies.
- Any other person whom the client considers they would like to invite.

For the second stage, service design may require the involvement of many people, some of whom may be:

- Service managers.
- Specialist professional staff (e.g. occupational therapists, psychologists).
- Direct care staff.
- Architects and building advisers.

- Planners and financial consultants.
- Local councillors/neighbours.
- Consumers.
- Neighbourhood representatives (e.g. clergymen, shopkeepers etc).
- Community health council or other designated bodies.

The norm is to include all those people identified as having an impact on the lives of the people concerned at the present time and those whom it is felt may facilitate their successful integration into their new home in the future. Professional advice such as that detailed above is essential to ensure realistic and appropriate service design.

# FUNDAMENTAL SERVICE PRINCIPLES

This chapter is not concerned with building design or the process of house acquisition, but with the fundamental principles within which the house will operate once it is commissioned. However, the latter is not possible without consideration of the former. Take, for example, a house that has been designed to meet the needs of a person with limited mobility which is purchased in an isolated position from the town or without adequate space for a wheelchair. Take also a house that is purchased for a group of four young people in an area predominately occupied by the elderly and distant from local amenities. The need for access to public transport routes, shops, friends and work all need to be considered as prerequisites to the principles of maintaining an ordinary life, which this chapter will go on to consider.

An agreement on our aims and objectives is required as a written statement by all the principal stakeholders. This is not always an easy process and time should be allowed for exploration of minority views and support offered to those who disagree. Most of the people involved will have a wealth of experience and advice to offer the planning team, who should nurture a feeling of trust within their working relationships together. Examples of poor teamwork have often been given for the failure of some projects: teams have not taken the time to plan according to the needs of the whole group or have not agreed the fundamental service principles first.

As a preliminary exercise the group should state the key components of its service and then agree on the client-centred principles it wishes to adopt. An example of the principles adopted by one authority is presented below:[1]

People living in the house will:
- Acquire new skills that enhance their ability to cope with the normal social environment.
- Engage in a wide range of ordinary activities to practice and consolidate skills they have acquired.
- Engage in a full range of home-making activities and household duties.
- Join in as many community-based activities as possible.
- Engage in as many new activities as possible outside the house.
- Use local facilities wherever possible.
- Be involved in all decisions affecting their lives.
- Lose disruptive behaviours that limit or deny access to ordinary activities.

This statement of client-focused objectives reflects the need for all services to be tailored to the indivdiual preferences, strengths and needs of its users, within the context of the least restrictive environment in which these objectives can be met. The service should also acknowledge that responses from staff should be offered in such a manner that is appropriate to the person's age and respect the dignity of its consumers and acknowledge their rights and responsibilities. To achieve this, individuals require opportunities for informed choice and autonomy over their own lives, which may involve taking defined risks (see Chapter 3).

## MAKING CHOICES

All people make choices of some kind or another about their lives. Some people express their needs and wishes verbally and explicitly, others through nonverbal and implicit methods depending upon their skills, previous experiences and opportunities. People with mental handicaps have always expressed their feelings but they have often been denied the opportunity or respect they require to have them noted or acted upon. People may need help to express themselves or to understand the implications of very complex or complicated options with which they may be confronted. There is a tremendous difference between choosing a familiar favourite sweet from a variety, to being asked if a move to a new home some miles from 'home' would be desirable. Before any choices can be made there are some basic questions to be considered:

- What will the change mean for me?
- Will there be any disadvantages to my choice?

- How much autonomy do I have to alter any possible predetermined outcome?
- Do I require help or further information before I make my decision?
- What past experiences do I need to recall to help me make my choice?

People with mental handicaps have often had decisions made on their behalf and they are not expected to make decisions. On many occasions decisions are made by people who do not even know them, but this is of course true of any citizen in society. People with mental handicaps have an additional problem in that they have often not been exposed to a variety of opportunities in their lives to experience alternatives or options. For many there will be little choice due to the restricted opportunities provided for them. Daily activities or job choice is a good example of this. Choices may be extremely limited depending on where you live, and the adult training centre (ATC) may provide the focus of experience for a person's total adult life. Opportunities for enrichment in life experiences is therefore a prerequisite for making informed choices.

Overprotection of some people has also complicated the matter and deprived them of the opportunity to gain some control over their lives. The burden of decision-making is something many people delegate, given the choice, but for this client group their disenfranchisement offers them little alternative to their acceptance of a passive role in this process.

The Campaign for the Mentally Handicapped identifies this problem as requiring a basic attitude change by those in close contact with people with mental handicaps:[2]

Being prepared to accept that a choice made by a person with mental handicaps is as valid as our own.

Being prepared to accept and support choices made by a person with mental handicaps.

Being prepared to look for imaginative and challenging ways of encouraging the person with mental handicaps to make choices in their own environment.

Being prepared to support bad choices (we all make them).

In the same document the authors outline a strategy to help people make choices about their own lives. It begins with the realistic assessment of their needs and the demonstration of possible choices and opportunities for people with limited experiences.

The challenge of providing choices for people with mental handicap may occasionally cause concern and in some cases genuine worries for people living with or caring for them. Issues charged with emotive feeling, such as emerging sexual awareness and risk-taking involved in independence training programmes are examples. However, we do have a responsibility to break the tradition of passivity in decision-making for people with learning difficulties, the first stage of which is the genuine commitment of professionals and carers to involve them in all decisions affecting their lives.

The CMH document[2] provides a model for facilitating this process (Figure 2.1):

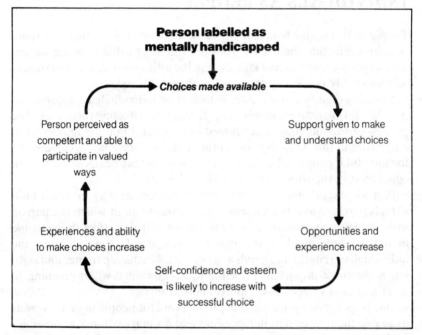

Figure 2.1  Breaking into the vicious circle (p. 41)

The advantages of gaining additional control over one's life are obvious, but with increased autonomy and awareness comes additional responsibilities and obligations. For people with mental handicaps this presents new challenges and opportunities. For example, acceptance in the community demands recognition of the local norms and rules enforced in the wider and local community. Protection from prosecution, for example, for those people who offend or infringe these rules can no longer be taken as a right for people who demand new powers of attorney in society and this needs to be balanced against each person's ability to make certain choices. It is up to professionals to draw attention to the consequences of any actions taken on the basis of informed choice.

Additional opportunities to make choices will be accompanied by an increase in the person's self-esteem and dignity which, in turn, may lead to more acceptable and constructive behaviours. The need to feel useful and valued underpins the whole philosophy of a meaningful lifestyle.

# INDIVIDUALS AS PEOPLE

People with mental handicaps may be dependent on others to share decisions effecting their lives. They are often regarded as being vulnerable to people's whims and fancies, and the attitudes of carers and society will inevitably determine the quality of their lifestyle.

Ensuring dignity and self-esteem require an individualized approach to people who are actively involved in all decisions affecting their lives. The process of life planning is developed in Chapter 3 but it is important to emphasize at this point that an appraisal of someone's needs can only be meaningful if people take the time to understand the needs of the person concerned in the total context of his or her life.

Past life experiences will inevitably influence the way in which individuals perceive another's needs. The environment in which the person lives and the people sharing his or her home will also affect the outcome of the decisions made about that person's life. Getting to know the individual's strengths and needs as a person takes time, patience and skill, but is the most important principle to acknowledge when planning to meet a person's needs in an individualized service.

One basic service principle is to provide care for people in such a way as to enable them to lead as independent and normal existence as possible. Such a service should be designed to meet individual needs in a manner to which they were accustomed to in their own homes and neighbourhoods.

While planning individual services there will always be conflict between the needs of individuals and the people who will share their home. It is unrealistic, although desirable, to state that all services will ensure the compatibility of all members of each household. Indeed, in some cases the sheer task of providing services for large numbers of people will highlight the enormity of this suggestion. However there are ways of ensuring that people are chosen and choose to live together based on the careful assessment of individual needs and preferences.

The selection of all people sharing a home with others should involve the householders in the selection procedure. Staff should be sensitive to potential conflicts or friendships among residents and should ensure that newcomers will not cause undue disruption or distress to the people living in the house. Resident committees and discussion groups can help to facilitate expression of people's feelings and solicit their opinions when such choices are to be made.

Service planners should agree with the concept of individually designed services and at a very early stage in the planning process should be aware of the needs and preferences of the people they are designing homes for. Such decisions will range from choice of colour schemes, to the individual design of the building to accommodate specific needs.

Standardized design models should also be discouraged since 'special buildings' create an image in the local community which sets the residents apart from their neighbours. Investments in large, specially designed estates also restrict opportunities for the residents to move onto other, more appropriate homes. Small, ordinary houses are much easier to sell and the occupants are freer to choose a new location; this is not easy with the larger estates built in previous years.

Access to various types of housing should not be restricted to any specific model, even in the open market. Some people may choose to live in flats, others in houses; some in the town and others in the country. It has been a misguided assumption that people with mental handicaps are different from other members of the population and in this respect account should be taken of the person's original life experiences and current preferences. The conclusion is that there is no one standard model for all people and that the only answers are the relevant ones which meet the individual housing needs of the people who will be living in them.

Sadly, individual choice is compromised by the availability of suitable houses in any given locality or by the amount of money available to purchase the homes required. This is particularly true in areas where property prices are high or in densely populated regions where property is unavailable. In such circumstances those concerned have to take their chances with other members of the locality in obtaining the homes of their choice. Where the problems relate to the lack of finance then pressure should be exerted on the authorities concerned; inappropriate or de-valued housing alternatives should not be accepted as a 'second best'.

This section has introduced the importance of planning the delivery of services to people with mental handicaps as individuals. The remainder of this chapter continues to explore some of the fundamental principles underpinning this approach.

# PRESENTING THE BEST OF ONESELF

Traditionally, people with mental handicaps have had to work extra hard to present themselves in society and to gain acceptance. History has dictated this and people with learning difficulties are at a constant risk of being cast into a deviancy role and being seen as different from others. For some people 'being different' is a reason for viewing others as devalued members of society with negative associations. Society and its interpretation of handicap presents people with mental handicaps with the considerable task of presenting themselves to acquire acceptance.

Imagery is associated with the way in which we regard people we meet in our everyday lives. The way in which we wear our hair and our clothes will convey specific messages to others from which they will make assumptions regarding our personalities and backgrounds. In the past, little attention was paid to helping people to select and purchase clothing in keeping with local and age-appropriate fashion. Hairstyles were often basic, lacking imagination, and the use of cosmetics to enhance appearance was rarely encouraged for people with mental handicaps. The result was to make people look different from their peers, and in many cases to encourage them to 'wear' the uniform of their group – standardized clothing, conventional hairstyles, sandals and drab fabrics.

The use of age-appropriate possessions is also significant in conveying positive messages to others. It is not acceptable for an adult woman to visit the shops pushing a doll's pram or to cuddle a doll on the bus, for example. Similarly, it is not acceptable for an adult man to 'play' with cars or to read childish picture books. However, it should be remembered that although it will enhance the person's acceptance in the community if they behave in accordance with the expectations of their age and sex, it may be at the loss of a very real attachment to a 'comforter' which will need to be replaced by more appropriate substitutes. This is not always as easy as it may sound and must be handled sensitively and introduced at a pace that the person can cope with.

The use of culturally valued means of presenting oneself is central to the principles of normalization which the author has so far tried to avoid labelling as a process in this chapter. However, to enhance one's behaviour, appearance, status and reputation in public is undisputedly important.

Implicit in this principle is the need to provide many varied learning opportunities to increase the greater likelihood of normative experiences. Access to valued peer models and exposure to a number of experiences will also be needed.

The key points raised so far in this section can be summarized thus:

- Provide opportunities to exercise autonomy, choice, citizenship privileges and freedom.
- Provide opportunities to meet a wide range of people, and form mutually satisfying relationships.
- Transfer the image of a devalued group of people to one of acceptance in the community and in society through the use of age-appropriate and normative behaviours and clothing.
- Enhancement of individual self-image and dignity.

These principles require that services are provided in such a way as to make them possible. Hence services should be:

- located within a cluster of the population;
- located within the centre of the locality;
- accessible to its consumers, their families and the public;
- accessible to a variety of resources (shops, post office etc);
- congrous with the local neighbourhood in design and appearance;
- planned to avoid saturation with other 'devalued' people.

Importance should also be attached to the way in which professionals address each other and their clients. The use of childish nicknames should be avoided and people should be addressed in a manner in keeping with their age. In the same way undue attention to the house where people live should be encouraged by avoiding the display of large devaluing signs dedicating the ownership of the property to a statutory agency. Entries in the telephone book should be discrete and the use of devaluing house names avoided, e.g. 'The Honey Pot' or 'The Annexe'.

Many of the services discussed in this book will be provided by the statutory sector, which will imply ownership of the properties and staff employed in them. The use of support services, for example, should be discreet and the use of large vans or lorries from central works departments should be discouraged from displaying logos advertising the fact that the inhabitants are 'dependent' on that agency for their homes. The use of local services and shops should be encouraged and this process is described further in Chapters 8 and 11.

This section has introduced the key components of normalization which implies that everybody should have the option of living in their own home. Too often people are expected to compromise their preferences and choices because of the lack of opportunities. Every person should be able to live in a comfortable setting which looks like, feels like and is considered as *their* home in the community of their choice and with which they are familiar. People should be able to choose with whom they would like to live and they should have control over the decisions taken within their home.

The principles of normalization imply that each person should be presented and interpreted to the community at large in as positive a manner as possible. Negative messages are too often conveyed to the community and these need to be positively discouraged and converted into positive messages. The names people are called, the way in which people are treated as mature individuals and the way in which services are provided will convey messages of this nature to the public.

The principles of normalization imply the need for people with mental handicaps to have the opportunity to experience new learning experiences. This will require the introduction of individualized learning programmes and opportunity plans as choices for independence are made (see Chapter 3).

The concepts of equality, rights and dignity are developed in the theory of normalization, which implies that people with mental handicaps have a right to share equally in the benefits and difficulties of life in their community. To do so they should be encouraged to participate in the life of the local community and its lifestyle as actively as possible. Integration into the community will provide opportunities for participation and learning. It will also allow members of the public to appreciate how similar people with mental handicaps are and how little relevance should be given to differences. Individuals should be able to participate individually and in small groups in a range of chosen resources in the community.

## NEIGHBOURS, FRIENDS AND NETWORKS

This topic is covered extensively in Chapter 4 but any discussion on the key components of maintaining an ordinary life would be incomplete without reference to the key principles in this chapter.

In order for people to gain acceptance in the community, they require opportunities to gain access to life experiences and other people in their neighbourhoods. To achieve this acceptance in the local neighbourhood is desirable and begins during the initial stages of a local property search.

When considering a locality within which to purchase a house, consideration should be given to choosing an area which meets the criteria mentioned above to enhance the quality of residents' lives. This may be in any part of the town although some areas may be considered to be undesirable due to the nature of the people who live there. People with mental handicaps do not need to ask permission to live anywhere. If they did this would be contrary to the acknowledgement to their basic rights as citizens, but it is important to assess the degree of welcome they are likely to receive once they have moved in.

Some members of the public still have stereotyped expectations of people with mental handicaps and occasionally feel concerned that any changes in the social balance of their neighbourhood should be resisted. This is often due to lack of information and experience and, on the basis of informed choice, potentially negative reactions can be converted to positive support for new neighbours.

Local councillors can be excellent allies in encouraging the integration of newcomers to the neighbourhood. Local shopkeepers may also sponsor their acceptance as they bring trade to their shops and offer to contribute to the economy of the area. Meeting local neighbours and inviting them in for coffee and sharing daily pleasantries when people meet in the street have been known to encourage the generation of meaningful networks for people with mental handicaps when they move into new areas. The fact that many people are being moved 'back home' is also helpful in staking the people's claim to their new home.

Once the initial contacts have been made there is still the need to encourage the formation of meaningful friendships for the newcomers. There is always a problem in knowing how far to sponsor new contacts or whether to leave things to occur naturally without drawing unnecessary attention to the house and its occupants. Perhaps one way of ensuring successful integration is to be seen as often as the opportunity presents itself to be sharing in the life of the community. Maintaining a high profile removes the possibility of false assumptions being made about the new occupants and provides opportunities for friendships to be developed on the basis of reciprocity. Attendance at the local church, youth club, adult education classes and in the shops are examples of this.

In some areas more structured approaches have been used to develop friendship groups to establish contact with non-handicapped people in the community. Volunteers may be willing to 'befriend' individuals and sponsor them into community-based activities. Walsh describes the establishment of such a scheme designed to 'build a person-orientated service' which she considers will not happen 'overnight'[3]. She sees the model as requiring some degree of promoting and sponsorship towards encouraging the real goal of friendship and integration:

This new model of care will be characterized by its flexibility, an emphasis on people's needs, whether handicapped or non-handicapped, and a de-emphasis on the provision of buildings or ability levels and on professionalism. The speed at which this happens will vary from place to place, it will be patchy, will move at different paces, in different ways; different practicalities will have to be faced and worked through and we will need to face many unanswered and unanswerable questions. It is the journey which will take us back towards meeting the most basic right of all: the right of us all to be treated as full human beings.

The Campaign for the Mentally Handicapped has also recognized the importance of building social relationships as part of the integration process:[4]

Without the active support and the opportunity to develop social relationships, there is a real danger that the often-voiced fears of opponents of community services will become true. Residents newly moved into the community may miss the readily available companionship and social activities available in hospital. They may become isolated, lonely and depressed . . .

At its simplest form, social integration means a sense of 'belonging'. On the one hand, it means feeling part of a social group or network. On the other hand, it means feeling part of the neighbourhood. In practice, the two often overlap. Joining in neighbourhood life involves making contacts with local people and becoming a part of local networks and relationships. Encouraging the social integration of people with mental handicaps involves a third dimension as well. The aim is that their relationships and social activities should not be confined to interactions with other people with handicaps but also include people who are not labelled 'handicapped' – people valued by the local community. In practice, a number of things can help, or hinder, with handicaps becoming socially integrated in their local community.

The whole concept of network building demands that people with mental handicaps acquire the social skills necessary to gain acceptance in the community, and opportunities and skills-based training programmes should be designed and implemented to facilitate this. The initial building phase can be manufactured but the maintenance of the network is left very much to the relationships of the people involved, including the person with a mental handicap who should be actively encouraged to 'own' and participate within it.

Helpers may be needed to achieve this initially, as discussed above, but in time the true success of the integration programme will be determined by the number of social contacts each person has maintained in the community. The aim is to replace the dependence that people with mental handicaps have on professionals with a self-support network of friends and associates in the neighbourhood. It is at this stage that integration and acceptance can be said to have occurred.

# MAINTAINING VARIETY IN EVERYDAY LIFE

As will be seen in Chapter 3, the importance of planning our lives and having a say in how we lead them is fundamental to maintaining an ordinary lifestyle. In this section the principle of variety in everyday life is considered.

Essentially, most people's lives revolve around their homes, friends, work and families, and the ways in which people choose to use their time will depend on personal choices and the demands made on their 'free time' by others. Another important determinant will be the range of activities or opportunities at their disposal and of course whether they can afford to use them.

People with mental handicaps have for many years been regarded as being incapable of handling their own financial affairs and in some cases people have not considered it necessary to give them access to their own money. Rules have been imposed by the DHSS and statutory agencies which positively discriminate against them and reduce their disposable incomes to a minimum. This will inevitably limit their choices in respect of leisure activities and may impose restrictions which require dependence using inferior services and 'charity' in order to gain any fulfilment in their lives.

In the past it was widely acknowledged that people with mental handicaps should engage in leisure pursuits with other people with learning difficulties. The segregation that such activities imposed served to set them further apart from their peers in the neighbourhood. A variety of 'special' clubs and social functions were provided by well-meaning people and in the absence of more valued alternatives, they certainly provided people with a welcome break from the boredom and routine of their lives. There were several reasons for the encouragement of segregated resources:

- They were often more accessible.
- They were cheaper.

● Attitudes amongst organisers considered them to be relevant to the needs of the client group 'who preferred their own company'.
● There were often considered to be few alternatives.

These factors raise several issues which require resolution before local facilities can be used. For example, many people with mental handicaps are dependent on others to facilitate their access to the community. This will require adequate numbers of staff or friends to be available to share their leisure or work pursuits and this, in turn, will require a commitment from their 'sponsors' to give time, energy and imagination to designing and exploiting local opportunities.

Staff time and resources should be planned flexibly to facilitate the use of leisure activities which may not fit cohesively into ordinary staff shift patterns. Managers will need to ensure that all staff contracts of employment make allowance for this and should allow staff the opportunity to work with individuals rather than to roster them onto rigid shifts without reference to the activities of the day or week. This matter will be discussed in Chapter 12.

Staff will also need to view their primary task as a commitment to enhancing the quality of life for the people they work with. Taking this to its logical conclusion, staff will need to recognize that their contractual obligations are individually led rather than service-dominated. This change in attitude from the more traditional approach of task allocation, so often seen in the past presents a real challenge to staff.

Similarly, financial procedures should allow immediate access to money when required rather than having to await lengthy requisition processes. Individuals should have their own, local bank accounts and where possible cash cards to allow flexibility in access. Knowledge of personal balances of accounts is also required when budgeting for outings and excursions. The whole process of adjusting staff and service attitudes towards the achievement of the maximum degree of independence and autonomy is therefore a prerequisite to expanding the variety and access to variety in one's life.

Once these procedural points have been covered, consideration needs to be given to assessing the range of possible opportunities available. These must match the needs and preferences of the people concerned. Decisions relating to work will be covered in Chapter 6, and it is sufficient to note the importance of valued work and daily activities for people with mental handicaps here within the total context of their lives.

Wherever possible, segregated activities should be discouraged in favour of integrating and sharing leisure time with our contemporaries and neighbours. The use of the local swimming pool, riding clubs and visits to the local pub and restaurant to celebrate birthdays or to entertain friends are examples. In one study the use of shops, cafés and public houses by people with mental handicaps in Andover emphasized the importance of maintaining a high profile in the local community.[5] Interviews were held with proprietors of local establishments and each suggested that the frequency with which their businesses were used was satisfactory; a third of the sample suggested that it could be more. The majority expressed good opinions of the clients' appearance and competence of the staff who accompanied them and, more importantly, acknowledged the importance of community integration and felt that their businesses had benefited.

The successful use of leisure facilities will also depend on the competencies of the staff concerned. Public attitudes are easily influenced if staff fail to present themselves and their companions in an acceptable fashion. Hence attention to dress sense, hairstyles and posture are important. It is also likely to improve the chances of successful integration if people engage in activities in small, discrete groups rather than in large numbers where public tolerance towards saturation may be unwelcome. This is of course true for those involved as well. Individuals stand to gain far more if they have the time and attention to devote to the activities concerned rather than having to constantly 'watch over' a large group of people. Care must be taken to organize activities sensitively and discretely and this is particularly true when organizing holidays.

Most people invest much of their energy during their work. For many, holidays form an important part of their lives and much time is often given to planning them and preparing for them. Holidays are also a time when companions are carefully chosen to share in the occasion. The same degree of consideration should be given to preparing holidays for people with mental handicaps, that is assuming that they want one at all! A variety of venues should be made available and personal choice exercised and attention paid to the number of people who will participate. The most important questions to ask are: Would you like to go on holiday? Where would you like to go for your holiday? Who would you chose to go with you?

Creating an exciting and stimulating learning environment for people with a mental handicap will require the provision of a wide variety of life experiences which will include some of the components discussed above. One must not ignore the importance of sharing in the home-making skills engaged in during everyday lives, all of which increase competences and self-awareness. More importantly, they imply ownership and mastery over one's own environment, all of which require the careful design of individual precision teaching programmes and opportunities.

The importance of widening our network of friends outside of the home and workplace is clearly important if people with mental handicaps are to establish control and choices in their own lives. However, retaining contact with relatives and old friends is also important if continuity in one's life is to be maintained.

Provision should also be made for individuals to continue to receive the respect and support they require to continue to practice their faith or religion. Ethnic considerations must also be integral to the design of a person's life plan, and opportunities provided for church attendance and choice of diet and clothes.

This section has emphasized the importance of designing a high quality lifestyle through the provision of a variety of opportunities ranging from the person's full involvement in the housekeeping arrangements of their home to the active pursuit of valued leisure and recreational activities.

# EXPLORING FEELINGS AND PAST EXPERIENCES

People who have entered residential care rarely have the opportunity to share their previous experiences with their peers and friends. All too often well-meaning care staff fail to recognize the importance of 'getting to know' a person's background and in some instances positively disregard the relevance of the person's family, old friends and acquaintances. However, it is impossible to fully understand a person's needs without considering the events that have influenced their thinking and shaped a person's perspective on life.

The choice of alternative homes for people close to their original home will provide many opportunities to familiarize and to share old memories within the context of previous experience. Visits to familiar places, meetings with old friends and the sharing of previous associations all form part of the process of reminiscence (see Chapter 10) which should remove the problems associated with the process of change when moving to a new home.

The way in which the physical and psychological environments are designed (see Chapters 8 and 11) should take account of the standards enjoyed by the people living in the house before their arrival. There is inherent in this statement a problem of definition. What standards should be imposed? What is normal? How are agreements reached on the needs of a group of people who will live together with differing needs and past experiences?

These questions will often present planners and carers with a dilemma, but they must be asked and the views of the people concerned, their friends and families should be sought in order to make their home as compatible as possible with their wishes and needs. This can often be achieved by visiting people in their family homes and by encouraging them to choose their own furnishings and, where they wish, to bring things with them from home.

Opportunities to have personal space and to display possessions and photographs of friends and family should be encouraged. Inviting people home for tea and to visit develops a feeling of pride in one's home and extends the opportunities people have to share their lives with others reciprocally. The sharing of important anniversaries, some happy and some sad, should be encouraged, with each person having the opportunity to express and to ventilate their feelings and emotions.

Living in the community may also bring certain rejections from people who do not wish to have their own privacy invaded by others. Rejection can be particularly painful and may diminish a person's confidence. Others may be particularly antisocial and hurtful in making the person concerned feel different and unwelcome. Preparation for such eventualities is difficult but opportunities for the exploration of feelings of rejection should be made and accommodated after the event and the person's concerns shared and supported.

For some people time may be needed for individual discussion and sharing of feelings and emotions. Often such opportunities have been denied in the past, and feelings surrounding loss, change and bereavement suppressed and introjected. It is a key component in our everyday lives to acknowledge that such feelings are an essential part of life and as such we must prepare ourselves for them and allow ourselves time to explore our feelings with the support of others. At times we may also wish to be alone and our right to privacy at such times should be acknowledged. A listening ear and a shoulder to lean on in times of trouble or distress are also needed by most of us occasionally; when this is needed, it should be available from people we trust and who respect us.

The right to give of oneself also demands the right to form relationships with others and to have the opportunity to feel valued and needed. A person with a mental handicap has the same right to and need for meaningful relationships with others. There is a need for age-appropriate sex and interpersonal education programmes for clients and guidelines for staff working with people with mental handicaps. There is often a lack of directives for staff who may find this area particularly difficult to define and work with. Some of the reasons for this may be as follows:[6]

- The whole area is highly emotive for all people involved and for the public at large.
- There is still a strong belief among some people that talking about 'sex' with clients will create rather than solve problems.
- The law is confusing and appears to operate double standards. We need to know where we stand.
- Sometimes it is easier to deny that our clients have 'sexual needs' – we can then consider all expressions of sexuality as 'problematic' and deal with it accordingly.
- If management issue guidelines, they will be making implicit if not explicit statements about clients' rights and needs. These may conflict with the views held by staff and the people concerned and may be highly controversial.

People with mental handicaps are people first and as such have the right to form relationships with others when they so choose. However, the people concerned must do so on the basis of informed choice and this implies that adequate training and preparation should be introduced and appropriate safeguards undertaken to avoid undue risks or hurt feelings. Taking risks will form a central part of the debate and it should be acknowledged that an environment which allows an appropriate degree of personal choice and privacy can never be risk-free.

Sadly, some people assume that personal relationships always involve sex and by so doing impose an injustice on people with mental handicaps who for the most part regard sex as a minor component in enjoying a personal relationship with another person. Questions relating to friendships, caring and sharing are of far greater significance in any preparatory programme.

All guidelines should be flexible because of the individualistic nature of the subject and should encourage the open discussion of the interpersonal needs of people with mental handicaps. Staff and carers should ensure that:

- All interpersonal needs are assessed individually by a multidisciplinary team.
- Opportunities for privacy are provided.
- Individually designed interpersonal training programmes are available.

- Guidelines should be available for staff on personal relationships.
- The views of parents should be noted.

The law acts as a safeguard, to protect people with mental handicaps from exploitation, but it does not impose restrictions on the people themselves. Where it can be shown that a service is acting on its professional judgement then it can expect to be acting within the terms of the law. However, readers are recommended to refer to a summary of the various relevant Acts concerning this topic before embarking on any programme which may be controversial or give rise to professional concern or debate.[7]

Personal relationships may lead to more permanent arrangements such as marriage. Marriage is a contract between two people of the opposite sex and the law regards this contract to be a very simple one.[8] Consequently most people with mental handicaps who express the desire to marry will be legally able to do so. Opportunities for people to have deeper relationships should be provided where members of the multidisciplinary team believe that both the parties involved fully understand the consequences of their wishes and actions. Support will also need to be offered in realizing the obligations of this arrangement. Appropriate advice on family planning and contraception should also be offered.

The questions to ask are:

- What will the person gain from the relationship?
- What are the possible 'risks' involved?
- Who needs to share the decision with them?
- Do they require any help to reach their decision?

Finally, this section considers the ways in which professionals express themselves to people with mental handicaps and the effect their methods of expression may have on them.

People communicate in many ways, speech being just one of them. Staff working as role models with people with mental handicap have to be particularly aware of how they approach and act with their clients. Appearance, posture, eye contact and gestures all send out signals long before a single word is uttered. Style of delivery, tone and volume, social distance and bodily contact are all important when working with others. The way in which messages are chosen and when will also have a profound effect on the success of professional interventions.

In some cases people use condescending language or simple speech forms to convey their message. On some occasions 'childish language' is used and at the other extreme 'bad language'. The importance of pitching one's conversation at a level which the person concerned can understand cannot be emphasized enough. Avoidance of jargon, gauging the speed of speech delivery and attention to avoid implied meanings will contribute to the successful delivery of messages to people with mental handicaps.

## PERSONAL RIGHTS AND RESPONSIBILITIES

Detailed reference to the concept of personal rights has been made in Chapter 1 but here it is necessary to reinforce an individual's right to live as an equal citizen. Indeed, all of the issues and principles explored in this chapter so far are based on the acceptance of everybody's fundamental right to be valued, needed and respected as a citizen in society, irrespective of their handicap or 'label'.

The dignity and self-esteem of others should be a primary consideration when working with people with mental handicaps. However, this is sometimes overlooked when planning and delivering services and may result in a failure to consult those that the service is aiming to provide for.

In April 1986 the Disabled Persons (Services, Consultation and Representation) Act sponsored by all parties in the House of Commons aimed to improve the rights of disabled persons by issuing a charter for change by making provision for the improvement of the effectiveness and co-ordination of services for this client group (and others).[9] It also establishes new procedures for the assessment of their individual needs.

The Act aims to:

- Allow a disabled person to have a 'representative' to help deal with the statutory services.
- Require Social Services to produce a formal statement of assessment of needs, if a person requests it, with full access to all nonconfidental information.
- Require Social Services to make assessment of a person's needs when school leaving occurs or when discharge takes place from a hospital.
- Require hospital authorities to inform the DHSS of all discharges from hospital at least 28 days in advance.
- Assess the needs and ability of carers to continue to provide primary and secondary care at home.
- Inform disabled people, by right, of services provided by public and voluntary bodies.

- Ensure that appropriate agencies are consulted whenever advice or support is required with special knowledge of the needs of people with mental handicaps.
- Procure from ministers an annual statement of the numbers of people remaining in mental handicap hospitals.
- Changing planning laws to improve access for disabled people.

This Act is far reaching in its requests to improve the rights and responsibilities of people with mental handicaps and reflects the interests and support of an impressive coalition of voluntary organizations determined to reduce the bureaucratic procedures that served to reduce the individual's right to determine their own future.

It has acknowledged the rights of people with mental handicaps to enjoy a meaningful life by inviting them to participate in designing their own futures and services. Those who are unable to plan their own futures should receive every support through the establishment of advocacy schemes to have their needs acknowledged (see Chapter 1). Service providers should also assume a proactive approach to providing services which are designed to meet the identified needs of individuals within the framework of a comprehensive life planning system (see Chapter 3).

Public acknowledgement and acceptance of the rights of people with mental handicaps is therefore an essential component in the realization of ordinary life experiences. To enable people to take full advantage of their rights, the need for sensitive and available representation and advocacy is needed whether it be through family, friends or through legal advocacy schemes.

In practical terms the whole concept of rights and advocacy continually affect the decisions professionals make regarding the way in which they plan and deliver their services. Occasionally, there will be conflicting values between the needs of one person and other members of the household, between the values held by staff members and people living in the house and between individuals and their families. Open and frank exploration of all the issues should be encouraged and decisions reached only after informed debate and consideration of as many views as possible. Inevitably, there will be disappointments for some people when their requests are considered to be too ambitious or unrealistic or in some cases too 'risky'. In such cases the benefits and consequences of each intended activity should be recorded and shared within the house and with all those people likely to be involved or affected by the decision. No matter how liberal professionals become in promoting the needs of people with mental handicaps, there still remain the professional's responsibility to promote client's interests in law and as citizens, which sometimes requires the introduction of sanctions to protect their interests.

Some of the basic rights to be encouraged in everyday life are the right to: privacy; to be treated with respect; to say no without feeling guilty; ask for what you want and need; choose not to assert yourself; make mistakes; be listened to; have and to express your own feelings and opinions; vote.

Dignity is defined as 'the state or quality of being worthy of honour or respect; sense of self-importance' and represents a goal to which all human services should aspire on behalf of clients. Self-esteem, 'a good opinion of oneself' is a natural progression associated with dignity and can be achieved when a person is valued, involved and accepted in the community in which he or she lives and when he or she feels that they have mastered the design of their own lives in partnership with others. For people working in human services the maintenance of a high quality living environment, designed to achieve this goal, requires constant defence.

# MAINTAINING THE QUALITY OF AN ORDINARY LIFE

When individuals from any social group are dependent on others to meet their daily living needs, a number of things may threaten their dignity and self-esteem. Changes in staff bring new threats and attitudes; changes in local policy and procedure may challenge the autonomy of the service to preserve its independence; and changes in the availability of resources may restrict opportunities for the service and its clients.

There are a number of safeguards which services should build into their operational policies to preserve the independence of the service whose primary aim should always be to enhance the quality of life of its users. Perhaps the most essential of these is to ensure that the various heads of department responsible for the management of various parts of the service are aware of the principles upon which the service is based. In any complex, public organization there will be heads of estate management, catering advisers, planners and financial advisers. With their functional responsibilities will be certain procedures and policies which may conflict with the maintenance of an ordinary lifestyle. For example, auditors may restrict the free choice exercised by residents to bank their money where they please. Trustees may refuse to give persmission to spend or release sums of money to enhance the quality of life of the beneficiary if they choose to oppose their request. Environmental health officers may insist on converting an ordinary domestic kitchen into an impersonal catering department and impose sanctions on the way in which people choose to maximize the space in their home. Building departments may insist on maintaining the estate without regard for the residents' privacy and may arrive to commence work in an ordinary street with large vans emblazoned with the logo of the local statutory authority and thus announce to the neighbours the status of the residents.

Many of these intrusions can be avoided if senior staff ensure that adequate preparation is provided with other service personnel to change traditional working arrangements and to replace inflexible procedures with more meaningful ones which accommodate the needs of the service users. Established services operating an ordinary life model have found that many of the established processes which previously mitigated against change and individualism are in fact able to accommodate the core principles underlying the new service model. Naturally, new policies and procedures will have to be introduced to replace the old to ensure that the quality of the total service is maintained, and some of these will be discussed in Chapter 12.

The quality of the service and the range of opportunities provided for service users will depend not only on the availability of local resources but also on the finances available. The service users will often have a limited income, either from their own earnings or more usually from state benefits. The statutory authorities sponsoring the service may also make provision through the allocation of service budgets but there will always be deficits in the amount of money available. In some cases the temptation may be to accept 'gifts' from local voluntary groups or from the public. This often presents services with a dilemma. In the first instance there is no doubt that many will quite rightly assume that to receive support from charitable bodies implies a dependency on others which may be seen as a threat to one's self-esteem. Others may see this as an acceptable opportunity to gain acceptance in the local community, since society is based on the principle of reciprocity and sharing.

It is not unusual, for example, for neighbours to welcome newcomers with a small gift or when guests come for dinner to accept flowers or other tokens. For many the sharing of tokens is an integral component of acceptance in a local community. Occasionally, sums of money or gifts may be offered by interested parties on an individual basis for the purchase of a 'non-essential' item of equipment. Such gifts should only be accepted if they are given anonymously and without unnecessary publicity. Press releases or publicity launches should be avoided and specific fund-raising activites for houses or individuals actively discouraged.

It is always difficult to prescribe policy statements of this nature and each case must be assessed on its individual merits, but as a general principle it is not appropriate for fund-raising activities to be encouraged in human services, although there is no doubt that the acceptance of gifts from local neighbours may help to build and encourage links with the community as a local gesture of goodwill. It will be for local personnel to consider whether the acceptance of gifts will enhance the quality of life for individuals or infringe their rights as ordinary members of society.

The preservation of privacy is one other area to be defended by everyone in the service. There are clear legal and local procedures and guidelines to protect service users from disclosure of personal and confidential information.[10] In small houses in the community this becomes even more important due to the close proximity with which each person lives with neighbours. Staff will need to be aware of certain facts regarding an individual's background in order to contribute meaningfully to planning to meet the person's needs. However, the amount of information available or shared with any one should be the minimum required to meet their needs as individuals.

One way of restricting the amount of information available is to introduce a key worker system with named staff working with one or two people on each shift they work. Their primary task is to monitor that a person's identified needs are being met and to ensure that agreed action is being taken. Key workers should restrict the number of staff that individuals relate to for the major part of the time at home. Key workers will be encouraged to take a specific interest in the needs of their client and will take responsibility for:

- Assisting people to manage their own finances and to budget accordingly to meet their identified needs.
- Encourage individuals to portray a positive and age-appropriate image to others, e.g. social behaviour, appearance and dress.
- Monitor on a regular basis the number and quality of the person's community contacts and valued experiences and adjust opportunities accordingly.
- Co-ordinate and assist the individual to participate in their own 'life planning' assessment (see Chapter 3) by: (1) liaising with participants, their families, professionals and others to prepare a 'strengths/needs' list for the meeting; (2) attending the meeting with the participant and

representing their interests and needs; (3) carrying out tasks agreed and delegated at the meeting.

- Participate in the design and implementation of opportunity plans.
- Assist in the choice, arrangement and participation of an annual holiday (if requested).
- Observe and record accomplishments and progress in the person's life, note changes in their physical and emotional needs and monitor progress.

The key worker concept is important for individuals if they are to realize stability and opportunities in their lives. Key workers should be flexible in approach and of course 'get on with their partner'. In some cases a change of key worker may be necessary due to a 'personality clash' or difference of opinion. Opportunities for the free exchange of feelings regarding this role are essential if the partnership is to work effectively and meaningfully. In most cases it works very well and provides an excellent opportunity to maintain appropriate contact between workers and clients which preserves their rights and restricts access of personal information to too many people.

The freedom to say no is perhaps one of the most important of all human rights and is also one of the most difficult to realize in human services. All too often people are expected to participate in joint activities or to receive visitors that they have not personally invited to their home. People will also be expected to attend outpatient appointments, to take medication or to participate in evaluation exercises designed to improve the quality of their home. All of these are sometimes taken for granted and explanations are not always called for.

Whenever people are expected to undertake procedures or to participate in activities which they have not requested they must be given the opportunity to consent and to state whether they agree or disagree with that procedure. Opportunity must be given to explain all changes in the person's environment and to receive this information in such a way that is meaningful to them and clearly understood. Procedures should be available to determine the number of 'external' visitors to the house and clearly defined guidelines should be provided for individual counselling and advice for clients. Each person has a right to expect to enjoy their life in relative privacy and to expect that any information given to others will be held in confidence and used only for the purpose for which it was given and not shared or released to others without their informed consent.

All persons living in accommodation other than their own should enjoy security of tenure through the provision of a tenancy agreement.

Agreements should contain statements regarding the conditions of the tenancy and should offer the tenant full consumer rights in the unlikely event of notice being served to move to another part of the service. Such agreements should be offered to all tenants and should be recognized in law. Many statutory authorities have in fact entered into such agreements or licences and as a result service users enjoy greater security of tenure in their 'own homes'.

Insurance cover for items of personal property should also be provided by agencies in respect of damage caused to personal property by others. This basic right should be secured either through private cover or through agreement with the statutory bodies responsible for the management of the property or for the employment of the staff who work there. Naturally, interpretations will differ from authority to authority and as in all insurance claims individual circumstances may mitigate in all claims. However, the basic principle of ensuring that appropriate cover is provided should be recognized.

## SHOULD ADDITIONAL SERVICES BE PROVIDED TO MEET 'SPECIAL NEEDS'?

This chapter has reinforced the view that all services should be planned to meet the needs of each individual. To assume that standard packages will accommodate all people would be incorrect and there will be as many variations on the ordinary life model as there will be individual needs. However, the basic principles outlined in this chapter are equally transferable to any setting and service since they do not rely upon special buildings or personnel for their realization or success.

There may be some people who will require services to meet their special needs due to the presence of acute physical or emotional needs. In the past the aim has been to provide special services for them and to segregate them from others. The additional services which some people will require to meet their needs are covered in Chapter 7.

## SUMMARY

The key issues involved in the maintenance of 'an ordinary life in the community' have been considered in this chapter. It argues for an individually based service, responsive to individual needs and flexible enough to accommodate changes in a person's everyday living arrangements. The model emphasizes an investment of highly motivated staff who will share their skills and experiences with the people with whom they work and to cultivate and exploit opportunities with them to integrate meaningfully into their local neighbourhoods.

The suggestions outlined in this chapter are practical and logical and more importantly achievable. The only constraints are human ones which can be overcome if people change their attitudes towards the rights of people with mental handicaps to live as equal members in society. Some people still argue to overprotect people with learning difficulties and deny them the right to enjoy life with its benefits and sometimes unpredictable outcomes.

For many, the constraints of specially designed services serve only to inhibit their integration into the community. For others the pace of change has been too fast for them to assimilate and accept, but for those who reflect on the 'impossibility' of the task of integration the less valued and enriched will be the lives of the people they work with.

Finally, all services must change as individual needs change. They require constant evaluation in respect of the quality of the service they are aiming to provide. In the final analysis, services must be judged against the quality of life they provide for their consumers within a framework of valued and accepted community-based provision.

# REFERENCES

1. Winchester Health Authority (1986) *Services for People with a Mental Handicap. Operational policy for staffed houses*, unpublished paper.
2. Campaign for People with a Mental Handicap (1986) Talking points No. 5, *Helping People to make Choices: Opportunities and Challenges*, North East CMH and Nan Carle, p. 5.
3. Walsh, J. (1986) *Let's Be Friends*, Human Horizons Series, Souvenir Press, London, p. 176.
4. Campaign for People with a Mental Handicap (1986) Talking Points No. 3, *A Part of the Community: social integration and neighbourhood networks*, Dorothy Atkinson and Linda Ward, pp. 1–2.
5. Felce, D., de Kock, U., Saxby, H. and Thomas, M. (1985) *Final Report: July 1985*, Health Care Evaluation Research Team, University of Southampton.
6. Report of a Working Party (Hampshire Multi-agency Group) (1985) *Guidelines on Personal Relationships and Sex Education for People with a Mental Handicap*, unpublished paper.
7. Craft, A. and Craft, M. (1986) *Sex and the Mentally Handicapped. A Guide for Parents and Carers*, Routledge & Kegan Paul, London.

8. Gunn, M. (1986) The law and mental handicap: Marriage, *Mental Handicap*, Vol. 14, March, pp. 37–8.
9. DHSS (1986) *The Disabled Persons (Services, Consultation and Representation) Act*, Chapter 33, HMSO, London.
10. DHSS (1984) *The Data Protection Act*, Chapter 35, HMSO, London.

# 3. Life Planning

*Peter Wilcock*

## INTRODUCTION

The increasing emphasis on providing individualized services for people with a mental handicap demands the development of service systems that will help identify the person's needs and plan to meet them. This chapter sets a context for these processes and describes approaches designed to ensure that they make decisions which are relevant to a person's life. A number of issues are explored in depth and the need to relate individual life planning to service management is emphasized.

## SETTING THE SCENE

As an ordinary part of their lives, most people organize their time so that they may participate in the range of activities that reflect what is important to them and the people they are. This may involve sorting out details relating to work and career development, to the maintenance of their homes and daily lives, or to planning their leisure activities. Some people plan their lives quite formally in order to fit things in and many will have to consult diaries before being able to confirm future arrangements. Other people may appear to lead quite disorganized lives, but even they will be making decisions about priorities as they encounter new opportunities and demands.

Many factors will influence what decisions are eventually made and indeed how they are made, as it will be necessary to recognize the constraints placed upon us by other people and circumstances. It may well be helpful to turn to others for advice and support, but we will usually expect to have the final say in the process.

Decisions will vary from person to person and will reflect, for example, previous life experiences, as a child and adult, feelings whether rational or not, and the needs of other important people in our lives. Awareness of what is available in the locality where we live and the interests and attitudes of our friends will also have an influence upon us. Finally, our own knowledge about the things we do well and the things that demand too much effort to make them worthwhile for us personally will have an effect on what we choose to do.

Once a decision is made, whether it is to move house, look for a new job, try a different sport or visit different shops, it is necessary to take action. The amount of effort involved will vary according to what that particular action is and how complicated our lives already are. One of the first tasks, therefore, will usually be to consider what needs to be done in order to achieve our ends. This may involve making contact with other people, finding out where to get hold of the things we need or discovering what is available locally. Some activities will demand skills and experience that we do not possess and hence it will be necessary to make arrangements to learn about these, either from friends or perhaps by taking formal lessons.

All these processes are undertaken as part of our daily lives and seem to be such an ordinary part of our lives that we undertake them without being explicitly aware of the amount of effort and planning involved.

The reasons for living in a particular area may be many and may also include forces outside our direct control, such as job moves and economic status. Thus, moving to a particular job will dictate the general area where we must live and our economic status will limit the part of that area where we can afford to buy a house or whether we can afford to. Once we have chosen a house and moved in, an early and important task is to explore the locality, meet neighbours and other local people, discover outlets for interests and ways of meeting needs and begin the process of forming new relationships.

We will become increasingly active as our network of contacts and knowledge of the community increases and after some time the questions about our lives are more concerned with how to fit everything in, rather than finding things to do. We will have met people with similar interests, whether they be work, leisure or social, and will be actively engaged as an equal member of our community. This will have a major impact on the way we perceive and value ourselves and on the way other people perceive and value us.

It is clear, therefore, that whether we realize it or not, we are involved in an ongoing and dynamic process of making decisions about our lives. Furthermore, this process is continually shaping us and has a fundamental influence upon the people we become. It is thus a continuous cycle which will determine at any point in time a lifestyle that reflects our individual interpretation of a high quality life.

As mentioned earlier, throughout this process we expect to be the main decision-maker and thus retain control over our own lives. In order to achieve this we must have the ability to make decisions, we must have gained the experience and knowledge to inform those decisions and, crucially, we must be able to make our views known. This latter point implies the presence of both skill and opportunity.

Until fairly recently, many people with a mental handicap have not been offered such opportunities, nor have they been helped to develop the skills necessary to make their views known. Their difficulties have been further compounded by the absence of opportunities for the ordinary life experiences that, as mentioned earlier, are of fundamental importance, not only to informed decision-making, but to the development of a positive self-concept.

Thus any consideration of issues related to life planning for people with a mental handicap must take into account the need to provide valued life experiences as well as establishing processes by which decisions are made. Unless there is a clear understanding about what living in the 'community' should mean, life planning will prove to be a mechanistic exercise which is irrelevant to the people it is supposed to be helping.

## CARE IN THE COMMUNITY

The Peter Bedford Trust argues that before care can legitimately be considered to be community-based, it must include the following five dimensions:[1]

- The opportunity for people to feel they belong to something they value.
- The prospect of others in the wider community sharing in some way in the lives of those with an institutional potential or background.
- The chance to count for something, to be a contributing member of the community.

- The prospect of increasing control over the events of one's life.
- The prospect of receiving the support, medical or otherwise, that is essential to allow everything else to happen.

This implies that we must move away from services that are seen as something that professionals provide for or do to others because the result of this is that opportunities for genuine sharing and collaboration are lost. The Peter Bedford Trust points out that this collaboration should be between the people who are the clients, the people who are paid to provide services, and other people living in the community who wish in some way to make contact with other people's lives.

People with a mental handicap rely upon help from others to develop the various networks that will give meaning to their lives and hence effort must be directed towards establishing ways to foster and support care by the community. The creation of positive links with local organizations and individuals is crucial if one is to avoid the mistake of imposing services that never really become integrated.[1] The task is that of helping the person with a mental handicap to make contact and establish relationships in much the same way as other people.

In order to help professionals look at the quality of people's experiences, a framework has been presented that will structure the approach and provide a common vocabularly.[2] Five areas of accomplishment which have a major impact on the quality of a person's life are described, which will demand hard work and co-operation between the person with a mental handicap and the other people he or she relies on as allies:[2]

- Community presence. This is the experience people have through the sharing of the ordinary places that define community life. This demands that care is taken to avoid segregated services and instead to increase the number and variety of ordinary places that a person knows and can use.
- Choice. This is the experience of growing autonomy in both small everyday matters (e.g. what to eat or wear) and large life-defining matters (e.g. who to live with, what work to do). It is pointed out that personal choice defines and expresses individual identity and it demands effort to avoid people with severe handicaps becoming passive receivers of services.[2] This area of accomplishment presents considerable challenges to others' ability to detect personal preferences, and it may sometimes require another person to make choices on behalf of someone who cannot make important decisions.
- Competence. This is the experience of growing ability to skilfully

perform functional and meaningful activities with whatever assistance is required. Focused effort is necessary to ensure that people with handicaps have expectations placed on them which must be accompanied by the opportunities, instruction and assistance necessary for development.

- Respect. This is the experience of having a valued place among a network of people and valued ideas in community life. Once again, focused effort is necessary to avoid confining people to a narrow range of stereotyped, low-status activities which restrict their opportunities to be seen and valued as individuals.
- Community participation. This is the experience of being part of a growing network of personal relationships which includes close friends. The effort here needs to be directed at providing opportunities for non-handicapped people in the community to meet those with severe handicaps as individuals. Assistance should be provided to support existing and growing relationships and thus ensure that a person's social network is not limited only to staff, family members and other clients.

A description is given of how each of these accomplishments can facilitate or inhibit each other; when considering priorities, the relative benefits and costs of achieving in one at the expense of another, need to be carefully considered. A clear message from this work relates to the amount of effort required to improve the quality of a person's life experiences; the rest of this chapter considers ways of tackling the necessary tasks.

## NEIGHBOURHOOD KNOWLEDGE

A detailed knowledge of a person's local neighbourhood will make an important contribution to the decisions about the lifestyle of that person. A number of writers have suggested ways of obtaining this information which will also help achieve the goal of stimulating care by the community rather than simply in the community.

A set of guidelines for the evolution of decentralized services have been produced.[3] It is pointed out that one of the first steps to be taken by local workers is to get to know their local patch and build up an understanding of the nature of the community. Identifying the community's strengths and weaknesses forms the basis of the approach, which has the objective of establishing partnerships with local people which, in turn, will facilitate the provision of help and support to those who need it.[3]

Knowing the community involves learning about the history of the neighbourhood, talking to local residents, becoming familiar with the local environment (e.g. houses, shops, recreation, industry, etc) and finding out how people who live and work locally view their neighbourhood. Other people considered worth contacting are local politicians, councils for voluntary services and other local networks.

The importance of such links is stressed to ensure that effective services are delivered at the right place and at the right time. Good links will provide a basis for increased co-operation and co-ordination of services as part of a collaborative approach. It is pointed out that this should be a two-way process. Local people and voluntary groups represent vital resources as well as the source of much knowledge, while local professionals have much to offer in the way of training, support and advice.

In a similar vein, the need for 'neighbourhood mapping' to provide a knowledge base about individual neighbourhoods is discussed.[4] It is emphasized that it is necessary to look at much smaller areas than community services traditionally cover and it is suggested that compiling a 'neighbourhood resources directory' is a prerequisite step for developing local services. This would provide a structured way of organizing information similar to that already recommended.[3]

Further, it is suggested that it would be worth the effort to identify local neighbourhood workers and prepare a 'neighbourhood workers' directory. It is pointed out that 'frequently key people whose involvement assists neighbourhood work are not paid workers in well defined work roles'.[4] Many key social interactions take place in informal meetings and in unstructured settings. These key people need to be identified, since they are often gatekeepers to services or provide substantial services themselves.[4] It is also emphasized that forming new networks and developing existing relationships demand considerable time and energy.

Another approach also talks about preparing a community services inventory which will include all services available to children and adults.[5] The point is made that although the needs assessment and planning processes must be based on each person's needs, the inventory gives an understanding about what is available and how flexibly it can be used.

# PLANNING AND MAKING DECISIONS

The availability of such information will provide the basis for an evaluation of the quality of a person's life in the context of that person's relationship to and use of resources in the neighbourhood. This evaluation needs to be organized to ensure that necessary information is available and that decisions are made. It is this formal organization of effort that is usually referred to as 'life planning'.

There are a number of different approaches to this, but currently most systems have been established and are managed by professionals employed to provide care and support to people with a mental handicap. However, the fundamental question as to whether it is appropriate for such systems to be managed by these professionals remains to be answered. There is a danger that keeping the ownership in professional hands may in itself present a barrier to real local collaboration due to other people's perceptions of professional roles and the status of professional organizations. As a result the decision-making process may be professionally dominated and more clinical than is appropriate.

## Approaches to the process

Life planning must be part of an ongoing process of obtaining information about a person's needs and desires and the neighbourhood in which he or she lives. To be successful, it must somehow mesh together the formal and informal services available. This should be a continuous feedback cycle, which allows relevant decisions to be made as flexibly as possible. A number of different approaches have been tried and some of these are described below.

### Personal futures planning

This approach is based on the five accomplishments mentioned earlier.[2] Two major dimensions are discussed: 'personal futures planning' and 'individual planning'. Personal futures planning involves people who have an important role in the life of the person being helped, and will include family members, important friends and other contacts as well as service workers. One important objective is to make a bridge between professionals and ordinary people as much as possible.

The personal future planning review is geared to social problem-solving to increase opportunities rather than the selection of the most effective intervention to remediate the person's problems. It is pointed out that if there is reason to believe that a person will benefit from clinical evaluation, this needs to be arranged and the results used to inform the decision-making processes in the review.[5]

A number of questions are suggested which form the basis for looking at the quality of a person's life with two main purposes in mind. The first reflects the desire to identify opportunities for better quality life experiences, and the second is to decide on strategies for accomplishing them. In order to facilitate the process, the questions review the person's current life experiences, look at what is changing locally or for the person that will influence his or her quality of life, and try to help describe what is an image of a desirable future for the person. An important area is the identification of barriers to progress and agreement about ways to overcome them.[2]

### Individual programme planning

A mechanism for providing a forum for multidisciplinary discussion where a co-ordinated practical plan can be drawn up has been described.[6] A detailed description of the roles of different people in ensuring the meeting is run efficiently and effectively is provided and will be referred to later.

The meeting uses a detailed pro forma to structure the discussion in a number of major areas. The headings ask questions about a person's need for major services such as education, accommodation and work, and includes a personal needs list to identify specific areas of priority such as self-care or communication skills. Skills to be acquired in the next nine months are discussed and agreed, objectives are set and the person responsible for a particular action is identified. This is then used to review progress at the next meeting for that person.

### Skills teaching, education and programme planning (STEP)[7]

STEP is a staff training package based on the principles of normalization and individual programme planning. It is accompanied by a life planning manual, which presents a very detailed approach to looking at the service a client receives from the client's own point of view. Following this a set of questions is included to identify the client's needs from the full range of ordinary life experiences and a third component demands that actions required to meet each need are specified in such a way that achievement can be monitored.

Each of these three stages is supported by a set of papers containing detailed questions, some of which need answering before a review meeting and some during it. STEP is also interesting in that the individual planning approach is built in as an integral part of staff training and hence may be expected to have an influence on their day-to-day working lives as well.

**Getting to know you[5]**

This approach is based on the premiss that the description of a person's disabilities is only relevant to the extent that they complicate the fulfilment of that person's needs. A number of dimensions are identified, such as autonomy, rights, personal growth and community participation, in which it is necessary to measure strengths and weaknesses. The process demands that one person gets to know the client very well, sees him or her in all significant settings and talks to other important people in his or her life. It depends on a trusting and personal relationship between the two people concerned. The information is used to prepare an individual needs summary, which is presented in the form of a sensitive description of the person, written by the assessor in the form of an essay, rather than a series of statements under a list of headings.

The aim is to produce a general service plan that assists in the identification, development and implementation of services and/or support that a person needs to live within a local community. More broadly, the information obtained can be used to stimulate the development of new services or identify the need for change within current systems. It is emphasized that the approach is not designed to serve as an individual programme plan which would require much more detail to specify goals and objectives and allow monitoring of achievement.[5]

# The place of meetings

Each of the approaches described above depends on significant people meeting together at some regular interval to conduct the business of making decisions and organizing the effort in support of the client. Indeed, it is difficult to see how any approach could work without some forum to allow the exchange of information and ensure that staff do not work in isolation from each other. There will usually be representatives from a number of different disciplines and agencies involved in a client's life, which would soon become confusing and chaotic unless their work was co-ordinated and directed towards agreed and common goals.

Within any system it is essential to be clear what the purpose of a particular meeting is. It will have been seen from the description of the four different approaches above that each has slightly different aims for meetings. The meetings described in one approach[2] use identified questions as an agenda to make broad statements about a person's needs. However, another approach plans a more detailed meeting where the emphasis is on forward planning, rather than current descriptions of a person's life.[6] The STEP approach[7] demands a similarly detailed meeting whereas another explicitly avoids a consideration of specific individual planning.[5]

Different meetings thus operate at different levels of individual and service planning and it is crucial that their explicit nature is clear to all participants during the information-gathering exercise before each meeting, as well as during it. Their place in the total process of life planning for a person must also be clearly understood to avoid the danger of being seen as the only forum within which decisions can be taken. This could result in a rigid and bureaucratic decision-making process, which would stifle the flexibility that must clearly be an essential component. The dangers of professional domination have already been mentioned and nowhere is this more likely to happen than in a meeting where they are likely to outnumber 'non-professionals'.

It must not be forgotten who the meeting is for and what the true nature of the workers' relationship to their client should be. It is too easy to convene such meetings because they meet the needs of the professionals attending them rather more than they are expected to change the lives of the clients. Indeed, the establishment of a process designed to help a person increase his or her quality of life could, unless sensitively managed, reduce the chances of this happening in ways that allow real individual choice.

## Administrative aspects

Whichever approach is adopted, there are a number of common administrative issues that need to be addressed in pursuit of efficiency and effectiveness.

### Frequency of meetings

At any time it is crucial that the people who are involved know the date for the next review of their client's progress. This is to ensure that they see the process as having timescales attached to goals and to give some incentive for taking action.

The time between meetings for a person will be influenced by a number of factors. Most important, it is necessary to allow enough time for action to have been implemented and progress to have occurred. If meetings are held too frequently it is possible that increasingly trivial objectives will be set in order that some sort of progress is seen to have taken place. This is a time-consuming, expensive and inefficient exercise.

Another major factor will be the number of people within the service who need to be reviewed and the staffing resources available to support them. There seems to be general agreement that reviews need to be held at least annually; six to nine months has been suggested as a reasonable compromise.[6] The actual time interval will need to be decided according to local factors and it is essential that positive monitoring procedures are introduced to ensure that major difficulties are identified as early as possible without necessarily having to wait until the next review.

### Chairing meetings

In order to be efficient and effective, meetings need to be skilfully chaired. Ideally, the chairperson should not be someone with a major contribution to make to the discussion, since these two demands can compete with each other.

The major task is to ensure that at the end of each meeting it is clear what action has been agreed and who is responsible for it. This means that the chairperson must be able to help participants articulate their views clearly, facilitate the very difficult process of agreeing priorities and make sure the meeting finishes on time. It has been pointed out that however conceptually perfect the process, it will be distorted by the values of the people implementing it and by the realities of opportunities and constraints.[5] The chairperson needs to plot a skilful course through such difficulties to ensure that although decisions reflect reality, they never-theless relate to the needs and desires of the client.

## The place of clients in the process

The person who is the focus of the efforts to help must be involved at all stages of the decision-making process. Professionals must remember that they are employed to support their clients, not supplant them. It is increasingly accepted that clients should attend meetings related to their lives, although there is still some dispute about this. Ideally, the meeting should be viewed as helping the person with a mental handicap make decisions about his or her life and thus he or she needs to be actively involved in the discussion. The person's physical presence in the meeting is likely to influence the quality of the discussion, even if he or she is unable to make a direct contribution. However, there is little point in insisting that he or she attends if he or she clearly does not wish to or if his or her behaviour would be so disruptive as to prevent coherent discussion.

For a client's contribution to be meaningful, he or she must have real information and experience of his or her world or potential world. Additional skills are those of making informed choice and being able to present views to other people.

Active steps must be taken to help clients develop this knowledge and these skills, otherwise the professionals and others present will continue to dominate, however well-meaning they are. It must therefore be seen as fundamental to life planning systems to ensure that coaching and support are available to individual people to help them learn these general skills. Great care and sensitivity are then needed to encourage and nurture their use in practice. Unless this happens, clients will be additionally penalized, because it may appear that they have been included in the decision-making process when, in fact, it has been going on around them.

## The need for advocacy

It will sometimes be the case that a person with a mental handicap will be unable to make an active and direct contribution to making decisions about his or her life. In these situations it is essential that a third and completely independent person is available to represent him or her.

This person will need to have the time to get to know the client, develop the skills to communicate with him or her, see him or her taking part in the important activities of life and meet other important people in his or her life. The advocate needs to be a person who is familiar with local neighbourhoods and knows about services that should be available.

The role of advocate is often picked up by staff working alongside the person with a mental handicap, but this is not really satisfactory. Being an advocate may bring a person into conflict with service providers and this will place staff undertaking the role into a very difficult position in which they will find it difficult to be completely independent.

Further questions to be considered relate to what status or authority advocates have when they do come into conflict with the service and what rights clients have to decide who shall or shall not be their advocates. The question may also arise about what rights a client has to veto a decision, if his or her advocate has been involved in making it.

It will be clear that developing an advocacy system needs very careful consideration and the issues are explored in greater depth in Chapter 1.

# The place of relatives

A particularly difficult set of questions arises when considering the place of relatives, especially parents, in the decision-making process. Traditionally, parents or other relatives have been considered to be the key decision-makers from whom permission was sought before major decisions about a person's life were made. This is, of course, appropriate for children, but is increasingly being challenged for adults with a mental handicap.

It is vital that within local services clear decisions are made about the rights and responsibilities of relatives of clients. Explicit guidelines need to be made available about how and when they should be involved in the life planning process and what their status is. The fundamental question about whether they can be the best advocates for their grown-up sons and daughters needs to be addressed, since they have a set of needs themselves that may be in conflict.

This must be handled with great sensitivity by the service professionals as it is all too easy to view parents as blocks to their clients' development and independence, and treat them in ways that makes them angry and hostile. When this happens, of course, it can then be used as evidence that it was right to view the parents with suspicion in the first place. It might be a salutory exercise for any professional to reflect on how they would feel if people outside their family became involved in making decisions about their own children and used a set of values with which they did not feel comfortable.

Thus it can be seen that without sensitive handling and genuine attempts to balance the needs of all family members, decisions designed to enhance the lives of our clients may have a destructive impact on the lives of their relatives.

# The place of the key worker

Most life planning systems include a key worker role as a vital part of the process. However, there are difficulties inherent in this approach that need to be understood if they are to be avoided.

One major difficulty is that this attractive concept does not always reflect the realities of the organization and structure within which key workers have to function. The role cuts across discipline boundaries and line management hierarchies. The key worker tasks are often picked up by junior members of staff whose authority, when monitoring action agreed by more senior colleagues, is uncertain, to say the least. The tasks may demand knowledge and skills beyond the experience of the key worker, who will thus be placed in a position of great difficulty. The tasks will inevitably be time-consuming and – bearing in mind we live and work in an imperfect world, where people forget or lose enthusiasm – the experience of being a key worker may be very frustrating.

Further difficulties relate to the conflict that very busy professional workers may have in picking up tasks not directly related to their primary skills. Apart from the obvious problems of time constraints, there may be issues of status here as well. Certain types of nonspecialist task may be viewed as being of lower value and hence demeaning, despite their obvious importance to the life of the person they are supposed to be helping.

The message appears to be that key worker systems are unlikely to be successful unless management boundaries are clear, communication channels are good and local staff have enough confidence in their own skills to allow them to trust and respect other working colleagues. It is only under these conditions that all professional energies can be truly directed to the people for whom they are employed to work. These particular issues of working together are addressed in more detail in Chapter 6.

Different systems have used keyworkers in different ways. For example, the approach described by two sources ties the role clearly into the effective running of the programme planning meeting.[6, 7] This includes some or all of the following tasks:

- Identifying all the people who should be attending a meeting and reminding them of the date, time and place of the next one.
- Making contact with these people to obtain their views about the person's current needs.
- Making sure the needs list is complete and circulated before the meeting.
- Making sure that the views of the person concerned are obtained either by direct contact or through someone who knows him or her well.
- Chasing up action between meetings.

The approach described by one source does not refer to a key worker as such, but the role assigned to the person called the 'assessor' is probably equivalent.[5] The tasks assigned to this person explicitly avoid measuring people's strengths and weaknesses because this is based on assumptions about our 'ability to discover and remedy various causal factors' which they claim does not hold up in practice. The role of the assessor in this approach is

> to work with a person (who happens to have a disability) and significant other people in his/her life to create a picture of that person that captures his/her uniqueness and humanity, in order to determine what forms of help the community needs to plan, arrange, provide and monitor to meet his/her individual and human needs.[5]

Similarly, another source avoids the use of the term keyworker, but refers to a person 'who has agreed to introduce the person's situation to the planning meeting'.[2] A guide has been prepared which poses a set of questions under each of the five accomplishments described earlier and which are used to prepare a summary of the findings about a person's current quality of life. This summary is prepared and presented by the person referred to above, who is recommended to use coloured marker pens on large sheets of paper which are hung on the wall.

A final point worth mentioning concerns possible confusion between the roles of key worker and advocate. It is natural that key workers will want to act as advocates on behalf of their clients by, for example, notifying service deficiencies through the appropriate channels. However, as mentioned earlier, it is not appropriate for them to pick up the broader responsibilities of advocacy, which must be entrusted to people who are not subjected to either the constraints or the managers of the service systems in operation.

## INTER-AGENCY ISSUES

The accelerating trend of dispersing services throughout local communities and the recognition that people with a mental handicap have a broad range of needs, necessarily demands co-operation between a number of different agencies. In addition to the major statutory services, the private and voluntary sectors are playing a more significant role and must be actively included in the collaborative process.

Traditionally, the major agencies have worked separately towards their own, not often very explicit and usually not very public goals. Suspicion and fear of each others' attempts to transfer the major costs of services to each other have in the past strangled attempts to work together and plan and provide services jointly.

This situation is now changing, partly as a result of government initiative,[8] and partly due to the presence of greater numbers of service workers with similar ideals. Paradoxically, this is happening at a time of increasing constraint and cuts in public expenditure.

One consequence of these difficulties could be a return to segregated, suspicious planning and service provision within agencies. Alternatively, the opportunity to share resources could be grasped to provide more integrated services, which do not require clients to be labelled in particular ways in order to gain access to one service rather than another. Such collaboration requires considerable time and effort, but is crucial if services are to develop which will ensure that meaningful life planning at an individual level can take place.

At a fundamental level, it is essential that senior managers and planners from different agencies can check to see whether they share the same vision about the pattern of future services. Unless they share the same goals and assumptions upon which decisions are made, conflict is likely to arise, however much goodwill is available.

It will also be helpful if workers from the different agencies can come together to share the difficulties and problems they face in their day-to-day work. A clearer understanding and knowledge about this will help to remove much suspicion and provide a base from which workers can plan joint strategies and work towards common goals.

One eventual aim of life planning systems must be to develop processes which bring together all the important people from whichever agency into a shared system of decision-making within which workers can support each other as well as their clients. If professionals are to stand any chance of providing an individual approach within services that plan for many, it is essential to avoid duplication of decision-making systems and promote active communication between all concerned.

In working towards this aim, it is probably not realistic to pursue one single agreed system across territories the size that most agencies have to cover. Indeed, bearing in mind the number and variety of different systems already operating, attempts to standardize may simply result in further argument and debate. A more realistic approach may be to agree broadly what principles should underpin life planning and what would be the characteristics of an approach that everybody would consider to be successful. These guidelines could then be used to look at more local systems and would serve as an aid to ensuring that the approach is flexible, understood and accepted by everybody as having authority. In this way the decisions made should be better informed and will stand a greater chance of being implemented.

# RISK-TAKING

One natural consequence of increased opportunities for ordinary living and encouraging people with a mental handicap to make their own decisions, is that they will be exposed to the hazards of daily living. Indeed, it can be claimed that this is their right. Staff will also be placed in the potentially difficult situation of being involved in making decisions that will actively introduce an element of risk into a person's life. It is important that they feel confident that providing they act in a professional and competent manner, their employers will support them, should incidents occur.

Therefore, it is crucial that risk-taking guidelines are prepared and agreed at the highest level of management. Otherwise life planning is likely to be severely restricted in its scope. Such guidelines need to consider the following areas:

## Kind of risk

Predicting the form that possible harm may take is the first step in preventing it. This may include physical harm to the person with a mental handicap, physical harm to other people or distress or misunderstanding by members of the public.

## Degree of risk

It is not easy to judge how likely the harm is to occur and past experiences must be used as a guide. Where such experience is not available, the best way forward is to test out the situation with careful monitoring, rather than decide not to proceed on purely hypothetical grounds.

## Priority of objectives

The importance of the objectives needs to be weighed against the possible degree of risk involved. The possible risks involved in not taking action must also be considered.

## Procedures of intervention

It is important to consider whether the same objectives can be achieved by less risky means. An apparently less risky and less efficient way of working may prove better in practice because workers may be more prepared to implement it consistently.

## Decision-making

The importance of shared decision-making has already been emphasized strongly and this is absolutely vital where risk-taking may be involved. If there is disagreement that cannot be resolved, whether it is to do with goals or methods, the majority view should usually prevail. Action should proceed with careful monitoring and be reviewed as soon as enough experience has been obtained about its implementation, to provide information which will resolve the disagreement. Once such decisions are taken, everybody involved has a responsibility to implement them faithfully, until the next review, even if they initially disagreed.

# IMPLEMENTATION ISSUES

There is little point in encouraging the development of life planning systems unless local structures ensure that decisions will be implemented. The approach will be doomed to failure if there is competition due to internal politics, lack of support from senior managers or the emphasis on individual planning is given low priority when compared to the day-to-day administration of the settings within which people live.[9] There are a number of issues to be considered and the most important of these are discussed below.

## Operational policies

The management systems for the service must be designed to reflect the fact that the major determinant of policy should be individual client needs. There may be a natural conflict between achieving this and organizing groups of staff efficiently and effectively and the outcome has traditionally been the establishment of staff-centred systems. It is therefore essential that clear operational policies are prepare to provide the framework for running the service and to identify dimensions for monitoring performance. Such operational policies must emphasize the core purpose of the service in providing a high quality lifestyle for its clients and describe the processes to be implemented in order to achieve this. They must place clients and life planning processes firmly at the centre of operations.

Each operational policy should begin with an explicit statement of the value base for the service and list the principles which will determine its nature.[10, 11] This needs to be translated into a set of objectives relevant to each part of the service which specify as clearly as possible what will be the outcomes of that service for each client.

The most crucial sections of the policy will be those that provide a detailed description of the processes that ensure client-centred planning and decision-making. The central plank to these will be the particular approach to life planning that is being adopted and which must be formally written into the policy. In this way its place as part of the day-to-day operation should be emphasized and secured. Although the operational policy is not the place for a very detailed description, the major dimensions with implications for staff time and action should be included. Issues identified in the earlier part of this chapter need to be addressed in this context.

The policy must also go further and build in the basic responsibilities for staff to provide opportunities for people with a mental handicap to gain the experience they need to help with their development and to inform their decision-making. This will only be achieved by efficient organization and hence strategies for planning the day ahead must be incorporated. This will ensure that staff are clear on what their tasks should be at any point in time during their working day and will help avoid situations where neither staff nor clients are engaged in purposeful activities.[12] Bearing in mind that not all staff will have been involved in the life planning decisions for each client, it is important that a process is established to share these decisions. This is discussed in more detail in the next section.

## Staff meetings

A dynamic service that continually responds to the changing needs and demands of a number of different clients presents particular challenges for keeping workers up-to-date and working relevantly.

Staff involved in the day-to-day operation of the setting must therefore be included in discussions about how best to implement decisions that have been made about individual people with a mental handicap. Regular meetings need to be held so that as new and different demands are identified, a process of negotiation can be undertaken at the end of which all staff are aware of the current tasks and have agreed practical ways forward. Such meetings will also help to maintain an overall perspective about the volume of current work being undertaken.

Additional benefits of such meetings are that they provide important staff opportunities for peer support and monitoring. Individual staff are less likely to be destructive or obstructive if they are not only involved in decision-making, but are also likely to be challenged by their own colleagues. The meetings also allow staff to share their difficulties and discuss constructive ways of avoiding them in the future. However, perhaps one of their greatest benefits is that they encourage the lowest status staff to make a valuable contribution to managing their own work environment, and this will greatly increase their motivation and result in better outcomes for their clients.[9, 13].

## Staff development

If life planning systems are to be implemented successfully it is crucial that staff have the necessary skills. Most of the staff working directly alongside people with a mental handicap will bring a range of skills and abilities based on previous life experiences, but will be unqualified in a formal sense. Thus they will lack the experience and knowledge about how to help the growing competence of people with severe learning difficulties. It is therefore essential that the skills necessary are clearly identified and a dynamic staff development culture generated so that individual staff members can themselves continually increase their competence. If this is done in a planned way, it will emphasize to staff the importance of their role and build their confidence. This will in turn have a major impact on the quality of the lives of their clients. Issues related to staff development are considered in more detail in Chapter 14.

## SUMMARY

It should be clear from this chapter that life planning is something that is crucial to all of us, whether we are aware of it or not. As we make decisions about our lives, we automatically take into account a number of factors relating to our circumstances, interests and abilities.

Many people with a mental handicap need particular help to make such important decisions and hence the process needs to be formalized and structured to organize the effort involved. There are many issues related to the organization of the effort and some of the key areas are discussed in detail within this chapter.

It is beyond dispute that wherever services exist, they should be

**Table 3.1   Some key questions related to the life planning process**

---

### 1. Looking at the quality of the person's current lifestyle

- Does the person live in a valued setting?
- Is the person familiar with the local neighbourhood?
- Has the person developed a range of activities that involve making use of the neighbourhood and having contact with other people?
- Does the person have autonomy and exercise choice in decisions about his/her life?

### 2. Looking at the person's desired lifestyle

- Is there a clear process which supports and encourages the person to make major decisions about his/her desired future?
- Are other important people in this person's life actively involved in this process?
- Is someone available to help the person make use of this process or make representations on his/her behalf?
- Does this process operate in a way which prevents it being dominated by service-based professionals?
- Does this process lead to a clear identification of the opportunities and skills that this person needs to enhance his/her quality of life?

### 3. Looking at the need to take action

- Is there a clear process which will identify the people who can help with the provision of opportunities and skills?
- Does this process ensure that action is taken by identified people and is monitored?
- Does information feed into the service network so that relevant professional staff are quickly made aware that their skills and expertise are needed?
- Is the work of service professionals organized to maximize efficiency and effectiveness and ensure co-ordination?
- Are service managers and planners kept informed about the changing demands of their clients?

### 4. Looking at the impact on the person's desired lifestyle

- Does a clear process exist which will allow the significant people in this person's life to monitor and comment upon the impact that is being made on moving towards his/her desired future (see 2)?

---

underpinned by processes that recognize the individuality of the people they serve and use the knowledge gained from this to direct the services themselves. The best way to do this is more debatable and will be subject to local circumstances.

It is therefore crucial that local managers identify what are the characteristics of a good process and this chapter has been prepared to support such discussion. Unless the key issues are explicitly addressed and positive decisions taken, life planning processes will exist in an atmosphere of uncertainty and confusion and may even do more harm than good to the people they are supposed to be serving. Table 3.1. presents some key questions related to the life planning process.

# REFERENCES

1. Peter Bedford Trust (1984) *Community Care – Which Community? What Care?* Peter Bedford Trust, London.
2. O'Brien, J. (1986) A guide to personal futures planning, in G. Thomas and B. Wilcox (eds.), *The Activities Catalogue: A Community Programming Guide for Youth and Adults with a Severe Disability.*
3. East Sussex Consultancy and Training Agency (1984) *Guidelines for Decentralised Teams*, East Sussex Consultancy and Training Agency, Brighton.
4. Baldwin, S. (1987) From communities to neighbourhoods, *Disability, Handicap and Society*, Vol. 2, No. 1, pp. 41–59.
5. Brost, N. and Johnson, J. (1982) *Getting to Know You*, Wisconsin Coalition for Advocacy, 2 West Mifflin Street, Madison, Wisconsin 53702.
6. Jenkins, J., Felce, D., Toogood, A. *et al.* (in press) *Individual Programme Planning*, British Institute for Mental Handicap, Kidderminster, England.
7. Chamberlain, P. (1985) *STEP Life Planning Manual*, British Association for Behavioural Psychotherapy, Rossendale, England.
8. DHSS (1981) *Care in the Community*, HMSO, London.
9. Wilcock, P. (1985) The role of the psychologist, in Craft, M., Bicknell, J. and Hollins, S. (eds.), *Mental Handicap*, Baillière Tindall, London.
10. King's Fund Centre (1980) *An Ordinary Life*, Project Paper No. 24, King's Fund Centre, London.
11. Independent Development Council for People with a Mental Handicap (1987) *Elements of a Comprehensive Local Service for People with a Mental Handicap*, IDC, London.
12. Winchester Health Authority (1986) *Services for People with a Mental Handicap*, Operational Policy for People Living in an Ordinary House, Winchester Health Authority, Winchester.
13. Mansell, J., Felce, D., Jenkins, J. *et al.* (1987) *Developing Staffed Housing for People with Mental Handicap*, Costello, Tunbridge Wells.

# 4. Towards Integration in the Local Community

*Ken Moore*

## INTRODUCTION

During the last decade there was little difficulty in differentiating between the choices available to people with mental handicaps and their families when it came to choosing alternatives to providing care at home. Quite simply, opportunities were allocated in response to a person's ability to fit into a restricted model of care linked to rigid divisions of dependency between health and social service departments.

In 1974 the government announced the creation of the National Development Group for people with a mental handicap, and during the next few years recommendations were made for the establishment of a new service for people with mental handicaps in their own homes. This signified the beginning of the now well-established community mental handicap team model which has been introduced within most health districts in the United Kingdom.

Parent groups demanded greater opportunities and choices for their offspring and the government responded by challenging the existing models of care in hospitals and local authority hostels as being uneconomical and certainly inefficient in the quality of care they provided, within a series of published reports and papers.[1-7]

During this period the inheritance of segregation between models of institutionalized care and care provided by the community was perpetuated by the creation of community mental handicap teams who found their bases in large mental handicap hospitals, often isolated from the very neighbourhoods they were designed to serve.

The Government Select Committee in its review of community care for people with a mental handicap supported this view and introduced the term 'transinstitutionalization' to describe the transfer of some people from hospital care into the community without integrating them into their new neighbourhoods as valued citizens.[8]

This chapter challenges the present model of community care and presents an alternative model encouraging the exploitation of naturally occurring opportunities in the community. By working from within the local neighbourhood it is possible to facilitate a partnership betweeen consumers, local stakeholders, residential and community-based professionals to achieve maximum acceptance for clients.

## WHAT IS MEANT BY THE COMMUNITY?

There are as many definitions of the term 'community' as there are examples of subcultures and minority groups in society, and it is not surprising that professionals planning services for others so often fail to match previous life experiences and expectations with new services.

Sociologists have acknowledged the influences that professionals bring to bear when designing support services to meet the needs of others and these are influenced by previous life experiences, attitudes and beliefs. The mental handicap profession has been particularly exploited in this arena and history has determined the model of care experienced by so many people with mental handicaps today.

One definition of a community is to bring together people with similar needs and to create a society to reinforce their common value systems and to 'protect' them from infiltration from other people's needs and exploitation. This model has been adopted by various religious groups, for example, the Moonies, and by fringe groups such as vagrants, 'hippies' and more extensively in the belief systems of some societies (Communism and the Kibbutz system in Israel, for example).

A more familiar definition refers to the local amenities which exist in a locality and are often evaluated in respect of the number of shops, public houses, leisure facilities and opportunities provided to the public. Schools and health facilities will also figure high in estate agents' information to prospective house-buyers, as will access to main public transport routes and major road links. The presence of community centres and local community groups will also influence a person's perception of the community and its inhabitants.

Where does the person with a mental handicap fit into this model? At the turn of this century the social scientists of the time determined that it was preferable for people who were 'feeble minded' or 'deficient' to live together in large colonies or hospitals, segregated from the local community. The development of self-sufficiency systems were encouraged and a new subculture emerged to support the 'new system'. Hence was born the mental handicap hospital and, surrounding its beliefs, staff were encouraged to move into hospital accommodation which in turn proliferated the value systems so important to a total institution. Finally, all this had an impact on the surrounding community and the institution gained its own value system which was often entrenched with mysticism and imagery.

More recently, the private sector has encouraged the development of larger 'communes' for people with mental handicaps; voluntary organizations have for some years invested in planning 'village communities' which are self-sufficient and often designed to reinforce belief systems, for example, Ravenswood Village Foundation for Jewish people in Berkshire and the Rudolph Steiner village communities seen in various parts of the country where an individualized work ethic is reinforced and practised.

The definition of the term 'community' is therefore open to wide and personal interpretation. The Select Committee report identified the difficulties inherent in the interpretation of the word 'community':[8]

> The phrase 'community care' means little in itself. It is a phrase used by some descriptively and others proscriptively: that is, by some as a shorthand way of describing certain specific services provided in certain ways and in certain places: by others as an ideal or principle, in the light of which existing services are to be judged and new ones developed. It has in fact come to have such general reference as to be virtually meaningless. It has become a slogan, with all the weaknesses that this implies. Pleasant commutations of the phrase can be misleading.

Some people have been relocated or resettled in communities without due regard being given to the process of encouraging their integration into local neighbourhoods. There is a basic misconception that community care is a natural progression in a modern society, but sadly inadequate thought has been given to the complex tacit rules which exist in society and which require nurturing and moulding before successful integration can be effected.

Some have also made the mistake of prescribing standard packages of 'community care models' which can be transferred to various parts of the country, and conference themes have reinforced this misconception. What is required is a framework for community integration which must be uniquely moulded to meet the needs of each locality. There are many 'models' of good practice and indeed there are many lessons to be learnt for each service, but it is a highly individualized service that is required.

In a response to a parliamentary question raised in the Lords by Baroness Trumpington on 21 April 1986, in respect of the government's intention to replace the director of the National Development Team for People with Mental Handicaps, the following statement was made:[9]

> The government's policy is that there should be good local services, capable of responding flexibly to differing needs and circumstances and provided by a variety of agencies working together both in the planning and delivery of services. They should be able to identify and to meet both the general and specific needs of people with mental handicaps and their families. We are talking about our relatives, friends and next door neighbours; but the better we know people the more keenly we are aware that they are all different and that standard packages will not do. The only right answers are the relevant ones, flexible enough to change with changing needs – and when necessary to promote change.

The Oxford and Chambers dictionaries provide the following definitions of the term 'community' which lead into the next section of this chapter: 'Joint ownership or liability; state of being held in common fellowship. Organizational social body; body of people living in the same locality; body of people with the same needs and interests in common' (*Oxford Concise*); 'Common agreement; people having common rights; a body of people living in the same locality' (*Chambers Concise*).

## THE PROCESS OF ACCEPTANCE

The successful development of local services for people with mental handicaps depends on the identification of those social rules and systems which operate in the locality. Each neighbourhood will have been shaped by past experience and history and will have its own unique identity. Any person wishing to enter and to gain acceptance as a fully integrated member will need to internalize these tacit rules and avoid their infringement.

For a person with a mental handicap, unfamiliar surroundings will complicate this process and for some deprivation of exposure to ordinary living experiences makes this even more difficult; negotiation of new skills and new opportunities within which to express them requires particular skill and understanding.

For many of us, the skills required to live in our own communities were acquired during our early lives through the process of socialization within our families. Skills such as those required to negotiate conversation with others, knowledge of when to withdraw from a situation and the skills required to keep within the accepted laws and rules of society are all examples of the interpretations of our social systems that we make daily as we go about our lives.

Society establishes laws and rules to ensure conformity among its members and successful integration demands the internalization of these tacit norms. Since so many of these are taken for granted in our everyday lives, we often forget that people with mental handicaps need help to negotiate these new requirements through trial and error or experiential learning.

All successful programmes of relocation in the community require the combination of skills-based programmes to prepare for more independent living and, more importantly, the exploration of individual needs and feelings in preparation for change.

The process of preparation for change falls into three main areas: client/family preparation; community preparation; and support staff preparation.

## Client/family preparation

People with mental handicaps are often seen in response to how others see them, rather than for how they feel or see themselves. This is partly as a result of the fact that society denies them the right to be individuals in their own right or to form the wide range of opportunities or relationships that many of us have. Implicit in this statement is the question of human rights to dignity and freedom to choose our friends, where we live, with whom and when.

For a large number of people with mental handicaps, it is not possible to discuss the development of human rights without linking the concept to meaningful life events and to present the subject at a practical and understandable level. Meaningful life events depends on the recognition of a personal identity and for some people who have had several changes in their lives, this fundamental need may have been missed or repressed.

For some there has been a conscious effort to deny the presence or expression of personal feelings and concentration on a behavioural approach to self-help skills and development has contributed to this process.

However, all individuals are people first with feelings, memories, previous life experiences and identities of their own. It is through the expression of these very basic qualities that we gain acceptance (or non-acceptance) in our local neighbourhoods. For people with mental handicaps, this seems to be a sensible place to start in preparing them for life away from the family home in the community.

While working as a community nurse with people with a mental handicap, the author became aware of the need to extend the range of opportunities to some of his clients but continually met opposition, not from society but from the very people he was trying to support. One way of answering this problem was to establish a psychotherapy group for 12 people with mental handicaps over a 52-week period.[10] The result was revealing to say the least, and required the skilful introduction of traditionally psychotherapeutic techniques combined with operant conditioning to facilitate client participation and self-expression.

Perhaps one of the most interesting conclusions was the exploration of previous life experiences and events which had never been worked through. Each group member had more in common with his/her peers than differences and often this was linked to the constant changes that had occurred in their lives. Changes in carers, staff support, friends, loss of family and loss of dignity. The group proved to be one way of encouraging self-expression for people who had not had the opportunity to do so before.

Denial of feelings in a field where emphasis is placed on behaviourism has been acknowledged – 'a philosophy of science where everything is reducible to the study of behaviour'.[11] For people with mental handicaps, communication may be limited and self-expression may be restricted to behavioural presentation. Life planning meetings should always take this into account and consider providing opportunities for speech therapy and alternative methods of communication.

The difficulties involved in recognizing people's feelings in respect of people who have difficulties in expressing their needs have been considered.[11] However, as a prerequisite, professionals need to consider the personal interpretation an individual gives to their feelings and the priority they give to them. Our own interpretation will often be linked subjectively to our own perception of the situation, and caution should be exercised to introduce objective methods of exploration to preserve their uniqueness as individuals.

Assessing feelings starts by asking people how they feel about certain things or changes in their lives. This is not so simple, even for those who can communicate for many have never been asked before and have consequently lost the skills of presenting a personal opinion or to reflect on their own needs. For those people who are unable to communicate, the situation is more complex and depends upon the establishment of a range of observation skills among those people who come into contact with the individual regularly. Nonverbal and verbal behaviours can provide objective indicators of feelings when opportunities are created for sharing different perceptions among significant people in the person's life.

One way to break into this arena is to ensure that people are involved in all decisions affecting their lives and by professionals discussing their own feelings with people with mental handicaps to act as role models in an effort to encourage the self-expression of *their* own needs. The first step is to motivate people to share their needs openly and to experiment with a range of opportunities for self-expression. The use of psychodrama, street theatre, puppetry, role play, art therapy, and calisthenics are some examples of creative therapeutic techniques employed to encourage this. However, there is one thing which cannot be denied – never take any-thing for granted, as the author learnt recently at a management group meeting which included a client representative:

> Mary had sat quietly through four meetings where aspects of management relating to the small, staffed house where she lived were discussed. She would politely 'listen' to staff comments and 'daydream'. We began to wonder if we had been mistaken in asking her to join us in the group. However, during the fifth meeting we were discussing the suitability of a senior member of staff to return to the house to work. The debate continued to a positive conclusion and Mary appeared to be passively listening as per normal. Suddenly she shrieked out a loud 'No!' when we recommended the staff member return and continued to attempt to articu-late the reasons for the concern she and her friends felt about the situation. Such was the power of her interjection that we were astounded and Mary 'had entered' the group. Needless to say, we supported her decision as a consumer and we have regarded her very differently now and facilitate her comments regularly.

This example serves to demonstrate the power of self-expression and self-advocacy which is rapidly gaining acceptance throughout the UK, but it does prove that so often professionals are to blame for denying self-expression. Another example of self-expression has been provided through the description of a project designed to help people adjust to change through the development of 'life story books' containing a constant record of their lives.[12]

> The life story book group project was a positive and valuable experience which gave the clients a structured and understandable way of talking about themselves and their past, present and future. I would stress that the preparation for the clients, carers and relatives was extremely important, because life story book work can and should begin to change mentally handicapped people's perception of themselves.

The exploration of feelings is an essential consideration in any programme of preparation for community care, but skills-based assessment and development is also necessary if one is to exploit the naturally occurring opportunities that will present themselves once access has been negotiated. These skills will need to be carefully assessed and related to the individual's own stage of development. There are many examples of such assessments and the application of learning theory to realize skill acquisition are well documented in the literature. For the purposes of this chapter, it is sufficient to include reference to the needs of people with mental handicaps to acquire competence in as many areas of social and self-help skill development as possible.

**Adjusting to change**
The presentation of change can be threatening for any person, but for people with mental handicaps this can be particularly traumatic. Stability of routine is most important to people with learning difficulties and it may be appropriate to consider using relaxation techniques to help people to adjust to change. Behavioural relaxation training is one such approach and a project to help people with mental handicaps to cope with change and anxiety in their lives has been described.[13] The most obvious use of this approach is to reduce the problems associated with physiological change which accompany anxiety and thus permit individuals to take advantage of the preparatory programmes outlined above.

Not only do individuals need to adjust to change but they so often continue to be integrated members of their nuclear families beyond the normal age experienced in Western society. Extended dependence on the family may make it particularly difficult for people to express their individuality and feelings, which may occasionally conflict with the perceptions of 'what is best for them' presented by parents. Transfer to community-based homes either from 'institutions' or from the parental home may present considerable difficulties for professionals and, of course, for the person concerned.

There are many examples of concern expressed by parents as their offspring aspire towards independence. These range from the free expression of sexuality, to moving to a home of their own. If community care is to be successful there is no doubt that these very real concerns cannot be denied, and opportunities for parents to discuss and work through these areas must be provided.

## Parent support groups

One example of meeting this need is through the establishment of parent support groups or through the introduction of parent workshops. In either case, the key aim is to provide parents with the opportunity for free expression and exploration of their anxieties with other parents for mutual support. Professionals may have a key part to play in facilitating these groups but the explicit aim must be to allow parents to reach their own decisions through informed choice. Other techniques have been used where parents are encouraged to participate in working groups where closure programmes are formulated and where opportunities for participation are provided. Shared learning opportunities may also prove to be important in reconciling parent feelings towards new ideas or suggestions. Examples of interpersonal skill training programmes shared with parents and their offspring have proven to bring about shared understanding.

In all of these schemes or ideas the main aim is to develop a meaningful rapport between parents, clients and professionals through sharing concerns and anxieties and through the introduction of new opportunities to enrich the person's life. Skills-based teaching programmes designed to develop self-awareness and independence all require adequate preparation and in most cases family involvement at individual life planning meetings and teaching programmes will usually be sufficient to enlist their support to achieve success.

However, in some cases there is a need for more intense casework; community mental handicap nurses and social workers may need to develop therapeutic strategies to meet the complex needs present in some families through the introduction of family therapy. The importance of whole family sessions to clarify perceptions and reorganize unwanted family behaviour have been described.[14] The dynamics of family interaction and presentation are often complex and may use a whole range of entrenched defence mechanisms surrounding the handicapped family member. The use of family therapy may help to untangle some of these issues and help the family to restore equilibrium while working through family needs and problems which may have been incorrectly assigned to the person with a mental handicap.

This section has considered the importance of ensuring that people are adequately prepared for changes in their lives. The individual does not exist in isolation from the family or from the wider society within which he/she lives. The importance of avoiding simplistic approaches to what is a highly complex area is recommended. However, this does not mean that the solutions rest with sophisticated intervention strategies, but rather in the use of imaginative and creative techniques designed to help individuals make the most of themselves and the communities in which they live. The model suggested in this chapter is an interactionist model between the individual, his/her family, the local community and the wider social system. The next section considers this model further.

## Preparing the local community

Much thought and time has been given to considering the most appropriate way to ensure the successful integration of people with mental handicaps into the community. Discussions have involved politicians, professionals, consumers and social scientists. The community itself has not been passive in the debate and has voiced many angry feelings of hostility against the methods employed for transferring services into neighbourhoods.

There is no one way to achieve success, but one thing is clear: success will only be achieved if the community is informed and able to make a conscious decision based on informed choice and knowledge of the needs of people with mental handicaps. Hence the community requires a comprehensive preparatory programme to promote positive attitudes towards this client group and to dispel many of the myths and images surrounding the needs and presentation of people with mental handicaps. Research and experience has shown that where this has occurred there is no reason to assume that integration should not take place effectively. The role of community support workers will therefore need to consider ways of promoting a positive presence in the local community.

For people moving from their own homes within local neighbourhoods the problem may not be so great, for neighbours may have known the family and 'owned' responsibility and consequently accepted responsibility for providing a home in the locality for their offspring. For others who may have spent much of their lives in institutions, the situation is different, with public attitudes being tarnished and conditioned to assume that institutions house people who are a potential threat to their lifestyles and families.

One way of breaking through this problem is to ensure that local support teams are established, with their bases being firmly established in the local town or area. The maintenance of an integrated community presence is a precursor to acceptance and staff may find it useful to begin a community education programme in local schools, voluntary groups, churches and community associations. In Exeter this approach has proven to be essential to ensure the successful integration of service users. They have transferred ownership of the service to the community through the establishment of local planning groups spanning several client-related groups and have encouraged membership to include local residents and people considered to represent the local community, for example, councillors, chemists, doctors and voluntary representatives.

This is one way of encouraging integration and there are many examples to prove that involvement of neighbours is an important area for consideration. The concept of exploiting the local community is not new and social workers have established 'patch teams', the police 'community policing schemes' and the voluntary sector 'community care groups'. It is from these models of community work that experience may be acquired when aiming to create new opportunities for people with mental handicaps.

Community care is about exploiting from within opportunities which already exist for members of society as naturally occurring friendship networks. Sadly, the concept of communities is challenged as general hospital sites are centralized, sub-post offices are closed, corner shops forced out of business and self-support networks dismantled. There needs to be a clear investment in preserving the integrated nature of local communities if people with mental handicaps are to be successfully assimilated and supported.

## Community support workers

The role of community support workers may therefore be to strengthen and forge close links with the very community to which professionals are transferring care. But before this can be assumed to be accomplished, there is need for a negotiating body to prepare the way. This responsibility may fall to the local community mental handicap team whose role and image has been reshaped in recent years to work from within the local neighbourhood rather than extending its previous advocacy role from the mental handicap hospital.

How can this be achieved? This section has already discussed the team's role in public education by raising local awareness of the needs of this client group. Perhaps a more useful way is through the encouragement of negotiating access to generic services in the locality. Hence the use of segregated services for leisure, occupation, community living and medical needs should be positively discouraged. People with mental handicaps should be seen to use public transport, wait their turn in doctors' surgeries and make local purchases in shops. This latter point also has another advantage – the introduction of purchasing power, which may be an incentive for local shopkeepers to encourage people with mental handicaps to use their facilities and thereby create opportunities to share in the daily routine of the town or village. The use of integrated leisure facilities such as the local swimming pool will similarly allow the general public to form their own opinions about people with learning needs, which previously may have been influenced subjectively by hearsay and concern.

## Housing
The choice of setting for house purchase is another important variable and should be planned carefully to provide individuals with opportunities to move into neighbourhoods which are familiar, close to home and compatible with their own life experiences and needs. Houses should be provided close to local amenities and shops, be close to public transport facilities, accessible for leisure pursuits and integrated in the local neighbourhood in properties chosen for their similarity to others in the street. It is only by providing a high profile within adequately supervised staffing levels that the local community will come to accept their new neighbours. Conversely, hiding away from the public view only serves to encourage the reinforcement of misperceptions and stigma.

There are other prepratory tasks which will encourage further acceptance and integration. The local police are one example of a group of people who can be particularly helpful in fulfilling this aim. Community support workers should ensure that they are known to the local police and introduce them to people moving into the locality. Acceptance is a two-way process and may well depend on the newcomer's immediate observation of local rules; any infringement of these may create an initial problem of acceptance in the neighbourhood, nurtured by local hostility as a 'self-fulfilling prophecy'. Experience has shown that early introductions to local councillors and community police officers will prove to be a worthwhile investment.

Voluntary organizations such as MIND and MENCAP have voiced

concern regarding the procedures used by the police when interviewing people with mental handicaps and have proposed a volunteer scheme to ensure that adequate numbers of trained people are available to represent people with mental handicaps should they have problems with the police.[15] However, not only can the local community assist in this area, but on a proactive basis can help to provide additional opportunities for people with mental handicaps in the community.

> Paul had a history of epilepsy and moved to a new staffed house in the town. He occasionally became frustrated and became troublesome at home and would shout and throw things. At a life planning meeting he expressed that the main cause of his frustration was the lack of opportunity to go out on his own to explore his new home. It was explained that his epilepsy was the main reason for this and although well controlled there was still a significant 'risk' involved to let him go out alone. Paul was determined. It was agreed that an identity bracelet should be purchased and that a programme should be introduced to assess Paul's social skills. His medication was reviewed and the local police invited to 'tea' to meet Paul and his peers. Paul explained his intentions to the community policeman and asked for his support should he 'fall' while out. A full assessment of the advantages for Paul and the disadvantages of his increased independence was made and it was agreed that Paul should begin his trip towards independence.

In Paul's case his 'new freedom' brought about a reduction in his inappropriate behaviours and he felt secure while out in the local town in the knowledge that a call to the emergency services should he have a seizure would result in constructive help rather than public 'panic'.

Similarly, some of the skills which people will need to live successfully in the community will need to be nurtured and acquired through practise and experience. Learning how to respect other people's property and to maintain personal privacy are skills which will be required, but occasional difficulties may occur initially which can be avoided if people are aware of the aims of training projects and can exercise discretion and tolerance.

Preparation of the local DHSS office is one other area to consider and many frustrations can be avoided if time is invested early on when people move into the community. Knowledge of the wide range of benefits and financial assistance available is essential if people are to take full advantage of opportunities in the community, but it is surprising how few DHSS officers are aware of the needs, or indeed rights, of disabled people.

## Adult education programmes

The Local Council for Voluntary Services is an important part of the equation and may negotiate access and practical support for people as they enter the neighbourhood. This is not so much through the provision of 'charity' but through the facilitation of membership to local, valued groups which may help to 'sponsor' people with mental handicaps into ordinary community schemes and ventures.

One example of this has been the rapid extension of adult education programmes to people with mental handicaps. It is well-acknowledged that the acquisition of new social skills and leisure opportunities needs adequate preparation and extensive programmes covering both these areas and adult basic education are becoming more available. To take full advantage of these classes, sponsorship into them is essential for people with mental handicaps. How to accomplish this without becoming patronizing is difficult. In Hampshire and in some of the London boroughs, a new approach to joint sponsorship has been developed. The introduction of the 'New Way' scheme demonstrates the value of exploiting the voluntary sector and provides people with mental handicaps with opportunities for coaching and new friendships in integrated classes with other adult members of the community. Classes in photography, cookery, literacy and design are some examples of courses available. So successful has the project been that demand has outstripped places and finance.

The advantages of such a joint approach are obvious. New skills are acquired, new friends made, the local community share their own learning with people with handicaps, and support is valued and provided without undue attention being drawn to the 'special learning needs of the individual'. Examples of programmes designed to increase competence in areas of daily living have extended to enable life skills to be learned by those who are attempting to live as near a normal life as possible in the neighbourhood. The use of joint finance is one way of encouraging the development of such schemes.

People moving from the parental home will also need new opportunities to acquire the necessary skills to live in the community. In one study, 20 per cent of a sample of 444 students with learning difficulties in the United States were found to interact exclusively with and within their own families.[16] There were few examples of socialization with others in local groups or clubs, and the emphasis appeared to be passively orientated activities conducted within their own homes. Some individuals made significant use of community facilities, although environments such as restaurants, post offices and banks were frequented by a relatively small number of people. Hence preparation for shared learning in the local community needs to be nurtured early on in life through the extension of home-based learning into the community. Community support workers can be particularly instrumental in encouraging the use of community facilities such as youth clubs, adventure groups and integrated sports activities:[16]

> The design and implementation of effective community integration training programs for persons with mental handicaps presents a challenge to professionals in schools and adult service programs. Successful community integration requires individuals to be independent within their homes and communities and to be socially integrated into all facets of community life. Although the majority of individuals surveyed engage in independent living activities and appear satisfied with their lives, many continue to be socially isolated within their own homes and fail to engage in active, structured recreational or social activities.

## Employment

The transition to work requires the extension of career opportunities, and the local careers office may be particularly helpful. The Department of Employment will also provide expert advice on employment for a wide range of people with special needs, but these need to be accessed and experience has again demonstrated that they do not present themselves easily. Maintaining close links with all statutory agencies is therefore important. The youth schemes are also available for extension to people with mental handicaps and local youth officers are well worth a visit.

Negotiating access to local employment schemes will require ongoing liaison between home, employers and community support services. Sponsorship schemes involving co-workers provide opportunities for skill acquisition which does not call undue attention to the handicapped person. On-the-job training programmes have proven to extend employment opportunities to people with mental handicaps. However, the maintenance of positive employment practices and skills within the work place depends on the free availability of advice to employers when required, and certainly before performance causes concern.

Members of the public will therefore have their own expectations and perceptions of people with mental handicaps; before acceptance can be guaranteed, people will need the opportunity to meet together to share joint experiences and remove some of the misconceptions associated with labelling and scapegoating. One recent article examines some of the reasons for the favourable integration of people with mental handicaps and, conversely, some of the reasons for their rejection.[17]

In Teignmouth and in all these studies we also see the positive aspects of social implications: where individuals appropriately dressed melt into the community, where group home residents become accepted by neighbours; where mentally handicapped workers in MENCAP's Pathway scheme become accepted by others in the factory as fellow co-workers. What these instances say is that successful retarded people melt into the community and when this happens their label melts with them. Before coming out of the mental handicap hospitals, whether for short-term holidays or for permanent living, they must have adequate social training beforehand.

Many people once given the freedom to choose, make choices in their own lives which in turn require new skills to help them to manage and cope with the consequences of their new behaviours. One woman worked in a hospital for people with mental handicaps and transferred to a house in the community. She found that transition difficult and traumatic, and she was a professional![18]

The sort of crises most of us have to face sooner or later in life, with the support of family and friends, can be far more daunting faced alone, handicapped, removed from the familiar surroundings that once provided at least security. Many of the mentally handicapped people who are learning to live independently are doing so with great success, but there are many who are not. It is to the professionals that they look for support – to the community nurses, the social workers, the adult training centre instructors, the GPs – and whose continued support may make the difference between coping with independence and succumbing to it.

## Preparing the professionals

One group studied nine family support systems in the United States provided by both statutory and voluntary agencies. Factors affecting the availability and accessibility of these services were examined and factors involved in the definition and variations in the location, type, auspice, size and structure of service agencies were shown to affect availability and access of family support services.[19]

the findings with respect to the clustering of family support services is particularly important because there is little evidence that suggests that advocacy for and development of these services have been built around the functional and organizational relationships that exist among groups of family support services. Increasing the availability and accessibility of these services would be enhanced by taking advantage of those linkages.

The relative high degree of eligibility criteria for family support services suggests that accepted notions of 'system' and 'network' often associated with community-based services do not accurately describe the family support services situation . . . there is a lack of the linkages and relationships between and among agencies that characterize a true network or system of services. Incentives to establish those linkages are required to take full advantage of the resources that can be devoted to these programs. It is also important to focus on the need for those services independent of an individual's enrolment in a core service program.

These researchers identified the key concerns that exist in the community when attempting to provide meaningful support services to people with mental handicaps and their families. Our own approach is often fragmented, directed by professionals and provided in isolation from experienced needs of consumers; certainly solutions are manufactured externally to the locality rather than from within.[19]

Policies that encourage the extension of family support services to families who may only need a minimal array of these services may stabilize a family environment and assist in keeping a member with developmental needs from placement in more restrictive settings.

The co-ordination of service delivery to people with mental handicaps and their families has been the subject of intense debate across agencies, within consumer groups and within the government. Catch phrases of 'towards collaboration', 'a joint partnership' and 'parents as partners' illustrate some of the thinking that has been involved in reshaping community-based services within the United Kingdom. The aims are simple but the lessons hard. Services are still provided by agencies determined to restrict fieldwork practice within bureaucratic boundaries and to jealously preserve the status quo within separate professions. Consequently, the community mental handicap team (CMHT) has developed in some areas as a group of individuals who meet together in the name of teamwork to facilitate opportunities in the community for this client group. There is an inherent danger in this approach to suggest that the team could become restrictive in its practice and serve to meet the needs of the organizations they represent without transferring ownership to the consumers.[20]

There is a tendency to regard the single title as indicative of a single role and even a single organization . . . it is not surprising that their functions and organizations differ. CMHTs carry the burden of promoting community services. There is a great deal of emphasis on this policy in the face of limited resources, practical problems and opposing philosophies. The work is and will continue to be difficult and uncertain. If the team can develop an identity, purpose(s) and function(s) which can be coherently presented they may stand a better chance of achieving at least their own objectives.

There is therefore a fundamental need to prepare professionals to give up ownership and to share across traditional professional boundaries and to emerge as a team of people working together to facilitate the transfer of support services to the very community in which the team works. If this philosophy is to be adopted, the team's boundaries will be limitless and its membership infinite, flexible and adaptable in the light of emerging needs.

This theme has been developed further:[21]

The CMHT will generate its own problems. It cannot be a panacea for all ills. One advantage of the Wells Road community support service has been that its small scale, patch base and its flexibility and lack of rigid constraints on how it should operate, has enabled staff and users together to think creatively, rather than in terms of orthodox, routine, service responses, when thinking about how best to meet people's needs. These are the elements of the community support service which we are now trying to preserve as CMHTs go into operation locally, and planning for the future transfer of the Wells Road service, and other community mental handicap services. . .

The Wells Road experience in Bristol provides useful lessons for all community-based services and emphasizes the importance of 'building fruitful networks of working relationships between local professionals'. The service has built on the following strengths:[21]

- The service has built upon, rather than supplanted, existing community networks and resources.
- It has operated very flexibly to meet individual, and changing, needs (no rigidly prescribed ways of doing things).
- It has worked with individuals already living in the community, rather than concentrating its energies exclusively on those being resettled from hospital.

- It has gone out to meet people, to knock on their doors and find out what they might want, rather than the more traditional passive service response to problems or to crises.
- It has placed the individual service consumer very much at the centre of the stage, considering their wants, their life, their needs and how best they can be met, so far as possible from their perspective.
- Most important, it has tried – and succeeded in – improving 'the quality of life' available to people with learning difficulties in the local area.

Much can be done to ensure that teamwork in the community is encouraged. The first principle is to ensure that a joint and shared philosophy is agreed and accepted between team members. Shared training opportunities across agencies and with consumers is one way to achieve this. Examples of such schemes are to be found in Wales where the statutory training authorities for nursing and social work the Welsh National Board for Nursing (WNB) and Central Council for the Education and Training of Social Workers (CCETSW) have agreed on a 60-day postbasic course which aims to bring nurses and social workers together to acquire the skills required to realize the aims of the All Wales Strategy. The course is open to other professionals and to consumers. A similar scheme is in operation in Exeter, and local districts are following a pattern of joint training for staff and parents.

Perhaps an overconcentration on professional training can alienate professionals from their clients and communities. This notion has been discussed:[22]

> But all down the line it was the untrained people who listened, saw the problems and helped me to apply the situation. The trained people, although I don't doubt that they had my interests at heart, seemed incapable of going beyond the obvious solution. Their training seemed to get in the way. So use instinct in social work situations as well as the knowledge gained through training. See the person, not the problem, or what you or your training think is the problem. And listen. The most important skill of all is the ability to listen.

This demonstrates the importance of human skills in working with people with mental handicaps and their families. Professional training skills provided in partnership with parents will serve to meet the experienced needs of clients in the community. Finally, it is important to stress the need to acquire skills of political awareness in order to develop responsive services which combine both residential and community services as one rather than as two separate services. A comprehensive service should therefore encourage the amalgamation of all available skills while recognizing that most opportunities already exist in the community and it is up to the professionals to exploit them.

One example of such opportunities presents as an alternative to residential care through the use of 'family placement schemes'.

## FAMILY PLACEMENT SCHEMES

Traditionally, residential care has been provided by service agencies in either purpose-built or adapted accommodation. Residential care is usually shared with other people with similar needs, and numbers may range from family groups of three up to larger groups of 40. Such 'homes' are usually staffed by professionals and direct care staff who receive a salary for their work in return for which they often work unsocial hours and provide care and support to their clients.

For consumers this represents security of routine, regular meals and so on. The only changes may be in the staff themselves who may leave and be replaced by others who are relative strangers. Some units also provide short-term care facilities, and different 'guests' may come to stay, which further disrupts life and routine. The residential model is fine up to a point but does not provide any substitute for home care within a family unit.

Obviously, the most appropriate way to provide care is to ensure that the family of origin receives all the support possible to continue caring for their handicapped offspring for as long as they both are able or wish to. However, reality will require the provision of substitute care provision at some point. When this occurs, opportunities should be available to provide each person with a range of choice to meet their needs. A range of provision may include the following:

- fully staffed support in a small house;
- group home provision;
- care with a substitute family;
- lodgings;
- warden-controlled housing;
- opportunities for independent living.

This section considers the development of family placement schemes for people with mental handicaps. A wide range of opportunities now exists in the community to provide alternatives to traditional residential care. Family placement schemes have been provided for many years by the local authority in response to meeting the needs of children taken into care. The schemes have been so successful with children that they have virtually overtaken the former 'children's home' model and have replaced them with foster and adoption schemes. For the former, new families apply for acceptance to become foster parents and in return receive a weekly allowance to cover incidental costs. Adoption is quite different and refers to the total acceptance of an individual as a full family member and for this no payment is made.

For adults with special needs, the extension of adult placement or family support schemes is becoming popular. Hampshire Social Services Department sponsors one such scheme which was developed from joint finance in 1979. The scheme was introduced to extend the range and choice available to consumers for residential care and to provide more appropriate home-based care. The scheme is not restricted to people with mental handicaps and extends to other client groups. It also provides opportunities to meet the needs of people with mental handicaps with identified 'special needs' and has several people with multiple needs placed successfully with 'new families' throughout the county.

The scheme employs a number of adult placement officers (APOs) who are responsible for the recruitment and selection of appropriate carers who receive training and support from adult placement social workers. The scheme insists that support is also provided from the local CMHT and that valued provision is made to meet occupation and leisure needs each day. All people using the scheme contribute towards the costs from their DHSS benefit, and carers receive a weekly allowance to cover their expenses.

The scheme does not aim to provide 'a home for life' but it does aim to provide additional stimulation and support for a significant period of time during a client's life, and aims towards full acceptance of the handicapped person within the family unit. Examples of improved performance, increased skill development and greater self-expression have encouraged the scheme to consider extending its services still further.

One of the obvious advantages of the scheme is that it brings care into local streets and neighbourhoods and aims to provide meaningful integration into the locality through one-to-one sponsorship, which has a greater chance of success. Family support schemes require full support and should be seen as an integrated part of a total comprehensive service, offering a range of facilities – and yet support should be provided in such a way that it does not detract from the main aim of the scheme, i.e. to provide a family-based service. Obviously, a balance has to be made between the formal offer of support and training of carers and self-support within the family.

For all placement schemes a contract should be issued to clients and carers outlining the terms and conditions of the scheme. Regular monitoring must be provided by a multidisciplinary team to ensure that the aims and objectives of the placement are realized. Professionals must recognize their obligations to 'share in the care with carers' to reduce the possibility of failure or inappropriate care.

Community support staff can help to realize the aims and objectives of the scheme by proving regular support to carers and by participating in training schemes for carers. Such courses are popular among carers although it is perhaps more beneficial to extend invitations to carers to join in training days organized for staff working in the statutory services. Such shared learning occasions provide opportunities to explore and to promote good practice. Carers have been found to require specific help, namely: medical needs; side-effects of medication; advice on psychiatric presentation; support in dealing with inappropriate behaviours; and advice on client self-awareness and sexuality.

## THE PRIVATE SECTOR

Family placement schemes are probably best regarded as an extension of statutory provision and home care but in any neighbourhood there may be other examples of residential care provision. The private sector may provide additional opportunities in residential facilities, which may range from small, family schemes to much larger concerns similar to those seen in the statutory sector. All facilities providing for more than three people are obliged to register with the local authority. Legislation under the 1984 Registered Homes Act places responsibility on the local authority to ensure that environmental and staffing conditions and standards are met.[23] However, it does not insist that quality of care or service provision is enforced. Apart from two statutory visits to the establishment each year, the Act fails to provide more than a basic safeguard for clients.

Responsibility for monitoring clients needs and for the evaluation of each placement should rest with the local CMHT, which should provide regular visits to clients and provide appropriate support services. Sadly, some professionals have disregarded this basic responsibility since they have regarded the placement as being a profit-making enterprise. Consequently, they have failed to provide support to the individuals living in the facility. However, all of these responsibilities need to be considered in the light of available resources; but it is essential that people living in private facilities are not deprived of their right to a valued life with provision of appropriate support when required. One way of ensuring this is through the introduction of similar guidelines to those outlined above for family placement schemes.

Some workers have described how a CMHT works in the 'private sector'.[24] Carers are provided with ongoing support and information – and the suitability of placements is assessed before they are made. Contracts are issued between landladies and clients; staff working in the Exeter CMHT have encouraged the development of a carers' group and it is hoped that in time the group will acquire its own status as an association, thus giving carers a voice in matters which affect their residents as well as 'promoting a greater appreciation of their role and commitment among those whose actions are governed solely by financial considerations'.

The Exeter staff were sceptical at first about the private sector, but as the report goes on to describe:[24]

> With the development of community homes, it seems that professionals and parents should rightly look to the statutory and voluntary bodies to provide care of a suitable standard. In Exeter, however, it has been found that there is also a place for the private sector and that this type of care satisfactorily extends the range of options open to people with mental handicaps. Provided that selection procedures are carefully observed and the active involvement of carers is sought, it is considered that private accommodation offers some clients the chance to become part of a family unit, which they might recently have lost or may not have experienced before, which they would not otherwise have. The level of commitment by the carers is impressive. They are keen to provide a professional service on a 24-hour basis. Moreover, this type of placement facilitates community integration, with carers involving residents in social activities locally. They have also proved to be excellent advocates for the people in their care.

# RESPITE CARE PROVISION

It is acknowledged by all statutory agencies that an essential element of a comprehensive service for people with mental handicaps must include flexible access to short-term care or respite care facilities. These should be provided as close to the person's home as possible, in keeping with 'the ordinary life' philosophy.

Perhaps one of the most important issues to clarify during any discussion regarding short-term care is its definition. For the purposes of this chapter the definition can be broken down into the following categories, which represent the main reasons for requests for admission.

### Emergency admission

No matter how well a service plans to meet the needs of its clients proactively, there may be occasions when an emergency at home, such as a sudden death or major illness of a principal carer, requires the service to respond immediately to provide emergency care.

### Phased care

Phased care is defined as a regular pattern of admission to a residential unit for a person who usually lives at home with his/her parents, but is gradually being introduced to a residential setting. Usually, clients using this service are being prepared for long-term admission and the frequency of long-term admissions for short-term care will depend on local needs, which is usually agreed between the family, community staff and the residential unit. The frequency may be for one weekend every month, one week every month, or even one night a week. The aim is to provide a flexible service to meet individual needs and the result is an efficient use of limited resources. In fact, up to six people may share one place over a one-month period.

### Assessment

This is perhaps the most unsatisfactory reason for all admissions. Occasions may arise when a person requires admission for acute observation, either for a clinical or a behavioural reason. The aim may be to stabilize and identify certain reasons for the presentation of certain symptoms and introduce procedures for their management. The CMHT will usually play an active role in liaising between the person's home, day placement and the residential care placement to ensure co-ordination of intervention.

### Respite provision

Occasionally, there may be no therapeutic reasons for admission, but a family may require the opportunity to spend time alone or with other siblings or to take a break from the day-to-day needs of caring for a handicapped person. Sometimes an admission may be required to provide this respite. The importance of respite care should not be underestimated, since experience has shown it to be an essential part of family support in community-based services, which may lead to meaningful and sustained care in the family home.

## Holidays

In the past some people saw short-term facilities as providing holidays for people with a mental handicap. Although there is obviously a need for holiday provision, it is not felt appropriate to provide holidays in a residential facility.

Almost everyone needs a break from others from time to time; people with mental handicaps are no exception. Traditionally, however, these needs have often gone unmet. Offers to provide 'sitting' services may be available occasionally for parents with handicapped children; but for adults it is often impossible to recruit assistance. Parents may also feel reluctant to share the care of their offspring if they have difficulty in making their needs known. Until recently, the main source of support was provided by mental handicap hospitals, which parents naturally viewed with suspicion and distaste. In the last few years the situation has begun to change and there are many examples of local schemes responding to local needs and circumstances provided by either statutory or voluntary organizations or in some cases as a partnership between the two.

As an alternative to residential short-term care, respite care schemes have been provided throughout the country and, although their method of operation differs widely, they tend to operate according to the principles outlined in 'Family Placement Schemes' (page 98). The scheme recruits local volunteers who offer short-term respite care to adults in their own homes. In return they receive payment for each session of care provided. Parents are usually assessed and provide a contribution to the cost of the scheme and are provided with vouchers depending on their needs. The vouchers are exchanged for sitting services received from carers who are reimbursed for the number of sessions of care provided.

In some areas, voluntary organizations have provided short-term care in separate houses in the community. In some schemes, families support each other on a shared self-help care rota. In one project, local university students provide rota care for a group of young people with mental handicaps in a local housing project on the campus.

For adults respite care services have been provided traditionally by health and social services departments, depending on the dependency of the person concerned. People with severe learning needs will often find themselves looking to the health authority to provide their care. In some areas this is still provided in large hospitals, where low staff to resident ratios result in impersonal care. In some health districts, short-term care 'houses' have been established and these may be administered as part of the CMHT in an effort to provide continuity of care between home and the community.

More usually, short-term care is provided in community houses or units and is shared with people who live permanently in the accommodation. Concern has been expressed by some parents and staff regarding the difficulties this sharing causes. The constant coming and going of some short-term users may disrupt the pattern of life for people who regard the house as their permanent home. Examples of accidental damage and the loss of personal effects are reasonably common and, not surprisingly, regular short-term care in an ordinary staffed house may cause considerable stress for residents, carers and for the short-stay user. However, for those people who are being 'phased' into a specific house, and who will regard it as their permant home at some point in the future, preparation for a life in the house is usually accepted.

Provision may also be made by the voluntary sector: MENCAP and Dr Barnados are two examples of agencies which provide a varied pattern of respite care provision in the community. Usually payment is provided by the local authority social services department. Parental involvement is always encouraged and the result is the emergence of a shared care philosophy. Religious organizations may also provide a range of services and this is particularly seen in the Catholic church.

Holidays may also be seen by some parents to be a welcome alternative to respite care, and there are many examples of adventure and individual holidays planned and provided for people with mental handicaps.

One other alternative to residential short-term care is through the provision of support in the person's own home by providing care attendants. In some areas, more regular help is provided through organized care attendant schemes. The Crossroads Scheme is one example where the philosophy of care attendants aims to ensure that parents are regarded as experts in the day-to-day care of their offspring.[25] Paid care attendants visit the family home to give the family relief from constant caring and, by working alongside parents, acquire many of their own skills, enabling the parents to share in the care required. Relief care may be provided for only a few hours at a time, but that respite may provide the means for parents to feel able to continue caring at home, rather than seeking alternative residential care. A particular value of these schemes is the consistency of support offered at a time when many services are increasingly discretionary and crisis-orientated.

Short-term or respite care cannot be provided in isolation from the individual's total life and should be regarded as a key component to be assessed whenever someone's needs are considered at review meetings. The CMHT may be involved particularly in co-ordinating services and liaising between its various agencies and professionals who may be involved with the individual and his/her family. Team members may be involved in booking and arranging short-term care and for providing ongoing communication between the family, the handicapped person and other significant people. Finally, members of the team will also be regular visitors at home and will provide a familiar face to individuals when short-term care is used; this may help to ensure a smooth transition.

This section has considered a variety of support networks and schemes providing short-term care for people with mental handicaps and their families. Models vary from district to district and where new schemes have developed, they have often been in response to the pioneering work of imaginative parents, determined to provide alternative systems to those available from statutory agencies. Perhaps the most common feature of those schemes evaluated by parents as being the most responsive to their needs are those that are flexible and fitting to the needs of parents and their offspring, and which provide opportunities to continue to share care, and which regard them as the principal carers in partnership with professionals when their support is required.

## SUMMARY

This chapter has considered those elements of a local, comprehensive service for people with mental handicaps in the community. It has recommended that service planners and professionals adopt a policy of exploiting naturally occurring opportunities in the community, rather than to design standard solutions to superimpose on local neighbourhoods.

The realization of integrated community care for people with mental handicaps will depend on the approach adopted by community support staff in preparing both clients and the locality into which they are to move. CMHTs should function within local neighbourhoods and should aim to extend membership to all people in the locality who have a stake in the service in order to facilitate the emergence of extended support systems within the community.

Like all social systems, the community aims to preserve social order and to avoid conflict through the maintenance of equilibrium. People with mental handicaps will be accepted if they observe the rules and norms of the locality and avoid their infringement. Given time and the opportunity to adapt to newcomers, the local community has the necessary skills and ability to adapt to change.

The future may prove that neighbourhood networks are flexible when opportunities are provided for them to share in the day-to-day lives of their inhabitants. For too long professionals have protected people with mental handicaps from the very communities in which they belong. If professionals reverse this process and nurture 'care and support by the community' then their aims will be realized and their professional skills used to good purpose in partnership with 'neighbours'.

# REFERENCES

1. DHSS (1971) White Paper *Better Services for the Mentally Handicapped*, Cmnd 4663, HMSO, London.
2. DHSS (1979) The Jay Report, *Report of the Committee of Enquiry into Mental Handicap Nursing and Care*, Cmnd 7468, HMSO, London.
3. DHSS (1980) *Development Team for the Mentally Handicapped*, Second Report 1978–9, HMSO, London.
4. DHSS (1980) *Mental Handicap: Progress, problems and priorities*. (A review of mental handicap services since the 1971 White Paper, Cmnd 4663), HMSO, London.
5. DHSS (1981) *Care in the Community: A consultative document for moving resources in England*, HMSO, London.
6. DHSS (1980) *Development Group for the Mentally Handicapped – a plan for action*, HMSO, London.
7. DHSS (1985) *Second Report of the Social Services Select Committee into the Care of Mentally Handicapped Adults with a Mental Handicap in the Community* (Chairman Rennie Short), HMSO, London.
8. DHSS (1985) *Government Response to the Social Services Select Committee into the Care of Mentally Handicapped Adults with a Mental Handicap in the Community*, HMSO, London, p. x, para. 8.
9. Hansard (1986) Government response to a question raised in the House of Lords in response to a question by The Baroness Trumpington, 21 April 1986.
10. Sines, D.T. and Moore, K. (1986) The magic shop, *Nursing Times*, Vol. 82, No. 11, p. 50–2.
11. Bailey, R., Matthews, F. and Leckie, C. (1986) Feelings – the way ahead in mental handicap, *Mental Handicap*, Vol. 14, pp. 65–7.
12. Frost, D. and Taylor, K. (1986) This is my life, *Community Care*, 21 August, pp. 28–9.
13. Lindsay, W. and Baty, F. (1986) Behavioural relaxation training: explorations with the mentally handicapped, *Mental Handicap*, Vol. 14, pp. 160–2.
14. Goodyer, I. (1986) Family therapy and the handicapped child, *Developmental Medicine and Neurology*, Vol. 28, pp. 244–50.

15. Jackson, T. (1986) Protecting the innocent . . . and the guilty, *Community Care*, 16 October, pp. 18–19.
16. Kregel, J., Wehman, P., Seyfarth, J. *et al.* (1986) Community integration of young adults with mental retardation: Transition from school to adulthood, *Journal of Education and Training of the Mentally Retarded*, March, pp. 35–42.
17. Wynn-Jones, A. (1986) The Teignmouth syndrome, *Community Care*, 21 August, pp. 18–19.
18. Balfour, E. (1986) Another world . . . Outside, *Social Work Today*, 24 February, p. 21.
19. Castelleni, P., Downey, N., Tausig, M. *et al.* (1986) Availability and accessibility of family support services, *Mental Retardation*, Vol. 24, No. 2, pp. 71–9.
20. Macdonald, I. (1986) *Community Mental Handicap Teams*, seminar paper from Brunel University Institute of Organisation and Social Studies.
21. Ward, L. (1987) Alternatives to CMHTs: Developing a community support service in south Bristol, in *Community Mental Handicap Teams: Theory and Practice*, British Institute of Mental Handicap conference series, p. 117.
22. Vernon, G. (1986) Untrained carers are the tops, *Community Care*, 11 September, pp. 28–9.
23. DHSS (1984) The Registered Homes Act, chapter 23, HMSO, London.
24. Ferrity, B., Ford, D. and Bratt, A. (1986) The private sector: Just landladies or carers? *Mental Handicap*, Vol. 14, December, pp. 166–9.
25. The Crossroads Scheme (1984) Association of Crossroad Care Attendant Schemes, 94 Coton Road, Rugby, Warwickshire.

# 5. Team Work in Small Houses

## *Joan Bicknell*

There's a story told about four people named Everybody, Somebody, Anybody and Nobody. There was an important job to do and Everybody was sure that Somebody would do it. Anybody could have done it but Nobody did it. Somebody got angry about that because it was Everybody's job. Everybody thought Anybody could do it but Nobody realized that Everybody wouldn't do it. It ended up that Everybody blamed Somebody and Nobody did what Anybody could have done![1]

## INTRODUCTION

The setting up of small houses for people with a mental handicap is outlined in Chapter 8. The type of clients who may live there and how their needs may be met, the staffing and management, are considered in other chapters. We can therefore concentrate here on a close examination of how teams work in such a residential setting and elsewhere. Much of the description of team work is based on various theoretical models of management and is applicable to teams anywhere in a caring service. Those working in small houses may apply these principles of team work to the situation in which they find themselves.

The chapter is divided into four parts. First, the structure and purpose of the team are discussed, looking at membership and roles within the team. Second, the team is examined in greater detail to look at the internal dynamics of the team; what can make or break the team, how team members relate to each other and how a team is led. The third part deals with the team and those around them, and the ways in which teams within organizations relate to other teams or hierarchies. Finally, the work of the team is examined to see whether the team is giving the best possible service under the inevitable constraints.

## DEFINITION OF A TEAM

A team may be defined as a group of individuals who contract to work together for an agreed goal. Teams readily come to mind from the sporting world; the team of footballers who need each other to work the ball across the field to score the goals, the cricketing team who need not only to shine individually when batting but must become acutely aware of each other when fielding, or the team of show jumpers who, in turn, excel to produce the lowest aggregate number of faults that may bring their country the medals.

In human services, working in a successful team can be exhilarating. Work will be well done with consumer satisfaction generating a feeling of personal worth and professional growth shared by other team members.

Team work does not happen automatically. Rather like a marriage, there needs to be hard work at times to bring the positive aspects of team work to the surface, and occasionally teams, like marriages, fail and break down. The above definition of a team includes four key words that each need to be further defined: a *group* – how cohesive is the group? the *contract* – what agreement has been made and with whom?; *work* – how much, how easy or difficult?; and *goal* – what goal and who chose the goal?

Within a team there may be unanswered questions for some members: some find themselves unwillingly a member of a team, others are not so convinced the goal is the right one, and some will be unsure how hard they are expected to work and what tasks they are to undertake. The rewards of good team work are many but the risks are great. Working in a team that is full of anger and conflict, with energy dissipated in rivalry, is destructive of personal well-being and brings no services to anyone; and yet being an isolationist in any part of the human service, and in particular in a close-knit community such as a small residential home, would at best be impossible and at worst chaotic.

Teamwork *must* be made to work and it is time well spent if teams will look at and learn about themselves so that each team member can contribute his skills as part of the total service given by the team, and experience personal growth through his day-to-day team contacts.

# TEAM TASK 1

Team work is hard work and requires individual commitment and effort, humility and a sense of humour to make it happen.

## Who is in the team?

Within a small residential home, a group of staff is appointed to care for those who live there and, to a greater or lesser extent, share their lives with the residents. However, there are many different models of staffing. Some homes will have residential house parents or home leaders with other nonresidential care staff where all the chores are shared, the main distinction being between residential and nonresidential. Others will have staff defined as cooks, cleaners, gardeners, drivers, care staff, where roles are outlined in job descriptions; the main distinction here is the type of work that is done. In other homes, staff will all be residential, sharing all the home-making tasks, and day and night staff are not distinguished. This pattern is becoming more common in all agencies where there is a strong permeating philosophy and the concept of living 'in community' is highly valued. Often, however, such staff stay for shorter periods than those making a less complete commitment as in other models of staffing. Here, the main distinction is between permanent staffing (or qualified) and shorter stay staff (probably unqualified).

Often, full-time staff are seen as more important than part-time staff, day staff than night staff, and direct care staff than those who care for the property or provide transport. The first decision is to identify team members and be aware of the important, but often only implicit, value judgements that may be used to devalue or split off some team members.

An example of how such potential splitting can be institutionalized is seen in the term, 'core' team, often used in CMHTs to pick out the full-time members and distinguish them from those who are part-time or advisory. The danger is that when such a split has already been made, potentially devaluing those who are outside the core, any conflict is likely to polarize team members and increase the splitting, for example, by restricting certain information or the power of decision-making to core-team members only.

# TEAM TASK 2

Decide who is in the team and then work hard to preserve the unity of the team by valuing each individual contribution as unique and important.

## Are the skills of team members defined and overlaps understood?

Every member of the team has a professional or technical role as well as a more diffuse role as a team member (see 'Roles of Team Members', p. 113). The role that is about contributing skills is the more easily defined. The home leader, for example, knows that his professional role is based on his training, his expectations of the post and his past experience in his working life. He may also have special interests developed along the way. He will be able to separate off some skills that are unique to a home leader

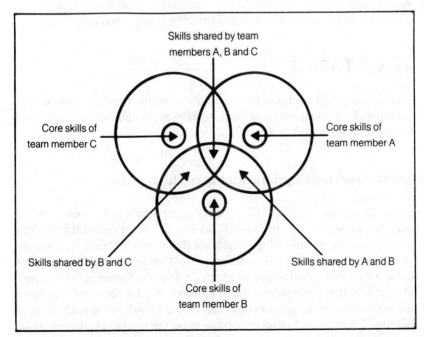

**Figure 5.1**  Core skills and shared skills

but other skills will be shared; for example, his skill in understanding family dynamics will also be found in the social worker, the psychologist and some of the direct care staff. Skills can therefore be referred to respectively as 'core' skills and 'shared' skills (Figure 5.1). A useful exercise for all team members is to identify core skills and shared skills in this way. An extension of this exercise is to ask the more senior members of a team to see if any skills have moved from 'core' to 'shared' during their years of practice. Beware of the team member who feels that all his skills are 'core' skills and none can be or are shared with anyone.

Often the shared skills have to do with special interests and further training, for example, counselling in bereavement or running social skills groups to encourage independence in decision-making and risk-taking. An awareness of skills shared with others can be put to good use when one member is hard pressed for time and another has not enough to do. At other times two heads may be better than one in very difficult tasks, and joint working can lead to success where one team member alone could have been overwhelmed.

If a team member fails to recognize that some of his skills are shared with others then he is unlikely to benefit from joint working and such possessiveness can lead to conflict between team members.

## TEAM TASK 3

Identify core skills and shared skills and with whom these are shared. Use shared skills to even out workloads, to help each other when needed and to come closer together as a team.

## Losses and new appointments to the team

The team in a small house is like an open group where individuals join and leave for personal and professional reasons but the team itself continues with a changing membership. Whatever the reason for leaving, the team will experience some reaction, a sense of loss when the team member has made a valuable contribution and perhaps a sense of relief at other times. One risk is that the valuable team member will be idealized and for a while the remaining members will feel that they will never recover from the loss. Likewise, when an unpopular team member goes, there may be scapegoating and all the blaming in the team placed on the outgoing member, with little inclination to examine the functioning of the remaining team.

The newly appointed team member will need to sense the welcome of this team as an open group and feel encouraged by friendship and professional support as they take up their roles in the team and in the service. It is a sad day for teams when a newly appointed member finds an impenetrable clique instead.

The loss of a team member may usefully be marked by the ritual of a party or a gift when the team has a chance to say goodbye, to feel the strength of the remaining team members and the readiness to welcome another in the empty space.

The readiness and confidence with which the team will accept a new member will depend in part on their involvement in the appointment. Have candidates been invited to meet team members formally or attend a team meeting? Ideally, where team work is an important function of the post then the team should be represented on the appointments committee irrespective of the profession involved. Sadly, this does not always happen and there is often work to do to overcome resentment to the new member and hostility to a profession when the team has been disregarded, and the new appointment has been made and imposed upon the team with no consultation.

## TEAM TASK 4

Teams can be enriched by the inevitable gains and losses of members, and team functioning strengthened if time is taken to acknowledge these. Involvement of teams in appointments committees may need to be worked towards and cannot be considered as inevitable.

### Roles of team members

The contribution of individual skills within the team has already been dealt with. The second and equally important role of each team member is the contribution that he makes by his personality, his relationship with and concern for others in the team. Leadership is often thought to be the only role of this type, with the rest of the team forming a homogeneous band of followers. This is totally untrue. The more individual contributions in the team are looked at, the more intricate and important they seem to be, with the total process of team work being greater than the sum of the individual contributions.

Here are some examples:

- The ideas man: 'Why don't we . . .?'
- The optimist: 'I am sure it will work!'
- The sceptic: 'I can't believe that's possible!'
- The pessimist: 'Yes, but . . .'
- The cautious: 'What if . . .'
- 'By the rules' man: 'Is it in accordance with the overall plan?'
- The peace maker: 'Perhaps we might all agree if . . .'
- The resource finder: 'Can anyone help us?'
- The tidy one: 'Let's finish this job before starting another!'
- The introvert: 'Let's take time to think.'
- The monitor: 'Have we done this well enough?'
- The community conscience: 'Is everyone involved?'
- And finally, the person with a sense of humour!

Each team will have some or all of these characteristics and each needs to be valued for the contribution he or she makes. A nice balance is to be aimed for. Too many optimists will mean that the team does not have its feet on the ground, but too few will mean that good chances for innovative schemes may be missed.

# TEAM TASK 5

Value the personal as well as the professional skills of team members.

## Leadership issues

Leadership is about being at the front of the team at a particular time for a certain purpose. Leadership skills are not restricted to certain professions and neither to positions of seniority. These skills have more to do with personality and inclination, and some team members will find that they can develop these skills by following good examples and with a little extra training. Others will never wish to be leaders but do other equally important team tasks (see Figure 5.3).

**What makes a leader?**
Someone who is well accepted by others; whose knowledge and wisdom

about the job are accepted; who values other people; who is ready to accept responsibility; who has interest and enthusiasm for the task; who has the time to do it; who can tolerate ambiguity.

At any one time within a team, several people may be exercising legitimate leadership skills.

## A leader by appointment

Leadership of an establishment, or less often of a team, will be contained within a job description and the details of that leadership role will be enumerated. For example, a home leader, appointed as the most senior person in a home, will carry the responsibility for the smooth running of that home and be accountable to a senior person or committee for progress and mistakes. Seniority, experience, wisdom, tolerance, creativity and positivity will be desired attributes in such a home leader.

## The chairman

The chairman is the leader of the team meeting and has an important role in calling, conducting and finishing meetings, ensuring that everyone is involved. He or she must be calm and face both crisis and controversy, and be tolerant, positive and creative and able to nurture the people within the team. Well conducted team meetings, where everyone feels that they are valued and that their voice is heard, will make a big contribution to the smooth running of work outside of team meetings. Many team members may have the qualities to be the chairman of the team, and teams often rotate the chairmanship position so that team members may try out their skills.

## The link person

One link person may represent the house team to another agency such as the local CMHT and another link person may represent the house to the local social services or voluntary agencies. The link person establishes a dialogue between the house and the outside agency; the link person thereby leading the team at the interface between the house and agencies that may wish to call upon the resources of the house or have something to offer. The link person is briefed by the house team and feeds back to the same team, dealing primarily with resources and not with individual clients.

## The key worker

This is the term used by many teams for the member who takes the leadership role for those in the team working with a particular client or resident. It is commonplace in small houses for every resident to have one member of staff as key worker who develops a close day-to-day relationship, being responsible with the resident for daily routines, behavioural programmes, leisure and work skills and who provides personal support and friendship. Other members of the team work with and through the key worker, who uses his leadership skills for that resident. This pattern of work within the team has been found to lead to clearer lines of responsibility and a chance for the special in-depth relationship between the resident and the team member who is his key worker.

But key workers cannot be with the resident at all times. A handover of information and tasks partly completed will be necessary when the key worker has time off and another must take a personal interest in the resident until the key worker returns. It is vital that this is understood otherwise the key worker system can lead paradoxically to neglect of the resident.

Key worker/resident relationships can become deep and fulfilling friendships, with reciprocity in learning. It is important that for some people with a mental handicap this may be one of a few meaningful adult to adult relationships that has been experienced. Small wonder, therefore, that the loss of a key worker through change of job or promotion, for example, can lead to a bereavement response that must be acknowledged and worked through before the resident can accept another key worker. Is this fair, you ask? Making and losing friends is part of the rich tapestry of life's experience, whereas the alternative – many carers, neutrality and social distance in relationships – only exercises one human response, that of loneliness.

## The democratic style of leadership

This is a popular style of leadership and works smoothly when a team is well established, stable and when the external pressures on the team are manageable. The democratic leader knows that he can delegate and needs the minimum of authority to bring together his team. He knows that the team respect him and are anxious to follow. He defines the limits and the team makes suggestions and decisions within those limits. He can present ideas, encourage others and allow the group to decide which way to go. Such permissive or democratic leadership is a pleasure to the leader and to the team but can be inadequate if major difficulties loom.

These difficulties may be: in the task to be done; in the skills and personalities of the team members; in the restraints imposed from outside.

At times like this, the leader may need to shift from a democratic to a

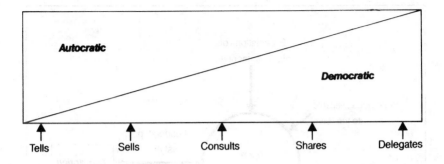

**Figure 5.2**  Styles of leadership

more autocratic position, taking more responsibility and power to himself, making decisions which he then may need to sell to the team and, in extreme situations, announcing the decisions and asking for action (Figure 5.2). This type of leadership is described as the authority-centred or autocratic leader.

### Authority-centred or autocratic leader

Such a leadership style feels uncomfortable, and is more at home in the cockpit of an aeroplane than in a human service; it tends to de-skill those team members with decision-making potential themselves. If felt to last too long, the team will split from the leader, who may fail to find loyalty and may need to rely on coersion. Such splits in teams may be seen when teams are told to do something that does not feel right: a useful service may have to be closed in the face of serious financial cuts or the team is asked to withdraw from serving a part of the catchment area. The team will resent and be distressed by this type of decision but the leader may have the delegated and thankless task to do. A lack of understanding by the team may cause the leader to separate from the team and become part of the management structure which is viewed as persecutory and of the unpleasant decision which is seen as destructive.

All teams will have good and bad times and the skilled leader is the one who can move along the democratic/autocratic spectrum just as much as is needed to keep the team together and in high morale, with the work progressing to satisfaction (Figure 5.3).

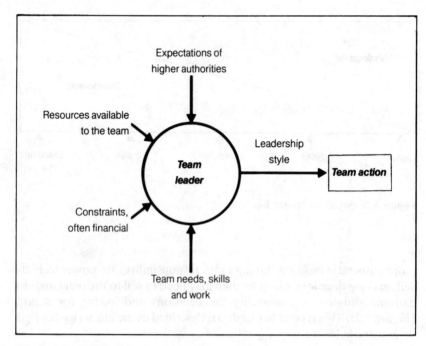

**Figure 5.3**   Leadership

# TEAM TASK 6

Examine the styles of leadership that you have in your team. When did you last congratulate the leader?

## Team agreements

These are essential and need to be constructed by team members and embodied in the *operational policy* of the team. They will probably cover the following:

- Arrangements, frequency and who can call a meeting.
- The powers of the chairman and election arrangements.
- Agendas for meetings.
- Appointments of key workers and link persons.

- Methods of record keeping.
- Confidentiality.
- Management of conflict.
- Responsibilities of team leader.
- Responsibilities of team members.

Of these, record keeping, confidentiality and the management of conflict will be considered further.

## Record keeping and confidentiality

A single central record keeping system for each resident, managed on his/her behalf by the key worker, and where everyone involved can make an entry often works very well. Everyone working with the resident has access to that information, and information known within the team is confidential to the team. Occasionally, a team member is given some information that they are told they cannot share with other team members. This may not be of vital importance to the care of the resident but will still create a dilemma.

> The mother of a resident confides in the key worker that her marriage is breaking down and the tension at home is distressing, but says that she does not want the staff in the house to know. The key worker has to accept this but the mother does agree that she can report back at the team meeting that there may be family-based reasons for the changes in behaviour of the resident.

In this example, it is important that the key worker does not break the bond of trust with the mother; her position in the team will not be jeopardized if she shares as much as she is allowed with the other team members. No difficulties are likely to occur if team members trust each other not to hold back on information that could be imparted. It is when information is held back as a means of holding onto power within the team that the team will suffer.

One way of allowing two levels of information to coexist within the recording system is, first, to have a single central record and, second, to allow all team members to keep their own confidential notes. If this is seen to be acceptable then the power of secrecy to divide is undermined at the very beginning.

# TEAM TASK 7

Confidentiality and communication are the opposite sides of the same coin. Can the team keep a balance between the two?

## Management of conflict

From time to time there will be differences of opinion regarding the management of a resident.

> Should Stephen go without his dinner if he refuses to come on time?

There are different ways this may be decided:

- The key worker decides.
- The home leader decides.
- There may be rules for the house which make the decision plain.
- His parents may have strong views.
- Stephen himself may be involved by showing him what might happen and his key worker may develop a 'contract' with him for the consequences of late arrival to meals.
- If there is a serious disagreement, the whole team may debate this until there is a resolution on which all can agree which is likely to be a compromise on the original proposal. This is *consensus decision-making*.

Serious disagreement is better brought out at a team meeting than argued behind closed doors. There will usually be someone who has peace-making skills who can encourage the necessary debate in a constructive way without the need to resort to decisions outside of the team, which will only weaken the team structure.

Each house will have its own operational policy and the decision-making process will be outlined in this document. The essential element is to ensure that, whatever the process, the team 'owns' the decision once made. In this respect, 'the power of veto' is particularly destructive of team dynamics and should only be exercised by someone who has sufficient seniority and wisdom to know when there is no alternative and to manage the repercussions that such an action will bring.

# Staff support

Team members each have their own needs and weaknesses as well as their skills and strengths. The joy of team work is that each team member can meet some of each other's needs and become more skilled and more mature themselves in the process. The following are needs that we all have in team work. Can you add any more?

- The need to be approved of and encouraged.
- The need to be supported and at times comforted.
- The need to be guided and checked.
- The need to be encouraged to work harder or, more commonly, less hard.
- The need to have time to think about team relationships.
- The need to think about the work that the team is asked to do.
- The need to be taught more skills.
- The need to laugh together and sometimes to cry.
- The need to be congratulated.

Much of this support will come from each other within the team, the team leader or individual supervisors who may not be team members. Most of this support will be informal and it is important for leaders to remember the need to praise progress and success and not to become preoccupied by unsolved problems and work that cannot be done. But who supports the leader? It is often lonely at the top and most team leaders will appreciate a word of encouragement for the difficult tasks they have to undertake.

There are at least two ways in which staff support may be intensified and have primacy in the team work at a particular time: a retreat and a search conference. Both require some organization but may be necessary for teams facing a great deal of stress or uncertainty.

## A retreat
A team that felt battered by the endless requests for client work, with inadequate resources and little recognition, began to register much internal disagreement, high sickness rates and very long hours of working. The team members decided to go away for a weekend together and with a group leader spent time looking at team relationships and the sources of stress. The destructive nature of the 'workaholic' model was recognized and team members gave each other permission to stop this from happening. The team never looked back from that weekend, more work was done in fewer hours and morale has remained high.

## A search conference

A large hospital needed to change but the future was uncertain. Many rumours started and staff began to leave. Two days were set aside to search for a new future for the residents and for the hospital. Three senior members of the staff were asked to pick three others who were regarded as fair-minded and who put the clients first in their everyday work. These three then picked another three and this continued until 30 people were chosen, with parents, residents, volunteers and staff members including the cook, hairdresser, the gardener, nurses and administrators. The rules of the two-day discussion were:

- Everyone's contribution is valuable.
- Let everyone share in the discussion.
- It is all right to disagree.
- Professional roles are not important.
- You are at the conference as yourself.
- Someone does not have to be wrong for you to be right.

Out of this sharing developed several exciting patterns for the future based on what the residents really needed. There was no longer any need for rumour and no more did the hospital feel the helpless victim of bureaucratic change.

## The team and the consumers

In a small home, the residents may be very much a team on their own, learning to live and work together, to share skills, to learn, mature and minimize their weaknesses. The same dynamics described for a team of staff may be seen within such a client group. They may be part of a more organized structure; there may be a residents' committee as a self-advocacy venture, and one resident may belong to the house team to represent the others. In a very small setting, residents and staff may belong to one team with no apparent divisions.

At times the (staff) team may need to discuss one resident. In the past that resident would not have been included in the discussion; latterly he would have been invited in at the end, but now he is more likely to be there throughout the meeting. It is important that everyone is prepared, especially the resident who may need help from his key worker before-hand to make the most of his own contribution. The presence of the resident alone is insufficient to safeguard the concept of equal involvement in decision-making; indeed if he is unprepared, cannot understand, is excluded by the use of jargon or talked down to, then the philosophy of self-advocacy has been completely undermined and his presence at the meeting has been a token gesture.

## TEAM TASK 8

Involve the residents or consumers as much as possible and give them the opportunities to be skilled and effective.

## To whom is the team accountable?

Teams are made up from many different professions, each representing a tradition, a skill and a professional loyalty and hierarchy. Such single

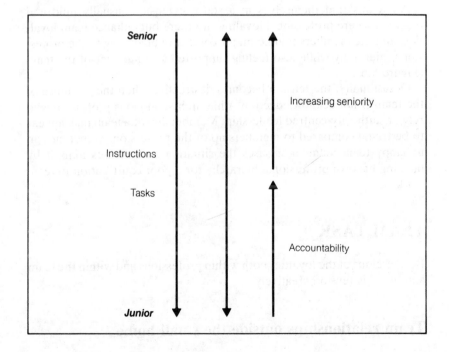

**Figure 5.4**   Single profession – vertical hierarchy

professional management structures are often of far longer standing than the existence of the team, which has become superimposed on such a 'vertical' structure (Figure 5.4).

The team can be visualized as a 'horizontal' line where loyalty and accountability is between professions, irrespective of seniority, and tasks are derived from team decisions and leadership action (Figure 5.5).

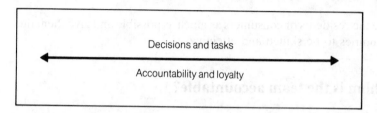

**Figure 5.5**   Horizontal structure of a team

All teams find themselves in a state of tension, usually mild and creative, where professional loyalties are there but enhance team loyalties, and the members find no major conflict in belonging to the professional hierarchy while also feeling supported as a member of the team (Figure 5.6).

Occasionally, the tension becomes destructive when the existence of the team is not acknowledged by a hierarchy-conscious profession who rely on authority-centred leadership. Membership of a team may appear to be trivial compared to membership of the profession. Sometimes an unhappy team member misuses the situation and excuses himself by blaming his own professional hierarchy for a poor contribution to team work.

## TEAM TASK 9

Be conscious of the loyalties both within professions and within the team and use this tension creatively.

### Team relationships outside the small home

Team work should ensure that: the appropriate skills, rightly timed, sensitively offered, in the 'best' place, by the 'best' person, and co-

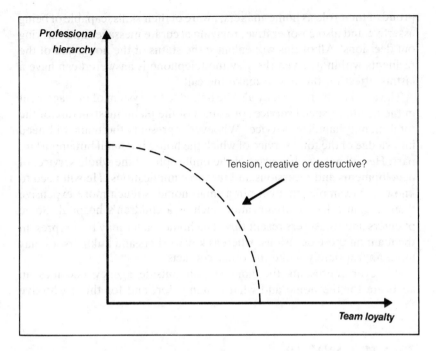

**Figure 5.6** One source of team tension

ordinated with other contributions, are offered to the client in need of the service.

What are these other contributions likely to be? For the small home for children, the school, the family and the voluntary agencies are going to play the major part; for adults, the school gives way to the social education centre, careers advisers and employment agencies and social organizations for adults, while the families gradually play a smaller part. An integrated lifestyle for each resident means contact will be made with, for example, sports centres, the launderette, shops, post offices, restaurants and above all neighbours.

Some of these contacts will be formal. The team of the home will be represented at the school leavers' conferences and at reviews at the social education centre. Other contacts will be much more informal, such as with the manager of the local swimming pool, and contacts are the most informal in local public houses!

The way in which these agencies view the team, and thereby the home, will reflect upon the residents. The team needs to be seen to be informed, proud of their role as home-makers, aware of their skills, capable of being assertive and also co-operative, relaying accurate messages and carrying out decisions. All of this will enhance the status of the home and of the residents within it. Even the way the telephone is answered can have a lasting effect on those who make the call.

The team in the home may also be linked to the system of management in the health or social services or as part of the planning structure of the total mental handicap service. Whoever represents the team will need knowledge of the total service of which the house is a small but important part. He will need to be aware of the philosophy of the whole service, of developments and recessions and resource implications. He will need to know, for example, that care in a small home is much more expensive than care in a larger organization such as a children's hospital. Some planners and treasurers resent this. The home leader may best represent the team on these occasions, whereas key workers and link persons may more appropriately make the other contacts.

Whoever represents the home to an outside agency becomes an advocate for the home and what it stands for, and for those who live there.

## TEAM TASK 10

No team stands alone. Teams relate to other teams, agencies and organizations. The point of interaction gives another chance to be an advocate for the clients that are served.

### Is there an overall philosophy?

There will be an agreed and understood philosophy for the home, the clients and the team which will give overall guidance on the direction in which the team must work. This will be stated clearly in the operational policy. This may be a philosophy of normalization, for example, with a set of underlying values against which the day-to-day work of the team will need to be checked.[2] There may be a high priority on the development of independence and allowing sensible risk-taking. On the other hand, the home may not place great value on integration but on developing a sense of community within the establishment. Some small homes will be part of an organization with a particular religious persuasion that will permeate the lives of the residents and the staff. Whatever the underlying value system, this will need to be explained and explored within the team, and new members of the team will need an introduction before they can be expected to understand how the team functions in the small home.

## What are the financial constraints?

The current trend is for devolution of budgetary control so that the unit for financial managment is becoming smaller, and it is quite likely that a small residential home will manage its own budget. This is probably the province of the home leader but the whole team will need to be financially aware; they need to know when money has to be saved and share the principles of sound financial management with the residents as they learn to manage their own money. Team members may often have good ideas on how money can be saved in the day-to-day setting, without affecting the quality of life of the residents. Such 'value for money' schemes will be far more effective than financial cuts imposed from outside of the home.

## What do others see as the service the team offers?

It is possible for a team to have a sound philosophy and good working relationships with those around them, and yet the team may not have communicated effectively with would-be consumers. There is an important public relations function for the team, very often taken on by the extrovert within the team. The service will need to be advertised for what it is so that expectations from the consumers are not too high nor too low. It is important too that misunderstandings are dealt with as soon as they arise. The home that offers respite care, for example, to the local community, may find that those living close by assume they have some priority over those who live further away. If this is not so, then this needs to be made clear before antagonisms arise.

## Are goals set for the team?

A goal is a long-range aim; objectives are aims in the shorter range that will enable the team to reach the goal. The goals for a team in a small home will probably be about the quality and range of services that the team expects to offer. There will also be individual goals and objectives set for and with the residents, but goal-setting for the team will be a closely related but different exercise.

## Is the team set in its ways?

From time to time the team may feel that new ideas are needed, that not all the options have been explored and that the service has become set in its ways. 'Brainstorming' is an exciting team exercise whereby the team gets together and the leader for the exercise asks for as many ideas as quickly as possible without stopping to evaluate or cost the ideas. Particular encouragement is given to unusual ideas and no one should hold back for fear his idea is silly or would not work. A list is made of all the ideas put forward and then, when no more ideas are forthcoming, each one is considered carefully, giving particular attention to the unexpected ones. This exercise can be great fun and everyone in the team can join in.

## Is everyone working to the best level of his ability?

The simplest form of work is the clearly defined task given to a team member, which consists of a direct action on the immediate environment, for example, cleaning the kitchen floor or laying out clothes for a child to wear the next day. The task is short, the end is clear and work of this nature can be readily checked. This is called *level 1* work.

*Level 2* work is somewhat more complex; a request to 'do whatever is necessary in the bedrooms' would involve bedmaking, tidying, sorting and putting away clean clothes, perhaps with a choice about the order of the work and the amount to be done. There would be the need for initiative and for choices to be made.

*Level 3* is more diffuse and not so easily measured or checked upon. Neither are the immediate results of the work quite so obvious as in levels 1 and 2. *Level 3* work might be taking responsibility for the goal-planning or the individual programme planning for the client. This could be described as a segment of the total service, the organization of which is *level 4*.

*Level 4* work is more complex and equates with the work of a home leader who needs to ensure that the home in so many different aspects functions well, that the residents at the heart of the service are doing well, that families feel secure, that staff are satisfied, that the home runs within the defined budget and is seen to be a valued part of the total service. The *level 4* worker will identify the deficiencies and gaps in the service and will make efforts to remedy these.[3]

Such an understanding of task complexity can be important for the team. There may be a tendency to value work according to its complexity but all tasks in a home are important, indeed vital, at whatever level. Some team members will function well at level 2, while others will be more challenged if they are stretched to level 3 and feel undervalued if doing only level 2 work. Occasionally, someone is asked to move from a routine of level 1 and 2 tasks to function at level 3 and fails, when blaming can start and unhappiness created within the team. Competence at any and every level is to be valued. The idea of *equality* within a team is probably not a useful one, but the concept of *differentness* with every contribution being valued on its own will lead to happy working relationships.

## TEAM TASK 11

Let each member examine their work and decide at which level or levels they are working. Is there a tendency to ascribe importance to those who are at the higher levels?

### How does the team plan?

Most teams learn to plan ahead for likely eventualities and crises. Is there sufficient food in the freezer for the Bank Holiday weekend and enough fuel in the minibus for the half-expected long journey? However, not all crises can be foreseen. The team that can respond to a crisis, live through it and laugh about it, is a team that is strong indeed, but too many crises detract from the day-to-day work and can weaken the team. Most teams in small homes will plan ahead, known as *proactive* planning. Much of the smooth team work is because crises are averted due to planning based on the assumption that certain events may happen. Planning in the spring for a summer programme of respite care to dovetail with residents' holiday arrangements is an example of a proactive plan.

Sometimes a need cannot be anticipated, in which case *reactive* planning is required; a rapid plan made when the need is felt. An example would be a quick response to the local family when mother falls ill, or the speedy arrangement for counselling following an unexpected bereavement for a client.

The third form of planning, the *retroactive* plan, is one that follows too late on an event or a crisis to be fully effective, meaning that the client or family is left unhelped for too long and the team loses credibility. A useful team exercise is to look at the events of the preceding week and see how many were managed by proactive planning or reactive planning. Hopefully, none were managed by retroactive plans!

# CONCLUSION

Team work is essential in human services and a good example is the team in a small home. Team work is not easy but can be exciting and challenging. The service offered by a team will vary according to need but the way in which any team works can with benefit be examined by the team members. Team work does not happen automatically. Relationships within the team, team member support, decision-making, communication and confidentiality, the management of conflict and the setting up of team agreements, must be understood and time given to this process of understanding.

The well functioning and stable team will then be able to provide the very best service for the residents and play a vital part in the total service for the client group whose needs are to be met and whose skills will be fully acknowledged.

# REFERENCES

1. Colby, M.S. (1984) *Test Your Management IQ*, Pan Books, London.
2. Tyne, A. (1981) *The Principle of Normalisation: A Foundation for Effective Services*, Campaign for People with a Mental Handicap, London.
3. Rowbotton and Billis (1978) in *Health Services*, E. Jaques (ed.), Chapter 7, The stratification of work and organizational design, Heinemann, London.

# FURTHER READING

Craft, M., Bicknell, J. and Hollins, S. (eds), (1985) in *Mental Handicap – A Multidisciplinary Approach*, Chapter 24, The dynamics of team work, Ballière Tindall, London.
Ovretveit, J. (1986) Organisation of multidisciplinary community teams, *The Health Services Centre Working Paper*, Brunel University. .

Woodcock, M. and Francis, D. (1981) *Organisation Development Through Team Building*, Gower, Aldershot, Hampshire.

# 6. Developing Day Services

*Rob Hancock*

## INTRODUCTION

This chapter is concerned with the provision of day services for people with mental handicap. As we approach the twenty-first century there is a growing awareness among service users (the consumer), service producers, parents and academics that day services, if they are to be of value, must meet the individual needs of the consumer.

Those involved with day services have begun to listen; to listen to, and value the wishes and needs of the consumer. Service producers are listening to researchers. Researchers are listening to parents and professionals. We are moving towards a partnership comprising all the people involved in day services. It is the age of achievement, a time of hope, as the challenge of providing meaningful day services is being taken up.

However, in any study of services for people, it is wise to consider the antecedents as well as the contemporary issues in order to gain a reasonable perspective of the complex elements involved. The purpose, content and practice of day services will be described and evaluated in the following four sections:

1. Day services – 'the log jam' – an evaluation of day services.
2. Tools for clearing 'the log jam' – contemporary issues and key concepts in day services.
3. Towards the twenty-first century – the essential ingredients for the future development of day services.

4. Meeting the needs of the consumer, finding the way – different ways of providing day services.

# DAY SERVICES

It must be a cardinal commitment for service providers to ensure people with mental handicaps are consulted and given an opportunity to express their preferences in respect of suggested services.[1]

## The consumers

Who are the consumers of day services? At present, 50,000 to 60,000 people aged between 16 and 65. Each one of these consumers is unique, each one is an individual. They are people with a mental handicap and, in some cases, with additional physical and sensory impairments. Each person has a range of individual needs, many of which will not remain constant.

They are not a neat homogeneous group called 'the mentally handicapped', all with the same or similar needs. Neither are they the same as, or have the same needs as, people who are mentally ill.

Society often fails to recognize what is dissimilar about people, their uniqueness and individuality. We have an innate need to classify and group; we look for common characteristics; and once these are discovered, a group can be categorized. People are categorized according to nationality, race, interests, religion, and so on. Such groups are given names, and in time the name conveys a stereotyped image of the individual members of such a group: for example, the French, football supporters, the mentally handicapped. Several writers have recognized such stereotyping as providing a handicap whereby consumers of day services were and are to some extent all thought to need the same type of day service.[2, 3]

Stereotyping causes people to be labelled. Such labels convey images; images that either aid or hinder a person's acceptance into his or her local community. Images help to decide whether a person can live an ordinary life or a special life within the community. A negative stereotype can be potentially as handicapping as a physical, sensory or mental impairment.

# What are day services?

One of the major tasks facing day services is to lessen the handicaps of its clients. How is this to be achieved, and what are day services? Although day services mainly consist of adult training centres (ATC) or social education centres (SEC) where large numbers of people with mental handicaps are catered for between 9 a.m. and 4 p.m., Monday to Friday, this need not be the case. Indeed, it is not the case in many day services and some day centres, as illustrated later in the chapter.

The provision of day services by some local authorities is a dynamic, not a static, service. They use ordinary established services and small, specially established services to create provision for people with mental handicap. To meet the individual needs of its consumers and lessen their handicaps, a service needs to be dynamic.

Guidelines for developing services are to be found in the King's Fund papers,[4-6] publications from the Independent Development Council for People with Mental Handicaps (IDC),[7-9] the Royal Society for Mentally Handicapped Children and Adults (MENCAP),[1, 10] the Campaign for People with a Mental Handicap (CMH),[11] National Development Group (NDG), and many other sources. Outlines and descriptions of dynamic developments have been well documented.[12-14] All argue for a dynamic, community-based service, developed according to the individual needs of the consumer.

# The providers

Day services are primarily the responsibility of local authorities. This responsibility is delegated to local authorities by central government. The local authority's social services department is usually chiefly responsible for the planning and day-to-day administration of day services. In some authorities the departments responsible for health and for education may also be involved.

The voluntary sector, consisting of charitable organizations, is often a provider of day services. The Wolfenden Committee[15] came to the conclusion that the voluntary sector contributes to local authority provision mainly in the following three ways: through extending the scope of existing provision; by improving the quality of government provision; and by being the sole/principal provider of services.

Local authorities are obliged to provide day services under the National Health Service Act of 1977. But, like most legislation concerning the disabled, it requires local authorities only to provide 'within the resources available'. Therefore, quality and consistency between authorities, and within authorities, varies. Consumers or their advocates are in no position to demand a particular type of day service, or that day services are of a specific quality; they are only in the position to accept what is provided.

However, the Disabled Persons (Consultation and Representation) Act makes recommendations for the assessment and provision of services (including access to day service provision/employment) and requires local authorities to produce a statement for each person with a mental handicap in respect of their needs and expectations.[16] The Act was the result of an all-party lobby to improve consumer involvement in choosing and receiving individually designed services (see Chapter 2). The success of these recommendations will depend on the availability of local resources and the response of individual local authorities to implement the main clauses; whatever the outcome, the Act demonstrates the importance of individual choice and consumer representation. (Chapter 1 provides a useful summary of consumer rights and advocacy.)

## THE LOG JAM

There is a great danger in generalizing about the present situation in adult training centres. The fact that such facilities are organized and provided for on a local basis has resulted in a wide variation in quality and quantity.[1]

Although MENCAP is correct in condemning sweeping generalizations about this subject, there is one factor that is true of most day services, i.e. there is little chance for all but a few consumers to move on or move up.

Day services for people with a mental handicap are segregated services; few people move on from ATCs or SECs. Consumers of day services have been, and often still are, forced to spend their adult lives in one centre. This 'log jam' can be better understood using a historical perspective of services for the mentally handicapped.

During the late nineteenth century and for much of this century, people with a mental handicap have been wrongly thought to have a disease, to be ineducable, and to be capable of passing on their handicap to the next generation. These false beliefs have led to segregation from mainstream society in isolated hospitals.

People incarcerated as inmates in so-called hospitals (12,000 in 1920, rising to 100,000 in 1950) were unable to benefit from day services which local authorities were obliged to provide following the 1913 Mental

Deficiency Act. Because of these factors there was no significant general development of day services until the late 1950s. The myth that people with a mental handicap were ineducable and in need of mainly medical care was still evident, in that during the 1950s and 1960s most junior training centres and adult training centres were the responsibility of local health authorities.

It was not until the late 1960s that the views of educationists who had been working with the mentally handicapped, such as Tizard, Gunsberg and Clarke, began to change established views.

Such research work, coupled with the appalling conditions exposed by the Ely Hospitals scandal in 1967,[17] the official recognition that mentally handicapped people *are* educable (the 1970 Education Act) and the 1971 White Paper,[18] led to a reappraisal of people with a mental handicap and their needs.

This brief historical perspective reveals the lack of value placed on the abilities of people with a mental handicap. Therefore, it is not surprising that the scope of day services up to and beyond the early 1970s was very limited. Indeed, despite the 1971 White Paper predicting a growth in the number of ATC places required from 25,000 in 1970 to 74,000 by the early 1990s, it was not until 1977 that the National Development Group (NDG) outlined its recommended reorganization of day services.[19] This provided an excellent analysis of the service and suggested a framework within which the service could be developed. Another publication in 1977 showed that centres were very poor at moving people out (less than 4 per cent), and they had low expectations of their clients' ability.[20] The time was ripe, therefore, to clear the log jam.

## Clearing the log jam

> We wish to emphasize that both research and practice have demonstrated beyond doubt that mentally handicapped people can learn.[19]

That it was necessary for the NDG to make such a statement indicates not only a lack of throughtput of people in day services, but also of ideas and knowledge. During the 1970s 'new' ideas which were both pervasive and persuasive did begin to emerge, influencing professionals, consumers, and planners of day services. These ideas sprang from research and projects in Britain, the USA and Western European countries.

Mentally handicapped people began to be acknowledged as human beings. In 1971 the United Nations' *Declaration on the Rights of the*

*Mentally Retarded* was published (see MENCAP (1968) p. 44). Minority groups of all kinds – including people with a mental handicap – began to demand their rights. These demands led to a reappraisal of 'old' ideas and a change in the traditional system.

Normalization, a system of values and beliefs developed by Nirje[21] in Sweden and refined in America by Wolfensberger,[22] became the ideas and beliefs on which to base services for people with a mental handicap. Normalization became the banner behind which those concerned with services for the mentally handicapped could unite. It is a powerful and valuable concept but many have debased it by never using it beyond the level of a slogan or mainly as rhetoric.

Rhetoric and slogans are useful in all areas of life to rally support and create interest. But, as Mittler points out, we need to be 'aware of the gap between rhetoric and reality, between what we would like to do and what we can actually achieve'.[24]

Important ideas and concepts such as normalization, individual rights and needs, and integration in the community, are important tools with which to break the log jam; but they need to be understood and assimilated beyond the level of rhetoric and slogans if they are to be effective tools in clearing the log jam.

## Tools for clearing the log jam

> If we were beginning afresh we wouldn't have long-stay hospitals; no hostels, and no adult training centres. Next time around we would be much more imaginative, more flexible.[25]

Many consumers and providers agree with this statement; many do not. But most agree that there should be change, be it by revolution, evolution, or by what some have termed, 'rapid evolution'.[3] However, whatever the method, whatever the chosen speed, all aspects of service provision require a system of values, beliefs, principles and practices on which to base services. Some of the tools for breaking through the log jam are outlined below as key components of a comprehensive consumer-led service which

● values the client as a full citizen with rights and responsibilities, entitled to be consulted about his or her needs and have a say about plans that are being made to meet those needs, no matter how severe his or her handicap may appear at first sight;

- aims to promote the independence and to develop the skills and abilities of both clients and families;
- aims to design, implement and evaluate a programme of support which is based on the unique needs of each individual;
- aims to help the client to use ordinary services and resources of the local community, e.g., primary care, education, health, social, employment, housing, welfare and recreational service;
- aims to meet special needs arising from disabilities by means of local, fully co-ordinated, multidisciplinary specialist services, delivered by appropriately trained staff;
- is easily accessible;
- is delivered to the client's home, school, AIC or work place;
- is delivered regardless of age or severity of disability;
- plans actively for people who are living in residential institutions to return to the locality to use its services;
- is staffed by locally based, small teams who are available to visit families in their own homes, and clients in their places of study and work.[7]

To this list I would add one more principle:

- ensures that all facets of the service are adult appropriate.

## TOWARDS THE TWENTY-FIRST CENTURY

People with mental handicaps are being helped to offer their presence and their contribution to the building of community. And that's not just worthwhile. It's something to celebrate – for them, for all those who help them and for anyone who has a care for the future of this society.[12]

As we move towards the twenty-first century and our understanding of the needs of people with mental handicaps slowly increases, it becomes increasingly apparent that there is no ideal model of day services – only examples and models of good practice. Indeed, the concept of day services or activities is undergoing constant revision. Many consumers, advocates and professionals are challenging the narrow concept of daytime activities or services as activities which take place only from 9 a.m. to 4 p.m. five days a week, or less. Those really concerned with meeting individual needs are including evenings and weekends as a legitimate part of services.

The concept of a service provided by one agency, e.g. social services, for a group called 'the mentally handicapped' is a redundant concept, even if it is still a working model in many local authorities. The concept of the diverse needs of over a hundred people often being met in one building, be it called an ATC or SEC, is also redundant but is still being practised to the detriment of people with a mental handicap.

Services need to be shaped by the individual needs of their consumers. (See Chapter 2 for an explanation of the principles of 'normalization'.) Therefore, services need to have a structure, but not a rigid structure. On the other hand, the structure should not be so flexible that its form is not recognizable to consumers, advocates and professionals, when they wish to plan individual pathways within it.

The structure of a service for the twenty-first century will be underpinned by four key elements, *purpose, practice, content* and *evaluation*. A consideration of these elements will give a perspective of the concept of a consumer-led service, which is coherent as a concept without being prescriptive in the service it recommends. Such a service is what is required to meet the needs of people with a mental handicap during the closing decade of the twentieth and into the twenty-first century.

## Purpose

> Good services must be based on explicit, coherent and carefully considered values and principles. These provide essential guidelines for determining both ends and means, for specifying what sort of life services should aim to support, and how services should be organized and delivered to provide that support. We must know *where* we want to get to and *why* before we can tackle the *how*.[11]

That the first priority for constructing good quality services is to establish the purpose of the service is supported by the King's Fund,[4, 5] the IDC,[7, 8] MENCAP,[1] MIND,[26] and many other individuals and organizations concerned for people with mental handicap. That their view of purpose may vary slightly in detail is of little or no consequence. Most of those concerned with defining the purpose or aims of a service for people with mental handicap would cite the principles of normalization as the essential guidelines of *where* we want to get to and *why*.

As some researchers have stated, when considering the purpose of their model of day services, 'Wolfensberger's conceptual model has implications for both policy and its translation into practice.'[27]

Wolfensberger and Thomas,[23] in their seven core themes of normalization, define the purpose of meaningful day services in a way which is
acceptable to consumers, advocates and providers. The seven core
themes are summarized as:

1. What happens in human services is often unconscious and destructive
   (e.g. treating mentally handicapped people as non-humans or as
   children) and needs to be made conscious and less destructive.
2. Negative role expectations of devalued people elicit negative behaviour and this vicious circle needs to be broken by establishing
   devalued people in positive social roles and having positive role
   expectations about them.
3. The more multiple the handicap a person has, the more exaggerated is
   the degree of apparent handicaps to the onlooker, an effect which also
   occurs in grouping numbers of handicapped people together. The way
   in which handicap is *presented* may exaggerate its reality. The effect
   needs to be reduced, e.g., by increasing the positive attributes of a
   handicapped person, or decreasing the number in a group.
4. Services should aim to increase clients' socially valued competences,
   which then offset handicaps.
5. Devalued people should have valued people as models to imitate, i.e.
   not only associate and identify with other devalued people.
6. The social image of devalued people should be made positive.
7. Integration into the life of normal society should be social and not just
   physical, i.e. involve socially valued participation.

Once the purpose and aims of the services have been defined it is
important that:

- The purpose is not subverted into rhetoric whereby a service is based
  only upon the stated purpose in words, and not deeds.
- The stated purpose should take account of what has gone before and
  what might follow.
- It is capable of encompassing the wide range of needs of people with
  mental handicaps.
- It actively strives to include all services and agencies, not only those
  specifically concerned with mental handicap.
- A well-defined purpose can act as a tool in evaluating if the services do
  not reflect the principles of the service.

# Practice

> The key factor in any organizational structure must be the needs of the
> mentally handicapped person.[19]

Practice has been defined by influential government reports, from the
White Paper, *Better Services for the Mentally Handicapped*[18] to the Social
Services Committee *Report on Adult Mentally Handicapped People*.[28]
Even though such reports have benefited from contributions and advice
from such bodies as the Campaign for People With a Mental Handicap,
CMH, NDG, MENCAP, IDC, and others, central government tends to
control the general direction of services and to set priorities.

Many believe that this policy of 'top down' planning has failed to meet
the needs of people with mental handicap.[4, 6, 7, 8, 26] The way forward is
seen to be in consumer-led, needs-based service, rather than a centralized
monopoly.

Comprehensive local services which are locally initiated, such as the
All Wales strategy, services in Winchester, North Western Regional
Health Authority, Northumberland and Bristol, are shaping models on
which practice for the twenty-first century can be based. Many of the
projects, such as New Ideas for the care of Mentally Retarded People in
Ordinary Dwellings (NIMROD) in Wales, are being closely monitored
so that an evaluation of their ability to meet the needs of the people they
serve can be judged.

Progress reports appear to support the views which were first put
forward in the Jay report[29] and the King's Fund Centre publication, *An
Ordinary Life*[4] that services will improve only through the partnership
and initiative of local people.

However, as the evaluation by one researcher in the London Boroughs
of Hounslow and Wandsworth has shown,[30] 'bottom up' planning, as
recommended by the Jay report and *An Ordinary Life*, needs a very
systematic and structured approach to bring together local services and
professionals in a service capable of meeting the individual needs of its
consumers.

An evaluation of the services developed in Sheffield concluded that,
despite extraordinary resources, there was a failure to establish a comprehensive community service as defined in the Jay report and *An Ordinary
Life*.[2] This was due, it would appear, to a lack of partnership regarding
the purpose, practice and content of the service. The judgement was that
money and political will do not make for a comprehensive community
service: 'Sheffield had its chance and muffed it.'[2]

The practice of meeting the individual needs of people with a mental handicap should, many believe, be supported by legislation.[10] In the USA such is the case, where projects such as the Eastern Nabraska Community Office for the Retarded (ENCOR), which inspired many people in this country,[4] are underpinned and supported by legislation concerned with the rights of the individual. It is doubtful if legislation in Britain will in the near future either support or underpin the individual rights of people with a mental handicap, but it is difficult to believe that such basic human rights can be ignored by all political parties far into the twenty-first century.

Without the general political will at the centre to create comprehensive local services, it would seem that a well structured 'bottom up' model is the method by which to establish them.

The following points may be helpful when considering *how* a local comprehensive service should be established (the IDC guideline principles for a local service quoted earlier need to be seen as a complement to these points):[8]

- Day services should be part of the network of special and ordinary services provided by all departments and divisions of local authority provision.
- Partnership between agencies and professionals is essential at all stages, from planning and resource management to daily provision.
- Local networks of resources within the community need to be identified and utilized.
- Practice should always seek to further the human rights of people with mental handicaps.
- Mechanisms, such as the Winchester model cited later in the chapter, should be established to set priorities, utilize ideas, and ensure that comprehensive local services are dynamic.

## Content

> When the centre manager arrived two years ago, craft work dominated. In his first week, he ordered eight corporation skips to dispose of all craft materials.[31]

The content of activities in day services is varied between social skills, work skills, further education and recreation skills. These elements have featured with varying degrees of prominence in day services since they began. They are subject to changes in name, emphasis and importance, depending on fashions. But they remain as the main content of day services.

It is hoped that in future services, which are based on individual needs, the content will be based only on needs and not fashions in research or professions. It is difficult to believe that the manager who decided that craft was not for those in his service really believed in a consumer-led needs-based service.

### What are the contents?
Broad areas of content can be identified; the most accepted are education, recreation, employment and social skills. However, if individual needs are to be paramount in future services, the content of services will be defined within these parameters by consumer needs. These key contents include: purpose; practice; and individual programme plans (IPPs) (see Chapter 3).

# Evaluation

Evaluation is fundamental to the process of developing services of quality for people with mental handicaps. Unless the purpose, content and practices of a service are continually evaluated, there will be no hope of better services for the consumer.[1, 4, 6, 7, 8, 11, 12, 23]

There are a number of methods of evaluating services as a whole or specific part(s) of the services. For example, if the purpose, content and practice of a service are governed by the principle of normalization, then Wolfensberger's *Program Analysis of Service Systems* can be used to assess how and if all elements of the service are meeting consumers' needs and the principles of normalization.[32]

Specific elements of services, e.g. community participation, staff performance and progress of individual consumers, can be assessed by quality action groups.[7]

Quality action groups consist of all who are stakeholders in the service, i.e. consumers, day services' staff, the CMHT, social workers, parents, service managers and so on. Such groups are not set but need to be convened to evaluate services in part, e.g. adult day classes or the service as a whole. The prerequisites and working details of quality action groups have been outlined.[7]

CMH considered that both external and internal evaluation is required if the quality of services is to be improved both in the statutory and voluntary sections.[11]

The Sheffield Development Project and (at the time) its unique evaluative study found many good points and flaws in Sheffield's strategic plan. But the conclusion was that, 'it is at least clear that the cost and effort of evaluation was not wasted. Where there was no firm basis for progress, one now exists.'[2]

No stronger argument can be made for the place of evaluation than its role in promoting quality and progress.

# MEETING THE NEEDS OF THE CONSUMER

## Day service models

There are a large variety of strategies and models for delivering day services to people with mental handicaps. At all levels, those involved with day services need to decide on the model or strategy which will best meet the consumer's need, and then shape the service to meet those needs. The seven models of day services (Table 6.1) provide an aid to such decisions by suggesting the different elements required for each type of service.[31] It is acknowledged that these are theoretical models, and in practice a day service may well be a mixture of one or more of the models.

The tools outlined and others will enable day services to be provided which meet the needs of people with a mental handicap into the twenty-first century. It is known the consumers can be educated; can make progress; can make choices; learn more quickly if taught skills in the same or a similar environment in which they will be used.

The principles on which to base services are self-evident – if consumer-led, needs-related day services are to be developed. Using the tools mentioned and others, negative attitudes towards people with a mental handicap can be changed.

# FINDING THE WAY

There is very general agreement as to why change is needed to pursue very generalized aims such as promoting independence; developing individual potential; and enabling people with mental handicap to live normal lives in the community; there is no agreed strategy or model to show the way forward to achieve these aims.[31]

That there is no agreed strategy or model for delivering day services could be a disadvantage if all consumers had the same needs. But if the aim is to meet individual needs in the community, there need be no disadvantage, for each day service will need to evolve its own strategies and models to meet the requirements of the consumers it serves. Planners, professional providers, consumers and parents may need to look at and read about how others have striven to meet the needs of the consumers. However, it is wise to remember when considering the strategies, models and ideas of others that no two consumers have the same needs and no two communities are the same. Not all good models or practices will work when transferred to new situations.

The services presented here have been created by providers and consumers who have been inspired to develop a service which responds to needs at an individual level. It is such inspiration that needs to be duplicated in day services, not just models or strategies. For it is a vision of what might be possible, as well as good models and strategies, that will widen the horizons of people with a mental handicap.

Community-based services have developed and are developing in many regions of the country. Only a few are outlined here. Their purpose, whether their content be employment, education, training or leisure, is to enable people with a mental handicap to become part of the mainstream of their community. One feature remains common to them all; they rely on local initiatives and imagination and have translated good 'ideas' into practice. The following examples build on this theme.

# MEETING THE CHALLENGE – THE HAMPSHIRE EXPERIENCE

Winchester, in Hampshire, has taken up the challenge of providing the members of its community who have a mental handicap with consumer-led, needs-related, day services. As in the rest of Hampshire, planning and provision for people with a mental handicap are often a result of joint planning between the social services department and the health authorities.

One of the main elements to develop is a core and satellite model. The existing day centre or ATC/SEC becomes the base from which a number of satellite bases and activiites are developed and resourced. The satellites are community-based and are as 'ordinary' as possible. Some already in use throughout the county include the use, as community bases, of

**Table 6.1 Seven models of day services**

| Features | Work model | Social care model | Further education model | Assessment and through-put model | Recreational model | Shared living model | Resource model |
|---|---|---|---|---|---|---|---|
| Objectives | To provide work experience and, where possible, preparation for employment | To develop normal living potential, and social skills in family and community context | To provide continuing education; to encourage assumption of adult responsibility | To channel people on to more appropriate (more normal) placements | To allow the person to develop a range of interests and activities | To provide a community within the ATC; to break down staff/trainee barriers | To provide access to a wide range of normal facilities |
| Methods | Work training Social skill | Social/behavioural assessment Problem-solving individualized programmes | Group learning Classes Projects Educational assessment | Assessment Schemes developed outside centre Short-term intensive training | Maximized choice Large range of activities Part-time attendance possible Contact when needed | Shared learning Shared residence/evening activities | 'Open door' advertised; information on aids, benefits etc. Family involvement |
| Assumptions | Society should provide employment for handicapped people | Social work has a role in meeting individual and family needs | Society should allow slow learners to develop to their potential as adults | Society should allow for a range of options for mentally handicapped people | Mentally handicapped people able to make choices about their lives and entitled to positive occupation leisure pursuits | Mentally handicapped people have a possible valued contribution to make to other people | Facility should be outward-looking to meet a variety of client and community needs |

| | | | | | | |
|---|---|---|---|---|---|---|
| ***Staffing implications*** | Craft/industrial instructors DRO Psychologists | CSS and CQSW | Teachers Lecturers | Assessors Instructors Linked personnel in facilities outside ATC | Instructors Craft workers Community workers Volunteers | Members | Mixed skills e.g. welfare rights, community workers |
| ***Administrative implications*** | 'Trainees/ workers' centres industrially located Separation of special care | 'Clients' Proximity to normal living situations Links with special housing | 'Students' Location with access to further education colleges and community facilities | Located close to range of community facilities | 'Members' Links with local leisure facilities | 'Members' Possible links with philosophical movement Mixed groups e.g. physically and mentally handicapped | 'Users'/ 'Visitors' Links with community groups |

Note: DRO – Disablement Resettlement Officer
CSS – Certificate in Social Services
CQSW – Certificate in Qualified Social Work

further education (FE) and higher education (HE) colleges, rented houses on short lease, leasing of shops, industrial units, market premises, short leasing of rooms within community centres, and so on. Indeed, it would appear that a satellite can be any feasible means of meeting the day services consumers' needs. The following description of the core and satellite model (Figure 6.1) is taken from work on this project in Hampshire.[33]

## The model

The core and satellite model is made up of an existing training centre at the core and a variety of small satellites such as those discussed above, spread around the catchment area of the day service. 'Satellite activities' may also be peripheral to the core centre, but are not physically located in its premises, or on land owned or leased by the day service. For example, a work placement scheme places people with employers and is mostly dependent on staffing support. If we were planning new services, the core would be relatively small, with numerous and varied satellites. As things are, we have large day centres which cannot be dismantled overnight, even if that were seen as desirable. Instead we are developing the satellites/ satellite activities in addition to the core.

## Types of satellite

Two main types of satellite have been developed to date. First, there is the community base which is located in a centre of population and aims to serve the people who live in the locality. It offers the possibility of teaching people to use the resources of their own neighbourhood, it enables local people to contribute to meeting needs; for some, it reduces the need to be bussed long distances every day . . . A community base can support about 20 people if at least half are out of the base most of the time. The second main type of satellite has a specific function. For example, a work base in an enterprise zone, a shop, a horticultural project or a day centre for the older person.

## The core

The core is the administrative base and also a base in which teaching, leisure and occupational activities take place. Large size is a drawback . . . the physical quality of the core environment and policies which reduce institutional practices also ameliorate the effect of size. Experience would suggest that good staffing ratios, plentiful transport and adequate social education budgets are key elements in transforming service quality based on existing core buildings.

## Activities

. . . Clearly, some resources will not be appropriate for everyone. But the ultimate aim is that there should be sufficient diversity within the service to provide an enjoyable needs-led service for everyone for most of their time of attendance.

## Cost and benefit

A truly needs-led service is very expensive, requiring much higher staffing ratios, more transport and larger budgets. When developing a new satellite, we attempt to get the quality of that satellite right . . . The choice of satellite development is a response to priorities derived from assessment of overall need.

## Assessment, tasters, collaboration

All service newcomers are assessed to determine their major needs. They also need to experience what is on offer, so they can make informed choices. In planning for individuals, day service staff often need to collaborate with those who can help and care for the person in their home life . . . they may find themselves advocating a high quality service for the person . . . Their views are given due weight, although the day services staff are ultimately responsible for overall fairness of the system. However, they can help to ensure that best use is made of their client's 'share of resources'.

The core and satellite model has demonstrated that several stages need to be identified in order to realize a community based day service:

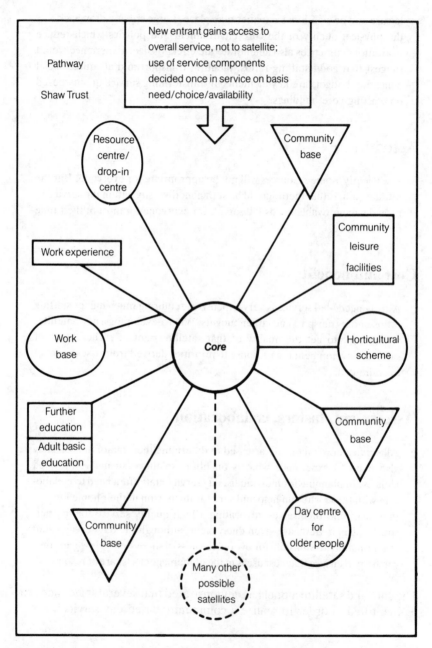

Pathway

Shaw Trust

New entrant gains access to overall service, not to satellite; use of service components decided once in service on basis need/choice/availability

Resource centre/drop-in centre

Community base

Community leisure facilities

Work experience

Work base

*Core*

Horticultural scheme

Community base

Further education

Adult basic education

Community base

Day centre for older people

Many other possible satellites

**Figure 6.1** Core and satellite model (reproduced by permission from Dr M. Shackleton-Bailey)

# Establishing a need

Day service staff and clients are expected to produce together clear statements of personal needs and wishes. These are recorded on an individual programme plan (IPP). Where possible, a computerized data base is used to record the results of IPP discussions. Consultation takes place with all people and agencies involved in the person's life.

# Ideas for meeting needs

Each project starts its life with an idea, often based on the imagination of consumers, their families or the people who work with them. In some areas, project officers have been appointed with the responsibility of promoting and matching identified needs to new resources in the community. Hampshire, for example, is now making use of specially appointed senior instructors for this purpose. Where possible, members of the community should be involved to build on their expertise and resourcefulness.

# Project design

The first stage is often informal, involving discussion with local consumers, managers and peers. Formal exploration/development of an idea follows once general support for the project has been received locally. The next stage is to provide a detailed description of the project to include the following information:

- brief description of the project;
- clients (numbers, needs, etc);
- approximate costs;
- origination of the project;
- project justification – what will clients do, how will they benefit?;
- value for money;
- main action required to implement the project;
- outcome of informal discussions (support and reservations);
- anticipating problems;
- timing.

## Desirability check

The Hampshire scheme incorporates a desirability check for all new projects, which considers the quality of the proposed project and the resources necessary for its realization. Questions regarding its position in relation to local service philosophy, practical logistical arrangements, personnel arrangements, issues of public acceptance, and value for money are included.

## Local implementation group

Local implementation groups with representatives from local services, consumers and managers should identify the key tasks to be undertaken and obtain detailed costings for the project. One of the major tasks of the group will be to allocate tasks and to design a written feasibility plan for each of its stages. Details such as premises, transport, meals, equipment, personnel and administrative details will need to be considered.

## Project proposal for approval/funding

The final stage before implementation will be a formal submission for costing/funding. The assistance of local administrative and project development staff should be enlisted. Consideration will be given to prioritizing the bid against other needs. Applications for funding may come from a variety of sources, e.g. joint finance.

## Summary

Many alternatives to the traditional day services model are seen as unobtainable or 'luxurious' in design, but the Hampshire model provides a very practical approach towards realizing community-based facilities as part of an evolutionary process. The core and satellite model attempts to provide an individually designed service within realistic resources and as a model possibly has universal application in new project design.

The key components of the model are:

- A common and shared philosophy between all persons concerned.
- The provision of informed choice/'tasters'/client involvement.

- The inclusion of a comprehensive resource search.
- The development of a partnership between all statutory and voluntary agencies in the project to share skills, funding and responsibilities.
- The devolution of planning and development to the 'grassroots' level (following the agreement of desirability/feasibility projects by managers).
- The promotion and involvement of local communities in the design and implementation of projects.
- The development of trust and partnership between fieldworkers and their managers as facilitators of local initiatives and their realization.

## THE RURAL ATC

Rural ATC . . . trainees were felt to model their behaviour very readily on staff members who found it particularly easy to relate informally to them as individuals and avoid unhelpful group stereotypes. To the extent that the training helped clients towards adult social values, it contributed to their normalization.[27]

This is one of the conclusions reached after research work was carried out on the rural ATC project. This unique and original day service brought day services for the *first time* to almost 50 per cent of the consumers who used the service.

As registers of people with a mental handicap are compiled throughout the country, it is becoming apparent that for many potential consumers there is no service at all – especially in rural areas. Such was the case in North Yorkshire, where the rural ATC project was conceived. The project was funded by the Rowntree Trust, with the DHSS funding the research side of the project.

The rural ATC itself was a re-fitted double decker bus, converted to provide facilities for education, skills, self-help skills, printing and so on. It serves two areas and has a permanent site on which to park in each area. Each site has a link-up for water, telephone, electricity and so on. In addition, other resources within the two areas are utilized – public houses, cafes, the village hall, an elderly person's home, and ground for gardening; numerous contacts with local people have been made.

Ten students were able to use the service at each site; one group for three days a week and the other for two days a week. A manager and two instructors staffed the service. Despite offering only a part-time service, the research findings show that the people using the rural ATC made as much progress as those attending ATCs full-time within the authority.

In other ways, part-time attendance was an advantage to some of the consumers who were able to continue to pursue, for example, part-time employment, running a home and community activities. However, some consumers did request a full-time placement in a conventional ATC.

The cost of providing the service was approximately 40 per cent more than funding a place with a conventional ATC within the authority. However, higher staff ratios in the rural ATC meant that consumers received as much individual attention as in a conventional ATC.

## Evaluation

That the rural ATC provided a service to about 50 per cent of those attending, who were receiving no day services, is to its credit. It is also an achievement that, even though the service was part-time, it met the needs of the people attending at least as well as full-time places within the authority's day services.

But perhaps the greatest asset lies in the researcher's conclusions, that 'the rural ATC may be better able to achieve the aim of normalization than larger ATCs.'[27] Perhaps the next step should be to analyse why the rural ATC is better equipped to achieve this aim.

# ENTERING THE MAINSTREAM OF ADULT EDUCATION

Both the MENCAP project,[34] and the work of Southwark Adult Education Institute[14] are examples of providing those with a mental handicap access to ordinary adult education services.

## Southwark Adult Education Institute

The Adult Education Institute (AEI) caters for a wide range of students whose ability ranges from students with multiple physical and mental handicaps to those with moderate learning difficulties; some students may have additional sensory handicaps.

Through its experience of providing courses over a number of years, the AEI has reached some conclusions that challenge the traditional stereotyped view of mentally handicapped people. It questions the notion that mentally handicapped people need to be taught specific social skills in order that they may successfully take part in adult education; it states that case studies show a lack of correlation between creative ability and assessed levels of IQ and social competence; and it has learnt from experience that professional attitudes, which, it is generally believed, know what is best for the student, are sometimes misplaced or wrong.

The AEI offers a range of subjects, including literacy/numeracy workshops, cookery, drama, music, painting, pottery and numerous other subjects. In addition to these classes, students are given the opportunity to join mainstream day and evening classes in a number of the AEI centres. Where necessary, students are supported using the same model as that developed by MENCAP.[34]

## Staff training

Tutors are given support and some in-service training on matters relating to mental handicap, but are encouraged to develop their classes in their own way. It is recognized that they are trained professionals in the subject they offer and will develop their curriculum according to the needs of the students.

## Consumer participation

Chris Lloyd, who has developed the project, considers it essential that students are seen as 'individuals who can work towards their own solutions, be they educational, personal or political, and not as a group on whom we impose a set of values and solutions which are in grave danger of being totally irrelevant'.[14]

## Evaluation

Southwark AEI has evolved a number of strategies and models so that people with a mental handicap can become part of the mainstream of adult education. It has learnt that preconceived ideas about people with a mental handicap are often false. It has also learnt that many, once they know how to choose and are given choice, know what they want to learn.

# A NEW WAY

## Purpose

*A New Way* was set up by MENCAP and assessed independently by the Thomas Coram Research Unit, to find out if it would be possible and desirable to integrate people with a mental handicap, who would need volunteer support, into adult education classes. This scheme ran for two years.

## Content

The scheme had a full-time co-ordinator who was responsible for running and taking part in the assessment of *A New Way* over a two-year period. Two adult centres, both in London (Hillingdon and Islington), were used, neither of which had previous experience of students with a mental handicap.

At the Islington centre students were to be paired with a volunteer student within each class. Not more than two sets of paired students would attend each class. Classes were selected from a normal range of educational/leisure adult education classes which took place mainly in the evenings. The classes selected included keep fit, swimming, dressmaking, pottery and so on. The tutors agreed to accept people with mental handicap into their classes.

Hillingdon AEI put on separate classes for students with a mental handicap and their volunteer students. Classes included cookery and pottery. The tutors to the classes were ordinary adult education tutors with no specific training in teaching adult students with a mental handicap.

## Practice

The co-ordinator worked closely with the adult education service and social services to organize *A New Way* and recruit volunteers. All volunteers, whether they were to be with students in classes or assist them in finding their way from home to the AEI, were first interviewed and references were taken up.

Day centres worked closely with the co-ordinator to select students who were thought to have the relevant skills and acceptable behaviour to attend an adult education class with the assistance of a student volunteer, but not on their own.

## Evaluation

*A New Way*, as the independent assessment by the Coram Research Unit showed,[34] was a positive learning experience for all those involved. No major difference emerged between the separate classes at Hillingdon and the integration into mainstream classes at Islington. However, at Islington the quality of integration was superior in that students with a mental handicap participated in an ordinary way.

Of the students attending Hillingdon, 19 out of 20 combined with adult classes. Of these, two entered mainstream classes. At Islington, 19 out of 23 students continued, four going on to attend classes without the support of a volunteer. All tutors, despite experiencing some difficulties, said they would continue to welcome students with a mental handicap into their classes.

The most encouraging point about *A New Way* is that both education authorities chose to continue the scheme after the two-year experiment, without the support of outside resources.

In Islington, the scheme (now called *Link*) has enabled over 80 students to participate in ordinary adult education. It is not a big drain on resources either, as it makes use of those already established for education within the community.

Southwark AEI also functions and continues to expand using a similar way, but both are 'a new way' for people with a mental handicap.

## THE SPECIALIZED TRAINING PROGRAMME (STP)

### Employment as an element of day services

Is employment an alternative to day services? A part of day services? A complement to day services? Or something you do if you are not in need of day services? A study of the various schemes (Pathway, l'Arche, The Wedge, Ravenswood Frans Deli; see 'Useful addresses', p. 162) and literature[4, 6, 7, 8, 33] offers no definitive answer. They all, in different ways, agree on one point – that work is important to people with a mental handicap.

Employment is often seen as the end product of day services, i.e. day services teach or train people in the skills and behaviour needed before they are ready for employment. Yet it is now known that not only is work a valuable motivator to the most able, but those with severe mental handicap and behaviour problems can and do become capable working adults. Through working, there is often an increase in skills in areas not directly related to work.

## Karl: one student's experience of the specialized training programme

People do need to be prepared, trained and educated for work, but they do not necessarily need either to possess or attain a certain level before they can work. This is demonstrated by the following example of Karl, a participant in the Specialized Training Programme (STP) at the University of Oregon:

> Karl is 51 years old. Thirty-five of those years were spent in large state institutions. His IQ is about 25. At the age of 28, he was said to be 'unable to carry out any work assignment'. When Karl came to his present job at STP benchwork site in 1976, his head was shaved and his clothes were dirty. He was missing a majority of his teeth and usually smelled bad. He had previously had an infection in his gum and jaw which resulted in surgery – and as a result his head and skull are noticeably misshapen. Karl has a history of inappropriate behaviour.[5]

Since joining the STP, Karl's earning power has increased by 400 per cent; he is now seen as a competent worker. With support, he lives in a flat within the community, shared with a friend. He is mostly now able to look after himself and move around the local community. Despite not being able to tell the time or read bus timetables, Karl, using a digital watch with an alarm as a functional aid, is able to go to and return from the library using the bus. His earning power allows Karl to buy the clothes and other consumer goods he wants, to eat out, take holidays with nonhandicapped friends, go to skiing lessons and take part in many other ordinary activities.

The STP perspective of day services and consumer abilities has given Karl the opportunity to have the lifestyle and dignity of an ordinary adult man. The work ethic provides status, dignity, financial security and companionship, yet with increasing unemployment in the Western World, additional time is also available for leisure study and recreation. Caution should therefore be applied to over-emphasizing the work ethic, although few would doubt the importance of having the opportunity to secure valued employment.

STP was set up as an alternative to the standard day services in Oregon. Like many of the services in Britain, in Oregon they were static with little or no throughput. Since its inception, STP, through its structured yet dynamic approach, has proved that employment is not only feasible for a few people with mental handicap, but that, given the right type of services, many more could become employed, adult people.

## Special features of the STP programme

- A person's assumed ability level should not preclude them from the opportunity to enter an employment programme.
- Low expectations can lead to low achievements, and often does, for people with mental handicap. This can lead to the mental handicap impairment becoming a greater handicap than it need be.
- Technology can lessen the handicapping effects of the impairment mental handicap.
- Services need to be structured to enable people to succeed.
- Success in one skill will often provide the foundation for learning other new skills.
- Services should never assume people with mental handicap cannot learn to develop.

# CONCLUSION – THE RIGHT TO BETTER SERVICES

The younger generations of people who have had the benefit of access to education, better recreational facilities, and improved health care, will expect and deserve something better.[1]

It is hoped that people with mental handicap, their advocates and those employed to provide day services and activities, will demand something better. Better services should not be made to compensate for neglect in the past, even though we are now aware this was considerable. Something better should be provided because it is what people with mental handicap have a right to.

Service providers now have the tools, IPPs, self-advocacy, a direction, normalization, and a will to provide a consumer-based, needs-led, comprehensive community service. But the task now is to turn rhetoric into reality; to turn theory into practice throughout Great Britain, not just in small pockets of development in local authorities such as Cardiff, Lewisham, Winchester and others. We need to plan, for those people who will enter the community from hospitals; for the people with complex needs for whom at present there is no place in our day service provision in many local authorities; for those people with mild mental handicap, who are no longer entering mainstream employment and are, in large and increasing numbers, rightly seeking the support of day services. In our changing world such people are being deprived of their right to an ordinary life, and this is a problem which policy makers and planners need to address. The question of providing appropriate day services to meet the needs of people at different stages of their lives also needs to be addressed.

There should be no illusions about the difficulties involved in meeting the individual needs of all people with mental handicap; nor should there be any illusions that, unless we meet this challenge, we will not have provided the service to which people with mental handicap are entitled.

# REFERENCES

1. MENCAP (1986) *Day Services Today and Tomorrow*, MENCAP, London.
2. Heron, A. and Myers, M. (1983) *Intellectual Impairment: The Battle Against Handicap*, Academic Press, London.
3. Shackleton-Bailey, M. (1984) *Adult Training Centres; Where do they go from here?*, MENCAP, South West Region.
4. King's Fund Centre (1980) *An Ordinary Life*, Project Paper No. 24, King's Fund Centre, London.
5. King's Fund Centre (1984) *An Ordinary Working Life*, Project Paper No. 50, King's Fund Centre, London.
6. King's Fund Centre (1982) *Better Services for the Mentally Handicapped*, Project Paper No. 34, King's Fund Centre, London.
7. Independent Development Council for People with Mental Handicaps (1986) *Pursuing Quality*, IDC, London.

8. Independent Development Council for People with Mental Handicaps (1984) *Living Like Other People*, IDC, London.
9. Independent Development Council for People with Mental Handicaps (1984) *Next Steps*, IDC, London.
10. MENCAP (1986) *Mental Handicaps – Partnership in the Community*, Office of Health Economics/MENCAP, London.
11. Campaign for People With a Mental Handicap (1984) *Hope for the Future*, CMH, London.
12. Shearer, A. (1986) *Building Community*, Campaign for People with Mental Handicaps, King's Fund Centre, London.
13. Wynn Jones, A. (ed.) (1984) *Adult Training Centres; Where do they go from here?* MENCAP, South West Region.
14. Dean, A. and Hegarty, S. (1984) *Learning for Independence*, Further Education Unit, London.
15. Wolfenden Committee (1978) *The Future of Voluntary Organizations*, Croom Helm, London.
16. DHSS (1986) *The Disabled Persons (Consultation and Representation) Act*, Chapter 35, HMSO, London.
17. NHS (1969) *Report of the Committee of Inquiry of Allegations of Ill-Treatment of Patients and Other Irregularities at the Ely Hospital, Cardiff*, Cmnd 3979, HMSO, London.
18. DHSS and Welsh Office (1971) *Better Services for the Mentally Handicapped*, HMSO, London.
19. National Development Group for the Mentally Handicapped (1977) *Day Services for Mentally Handicapped Adults*, DHSS, London.
20. Whelan, E. and Speake, B. (1977) *Adult Training Centres: Report of the First National Survey*, University of Manchester.
21. Nirje, R. (1980) The normalisation principle, in R.J. Flynn and K.E. Nitsch (eds.), *Normalisation, Social Integration and Community Services*, University Park Press, Baltimore.
22. Wolfensberger, W. (1972) *The Principle of Normalization in Human Services*, National Institute of Mental Retardation, Toronto.
23. Wolfensberger, W. and Thomas, S. (1981) The principle of normalisation in human services, *Research Highlights*, Vol. 2.
24. Mittler, P. (1983) In Heron and Myers (eds.), *Intellectual Impairment: the Battle Against Handicaps*, Academic Press, London.
25. Brandon, D. (1984) The ATC is irrelevant, in *Adult Training Centres: Where do they go from here?*, Report of the 17th Spring Conference on Mental Regardation, SW Region, Exeter, MENCAP, London.
26. Bosanquet, N. (1984) *Extending Choice for Mentally Handicapped People*, MIND, London.
26. Ward, L. (1982) *People First*, Project Paper No. 37. King's Fund Centre, London.
27. James, S. and Martin, D. (1984) *The Rural ATC*, University of Sheffield.
28. DHSS (1985) Second Report of the Social Services Select Committee on Community Care (Chairman, Renee Short), *Adult Mentally Handicapped People*, HMSO, London.
29. DHSS (1979) *Report of the Committee of Inquiry into Mental Handicaps, Nursing and Care* (Jay Report), HMSO, London.

30. Glennester, H. (1983) *Planning for Priority Groups*, Martin Robertson, Oxford.
31. Seed, P., Thomson, M., Pikington, F. *et al.* (1986) *Which 'Best Way'?*, Costello, University of Aberdeen.
32. Wolfensberger, W. and Glen, L. (1975) *Program Analysis of Service Systems: A Method for the Quantitative Evaluation of Human Services*, Volume 2 (3rd edition) National Institute of Mental Retardation, Toronto.
33. Shackleton-Bailey, M. (1986) Unpublished material, Hampshire Social Services.
34. Kiernan, C. and Willis, P. (1984) *A New Way*, Thomas Coram Research Unit/MENCAP, London.

## USEFUL ADDRESSES

1. Pathway Employment Service, 169A City Road, Cardiff CF2 3JB.
2. L'Arche, 127 Prescott Road, Newsham Park, Liverpool 6.
3. The Wedge, 11 Norwood High Street, London SE27.
4. Ravenswood Village Foundation, Centre for Continuing Learning, Nine Mile Ride, Crowthorne, Berkshire.

# Section Two: Providing Opportunities to Meet Residential Care Needs

# 7. Towards a Comprehensive Service: Its Nature and Design

*David Sines*

## INTRODUCTION

This chapter considers those elements of a community-based service which have been identified throughout the book. It attempts to identify the key components and to highlight the main issues involved in the design and maintenance of services for people with mental handicaps in non-institutional settings.

Some have suggested that a 'model service' exists for all people and that within any locality services may be replicated as 'standard packages'. In fact, nothing could be further from the truth and rather than leading the reader into the trap of prescription, this chapter emphasizes the need for all services to be tailored to individual needs.

The basic principles of 'an ordinary life' remain as the foundation of human service design and are complemented with suggestions for services for those people with additional needs. This chapter does not take into account the specific service needs of children or older people as these are covered in Chapters 9 and 10.

## A QUESTION OF OWNERSHIP

Perhaps the most fundamental question relates to the ownership of services and the choice that is afforded to consumers when in need of support.

To date, residential services have been provided for this client group by health and social services departments, which have often failed to consult consumers in respect of service design and needs. As a result local services have become fragmented and in some cases outdated before they leave the drawing board stage of design. Consumers have often been unable to understand the apparent disparity of service provision in different parts of the country and it has not been unknown for people to move to acquire appropriate facilities where authorities have been more forward thinking than in their home area.

In fact, to deny that disparity exists in the services provided by these two main statutory agencies would be naïve. In the past decade, as a result of changes in government policy, parent involvement and professional practice, the sum total of agencies and personnel involved in the provision of a community-based service for people with a mental handicap has been further complicated through the introduction of a matrix of bureaucratization.

Into the arena have entered a vast array of voluntary and statutory departments to provide new opportunities for people with mental handicaps and their families with access to an expanded range of facilities in the community. These have replaced the services provided by the older and outdated hospitals whose previous role, among others, was to advise parents of their rights and to provide for the total needs of the individual 'under one roof'.

The following list provides some illustration of the agencies now involved in the provision of services for people with mental handicaps and their families:

- local social security offices;
- family practitioner committees;
- social services departments;
- health authorities;
- the Housing Corporation;
- Manpower Services Commission;
- education department;
- local authority housing department;
- voluntary organizations.

This list is far from exhaustive and represents no less than four main government departments who all have a stake in the provision of today's services for this client group. In fact, consumers are justified in their complaints that they have little idea of who provides which service and to what end. This is further complicated by the array of professionals who will lay claim to the consumer at variable intervals throughout their life. A vast number of people will duplicate the collection of 'essential' information about service needs and will expect to share in the person's life and in its design.

The planning and organization of services is therefore becoming increasingly complex all the time and this presents consumers with additional hurdles to climb, without any logical outcome being apparent; indeed, in some cases without any 'safety net' within which to break their fall should services fail to meet their needs.

In December 1986 the government published a report from the Audit Commission which called for action to improve the co-ordination and delivery of community care.[1] The report highlighted many of the problems identified above and criticized the government for failing to co-ordinate its community care policies to the advantage of the consumers, who they felt were all too often denied opportunities to fulfil their potential in the community.

In a press release the Audit Commission stated:[2]

> if the opportunity is not taken now to establish an effective community-based service, a new pattern of care will emerge, based on residential care. The result will be a continued waste of scarce resources and, worse still, care and support that is inappropriate to some of the most disadvantaged members of society and the relatives who seek to care for them.

The report confirmed that progress had been 'slow and uneven':

> Community care is about changing the balance of services and finding the most suitable placement for people from a wide range of options. It is not about imposing a community solution as the only option is the way that institutional care has been the only option for many people in the past. Although there has been worthwhile progress in some areas, and most authorities have at least made a start, care in the community is far from a reality in many places.

The report confirmed the feelings of many consumers and professionals who believed that the uneven rate of progress in making more meaningful provision for people with mental handicaps was due mainly to a lack of foresight among planners and managerial inadequacy at local level. Naturally, budgets and available staff resources also determined the future of local services, but the involvement of consumers in the planning and delivery of 'their own' services was denied to all but a few. It is the sharing of the ownership and design of local services that managers had within their grasp but failed to facilitate.

Some degree of sympathy is required for the managers of such new services, whose task was formidable to say the least. Many new services required the closure of vast hospital estates, and in some areas where two or three hospitals were all contracting the concept of community care in an already saturated area, the task must be onerous. Staff also raised their objections to change and were in some cases joined by angry parents who called for the retention of the hospitals. Indeed, if consumerism and the sharing of services were to be realized, then in some areas parent pressure groups were actively campaigning against community care in favour of the hospital.

Perhaps one of the most fundamental problems to be tackled was that of designing services to meet the needs of all its consumers in such a way that enhanced their lifestyle as individuals, and ensured that adequate choice and involvement in the project was assured at the earliest possible opportunity. Many of the complaints of consumers and their families have in fact been justified in that they have not received adequate involvement in the assessment of their offspring or in the planning or choice of alternative living accommodation for them. It is not to be unexpected that such omissions in consultation resulted in distressed and sometimes angry letters to ministers and local service managers about the inappropriateness of community care provision.

Press reports about unco-ordinated community care projects also contributed to the concern shown by a large number of people who interpreted hospital closure programmes as a 'cost cutting exercise' and poorly resourced projects had little chance of success. In fact, the move towards community care represented little less than a revolution in social policy and service design, and it is little wonder that mistakes were made in some areas with little or no previous community-based services to model from. It is true to say that the USA and Scandinavia had pioneered similar projects in the past, but if the problems associated with translating service design within a county are compared to the differences between two completely different cultures, then the lessons to be learnt were possibly of limited use when transferred to the United Kingdom.

Despite the lack of previous experiences, new opportunities have been provided for people with mental handicaps in the community, of which some of the most successful have been those which have evolved to meet local circumstances, resources and needs. The only answers, therefore, appear to be those which have been designed to meet the needs of local consumers. As a result, any 'blueprint' for future service development may be impossible to determine. The Government has shown some concern for this approach since it provides opportunities for the piecemeal development of services. The Social Services Select Committee confirmed this view:[3]

> The phrase 'community care' means little by itself. It is a phrase used by some descriptively and others prescriptively; that is, by some as a shorthand way of describing certain specific services provided in certain ways and in certain places; by others as an ideal or principle in the light of which other services are to be judged and new ones developed. It has in fact come to have such general reference as to be virtually meaningless. It has become a slogan, with all the weaknesses that implies. The pleasant connotations of this phrase can be misleading.

Following the publication of the Audit Commission report,[1] the government announced the launch of a review of community care policy under the chairmanship of Sir Roy Griffiths.[4] The review aimed to ensure that the social security system was sensitive to individual requirements and provided a range of choice for consumers when determining their future needs. The review also acknowledged that substantial public funds are afforded to community care programmes through social security, through personal social services run by local authorities and through the health service, and that these funds are not always used effectively or efficiently.

The ownership and funding mechanisms of services for people with mental handicaps is under scrutiny and there is little doubt that the time has come for consumers to be given more choice and opportunity in determining the direction in which they are going. Discussions on 'lead agencies', professional roles and responsibilities will all figure in the debate that will ensue, but the realization of a more efficient and 'shared' social service for this client group appears to be becoming a reality.

## DETERMINANTS OF SERVICE PROVISION

Historically, eligibility for service provision depended upon the abilities of the person concerned. A rigid division between 'health' and 'social service' responsibility was reinforced through the introduction of 'dependency schedules' and local 'registers'. Services were calculated in response to national trends and norms based on outdated estimates of incidence and prevalence; the planning of new services often took place within health and local authorities without reference to joint planning machinery. Services were also designed in isolation from consumers, who were afforded little choice of residence. The two main service providers jealously guarded their resources to the exclusion of mutual co-operation and skill sharing.

Other determinants of service provision are:

- relationships between agencies;
- professional fragmentation;
- differences in service boundaries (the absence of co-terminosity);
- the presence of private sector facilities (the supplementary benefit system favours residential care);
- differences in style between agencies;
- lack of incentives to move between agencies;
- different priorities between agencies;
- geographical inequalities;
- organizational fragmentation;
- availability of finances;
- the efficiency of a comprehensive data base from which to plan services.

Other determinants depended on well-established working relationships between personnel in the lead agencies and their willingness to work together to develop services for people with mental handicaps based on a common philosophy. The support of health authorities and social service committees is also needed, and it is only recently that it has become necessary for agencies to demonstrate to their superiors that they have developed joint strategies to work together to design services to meet the needs of this client group.

The success of local joint planning and service delivery will also depend to some extent on the attitudes of the service managers and their personal commitment to service change. Most successful projects have identified the presence of a charismatic figure in their midst who has been prepared to take risks and to promote the project among his/her fellow workers.

Project or service design begins with the establishment of an agreed set of service principles as a foundation to determine the pattern of service provision. Many of the basic principles are outlined in Chapter 2 within the concept of 'an ordinary life' and these should form the basis of any service model. The key principles are:

- an acceptable/secure place to live;

- choice with whom you live;
- reasonable access to services wherever you may live and in accordance with individual need;
- the best possible income available;
- valued and meaningful day/employment opportunities;
- freedom to associate with others and protection from severe risk;
- accessible and locally managed services;
- full involvement in service design and delivery.

All services should afford the same rights and value as any other person in society and should be designed to ensure that consumers develop to their maximum developmental ability. In order to realize these objectives, the determinants of service provision should be based on the identified needs of consumers through the introduction of comprehensive and shared individual programme/life planning meetings (see Chapter 3).

Consumers and their families will need to be involved in all stages of the planning process, and service managers should take account of their views, opinions and requirements. Flexibility in providing resources to meet emerging needs will be a prerequisite to a shared service. The identification of priorities and the allocation of resources both human and financial should be determined by local staff with consumer involvement.

## RATE OF SERVICE CHANGE

Consumers and professionals have been concerned that the pace of change in service provision for people with mental handicaps has been too rapid. Adverse reports regarding insensitive closure programmes of large hospitals and of people being ill-prepared to move into the community have further compounded the call for incremental change rather than radical approaches to establish alternative services.

Certainly, the dismantling of existing services should not be embarked upon until alternatives have been provided that are sensitive and able to meet the needs of their users. However, the pace at which these developments take place will often be determined by financial policies and procedures and will need to be planned tactfully and strategically to ensure that the quality and continuity of services is maintained during the transition.

The rate of service change will be affected by the amount of time that is invested in the preparation of consumers, their families and professionals. Some successful services have deliberately avoided an incremental approach to hospital closure and have managed to secure the full support of their staff and consumers in the process of change. Such projects have been characterized by extensive preparatory programmes for all people involved in the project and have taken account of each person's individual needs. Conversely, those services that have assumed a more conservative approach have often failed to realize their objective of service change as finances and motivation diminish over time. In fact, people seem to respond more positively when they have been fully involved in the project and when they can see a realistic date for its completion.

Services should ideally work towards the realization of local delegation of responsibility to the people who are in direct contact with the clients. They should also meet the expectations of consumers and local staff and ensure their full participation in the project with their full commitment, regardless of their professional training or experience. The accomplishment of this goal will require opportunities for the following:

- The need for comprehensive service developments in response to consumer needs.
- Delegation of decision-making to local staff and consumers.
- The status and rights of consumers and their families to be elevated as equal contributors to service planning.
- Opportunities for professionals from all agencies and consumers to 'train' together and to share skills.
- The need for the monitoring of service delivery by the local community and its representatives.

## ELEMENTS OF A COMPREHENSIVE SERVICE

Having agreed upon a comprehensive life planning system and a philosophy of care which is subscribed to by service users and their carers, the basic components of the service should be identified. Although this chapter has argued against prescribing any one model of care, it is pertinent to base all services on the premiss of a basic, needs-led charter which enhances the rights of the individual:

- to meet the developmental potential of the individual;
- to recognize their rights as people;

● to recognize the dignity of risk;
● to accommodate the principles of normalization;
● to facilitate the use of generic services wherever possible.

Many of the elements of a comprehensive service have already been described in this book, and this chapter will concentrate on those areas that have not been covered elsewhere. It would be useful for the reader to refer to other sections in the book:

● self-advocacy and consumer representation (Chapter 1);
● life planning systems and individual programme plans (Chapter 3);
● the philosophy of an 'ordinary life' and the principles of normalization (Chapter 2);
● valued occupation/daily activities (Chapter 6);
● age-appropriate services (Chapters 2 and 3);
● ordinary housing with appropriate support (Chapters 4, 8 and 11);
● short-term care (Chapter 4);
● effective professional support and team work (Chapter 5).

Perhaps the first and most difficult concept is to identify what people mean by a comprehensive service. Certainly, some people see 'comprehensive' as being a model of service delivery on one campus with easy access to a range of services, such as those models seen in the United States and in Scandinavia where small village communities provide for the total needs of their residents. For others it may mean the total range of services provided by one agency without regard for those services provided by others in any given locality.

The whole concept of the term 'comprehensive' is in danger of becoming yet another catchword of the 1980s with all the inherent problems that popular themes pose. However, the true nature of a community-based service should be to facilitate opportunities for consumers to integrate into their local neighbourhoods and to develop local friendship networks. This requires the provision of individually designed services within easy reach of 'home' and when required should impose the minimum of disruption to the person's life. This then is a valued interpretation of 'a comprehensive service'.

Carle has identified the following key elements within a comprehensive service:[5]

● a wide range of services to meet individual needs and to provide choice;

- effective co-ordination of local services which are designed to facilitate access;
- a manageable area should be identified with coterminous boundaries to match other services;
- a workable population size should be identified which is both manageable and efficient (page 5).

In the same paper she goes on to list the key design principles upon which services should be based:

1.  The service system should work to improve the quality of life of the whole community by using available resources to integrate people with special needs and their families into its life.
2.  No one, whatever his or her handicap, should be excluded from community services.
3.  Wherever possible, people who are mentally handicapped should use services already used by other members of the community, rather than separate or segregated ones.
4.  Services should be distributed through the area in a pattern which reflects the distribution of the population.
5.  For each individual consumer, there should be as little use as possible of the service system and as much effort as possible to support their natural networks of family and friends.
6.  Services should be arranged to reflect the ordinary pattern of life – with their different activities and rhythms for daytime, night-time, evenings and weekends.
7.  Services should be designed to meet the particular needs of individuals rather than standardized for groups.
8.  Services should promote and maintain the development of valued skills.
9.  Services for people who are severely handicapped should use every contribution of technology that is relevant. The more severely handicapped the consumer, the more highly trained staff will need to be and the more equipment they will need to use.
10. Each consumer should be enabled to participate in arranging and monitoring the services he or she needs (page 6).

What is clear from this list of design principles is that the services are not necessarily dependent on support or back up from large hospitals or from specialist services. Rather, many of the additional services that will be required for even the most handicapped person can be provided through the imaginative deployment of specialist resources within people's own homes and in community-based services.

Perhaps it is also important in this section to dispel another myth and that is the inaccurate belief held by some that all services must be provided by highly skiiled professionals in 'special' buildings or specially designed units or campuses. Indeed, for most people with mental handicaps, the 'expert' for the larger portion of their lives has in fact been their parents, who have acquired over the years the experience and 'expertise' necessary for their child's needs in their own homes.

It is also inaccurate to assume that the statutory services are the only agencies to be capable of providing the degree of care, training and support required by some of the more dependent members of this client group. For many years parents have looked to voluntary groups such as MENCAP and the National Autistic Society to meet the needs of their children when the statutory services were unable to provide them with acceptable alternatives. Similarly, the private sector has recently emerged as a firm contender to provide care for people with mental handicaps, and has been encouraged to do so in some areas as local services are redesigned and developed.

A comprehensive service therefore requires an investment in human skills, resources and imagination. Its very success depends on its ability to adapt to meet the needs of its consumers and should be designed to accommodate service change. Investments in large, outdated buildings restrict the process of service development and should be avoided; buildings should only be purchased following an assessment of their resale potential and of course their ability to meet presenting needs. A comprehensive service must also acknowledge its limitations in providing 'all things to all men' and must take account of its present financial and human resources both in terms of available manpower and skills.

This latter point should not be dismissed lightly for it is often the most contentious of all arguments presented in favour of maintaining the status quo and resisting change. Some people have assumed that all people with mental handicaps will wish to or be able to live in small houses in local communities. Some people will in fact have great difficulty in realizing this aim because of previously acquired behaviours which have restricted their opportunities in many cases to hospitals. Others may have associated psychiatric illnesses or physical handicaps which require specific skills and facilities for their treatment.

The reality is that even of this group of people with special needs, the majority will be able to live in ordinary houses given adequate support, preparation and training. There will remain, however, a minority of people whose needs will require additional facilities, and it is for this group that some authorities are ill-prepared or unable to provide community-based alternatives to the hospital. In part it may be true to say that much may be attributed to inappropriate housing facilities or to 'hostility' from the neighbours, but in reality it is often due to inadequate numbers of staff being available with the necessary skills to provide individual services for people in the community with special needs. It is to consider this area further that this chapter now turns.

# PROVIDING SERVICES FOR PEOPLE WITH 'CHALLENGING BEHAVIOURS'

Over the past ten years the number of people resident in mental handicap hospitals has fallen by 27 per cent and, of these, a significant number were identified as presenting challenging behaviours. The whole question of service provision for people with challenging behaviour, has been charged with emotive debate, and statistics have been bandied about suggesting that the incidence of disturbed behaviour is far higher than it is. Some have suggested that all people can live in ordinary houses irrespective of behaviour; at the other end of the spectrum, people have recommended the retention of large hospital units of up to 200 places in certain health regions.

In practice this client group has traditionally received services from the health service but the development of needs-led services has removed the franchise from the health service; in all agencies people are to be found who exhibit disturbed behaviour from time to time. For most the presentation of such behaviours will be transitory and will not represent a permanent problem for their carers. However, it is essential at these times that families and day and residential care staff receive adequate support from appropriately skilled staff in order to prevent situations becoming out of hand.

However, before considering appropriate interveniton strategies a definition of what constitutes 'challenging behaviour' is required. In fact, the most difficult area upon which professionals can reach agreement is often on the definition of this client group. Definitions vary in the light of the previous training and experience of staff working with people with mental handicaps and in the degree of success people have had in 'modifying' behaviours which may appear to be disruptive according to the norm of the group in which an individual lives.

Emphasis should be placed on an individual's needs; any service tailored to meet those needs must be individual in design and aim to provide service users with opportunities to maximize their integration in the community and in the mainstream of services available. For those people whose behaviour is of such an intensity, frequency or duration as to threaten the physical safety of themselves or others, access to community-based services may be severely limited. It is these people who are often identified as presenting 'challenging behaviours' and may demonstrate their needs antisocially through occasional violence to themselves or to others or by engaging in less extreme forms of disturbed behaviour, e.g. swearing in public, 'absconding' or refusing to dress appropriately in public.

The identification of people with challenging behaviours should be based on the process of individual programme planning shown in Chapter 3. Such plans should identify the specific needs presented by each individual and should detail the support that would be required to enable the person to participate within a normal community in such a way to enhance their level of competence and status. The individual programme planning system should therefore provide the basis for the planning of all services to people with challenging behaviours, based on an assessment of their unique needs as individuals rather than by a predetermined assessment within a 'specialist facility' for people with similar needs. Should the latter be chosen it is possible that the behaviour of others at a particularly acute time in the person's life may reinforce inappropriate behaviours to such an extent that they may be stereotyped as 'deviant' and be forced to embark on a 'predetermined' career.

The number of people who have exhibited disturbed behaviour at any one time would indeed be high but when further analysis of behaviour patterns and their frequency is carried out, this number may be drastically reduced to a few remaining people whose behaviour requires specialist attention. In one study (unpublished) in Winchester, for example, 18 people were identified from the local register as having had a significant degree of severe behaviour disorder when they were admitted to the district's community-based service. It is perhaps interesting to note the success there had been when working with these individuals who were diagnosed as having severely challenging behaviours in other settings such as long-stay hospitals and other units. The success of their integration has undoubtedly been due to the philosophy which is adopted in that area of developing individual services and by investing in staff skills, rather than specialist residential facilities.

The lessons to be learnt from the Winchester experience have been applied in other areas throughout the country and have indeed formed the philosophy of many other services which have actively discouraged the development of specialist facilities for this client group. However, the number of appropriately skilled and experienced staff that are available in local districts may severely limit the development of individually designed services for some people with special needs. Certainly, direct care staff require additional support in times of 'crisis' and the availability of specialist staff when they are needed may determine the ability of local services to cope rather than having to rely on neighbouring authorities to provide specialist residential facilities.

Some services have invested in specialist support teams comprising a number of skilled and experienced practitioners who work as peripatetic staff to support direct care workers in ordinary life services in the community. Such teams are usually made up of clinical psychologists and nurses who work closely with local staff to enhance their own coping skills and abilities. Their aim is not to provide a substitute for the person's home or to take over their direct care, but rather to provide intensive back-up support when it is required. Advice will be required from the consultant psychiatrist and this is usually provided either through the CMHT or through the local residential service. The teams usually continue to monitor the local service and to offer advice when the 'problem' is solved.

In other areas the role and function of the community specialist teams have been extended to provide advice and support to residential staff when the need arises. However, this has often proved to be disruptive to the day-to-day work of the community staff and problems have arisen in respect of the availability of support when required by staff in the residential service in times of acute need.

Demographic changes and changes in social policy have also influenced the nature of this client group to the extent that several people with mild learning difficulties are now deprived of appropriate opportunities with which to maintain a valued lifestyle. Emotional difficulties have some-times resulted in referrals being made to services for people with mental handicaps for those who would have otherwise found mainstream employment and support in generic services. This client group represents a grey area and requires further research in order to determine the exact nature of the needs of this client group. However, it is important to acknowledge their existence and right to a service since, undoubtedly, many will look to the mental handicap service and its specialist staff for support and intervention.

Many of the needs of people with challenging behaviours can be met within the community in individually designed services. Each person will require an individual service plan designed to identify the support they will require to maintain their lives in the mainstream of community provision. An investment in appropriately skilled and experienced staff will be a prerequisite to any service development and this must be supplemented with ongoing staff training and development. In addition, staff will require support themselves from senior managers and professionals in order to provide available services flexibly when required.

There will inevitably be some people whose needs cannot be met in ordinary services of the type discussed throughout this book. Although in the minority, their needs cannot be dismissed, and for them there will be a need to create a fallback position to meet both their needs and the needs of society. This group represents those people who present serious risk to themselves and to the community in which they live. They will usually have been in receipt of valued and individual services but are unable to manage within the resources available, or choose to reject the service model which appears to suit many of their peers.

This group of people may be detained forcibly under one of the relevant sections of the 1983 Mental Health Act[6] or may be resident in one of the special secure units provided for 'offenders' throughout the country. Examples of such offences may range from frequent demonstrations of violent behaviour towards themselves or to others, arson and sexual offences. Others may live in 'locked wards' in mental handicap hospitals, while some may receive residential care in the private sector. Wherever their needs are met, the treatment strategy appears to be a mix of active corrective therapy and asylum, with an emphasis on custodial care. The importance of maintaining a 'safety net' of specialist provision to back up all local service developments should be acknowledged. What is less clear is the number of such places that will be required in the future as traditional mental handicap hospitals close and as the law redefines its approach to 'mentally handicapped offenders'.

In summary, the following key issues should be considered when designing services for people with 'challenging needs':

- There must be flexibility in all aspects of the service. As clients are expected to change their behaviours, so staff and services must change around them, e.g. adjusting housing and staffing requirements.
- Clients need very skilled, experienced and competent staff to work with them and their direct care staff.
- Trained staff are not always required to work with people face to face

but must be available to provide adequate support when required.

- People providing the service should have the necessary authority to provide flexible services when required, e.g. adjustments to staffing levels.
- Relationships should be consolidated between staff and clients before embarking on any therapeutic programmes.
- Communication skills should be developed with clients in order to remove possible sources of frustration.
- Staff and clients need to be individually matched with client involvement in staff selection.
- Residential care should be provided in the least restrictive environment possible.
- Special treatment should not prevent people having access to ordinary living experiences.
- Safety should be obtained by staffing levels and skilled management and not just by building design.
- Treatment plans should be designed individually and delivered in accordance with written programme plans by all people involved in their care.
- Funding for specialist placements should be reserved as a 'safety net' should they be required in exceptional circumstances.

# FACILITATING ACCESS TO GENERIC SERVICES

In accordance with the principles identified in the ordinary life model, people with mental handicaps should be encouraged to make use of generic services wherever possible and the development of special services should be discouraged. In practice, this requires constant effort on the part of service providers to pioneer access to a wide range of services, e.g. visits to local dentists, or visits to the duty room at the local social services department.

In the past a 'comprehensive' service boasted the provision of all services on one site with all specialist support being available within one campus. Arrangements were made to provide general and psychiatric care for people with mental handicaps within their own hospitals and visits to generic services were extremely limited. Consequently, visits were not unusual to the mental handicap hospital from specialists and hospital social workers provided for their social needs in hospital social work departments. Even spiritual needs were not neglected in this model and each hospital had the privilege of its own chaplain. Sick wards were provided and elaborate clinics established to meet the needs of people living in the hospital and of people with mental handicaps in the community.

General medical care was provided by resident medical officers, and only in the past ten years have general practitioners been employed as clinical assistants to meet their medical needs. In fact, the introduction of general practice in mental handicap care marked a change in the way in which clinical services were to be delivered to people with mental handicaps, which was to have a marked effect among professionals in all fields of health-related care.

Perhaps the most recent of all revolutions in moves towards generic health care have been the changes in primary health care practice in the United Kingdom. Certainly, the publication of the *Community Nursing Review in England and Wales* made this point clear by recommending the erosion of traditional boundaries in community nursing, which often excluded people with mental handicaps when they reached adulthood.[7] In fact, the new recommendations acknowledge the specialist needs of this client group but have emphasized the right of people with mental handicaps to receive generic primary health care directly from community medical and nursing practitioners for the majority of their health-related needs.

The establishment of CMHTs in the mid-1970s encouraged community specialists to work together in teams (see Chapters 4 and 5) in the community with people with mental handicaps and their families. The teams may also provide a focus for specialists to share in case discussions and to plan intervention strategies for their clients. The teams also aim to develop access to generic health and social services, and much of their day-to-day work is involved in negotiating new services or opportunities.

The co-ordination of staff support has been explored.[8] It is argued that much valuable time is wasted among professionals who tend to regard their contribution to the care process as being preferable to that of others.

> In a health service which is continually under pressure as a result of finite resources and infinite demand, it seems sad that we waste time on needless argument between the professions. There are plenty of people using the service with plenty of unmet needs, so who cares who meets the needs? Each profession has a thorough training which imparts a set of core skills, a unique body of knowledge. But examination of the content of different syllabi for health care professions will reveal a good deal of common

ground, particularly in regard to 'people skills' – that is, how to communicate with people who find themselves in the role of patient or client. . . I would make an urgent plea for more joint training initiatives. In many districts in the UK we have multi-professional centres of education, yet how often do medical students, nursing students, social work students, physiotherapy students and others sit down together and share learning?

Successful access to generic services must therefore combine specialist skills within a framework of valued service delivery in the community. Such services are already emerging, providing people with mental handicaps and their families with new and valued alternatives to segregated service provision, without any reduction in the skill base or role contribution of the professionals who work with them.

Hence general health care needs are now being met by the local primary health care team and by local district general hospitals; dental services are provided by local dentists; and the needs of elderly people with mental handicaps by services for the elderly. At the other end of the scale, children with mental handicaps are increasingly being regarded as 'children' first and their needs met by services designed to work exclusively with all children in the community irrespective of their handicaps. The local education and social services departments are providing equal opportunities for all people within the mainstream of their service provision and housing, and the department of employment is extending its facilities to people with learning disabilities. All in all there has been a major shift in emphasis from segregated services to one of equality in local neighbourhood provision. There is still a long way to go in realizing the objective of a totally accessible and generic service, but there is no doubt that progress had been made towards its accomplishment through the introduction of flexible services and changes in professional attitude and practice.

## MEETING ADDITIONAL SPECIALIST NEEDS

Some people with mental handicaps will have additional needs which will require access to more specialist services. However, in the general community many people live at home with their families or in their own homes with support from individually designed service systems. In actual fact, there are very few people with physical handicaps who require specialist, residential facilities; the introduction of community care schemes and advances in new technology have made community living more accessible to many people with multiple handicaps.

The main focus of care for many people with additional needs is, in fact, the family: many people will live at home in ordinary, adapted housing. Services should be provided following a comprehensive assessment of the individual's needs and should determine the support services that will be required to encourage the person to develop to his/her full potential. This in itself is a complex task and requires the co-ordination of many services, which will include the contribution made by specialists. They will be required to work with the family in designing and delivering the support required.

The role of the key worker is worthy of particular emphasis at this stage, since it will be this person's task to ensure that all services are efficiently co-ordinated and accessible (see Chapter 2). Professionals will need to clarify their own individual contributions to the care process and be willing to work in partnership with families and care staff to transfer skills and experience to provide continuity of care and treatment. Shared training opportunities should also be provided to allow professionals and informal carers to acquire new knowledge and to support each other in the realization of a 'person-led' rather than a 'professional-led' service. Particular attention should be given to providing instruction in the use of new technology, aids and equipment, communication skills and to facilitating meaningful teamwork among participants.

Perhaps the first step in realizing this aim is to ensure that comprehensive assessment facilities are available to all people with mental handicaps and their families. Such facilities should be provided locally in the community and should encourage the full involvement of consumers and their families in determining their own needs and services. Multidisciplinary teamwork will be required and a range of professionals from a variety of agencies will be accessible to contribute to the assessment process. Assessment must also lead to positive action and result in the delivery of effective intervention in accordance with the predetermined needs of each person using the service. The elements of life planning have already been described in Chapter 3 and are particularly relevant when co-ordinating services for people with additional needs.

In any consumer-led service, the results of individual assessments should provide managers with some degree of insight into the range of services required to meet the needs of their consumers. In the past these were often categorized in terms of the person's disabilities, and the following list may serve to illustrate some of these groups:[9]

● People who are profoundly mentally handicapped.

- People who are blind or partially sighted.
- People with mental handicaps, unable to communicate or who have severe communication difficulties.
- People with mental handicaps who are also profoundly physically handicapped.
- People who are behaviourally disturbed as a result of their mental handicap.
- People suffering from a severe progressive disability.
- People with mental handicaps who have an additional mental illness.

This approach focuses on the person's disabilities and encourages the development of segregated services, which may remove the focus of care from the individual to one which is constrained by an overemphasis on specialist function. The arguments against segregated services have been well described by the North Western Regional Health Authority:[10]

> It is sometimes suggested that specialist assessment and treatment units are required for people with special needs. However, removing a person from his usual setting removes the opportunity to observe and analyse the interaction of the person and the environment. Assessment therefore usually requires the person to be observed in his natural surroundings and not in artificial environments which should be avoided if at all possible.
>
> Once segregated, opportunities to learn how to adapt to living in the community are reduced.
>
> Segregation makes it difficult to reintroduce a person to less restrictive settings . . .
>
> Personal relationships with friends, family and neighbours are disrupted by segregation and can become difficult to re-establish.
>
> Segregation reduces the opportunity to learn appropriate behaviour from nonhandicapped peers. . .
>
> There is a danger of segregated settings being used unnecessarily because staff in ordinary settings may become less able to serve people who present a challenge when they know that an alternative exists. As has frequently happened in the past, they may also be used unnecessarily when resources provided in less restrictive settings have been insufficient.

The identification of people's needs should begin very early on in the person's life and should be accompanied by counselling services for families. The introduction of key workers at this time is essential to provide liaison between the needs of consumers and service managers, and will play a central role in determining access to support services throughout the person's life. Examples of such services may involve access to:

- Assessment facilities.
- Respite care schemes (see Chapter 4).
- Education, employment or valued daily opportunities.
- Generic services in the community.
- Community specialist staff to meet individual needs.
- Introduction to an alternative home.
- Leisure facilities.

This list is far from complete, but serves to illustrate how similar the needs of people with additional needs are to other people in the community. The task is only complicated by the number of people who will become involved in meeting their needs and the task of co-ordination becomes all the more essential. Of equal importance is the need to ensure that people are not deprived of essential services they require to meet their needs when access is required to specialist facilities. Multidisciplinary teamwork will be required to avoid this. People with additional needs therefore require the same range of services as others, and within an individually designed service should find those needs met in the mainstream of community provision.

Integration of people with additional needs in ordinary living projects is not uncommon and many new service developments for people with mental handicaps make provision for people with physical handicaps in their design. It is important to involve a wide range of specialists at the design stage of the project to ensure that the accommodation will meet the needs of its residents. Avoidance of obvious adaptations is important if the house is to merge with the local neighbourhood; aids and adaptations should be chosen sensitively to complement the design of the house.

The use of care support schemes and the relationship between disabled users and their care workers has been described in Chapter 4[11]. The project illustrates the possible options which people with additional needs have to live in the community with additional support and finance. The project demonstrates the images of possibility for disabled people to sustain meaningful lives in ordinary houses, irrespective of their level of dependency. Contracts and agreements are referred to between consumers and their carers and the imaginative use of the redirection of finances is explored to give people new opportunities to 'purchase' their own care programme in their own homes. The use of informal carers is also explored and suggestions for training programmes for them are provided.

The result is to provide people with severe handicaps with the option of controlling their own lives through the provision of imaginative support services.

Similarly, the Crossroads Care Attendant Scheme,[12] originally designed to support disabled people in their own homes, has extended its work to include people with mental handicaps, and there are examples of schemes in operation throughout the United Kingdom. The objectives of the scheme are:

- To relieve stress in families or persons responsible for the care of disabled persons and, exceptionally, in suitable circumstances, to help such disabled persons who live alone.
- To avoid admission to hospital or residential care of such disabled persons should a breakdown or other failure occur in the family.
- To supplement and complement, not to replace, existing statutory services and to work closely with them.
- To strive to maintain a high standard of care.

The Crossroads Scheme functions as a voluntary body and receives finances from statutory services, which demonstrates the importance of forming a partnership in the community to provide services for people with additional needs. Such care attendant schemes are in their infancy in the provision of care to mentally handicapped people and their families, but their potential to expand the range of opportunities for ordinary living for this client group is enormous.

# THE PROVISION OF PSYCHIATRIC SERVICES

The role of the psychiatrist for people with a mental handicap requires special mention due to the changes that have occurred in the provision of psychiatric services for this client group. Certainly, these have been accompanied by changes in the role of the psychiatrist who, historically, had the franchise of care for all people resident in mental handicap hospitals. The situation is very different today, with psychiatrists playing key roles in multidisciplinary teams, providing advice and treatment to individuals in association with other professional colleagues.

For most people with mental handicaps, the provision of psychiatric services will be made by general psychiatric services. However, it is generally accepted that the incidence of mental illness among this client group is higher than that of the general population, and its presentation may require intervention from psychiatrists who are experienced in caring for people with mental handicaps. The nature of presenting handicaps (often involving difficulties in communication) may make diagnosis particularly difficult for the general psychiatrist; clients may well benefit from the additional support offered by specialists.

Ideally, specialized services for people with mental handicaps should be integrated with the other psychiatric specialities as part of a comprehensive psychiatric service to a locality. Close links will also need to be maintained with local general practitioners and community medical staff who will be responsible for the screening and treatment of the medical needs of people with mental handicaps. Liaison with other community specialists will form an essential part of the psychiatrist's day-to-day work. The model which is developing is one of partnership between psychiatrists in mental handicap and general psychiatric services. The skills of the former are a prerequisite to realizing accurate diagnosis and treatment strategies for their clients.

The Royal College of Psychiatrists has confirmed this view in a report approved by Council in January 1983:[13]

> The heterogeneous nature of the mentally handicapped population and the multiplicity of their problems require a wide variety of skills and services to deal with these efficiently. At present there are a large number of people in mental handicap hospitals who do not have psychiatric problems and are the proper responsibility of other services. Mentally handicapped people, like others, need services which are social and educational in nature, but some of them and their families have a variety of problems which require psychiatric services and other medical services. The psychiatrist with a special training in mental handicap would be in the best position to provide the clinical input. . .

The nature of psychiatric service provision is changing to provide people with mental handicaps with a specialist service which is firmly rooted in the mainstream of community provision.

## THE POLITICS OF CARE

This chapter has shown that in the development of comprehensive services for people with mental handicaps and their families, there will inevitably be changes in established patterns of service provision. This will often require changes in attitudes among service users and professionals, and will also be determined by the influence of both local and national government.

During the past decade, most people involved in the provision of services to this client group have increasingly acknowledged the need for service change. This change in direction towards valued community care programmes has been reinforced by government policy:[14]

> The Government's overall objectives are to develop a comprehensive range of co-ordinated health and social services for mentally handicapped people and their families, including assessment, day services and long-term and respite residential care in each locality; and to achieve a major shift from institutional care for mentally handicapped people to a range of community care according to individual needs, with a corresponding shift of resources. This will go along with a continued run-down of large mental handicap hospitals, but specialized residential health provision, which may be in small units in the community, will continue to be needed for people with special medical or nursing needs, as well as specialist support for those in other settings.

The last decade has also seen a shift in thinking in respect of the planning base for new services. Acknowledgement of the principles of 'the ordinary life model' have predominated in many areas, and joint planning machinery has produced many strategic plans which reflect the nature of the partnership between health and social service departments and consumers. The scale of these changes is often quite small in some places, but these may conflict with pressure exerted by managers anxious to realize new community-based services and hospital closure.

There is also evidence that the machinery currently provided for joint planning is not as efficient as it may need to be to make the massive shift required to realize the Government's objectives of community care. The Audit Commission has drawn attention to the inefficient deployment of resources and skills at local level.[1] Duplication of services is still seen in those areas where statutory and voluntary services have failed to identify meaningful working relationships, and the allocation of finances to fund new services may be dominated by cumbersome machinery which mitigates against individual services and local service management.

Perhaps the biggest of all necessary changes will continue to be in the training and preparation of all people involved in the provision of community-based services. This will include government personnel, service managers, professionals, consumers and the electorate. Similarly, there must be opportunities to monitor the effectiveness and efficiency of new services and to encourage the continued expansion and improvement in all areas of provision.

Financial constraints will also determine the rate at which services may improve and expand their capacity to meet the identified needs of their consumers. The allocation of finances will also be determined by national and local trends in government expenditure and may also reflect changes in political policy. Human services require immunity from the changes imposed by changes in political parties and services should continue to enjoy the freedom to determine their own pattern and pace of development in accordance with local service planning procedures with consumers. In practice, this is not always easy to realize as budgets continue to be cut and priorities in service delivery changed in accordance with new demands within multi-agency departments. However, if true community care is to be achieved then there is little doubt that immunity from cutbacks in expenditure and continued investment in care provision for people with mental handicaps will be required as a priority.

A framework has been identified within which to map key issues involved for the realization of a comprehensive community-based service for this client group (Figure 7.1).[15]

The direction of future services will therefore depend on the establishment of new provision for this client group, which is both responsive and sensitive to their needs. Consumer research is already dictating the way forward in many areas and pressure groups such as the Royal Society for Mentally Handicapped Children and Adults and Campaign for Mentally Handicapped People have reinforced the view that community care is indeed the way forward. However, the allocation of additional resources will be required to provide high quality, replacement services and the emphasis must be on their development rather than dismantling the 'old' service as a priority.

The success of the new service will also depend on the way in which it is 'marketed' and introduced to service users, neighbours, politicians and professionals. Seminars, conferences and local discussion on the advantages of community care will provide opportunities for consultation with all people involved in the service and will gradually reshape the pattern of national policy in favour of local services. At a local level this will be particularly important to ensure that access is provided to local services and to facilitate integration in local neighbourhoods.

The latter will require support from local councillors when applications are made to local councils for the change of use of residential properties

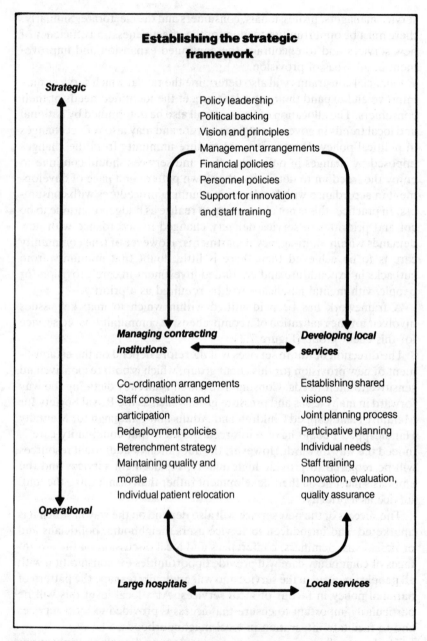

**Figure 7.1** Mapping key issues in a concerted strategy for change[15]

for people with mental handicaps. Local legislation may in fact reduce ordinary living opportunities by imposing unnecessary restrictions on planning, fire and building regulations for projects designed to function as ordinary houses. In some cases, local politics have also been responsible for the acceptance (or sadly the rejection) of people with mental handicaps in local neighbourhoods, and service managers are rapidly learning how to influence local politicians to accept the principles of good community care practice through informed choice and marketing.

The pattern of local and national politics will have a crucial influence on the direction, and provision of services changes in policy should not restrict service growth or reduce the stability of services which people have chosen to meet their needs. Care provision must be stable and not dependent on the support of any one political party or on the strength of the opposition of those wishing to maintain the status quo.

# THE PRIVATE SECTOR

The Government has recognized the private sector's role in providing residential services for people with a mental handicap in the community. In fact in the past few years there has been a surge in the number of residential units which have been opened to provide alternatives to residential care provided in the statutory sector. The increase in private sector developments has now enlarged the choice available to mentally handicapped people and their families. However, the standards of care provided in private homes should be subject to regular inspection and control. The Royal College of Nursing has reinforced this view:[16]

> It is vitally important for a vulnerable group such as the mentally handicapped to be protected, especially now that a variety of provision in a range of settings has been provided. While professionals care for this group of people and the statutory bodies ensure that high professional standards are maintained, a degree of protection is guaranteed. Removal of this safeguard would inevitably result in poorer standards.

Developments in the private sector offer new opportunities which range from adult placement schemes (see Chapter 4) to the emergence and provision of new, large residential facilities. The majority of services in this sector are aimed at the provision of small, homely environments, based on the principles of community integration. To achieve these aims, local agreements need to be reached between the statutory authorities and people involved in providing residential facilities in the private sector.

The concept of multidisciplinary team work and the sharing of resources should be extended to the private sector in order to ensure that consumers receive adequate support from a wide range of professionals when required to meet their individual needs. Similarly, staff employed in private establishments should receive regular in-service training in order to increase their skills and to provide a high quality service. The danger of isolation within this sector needs particular attention, which may lead to reduced standards of care should opportunities to share skills and experiences with staff in statutory services be denied or unavailable.

The development of new facilities in the private sector should be co-ordinated with local district plans and should complement the range of existing residential facilities. Assurances should also be sought to ensure that the philosophy of care to be employed is acceptable and in keeping with the principles of 'an ordinary life'. Consequently, staff should work to facilitate the positive integration of residents into local neighbourhoods by participating in local activities without violating local norms or expectations.

The development of care in the private sector should have as its primary objective the provision of increased opportunities for people with mental handicaps to live, learn and participate in ordinary, community-based activities. Naturally, there will be a price to pay in the quality of services received and delivered and the private sector demonstrates an alternative to those services provided in the statutoty sector. This was further acknowledged by the Royal College of Nursing:[17]

> This document has identified the importance of multidisciplinary team work and the identification of an individual programme plan for each person with a mental handicap. The aims and objectives of each person's care plan should be translated into meaningful opportunities in residential care through the introduction of formal agreements between prospective carers and clients. To ensure that the objectives identified for each person are achieved, local community mental handicap teams should have the authorization to visit, monitor and follow up individuals in private establishments so that the highest possible quality of service delivery is available in accordance with the original contract signed between the carers and clients.
>
> Should the secondary recommendations be accepted and built into the statutory framework for the monitoring of care, these would complement existing legislation which regulates the environmental aspects of private

residential services. Accordingly, the status of private residential units would be enhanced.

# THE NATURE OF A COMPREHENSIVE COMMUNITY SERVICE

This chapter has considered many of the elements and components of a comprehensive service for people with mental handicaps and their families. The structure and management of such services will need to be flexible and responsive to accommodate the emerging and identified needs of its consumers. Traditionally, the nature of these services has been shaped by professionals and their managers, often responding reactively to changes in government and social policy.

Knowledge of the local communities within which services were to be provided was sometimes neglected and services superimposed on existing neighbourhoods without preparation or regard for natural strengths which the community had to offer to the success of the project. This approach implies a sharing of resources from within the community rather than relying on an 'imported' support structure from professional services. The goal of meaningful integration in the community therefore requires the sensitive introduction of new services, which must be preceded by participation and preparation of the chosen neighbourhood before services are planned.

This approach acknowledges the principles of 'an ordinary life' and aims to ensure that people with mental handicaps receive integrated support from and within their 'new' communities. It also has to make provision for the delivery of specialist support to provide individuals with the services they require in order to maintain and develop their lives beneficially. These services should be provided sensitively and support and encourage the development of access to generic services.

Perhaps one of the most obvious factors which will determine the success of an integrated service will be the extent to which it merges naturally with other parts of the neighbourhood. To develop new and incongruous services will imply a rejection of local norms and encourage newcomers to be labelled as 'different', which may in turn deny them access and acceptance. Conversely, a service which is shared with neighbours and which ensures that a 'community presence' is maintained may in time encourage the full participation of people with mental handicaps in the community.

Before this goal can be fully realized professionals will need to reconcile their own perceptions of 'community care' and strive to remove many of the outdated attitudes to professionalism that have been reinforced over many years as a result of institutional care. Indeed, some staff may find it particularly difficult to integrate into local communities themselves, having been dependent on hospital support systems in the 'old model'. Others may find multidisciplinary and multi-agency team work particularly difficult to accept. There is much preparatory work to be done to encourage the development of joint training and sharing of skills between professionals and parents. In summary, there are a number of precursors to meaningful integration in the community and support staff will require opportunities to adjust to new ways of working if services are to be successful.

It would be inappropriate to prescribe any one model of a comprehensive service since, by their very nature, they must all be adapted to meet individual needs and will differ from area to area. However, there are some common elements and principles that together form the basis of an individually determined service, as is now described.

## Services for children

- All services should be needs-led and provided locally.
- Parents should receive access to appropriate counselling services following the birth of their child.
- Facilities for the assessment of all children should be provided.
- Short-term care and respite care facilities should be provided according to parents' needs and should present a range of options ranging from family-based care to residential provision.
- Community specialist support should be available to all children and their families, which should acknowledge the role of the primary care team and children's service as the lead agency for the co-ordination of their needs.
- There should be a clearly identified interface between children's services and the local mental handicap service to ensure that specialist support is provided when required.
- The development of self-support groups for parents should be encouraged to provide mutual support and to identify local needs.
- Access to appropriate and integrated educational services should be provided as a matter of right.
- Parents should be involved in the planning of all new services and, as

they will only be able to contribute if they are informed, opportunities should be provided to share information and skills with them.
- The introduction of pre-school teaching programmes should be encouraged and opportunity groups provided.
- Holiday play schemes, home sitting services and other family support services should be provided.
- All service developments should be planned jointly with consumers and representatives from all agencies involved in the delivery of child care services.

Many of the principles surrounding the provision of services for children will apply equally to adult services. These have been elaborated throughout this chapter and elsewhere in the book (see Chapter 2). The following identifies those components of a service for adults which require particular mention.

## Services for adults

- Appropriate and sensitive arrangements should be made for adolescents transferring to the adult service.
- Opportunities should be provided for educational needs to continue to be met through the provision of adult and further education.
- Valued employment, leisure and a wide range of integrated daily activities should be made available.
- Access to a full range of financial support should be made available to encourage independence and choice in all areas of life.
- Opportunities should be extended for people to develop friendships and personal relationships which will imply the need for individual teaching programmes.
- Opportunities to take calculated risks and to take responsibility for decisions they may make affecting their lives.
- Services which are sensitive to meet the religious and ethnic needs of consumers.
- Access to generic health and social services and, where appropriate, specialist support.
- The right to an alternative home. This is perhaps the most important of all service requirements. A wide range of choice should be provided and should include opportunities for housing from the following agencies: local authority housing department; housing associations; local authority social service department; local health authority;

voluntary agencies; the private sector; family placement schemes.

Opportunities should also be provided for people to purchase their own homes and to obtain mortgages like others in the community and to obtain support in acquiring properties to meet their own needs. Houses should be provided as near to the person's home as he/she chooses, and should be small enough to provide for the creation of a 'family' atmosphere. Large, purpose-built developments should be avoided and all houses should be designed to complement the local neighbourhood. They should be located in the centre of local community life and should be accessible to local facilities and amenities.

Support staff should be provided to meet the identified needs of people living in the house and should be chosen for their skills, experience and willingness to enhance the potential of the residents. The number of staff should be determined according to the needs of people living in the house, and will range from minimal staffing levels to the provision of intense, specialist support.

## CONCLUSION

This chapter has considered those components and service systems that constitute a comprehensive service for people with mental handicaps and their families. Consumers require access to information, advice and support regarding the range of services available to them. They will also require reassurance that new services will be high in quality and realistically planned and delivered to meet the needs of their family members. They will require access to emergency services in the event of crises and the support of specialist staff when needed.

The pace of change and the preparation of both consumers and support staff should be planned strategically to enlist the commitment and involvement of all people involved in the project. Professional skills will require revision and the altered images of staff involved in the care process understood and revalued.

The task now remains to spread the good news regarding valued service developments in this country and to ensure that consumers, their families, their neighbours and professionals involved in the delivery of services facilitate opportunities for the realization of such services.

This chapter ends with two quotations which suggest the way forward towards the realization of a comprehensive, community-based service:

The idea of a fully integrated single authority service seems to be reaching out for the sort of 'total service' envisaged when the large, self-contained mental hospitals were envisaged. It is not clear how this might be achieved in a community-orientated service. . . Mentally disordered people require access to a range of services according to their varying and varied needs, many of them shared with others: primary health care, social work support, specialist health care, education, employment and leisure services, social security etc. . . The way ahead lies in better co-ordination and co-operation rather than in amalgamation.[3]

. . . in the end, a comprehensive locally based residential service for mentally handicapped people will grow from the enthusiasm, initiatives and sheer doggedness of local people. That is the challenge to everyone who reads this paper. We believe that mentally handicapped people have the right to expect that it will be taken up.[18]

# REFERENCES

1. Audit Commission (1986) *Making a Reality of Community Care. A Report by the Audit Commission*, The Audit Commission for Local Authorities in England and Wales, HMSO, London.
2. Audit Commission (1986) *Audit Commission Calls for Action to Improve Community Care*, Press Release 86/16, HMSO, London, pp. 1–2.
3. DHSS (1985) *Second Report of the Social Services Select Committee on Community Care with special reference to Adult Mentally Ill and Mentally Handicapped People* . . . (Chairman Renee Short), HMSO, London.
4. DHSS (1988) *Community Care: Agenda for Action, Report to the Secretary of State for Social Services by Sir Roy Griffiths*, HMSO, London.
5. Carle, N. (1984) *Key Concepts in Community-Based Services*, The Campaign for Mentally Handicapped People, London.
6. DHSS (1983) *The Mental Health Act*, Chapter 20, HMSO, London.
7. DHSS (1986) *The Cumberlege Report: Neighbourhood Nursing – A Focus for Care, Report of the Community Nursing Review in England and Wales*, HMSO, London.
8. Rowden, R. (1987) Whose patient is it anyway? *Nursing Times*, 7 January, Vol. 83, No. 1, p. 22.
9. DHSS (1984) *Helping Mentally Handicapped People with Special Problems*, HMSO, London.
10. North Western Regional Health Authority (1985) *Services for People with Additional Special Needs*, NWRHA, p. 2.
11. Hampshire Council for Independent Living (1986) *Source Book Towards Independent Living* . . . *Care Support Ideas*, (Chairman Rachel Hurst), HCIL.
12. Bristow, A. and Brenig-Jones, J. (1984) *A Study of Four Crossroads Schemes Which Extended their Care to Include People Who Have a Mental Handicap*, Assoc. of Crossroad Care Attendant Schemes.

13. Royal College of Psychiatrists (1983) *Mental Handicap – The Future*, Bulletin of the Royal College of Psychiatrists, Vol. 7, Part 7, pp. 131–4.
14. Hansard (1987) Parliamentary answer by the Minister of Health Edwina Currie, to a question raised in the House of Commons by Sir Fergus Montgomery on 20 January, House of Commons Hansard, Part answer column 530.
15. Towell, D, and Brazil, R. (1986) *Promoting Informed Strategies for Developing Community-Based Mental Handicap Services*, King's Fund Centre, London, p. 6.
16. Royal College of Nursing (1986) *Letter from the Deputy General Secretary of the Royal College of Nursing, Miss Gillian Sandford, to the Secretary of State for Social Services*, 18 July.
17. Royal College Nursing (1987) *Assuring Quality in the Private Sector – Residential Services for People with Mental Handicaps in the Community* (Chairman David Sines) RCN, London, p. 25.
18. King's Fund Centre (1980) *An Ordinary Life – Comprehensive locally based residential services for mentally handicapped people*, Project Paper No. 24, King's Fund Centre, London, p. 42.

# 8. Setting Up Home – The Winchester Experience

*Connie Flight*

## INTRODUCTION

Home is a large, family house in a middle-class district outside Winchester. The house was purchased on the open market for the average price in that area. Half as much again was spent in re-wiring, re-plumbing, fitting a new kitchen and complete redecoration inside and outside.

Certain features were installed to comply with fire regulations and Health and Safety recommendations. No external building or major structural alterations were necessary. Essentially, the house remains very much as it was when purchased, therefore blending in with the local neighbourhood with no indication of who lives there. Five people with varying degrees of learning difficulties live in the house supported by a team of people employed by the health authority.

## COMMISSIONING THE HOUSE

This involves the total preparation of the house for the requirements of the people going to live there. Prior to purchase there are basic requirements such as locality of property, size, number of bedrooms, planning permission availability, local amenities and ground floor accommodation for physically disabled people if required.

Following purchase and the granting of planning permission for change of use of the property (if required; this depends on local policies and numbers of people living in the house), the property has to be registered with the local authority. It is subject to building controls and Health and Safety regulations and environmental health requirements. There are many agencies involved, therefore, and to co-ordinate all these for one property takes time and careful planning.

The architect and the link person from the health authority have to work closely together to draw up the schedules of work involved prior to the work going to tender. Contractors putting in a bid for the tender are given the schedules of work and job specifications to the standards required; they are then taken to the property and invited to submit the tender.

All applications are scrutinized and the contract is given to the tender offering the best value for money within the specified budget and time allocation. Once the contractors take over the site, only nominated members of the health authority are allowed on site due to insurance restricting access to the site by unlawful persons.

Site meetings with the contractors are held on site, as the title suggests, and involve discussion on progress of work, difficulties encountered, changes required and a site inspection each visit. The person who is going to be responsible for running the house is involved in all these meetings and is able to negotiate changes if required.

At the signing of the contract, a completion date is agreed and penalties imposed if that date is exceeded. The person in charge of running the house knows how long he or she has before the house opens, so is able to order curtains, furniture and so on, and advertise for staff at the appropriate time prior to opening.

Usually the person in charge knows the residents who are going to live in the house and is able to involve them in choices of colour, decoration, furniture and curtains. Ideally, this is done in a local store, but has to be to the required standard of fire retardancy as set by the DHSS. Most large stores carry a range that meet these requirements, so the houses are able to be decorated and furnished in a domestic style and prospective residents can be involved in visiting the store, seeing a range of suitable furniture and furnishings and are able to choose within that range.

When these items are selected the delivery date can be agreed with the store and conditions of delivery can be negotiated. During this time the adverts for staff must be placed, usually three months before the house is due to open. This allows two months to recruit and one month for induction, but this may vary depending on local response to advertisements.

The person in charge needs to draw up an induction programme with the staff development officer, and has to write to prospective speakers and agree dates and times for their sessions. A venue needs to be selected for the induction programme to be held and could be held in the house, if it will be opened in time.

A sample of induction programmes for care staff is contained in Chapter 14. Many of the sessions will be forgotten; this is certainly no reflection on the speakers, but will need to be repeated during the first six months after the house is opened. The real value of induction is for staff to become comfortable with each other, and in discussions and during lunches and coffee breaks a great deal of ice is broken. In fact, the beginnings of team building take place, agreement can be reached on how the house will run, the residents and staff can become acquainted and, hopefully, the move to the new house is made as painless as possible.

It was during the last week of the induction programme that agreement was reached to discharge all the residents, so procedures had to be followed to obtain DHSS benefits for the residents (procedures in Appendix A).

The Winchester house was not handed over by the contractors to the health authority until the day before the furniture was due to arrive and two days before the residents were due to move. The handover is a formal meeting between health authority and the contractors, where the whole site is inspected and defects are noted. The contractors are obliged to put right the defects and there follows a six-month period after handover where the contractors are liable for any defects occurring in the house or on the site. There is a further inspection by both parties exactly six months after handover; anything outstanding is corrected by the contractor and after that, responsibility for repairs or defects belongs to the health authority.

## NEIGHBOURS

There was a great deal of ill-feeling about the proposed use of the house among the neighbours, and there were several meetings with members of the health authority. Many visits were made to neighbours during the commissioning period, and although feelings were still expressed against the residents moving in, a certain rapport was established. Another house opening in the same district approximately one mile away had even more trouble with neighbours, culminating in the health service commissioner being called in and a full enquiry being held. This went in favour of the health authority, but did make recommendations regarding the approach with similar projects in the future.

On moving in, it was found that local people (apart from immediate neighbours) were pleasant and helpful and shopkeepers were welcoming, although a decision was made to move into the immediate community gradually, and in hindsight this appears to have been the correct decision.

The immediate neighbours began to complain about everything and anything, and the telephone calls and subsequent visits became very stressful to the staff working in the house. After a time they diminished and 13 months after the house opened, the neighbours came to the door to make peace; there has been harmony since that visit.

One of the main worries appeared to be the drop in property values and although assurance was given that this could be the case for the first few months, it has been demonstrated that, in fact, it makes no difference to local property values. The health authority also tends to look after its properties so that it enhances rather than detracts from property values.

## SELECTION OF RESIDENTS

It would be useful to give a 'magic formula' to help those embarking on a similar exercise, but standard solutions may not be appropriate when adapted to local circumstances. Decisions were influenced by the closure of a long-stay hospital, with the result that people leaving the hospital required alternative homes. Inevitably, this meant that some people would not know the people with whom they would be living, and for those who were unable to be involved in the decision, it proved to be a very traumatic experience.

The proposed groups of people were altered on paper and regrouped many times in an effort to achieve the best results for the residents; the final groups were totally different from the originals. Valid reasons for suggesting the original groups went out of the window and the group of people going into the house was not agreed upon until three weeks before moving in. For some people the move was very difficult; one person in particular took some considerable time to settle.

Eighteen months after the setting up of their home, the five people living there are not really friends; they live together fairly comfortably as a group but do not share common interests. They accept and tolerate each other, possibly because that is what their previous life experience had taught them, and because there were no other available options at the time.

When people are unable to express their choices it is very difficult to make decisions on their behalf, even for someone who knows them well.

What appears to be the best option to meet their needs may prove to be less effective or acceptable than anticipated.

## Residents' status and finances

Since only two of the five people were 'in-patients' of the health authority, it seemed reasonable to discharge them and have all five receiving their own benefits and jointly renting the property with rent agreements. Two weeks before moving, it was agreed that all five people would be discharged according to local guidelines (see Appendix A). A written procedure at the outset is time-saving both when searching for information and avoiding delays in receipt of benefits.

All five people need staff support, and the health authority employed 9.5 whole-time equivalent staff to undertake this task. Therefore, a budget was required to cover staff and administration costs. Other costs were met by the residents from their DHSS benefits. The house expenditure is subject to audit and procedures for the safe-keeping of valuables and, of course, guidelines have been recommended by auditors. Most of them have been implemented, although some were challenged as being against the principles of normalization and ordinary living, and unnecessarily rigid in their insistence on the introduction of outdated and intrusive procedures.

Each resident receives his/her own allowance book from the DHSS and goes independently or with a member of staff to cash the voucher. This voucher is made up from Severe Disability Allowance at the current rate and Supplementary Benefit; this benefit is determined after an assessment of personal circumstances by an officer from the Supplementary Benefit Section of the DHSS.

Residents cash their vouchers at a local nominated post office and upon returning to the house, each resident (together with a member of staff) aportions the money as follows:

- Housekeeping: regular weekly amount agreed in house.
- Training centre money: this amount is deducted from the housekeeping if the resident attends the adult training centre.
- Window cleaning money: it was thought that the appearance of the windows of a house is important to its image, so professional window cleaners appear every six weeks to clean all the windows inside and outside the house. Residents contribute weekly to the cost.
- Heating and lighting costs: money is collected weekly from each

resident, who receives a receipt and the money is paid to the landlord.

- An amount of money is kept in personal cash boxes in the house for personal use, and expenditure is always recorded.
- Deposit account or similar, for savings towards clothes, holidays and so on.

The residents are responsible for paying rent for the property they live in and each person receives a rent rebate as all people in the house are in receipt of Supplementary Benefit. Rent is paid directly from the local housing department to the landlord, which is an acceptable arrangement chosen by many people entitled to and receiving rent rebate. One person living in the house receives Mobility Allowance which is paid into an account administered by the health authority. Although discharged, the health authority agreed to continue to receive and manage the money on his behalf.

Supervising a system such as this makes the administration of the finances much simpler and less time-consuming than having to acquire money through the finance department of the health authority, and has the following advantages:

- Money is readily accessible to the residents.
- It is easier to budget on a weekly basis rather than having a year's allocation of money to monitor and control.

There is certainly less paperwork and time spent filling out request forms for monies, so more time can be allocated to staff and residents' needs. All staff have access to the housekeeping money through a nominated keyholder, who may not necessarily be the most senior person on duty, but is the person who is on duty for the longest period of time, and this saves frequent changes of keyholder. On changeover of keyholder, all monies in the house have to be accounted for and cash boxes checked and signed for by new keyholder.

The housekeeping money covers all food, cleaning materials and such sundries as may be required. To keep account of expenditure, the following processes are required:

- All expenditure must be receipted.
- All receipts are numbered and entered on a cash sheet.
- All meals are planned a week in advance to identify items for shopping lists.
- All receipts for food and so on must itemize each purchase.

The residents cash held in the house is kept in individual cash boxes and each person has a cash book. All monies must have receipts for expenditure except: small spending (money given to residents to spend unsupervised); ice creams and miscellaneous expenditure (not appropriate to ask for receipts); pub spending (again, not appropriate). For all other occasions it is reasonable to demand and expect a receipt. Personal savings are used for holidays, outings and clothing or anything else that may be needed or chosen by the individual to meet his/her needs. (There is no budget available for these items from the health authority funds.)

# MENU PLANNING

When the house opened, lists were made of people's likes and dislikes. This obviously included food; one of the early things to be identified was that people did not know the names of different items of food and so it was difficult to involve them in menu planning. A point was made of telling people in the house the names of food they were eating and what they contained. This became easier to identify as the residents became involved with cooking their own meals and doing the shopping.

The menus are planned a week in advance. The residents and staff plan them together, not for set days but as a week's supply of menus, i.e. a breakfast, a light meal and a main meal each day. These are recorded in a book and a decision is made on the day as to which menu is to be chosen, which is entered on the day sheet and ticked off in the menu book, thus ensuring that the meals are not repeated two days running. The menu book also provides a basis for the week's shopping, and flexibility of choice, since meals are chosen to suit individual preferences and are flexible in timing and content.

There is provision for two members of staff to eat with the residents at any one time, and the health authority provides a sum of money each week to cover the cost of this so that the residents are not required to subsidize staff meals.

All meals prepared in the house are cooked by residents with staff support and only the minimum amount of support required is given to ensure success. There are some occasions when the task is shared on an even basis, as a semi-social occasion to reduce the training emphasis of the procedure. Meals are also eaten in restaurants and so on, and quite often a 'take-away' is bought jointly to be shared in the evenings.

# STAFFING

Staffing is the main resource. It is the most costly and the most important to get right. In some ways it is easier to interview applicants when setting up a new house, than to try and select someone to fit into an existing team.

Selecting staff for the opening of a new house requires careful planning. The likelihood of recruiting everyone in the first 'trawl' is remote, so several months is needed (at least three) before opening, for the first advertisements. Use should be made of the local press, internal advertisements and the local Job Centre. Decisions have to be made about whether full-time or part-time hours are required, a sample rota needs to be prepared, as do a job description, a brief outline of the project and, of course, carefully worded advertisements.

The interview panel for this house consisted of the person in charge, the senior nurse for the community in that sector, the personnel officer and one of the residents. It was felt important not to interview too many candidates at one session and to allow time for discussion between interviews.

On reflection, people were selected to suit the interpersonal needs of the staff team; they were people who would be easy to work with, and with whom an instant rapport was established. Fortunately, a team of people was recruited with enthusiasm and good ideas and they were prepared to put their ideas into action. Best of all, they had the residents' interests at heart. However, as time went on, it became apparent that with the ages of the people selected, some staff looked very much like 'escorts' rather than friends when out with residents. This may be illustrated by the following example: one young man was out shopping with an elderly gentleman who stumbled, fell and cut his face quite badly. The young man, a member of staff, went to assist him and a passerby thought the young man was assaulting him.

When participating in social excursions, the age gap became increasingly inappropriate and as some staff members left, they were replaced with more mature part-time people. This has proved to be beneficial to all concerned.

A sample duty rota may be found in Appendix B with an explanation of how it functions. 'Sleep in/standby' staff are employed rather than 'waking night staff' and this provides far more people available to work during the day within the staffing establishment. Although remuneration is less than for 'waking night staff', it seems to be more appropriate, since everyone in the house goes to bed at night instead of somebody sitting up, awake and waiting for morning.

Having said that a sample duty rota needs to be prepared prior to interview, in this instance, one was not prepared; instead, candidates were given outlines of suggested hours, and applicants for part-time posts said how many hours they were able to work.

The duty rota was developed during the induction period, where there was agreement about how early to start the day and how late to finish. The day for the staff meeting was also agreed, chosen partly as it was the half-day closing of the local shops. All staff are on duty every Thursday afternoon regardless of how many hours they do, for two hours for the staff meeting, since the weekly meeting is compulsory.

Prior to appointment, applicants had agreed that they would be flexible, and as time went on this proved to be the case. This is essential to cover the needs of the house and residents, and particularly to cover annual leave, courses, and residents going to work, and attending outings and appointments.

A nonsmoking policy was adopted by all staff and agreed at interview, as none of the residents in the house smoke.

## STAFF TRAINING

All the new staff started on the same day, three weeks before the house was opened and attended an induction course. There were compulsory talks and presentations and many of these were repeated within the following six months as a refresher update as it was found that many people require opportunities to receive ongoing teaching support. Many were new to client centred work and as such, personal issues tended to infiltrate a relaxed approach to learning. Therefore it appears essential to repeat sessions later when staff have acquired new confidence and skills.

During the induction, discussions ranged from how duty rotas would work, how staff meetings would run, on the philosophy of the house and the aims of the service. 'Getting to know one another' was another important aspect, as was meeting the residents, of course. There were also teaching sessions from therapists, psychologists, the community team and other specialists.

Apart from repeating some of the induction sessions, some time during staff meetings is used for training such as: how to record accurately, relevant information; techniques in coping with challenging behaviours; first aid; food handling; discussions on how staff talk to each other and the residents; and fire lectures.

Staff are sent in turn to 'out of district' courses and workshops, so that they meet other people working in similar situations and they are able to acquire and share knowledge and experiences with others and to develop new skills for their clients.

A new curriculum of training for staff has been developed in Winchester, so that all care staff are given continuous education to develop their skills and help to integrate them with other staff in other houses in order to prevent professional isolation. Staff are also given articles to read and have to keep up to date on all policies – some of which are developed in house with full staff involvement.

## Policies and procedures

In every residential establishment within Winchester Health Authority that cares for people with a mental handicap are written policies, procedures and guidelines for all staff. These include a house operational policy and risk-taking guidelines.

All staff are expected to be familiar with these documents, and to have read, signed and dated them. Some of these documents will be referred to in this chapter and copies may be obtained from Winchester Health Authority by specific request.*

*During the commissioning period, regard to the following important policies and regulations will be necessary*
1. Local authority registration requirements.
2. Planning permission procedures.
3. Building regulations.
4. Contractors insurance regulations.
5. Environmental health requirements.
6. Fire regulations.
7. Health and Safety at Work requirements.
8. Health authorities' own policies on standards of work and quality of equipment.
9. Regulations and standards set out in the schedules of work for the project as determined by the health authority.

*Staffing procedures include*
1. Whitley Council Conditions of Service.

* *Services for People with a Mental Handicap*, Winchester Health Authority, Silverhill, King's Walk, Winchester, Hants SO23 8AF.

2. Advertising and interviewing procedures.
3. Contracts of employment.
4. Personnel procedures including:
   District grievance procedure.
   District disciplinary procedure
   District disputes procedure (industrial action).
   Sickness and absenteeism.
   Maternity leave.
   Annual leave recording
   District retirement policy and procedure.
   District training procedures.
   District complaints procedure.
   Confidentiality.
   Health and Safety accident and hazard reporting procedures.
   Staff record-keeping.
5. Security.
6. Missing persons reporting procedure.
7. Volunteers (every service should have one!)
8. Driving of vehicles and carriage of residents/clients.
9. Risk-taking.
10. District smoking policy.
11. Dealing with the Press and media.
12. Prescribing arrangements and storage of drugs.
13. Visitors' policy.
14. Management of disturbed behaviour guidelines.
15. Maintenance policy for buildings and estates.

Many of these policies are summarized in a local handbook designed by Winchester Health Authority for the guidance of staff.[1].

During the first six months of the running of the house, the staff group devised an operational policy for the house, based on the core principles used for all small houses within the service.

## Service systems in the house

### Key workers
During the induction training period, each resident was allocated two key workers, who were jointly responsible for all aspects of care for that resident. They checked that: residents have all their health needs met, e.g. doctors, dentist, hospital appointments etc; finances are monitored

and controlled if a resident needs help; clothing is checked for cleanliness, repair or replacement; hair appointments and general hair care are arranged; special outings and holidays are organized; liaison with other agencies (ATCs, parents, volunteers, adult education etc.) takes place; opportunity plans are written with residents. They also act as the reference point for other staff in the house and liaise with therapists on individual training needs, arranging and implementing individual programme plans, and organizing clubs and visits to friends as required by the resident.

In addition to being key workers, staff supervise the needs of others in the house during their span of duty. Key workers would be expected by the person in charge to act as advocate for that person if required, to help and support that person in all areas of expressed or demonstrated need.

### Organizing residents' training

The key workers were responsible initially in drawing up a list of strengths, needs, likes and dislikes for each resident. All staff contributed to these lists as they became familiar with the residents' needs, and their lists formed the basis for the design and introduction of opportunity plans.

Residents were not put under any pressure initially to engage in tasks about the house, but were invited to participate, so that assessments could be made regarding each individual's skill base. As training needs were identified for the residents, so the opportunity plans were introduced as a means of teaching residents new skills by identifying a series of opportunities throughout the day. It is interesting to note that the initial six months provided staff and residents with an opportunity to identify and clarify individual needs and preferences within the context of 'their new home'. Many preconceived ideas and initial assessments were changed radically in the light of practical evidence and new opportunities.

### Individual programme planning meetings

The first meetings for residents began three months after the house opened and were reviewed at six-monthly intervals. The meetings were attended by all staff initially to develop their skills and confidence in running meetings for residents as their key workers, and were chaired and minuted by the person in charge and senior staff.

Parents and/or selected friends or advocates were invited, as were therapists who may be involved with the resident, representatives from the ATC in question, and the sector psychologist, who chaired one of the meetings. Therapists not involved with the residents, but thought to be necessary for developing other skills, were invited by letter in order to facilitate their assessment of needs. The meetings follow an agenda and key workers and client are jointly responsible for acquiring information, inviting guests, presenting a written profile of a typical day for the resident, providing a summary of new skills learned since the previous meeting, stating whether all previous set objectives have been met (with an explanation for non-accomplishment), and listing the needs identified to develop before the next meeting. The key workers jointly present the information on behalf of the resident and the resident is always present.

After the first meeting, the key workers chaired and minuted the meeting and presented information summaries, and only people actively participating in the residents' lives were invited to meetings in order to reduce the size of the meeting and help individuals feel at ease. The meetings are held in the house and the minutes are circulated only to those involved in the meeting.

### Day planning sheet
These were introduced after the house had been open for one year, and were adapted to suit the needs of the house (from an original format and ideas developed in another sector) by staff working in the home. Several changes were made and tested until a final draft was agreed and included in the work/task book for the house (see below). Day sheets were used to help the staff plan daily activities with residents, but were not so binding as to prevent spontaneous changes of plan or provide opportunities to be missed for a more enriching experience than that which had been planned. The system assists the deployment of staff, prevents staff duplicating work and ensures even distribution of workload.

### Hygiene standards in the house
It was agreed at one of the early staff meetings that the cleanliness of the house should be maintained to an acceptable standard. Staff were allocated specific areas of responsibility in the house and garden, and were required to produce written standards for that area. For kitchen cleaning, the catering service manager was asked to comment on and amend written standard statements; similarly for cleaning, the domestic services manager was asked for opinion and advice. They were both invited to assist in the ongoing monitoring of satisfactory standards in the house. These standards were collated and suggested tasks for daily, weekly and monthly cleaning were listed and made available to all staff for guidance.

**The 'work/task book'**

This was completed and introduced 18 months after the house opened in an attempt to rationalize many of the separate information and recording systems that were in use at the house. This was highlighted when introducing new staff to in-house procedures and, as a result, the book was developed.

It covers four-week periods and should be used to plan outings, activities, daily routines and the allocation of staff resources to meet these commitments.

The book contains: sheets to record residents' income and expenditure; sheets to record handover of keys and monies and to record income and expenditure in respect of housekeeping; sheets to plan daily activities for residents; sheets to record opportunity plans for residents; duty rotas; standards for the hygiene of the house; plain sheets of lined paper for conversation/communication for the four weeks.

These papers are spiral-bound and, along with a diary, provide all that is necessary for the day-to-day running of the house (apart from the residents' personal cash books). It is also proposed to introduce a system to record each resident's skill level and accomplishments, so that new staff know how much support is required by each resident to complete specific tasks. This system will complement the work/task book. The Bereweeke Skill Teaching System[2] is being introduced to teach those skills that are not learned from opportunity plans.[3]

# RESIDENTS' DAILY OCCUPATION, WORK AND LEISURE

A small working party was established within the house to research and list available resources for work, leisure and educational opportunities. One resident already uses the local ATC three days each week, but the others were engaged only in domestic chores, shopping and outings to the more obvious places of leisure, e.g. recreation centres, gardens, cinemas and so on.

Surprisingly, several opportunities were offered but involved skills such as reading, writing messages and answering telephones, skills the residents did not have. Two 'cleaning jobs' were offered, both in factories, one with workers present, the other after-hours when the factory was empty. The residents were offered the 'going rate' for the work and with intensive staff support including good will, these jobs provided a rewarding learning experience in valued environments for two of the residents. The DHSS was notified of the change in financial circumstances and in one case all benefits stopped. The Severe Disability Allowance stopped because it was said that the resident had proved to be capable of work despite the fact that without full staff support that person would not have been able to work; consequently all other benefit stopped.

The cleaning contract ended and was not renewed, so the resident lost the job through no fault of his own. No further work was offered that was suitable for that person's needs, and a great many letters had to be written to have the three benefits reinstated.

The other resident gave up her job, because it was too tiring to have an evening job after a day at the ATC, but the work had proved to be a useful experience. A private cleaning job for two evenings a week was offered and accepted, and was much easier to cope with, but the employer left the district and thus ended another job!

Two people had places for 10 weeks on a course for one full day a week working one-to-one with a student teacher, which proved to be a very enjoyable experience, but had nothing with which to replace it after the ten weeks ended. Two people had places on the 'New Way Scheme' which offers places to people with a mental handicap in adult education classes, such as cooking, yoga or keep-fit, and each resident attends the class of his/her choice with a volunteer.

These classes have been very successful and most enjoyable. One resident attends a pensioners' club one afternoon each week with a member of staff and joins in the full range of activities offered with everyone else. There are 'taster days' during the term-time at the local further education colleges for people to experience new activities and to see if they would like to join in. These have proved to be very enjoyable and are sponsored by the local adult education department.

A local working party continues to search for new resources and some that were not able to be used by the house have been passed on to other houses or agencies in the area for their consideration. The health authority and local authority social services department have established a working party to identify resources and fund day-time occupation for people living in residential homes through the use of joint finance schemes.

# CONCLUSION

On reflection, 18 months after establishing the house, the residents appear to use it as their home and have developed new skills and grown in confidence. Although, inevitably, there have to be service systems introduced within such residential establishments, they are hopefully as unobtrusive as is practicable and enhance rather than disrupt the lives of the people living in the house. The Winchester experience may help others embarking on a similar project to clarify thoughts, assist in the promotion of ideas and avoid some of the pitfalls.

# APPENDIX A

## Procedures for discharging long-stay patients to the community and to obtain DHSS benefits

A covering letter needs to be written to the local DHSS office two weeks before the date of people moving from hospital accommodation to their new home. The information required is:

- A form (SB1) obtainable from the local DHSS office to claim supplementary benefit; one form for each client.
- The date of moving into the new house.
- The discharge date (this may be the same as above).
- The discharge certificate (signed and dated).
- Where the person is to be discharged from.
- Full name and date of birth.
- The amount of money held by clients in savings, or on their behalf by banks, health authority, court of protection etc.
- Rent breakdown of house they are moving to (identifying rent, rates, general and water, repairs and decoration, furniture, heating and lighting and telephone rental costs. To give all this information at the time of writing saves everyone a lot of time).

The DHSS sends an appointment date and time for each client to be seen and assessed for benefit by one of their officers from the Supplementary Benefits Section at the resident's new home. The DHSS will not assess or visit before this client moves to his/her new home.

The clients need to register with a GP immediately they move, as the assessor needs to know the name and address of the GP. For the assessor's visit, each client needs:

- To have joined the list of a GP and have a medical card.
- A (MED3) form from the GP, who will need to see the client, stating why client is unfit for work. The certificate is usually for 6 months' duration.
- Any pension or Severe Disability Allowance books, or other benefit. The assessors will take the books away and issue a receipt for them.
- A list of any savings or monies held by any agency for the client.
- The client *must* be present.

If the clients have come from long-stay units or hospital, they often do not have medical cards. Temporary medical cards obtainable from the surgery of choice can be filled in and given to the GP of choice for acceptance by him/her, onto his/her list. On the card is a section for place of birth; sometimes this is unknown which can cause problems, but with a little time and research, these problems are not insurmountable.

The information required for the cards is: full name; new address and post code; previous GP and address; previous address of applicant; date of birth; place of birth. The cards go from the surgery to the family practitioner service for processing, and permanent medical cards will be issued in due course.

- When the benefit comes through, the client receives from the Supplementary Benefit Section, a form (either blue or yellow, depending on finances of the client) to enable rent rebate to be claimed. The form has four or five pages of questions, but is not complicated, and the previously mentioned rent breakdown for the house is very helpful. The client has to sign the form, and if above the signature is written 'please pay direct to landlord', the money goes direct to the landlord and saves the person in charge a lot of paperwork.
- A little time spent filling the forms in correctly helps the rebate office and speeds up the system and the receipt of payment. If a client has a lot of money saved, the whole of the rent may have to be paid until these savings are reduced to a level when they become eligible for rebate.
- Any savings from Mobility Allowance do not count as it is considered reasonable to accrue a lot of money if saving for a car or similar.
- When the rebate goes through it does not cover heating/lighting; this has to be collected by the person in charge from each client, each week

and paid into an account designated by the landlord.

- The rent may take a little while to process by the rebate office, but is back-dated when it arrives. Because of this, the landlord must understand that a couple of months may pass before money is received.
- Since benefits may take a few weeks to work out, the person in charge should organize a temporary petty cash system, on the understanding that all monies will be repaid by the residents when the back-dated benefits arrive.
- It should also be borne in mind, because this money has to be repaid, that just because it is 'petty cash' it is not a bottomless pit, as enthusiasm in setting up the house tends to encourage residents and staff to overspend.
- The benefit of this system is that budgeting is much easier; a weekly amount is dealt with and the money is very accessible. Residents are financially better off, and in line with the principles of normalization and valued 'ordinary living'; it is of course normal and more dignified to pay rent, housekeeping and so on than to receive pocket money on a voucher system.
- The administration of such a system is also comprehensive and less time-consuming.

## APPENDIX B

### Sample of duty rota for house

This rota is part of the rota for the house. The person in charge does not appear on the rota as he/she attends meetings and tends to work from 9 a.m. to 5 p.m., but is flexible to the demands upon his/her time and the needs of the house.

Seniors 1 and 2 work full time and opposite weekends to each other; they also work long days and share 'on call' with the person in charge. Care staff 1 to 4 inclusive work full time, do some sleep-ins and follow each other on their four week rota. Number 1 goes to Number 2 the following week and so on, and Number 4 goes to Number 1. Care staff 5 works 27 hours and two sleep-ins the same nights every week, and the house is covered subject to flexibility between rotas and staff agreement.

Care staff 6 works the same 10½ hours each week unless the house requires different times; the hours worked are to cover a specific activity with one of the residents.

| | Sun-<br>day | Mon-<br>day | Tues-<br>day | Wed-<br>nesday | Thurs-<br>day | Fri-<br>day | Satur-<br>day |
|---|---|---|---|---|---|---|---|
| **Senior 1 F/T** | 8–6 | 8–6 | **Off** | 8–6 | 8–3.30 | **Off** | **Off** |
| **Senior 2 F/T** | Off | Off | 8–6 | Off | 1–8.30 | 8–6 | 8–6 |
| **N/A 1 F/T**<br>**37½** | Off | Off | Off | 2–12<br>MN SI | 6.30–<br>3 | 12MD–<br>10 p.m. | 3 p.m.<br>MN SI |
| **N/A 2 F/T**<br>**37½** | 6.30–<br>3 p.m. | 7.30–<br>4 | Off | 7.30–<br>7.30 | 7.30–<br>4 | Off | Off |
| **N/A 3 F/T**<br>**37½** | Off | 2–<br>10.30 | 2.30<br>12 MN | SI 6.30–<br>1 p.m. | 12 MD–<br>3.30 | Off | 8–<br>5.30 |
| **N/A 4 F/T**<br>**37½** | 2.30–<br>MN SI | 6.30–<br>8.30 | 7.30–<br>4.30 | Off | 1–12<br>MN SI | 6.30–<br>12MD | Off |
| **N/A 5 P/T**<br>**27** | Off | 6 p.m.–<br>12MN<br>SI | 6.30–<br>1 p.m. | Off | 1 p.m.–<br>3 p.m. | 6 p.m.–<br>12MN<br>SI | 6.30–<br>1 p.m. |
| **N/A 6 P/T**<br>**10** | Off | Off | 1–<br>9.30 p.m. | Off | 1–3 p.m.<br>Staff<br>Meeting<br>1–3 p.m. | Off | Off |

Note: MN – midnight
     MD – midday
     SI – sleep-in duty
     F/T – full-time
     P/T – part-time
     N/A – nursing assistant

There is still a 1.5 whole-time equivalent (WTE) establishment left. Currently, these are filled by part-timers to suit the needs of the house and particularly the residents. It will be noted that *all* staff, no matter how few their hours, are put on the rota for Thursday staff meetings. This meeting has to be compulsory and is *vital* to the running of the house.

# REFERENCES

1. Winchester Health Authority (1986) *Operational Guidelines for Persons in Charge of Small Houses for People with a Mental Handicap*, Winchester HA.
2. Mansell, J., Felce, D., Flight, C, *et al.* (1984) *The Bereweeke Skills Teaching System*, Programme Writers' Handbook, NFER-Nelson, Oxford, p. 245.
3. Felce, D., Jenkins, J., de Kock, U. *et al.* (1984) *Day Sheets to Accompany Opportunity Plans* (unpublished), p. 241.

# BIBLIOGRAPHY

Wolfensberger, W.A. (1972) *The Principles of Normalization in Human Services*, National Institute of Mental Retardation, Toronto.

King's Fund Centre (1980) *An Ordinary Life*, Project Paper No. 24, King's Fund Centre, London.

# 9. Residential Services for Children
## *Diane Worsley*

## INTRODUCTION

> I didn't like to be disabled so it is bitter in my heart. I would like to be taken
> care of. I would like to be loved. I would like to be respected and trusted. I
> would like to be considered too.
>
> I see through your eyes pity for me
> I don't want your pity or your lies
> You see my chair instead of me
> You see many things wrong with me
> Instead of just me[1]

Children, all children, have some needs in common. The need for food,
warmth, shelter, to be protected from danger, to have the affection and
approval of a care-taking adult, to have the opportunity to grow and
develop to the maximum of their abilities in a stable environment.
Children who are physically and/or mentally handicapped are no different.

However, children are individuals. They have individual personalities,
abilities, families, social background, cultural influences and life experiences. Children who are handicapped are no different, except perhaps
one might add to this list, the limitations of their handicaps, their
perception of these and of themselves.

Since the Elizabethan Poor Law, care of children in need has been subjected to fashions of public care. From the village and extended family they moved to a hopefully benign, institutional care. There have been many changes since then. Large institutions fell into disrepute, 'family' groups, smaller homes or communities became established. These changed to group homes and, currently, foster care. So often one mould is deemed suitable for all of them because they are children. If it is accepted that children are individuals and have therefore individual needs then a variety of facilities must be provided to give the best possible service to them. They have a right to this – to have the opportunity to grow up in an environment that will allow them to develop to the maximum of their potential. Some children, unable to live with their natural parents, will desperately need the warmth of an alternative family, and every effort must be made to find them a suitable foster family. Other children may be so damaged by life's experiences they need time and space and will respond more quickly to a less emotionally demanding environment, as found in a children's home.

This chapter examines residential care for children who are handicapped. Clearly, the first and most obvious care is within his natural family. However, where this is not possible or perhaps desirable, what are the other options? Some alternatives are looked at, such as foster families, children's homes and boarding schools. Supportive services are also examined, such as the availability of professional expertise, short-term or respite care, and self-help groups within the community.

# NATURAL PARENTS

It is worthwhile to stop and consider for a moment the child's natural (biological) family. This is his first and most desirable residential care. Whether he can remain in it while he grows up will depend on factors over which he will have little control. These are factors within the family. First, how has his arrival been accepted by his family? When parents are told their child has a limiting handicap their response is similar to that of bereavement – a loss of the child they were expecting, hoping and planning for. Bereavement responses follow a well-recognized pattern. Initially, shock – a paralysing disbelief; panic ('We can't cope'); denial ('There is a mix-up, he's not ours') or ('The doctor has made a mistake') or endlessly seeking other opinions. This leads to grief; tears yearning for the baby that might have been; then projected grief (anger – 'Why me?') and guilt ('If only we had (or hadn't)'). Then there is bargaining ('We will accept him if he can walk'). Finally, acceptance – of the child as he is, and constructive interest in his development.

This latter stage is followed by interest in other families with a similar problem. It is then that parents become most active members of self-help groups and can give a lot of support to other families, in earlier stages of feeling. There are no rigid lines to the pattern of bereavement and no guarantee that both parents will be at the same stage at the same time. Most families are able to work their way through to acceptance using their own resources, but some need outside help – some become stuck along the way. These are the families always seeing a new doctor, always trying a new treatment or perhaps finally rejecting their child.

Some families already have internal problems: accommodation, finance, an unsteady marriage, unemployment and so on, and the birth of this child is the last straw before the break up of the family.

Second, the child's long-term future will depend on his family's understanding of his condition and management of it. This does not mean the acquisition of reams of technical data – though some parents do become very knowledgeable about their child's condition – rather, what it is and what it will mean in relation to everyday living within the family. A chairbound child with cerebral palsy who has frequent and severe fits will bring an added stress to an outdoor, athletic family, as will a severely mentally handicapped child with physical deformities, who is overactive and destructive in a 'show business' family. Other parents with similar children can be particularly helpful in giving suggestions from their experience about coping with the sometimes quite trivial problems of daily life.

The child, too, will be making his own impact on his family, e.g. a child with autistic behaviours who is also very active, needs little sleep and is destructive, will tax the resources of any family. Community support is essential if these families are to continue to manage. This support should include both professional help and nonprofessional help, as found in local organizations and self-help groups.

## PROFESSIONAL HELP

Professional help will be required and influenced by legislation and available resources. The way in which services are delivered will vary, of course, from area to area. Help should certainly include information, preferably printed, that can be digested and referred back to at the right moment, on the facilities available to the child. Thus it is possible for the family to make informed choices about the most suitable service available to the child at each stage of development.

# CHRONICALLY SICK AND DISABLED PERSONS ACT, 1970[2]

This Act obliged local authorities to provide practical support for people who are 'substantially and permanently handicapped' by illness, injury, congenital deformity, old age and mental disorders of any description. This support includes short-term care, day care, home adaptations (i.e. downstairs bedroom/toilet), holidays, assistance in obtaining a telephone and any adaptations for its use, and so on. There is no compulsion placed on the local authority to provide a service unless in their assessment of an individual a particular need has been recognized. Anyone can apply to the local authority, which will also take into account individual circumstances.

The reality of implementation has meant a patchy service with different standards and variations in interpretation, influenced by the cash flow within the local authority.

# THE EDUCATION ACT, 1981[3]

This long awaited Act provided parents and children with a mental handicap their first opportunity to be actively involved in designing the pattern of their education. The implications of the 1981 Act provided teachers and parents with the challenge of revising their curriculum to meet each child's changing needs.

Perhaps the most important feature of this Act is the requirement to provide a regular multidisciplinary assessment of the child's educational needs in the context of their 'total life', and to provide a written 'statement' of the aims and objectives for the child's education at school. The 'statementing' process takes place at regular intervals throughout the child's school life and becomes particularly important during adolescence when future plans are being made.

The Act also makes provision for parents to appeal against decisions made by the education authorities, both in respect of curriculum design and in choice of school for their child. Additional rights are provided to parents and their children to ensure that they are actively involved in all aspects of their child's education.

Regrettably, some schools interpret the 'statementing' process to be exclusively their own assessment and fail to implement or to realize the true philosophy of multidisciplinary assessment and shared involvement with parents.

The Act also makes recommendations for the integration of children with a mental handicap into ordinary schools, and advocates that further education be provided for all children up to the age of 19 as a matter of right.

# DISTRICT HANDICAP TEAM

The Court report of 1976 reviewed the existing health services for children and made practical recommendations for a new integrated child health service (ICHS).[4] One such recommendation was the setting up of a district handicap team in every health district. The team would consist of a core of professionals – paediatrician, clinical medical officer (child health), social worker, psychologist and a representative of the community nursing services (health visitor), with others being co-opted as necessary, e.g. physiotherapists, speech therapists or a specialist teacher for the blind. This team was to co-ordinate the service received by the family, and a key worker was appointed from the team to be the contact person for the family – a named person who could make regular visits and would report back to the team. The family would also be able to meet the whole team.

The team was to make a thorough assessment of the child and his needs by a summary of individual member's reports; then, with the family, plan for the needs of the child and monitor his progress. It is frustratingly futile, however, to provide a comprehensive report only to discover there are no facilities available to meet the needs identified. On many occasions this has been yet another reason for the child to leave the parental home and move into considerably more costly residential care. The development of ICHS has varied from district to district. Some teams are established as part of the local general hospital; others are based in child assessment centres, where playgroups and short-term care may be also available.

When the child is grown up he is referred on to the community mental handicap team. Somewhere between the age of 16 and 19 is the usual time for this transfer, but it needs to be a flexible arrangement based on the child's development rather than some chronological rule.

# THE FAMILY FUND[5]

This fund provides practical help not covered by the Chronically Sick and Disabled Persons Act. In 1976 the government set aside funds to be administered by the Joseph Rowntree Memorial Fund to provide essential equipment or other financial or practial help for parents caring for a severely handicapped child at home. This help is outside the facilities provided by the local authorities. For example, it will not pay for short-term care, but may buy a tumble dryer for an incontinent child. It may provide a freezer for a family where shopping is difficult or pay for driving lessons for parents.

There is no doubt that the Family Fund has inspired much valuable research into ways of alleviating stress relating to caring for severely handicapped children at home. The true value of support received by families from the Fund should not be underestimated. For many it has been a lifeline to survival.

# SELF-HELP GROUPS

Self-help groups provide another means of family support. These groups start usually in a small way by a group of people with a similar problem or need, who often have been frustrated by lack of facilities and understanding. Thus they set about to meet their own needs and provide the lacking resource. This could be a temporary resource, such as playgroups for severely handicapped pre-school children, that ceases to be necessary once the local school for severe learning difficulties has provided a nursery class. Here, the group has established the need, which has been accepted by the statutory body and taken on by them. The advantage of self-help groups is that they are able to be flexible and direct their attentions to the changing needs within the group.

They may provide an ongoing commitment to particular resources; for example, even though local authority funding meets the educational needs in Spastic Society schools, many local groups are still supporting the schools for extras, equipment, short-term care and pre-school therapies. Leading groups such as MENCAP and the Spastic Society began in these ways and have developed into national bodies with many specialist resources of their own.

Stories abound of many voluntary self-help groups set up across the country. Other special resources like the toy libraries association help to fill different gaps. They provide a variety of often very expensive toys on loan to families with a handicapped child, to help encourage development or just for enjoyment.

## TAKING A BREAK

A bewildering number of new terms have entered the maze of popular professional jargon – respite care, short-term care, phased care and so on. What do they all mean? Respite care means to give families or parents some break or respite from the demanding routine of caring for their child. Short-term care can mean anything from a few hours to a weekend, a residential assessment, or emergency care to a summer holiday. Phased care means planned weekends or perhaps a preparation for long-term care.

Basically, they all mean the same; a child will be leaving his family and coming into some form of residential accommodation for a short time. To serve the needs of both the child and his family, it should be possible for them to make an informed choice of facilities and to select the most suitable to meet their needs. What will they be looking for?

## Local services

First, a local service, somewhere close enough to home to be accessible for the family. There are many obvious advantages. It is possible for the family to get to know the staff and placement on a more informal level. Locally placed, the child may be able to continue uninterrupted at school, and thus it becomes then a less traumatic upheaval for him. It is also probable that other children at the home will be attending the same school. There can be a connotation of going to stay with school friends, an opportunity often not possible for children who are handicapped. The school will also have links with the home. Indeed, some special schools are setting up their own short-stay units close to the school. Training programmes can also be maintained with a minimum of fuss.

Travel will play a big part for families. A place situated 30 miles from home means the family have to contemplate a journey of 120 miles for the weekend. Many families have said that where this is acceptable for an annual holiday, it is too daunting for regular weekends. It is certainly out of the question for short breaks such as afternoons or an evening. Where this is the only option, families have often gone without. This is particularly so in rural areas where it is difficult to set up a local service because of the large, thinly populated areas covered.

## Flexibility

Second, how flexible is the service able to be? Is it possible to offer care for only a couple of hours to allow parents to go shopping, attend a prize-giving for another child, attend a wedding? Is it possible to offer regular planned weekends or annual holidays along with less planned breaks? An emergency service in some form is essential. Parents have said that this is the real life-saver. Just to know that it is available is a great reassurance. Undoubtedly, a planned series of booked weekends is something to hold on to and enables other things to be planned for, but you cannot rely on elderly relatives dying on the right weekend, you cannot plan for the mains pipe bursting in the kitchen – and four inches of water in the kitchen is as much an emergency as sudden illness. To know that help is available strengthens the family and holds it together.

In practical terms, the currently popular small facilities taking four to six children are often counterproductive for flexibility. Having so few places, it is economically necessary to have 'the beds full'; a slightly larger facility is more able to withstand the need to have one or some beds empty to allow for emergencies.

Booking arrangements also need to be flexible. Much will be dictated by the agency providing the service, i.e. social services, the NHS or voluntary/charity. Each have their own systems. One father recently explained he was offered a place in a small specialist unit for his profoundly multiple handicapped daughter, but first he had to see the doctor associated with the unit and then he would need to fill out a series of forms each time she came. He said he was 'sick to death' of seeing different doctors, and the apparently endless formality had put him off. There is no doubt information about the child is needed within the unit, but does the same information need to be taken every time? Where the child is known or is a regular visitor, a less formal arrangement should be possible. Changes, medication and emergency telephone numbers are the essentials to note.

## Large or small?

Third, what size of facility will the family be looking for? The days of large institutions are over (almost). Wards of 30-plus are not now seen as appropriate for children because of their more formal, institutional and less personal approach, and inability to respond to individual needs. Currently, small local facilities are favoured. Those offering four to six places are much more able to offer a homely atmosphere and give more individual attention. Staffing these facilities is a costly business. It is possible to create a homely environment in a slightly larger unit of, say, 10 to 12 places, and these should not be discounted out of hand because of fashion. In recent years many local authorities have encouraged a scheme of what is basically very short-term foster care. Sometimes these are called 'Link and Befriending Schemes', where the scheme links a family with another local family. Appropriate short-term care is then arranged between the families and is usually paid for by the local authority. The obvious advantage is the new family can become part of the extended family with a building of friendships and mutual support between the two families, while caring for the child. In rural areas these schemes can provide a service where other alternatives are few and very far between. The danger as with longer term foster care is feelings of guilt in the natural family that another family can cope where they cannot. Most of these schemes work very well indeed but, like everything else, are not suitable for everybody.

## Type of facility

Is the facility especially and only for short-term care and therefore with a mobile population, or is it a home with some short-term care places? It is certainly more difficult to create a stable homely environment where people are just passing through. Everyone is unsettled. Staff experience a reduction of job satisfaction when relationships with the children are so transient, and it often means a high turnover of staff. They, too, are just passing through.

These problems are perhaps lessened where there is a common factor, e.g. the facility is linked to a school. If the facility is a home for a number of long-staying children, how are they affected by a continual stream of others coming and going again? It can be a fairly unsettling experience not to know who you may be sharing your bedroom with each night. It is heartbreaking and unfair if a child's prized possessions are inadvertently smashed, misused or lost by a visitor, and great care should be taken to see that these are protected. The resident children will cope much better with some privacy. If, for example, there is a special visitor's bedroom, the 'long-stay' children will be more prepared to share the communal rooms of the house.

In a local scheme the children will become regular visitors and perhaps ultimately friends, which does help to alleviate the isolation often expressed by children who are handicapped. Their school friends often come from a wide local area and rarely live next door or even in the same street which may be the experience of their brothers and sisters.

## Settling in

How the child settles depends as much on his reception as his suitability for that unit. Several short visits, at least one with his parents, will often ease the way for him and those already in the unit, including the staff. Some general information on the child should be available but endless pages of 'case histories' are often counterproductive. Children do not always behave in the same way at different places. Parents of normal children often say how differently their child behaves away from home, either better or worse. There is no reason to imagine that children with a handicap should be different. One such little boy stays occasionally in a local home. He is very small, plays happily and is 'no trouble' in the home. At home he is very naughty for his mother and, on seeing her, switches from being a sweet little boy to a little fiend, slapping her around the face.

Sometimes, noisy or overactive children can be a real trial, say, in a small council house, but in larger, safely enclosed grounds with more space they present no problems at all. Parents feel safe, too, with the security of these grounds. Sometimes, of course, this can work the other way; through anxiety or whatever reason, the child is more difficult, more upset or behaves differently.

A key worker helps to ease the passage for a child entering a new environment. Even in small homes everyone will be new to the child, as will the routine, where to find things and whom to ask for what. It can become an added anxiety for him. This can be alleviated by having one person admitting the child, taking a particular interest in him during the day, giving him someone to relate to, and who will be available the next time he comes to stay. A key worker is more able to maintain many rituals of home, play in the bath, bedtime stories and the like. Obviously, the child will not be in that person's sole charge, but a key worker system will give him someone to relate to. This will be more important to some children than to others.

## Staff attitudes

What of staff attitudes to these youngsters, and to their families? A parent once related her experiences with her son Geoffrey. He was a very difficult little boy, and this was why his mother needed a break. At one short-term care unit, the staff seemed to wait together for her return to collect Geoffrey. They were ready with a catalogue of his misdeeds for the day. She so dreaded collecting him that the break was hardly worthwhile. She often cried all the way home. The alternative extreme, where the staff comment in a fairly superior way that 'Of course, he's no trouble here' is equally unhelpful. Honesty is needed, but in a constructive and positive way, with a view to working together with the parents to help the child.

What is the programme of the facility? Will the child play inside or out? Is it just a minding service with supervision or can he be absorbed into the normal routine of the home? This may include play and also helping to prepare lunch, if residents do that. During holiday times some units run special play activities or outings. The school holidays are very long for all children and they are sometimes bored. Children with handicaps who are often isolated from their friends can find holidays very long indeed.

Will there be one place for short-term care for the child or a variety? Sometimes parents are pushed to use a variety of facilities to get enough breaks. Ideally, it is of more benefit to the child to pursue one alternative if this is able to provide the appropriate quantity of care needed. A regulated amount of, say, one weekend in four may be too much for one family and not enough for another. Parents of an active and possibly destructive child who sleeps little are clearly going to need more breaks and support, yet these are often the families who have difficulty in obtaining *any* breaks. One hears stories of families going further and further afield in search of facilities, or of total family breakdown.

## Who pays?

The NHS has always provided a free service and, until recently, so have local authority social services. Some authorities are now means-testing families for a contribution to care in one of their homes. Voluntary homes or charities have always had to make a charge to make ends meet. The cost of these placements are borne by the NHS and local authority social services, raised through joint funding or other more personal sponsorship schemes. Sometimes they are paid by the parents. In any case, lack of funds should not be the deciding factor in short-term care.

## Plus points

What is it, then, that makes a good facility for short-term care?

- A local, easily accessible place in the community.
- Flexibility: in the length of care offered (can it be hours or weeks?); in booking arrangements (a planned holiday or an emergency at two hours' notice); in daily programmes within the facility to meet individual needs.
- Quality of care: a child-centred place, not staff- or organization-centred. One where the child has a full, interesting and stimulating day, and which is safe and free from unnecessary risk.
- Recognition of individuality – where the child is accepted, foibles and all. Where rituals of home are continued, i.e. where he can wear a blue hat in bed if he wants to. Where individual training programmes can be continued.
- Involvement of parents – where they can feel accepted and part of a team, and not failures.

Short-term care should be a positive experience for both the child and his family and flexible enough to meet real need without deskilling the family.

## GOING AWAY TO SCHOOL

Boarding schools have made a major contribution to the field of mental handicap. Many cater for special behaviours such as autism or other special needs such as cerebral palsy. These schools have developed as centres of expertise. They are staff-intensive, with most therapies available. Usually this means the therapist, e.g. speech or physiotherapist, is on the staff and available to contribute to individual programmes. This compares very favourably with local schools, where such therapists are only available for a limited number of sessions each week.

Boarding schools are of necessity highly structured and geared to help the student make maximum use of his abilities, as well as to provide a basic education. Since the 1981 Education Act made provision for the education of children who are handicapped to remain at school until 19 years,[3] new units have been springing up everywhere, and established schools have developed a 'further education unit' to cater for the 16 to 19 age group.

It is something of an anomaly that the residential aspects of schools come under different regulations to those now applicable to residential homes in the community. Schools, for example, are still able to use dormitories or at least multiple (four to six) occupancy rooms, whereas these are not acceptable in homes. To be fair, most boarding schools have now established smaller 'family units' within the school.

One of the difficulties confronting boarding schools serving a special need is that they can only be in one place and have a wide catchment area or perhaps no catchment area at all. These schools are scattered across the country. The children, then, are likely to have little in common, save their handicap. It means most children attending are a long way from home.

Most schools encourage parental involvement and hold open days, fête days and so on, but it can be difficult to maintain close links from a distance. For example, parents travelling from Surrey to Shropshire will be unable to visit every weekend, if they are able to visit mid-term at all. Equally, for the child it is not possible to have school friends home to tea. During school holidays they are long way from most of their school friends, who could be scattered the length and breadth of the country. During absences at school, these children lose touch with local friends. They can only attend local clubs in holiday times and they often close for the holidays. Sometimes a local group provides a holiday play scheme, but this is not always the case, and often it is a different group of children attending the group each day.

It is ironic that schools taking some of the most difficult children have such long holidays. This has meant long unrelieved periods for the family and boredom for the child, often with disastrous results. It must be noted, however, that some schools are now staying open most of the year, and although the school itself is closed, the family groups continue with a holiday programme. For some children unable to return home, the holidays mean admission to some short-term care facility. Sadly, this is not always the same place. Indeed, sometimes it is a different place for each holiday or, even worse, several places during a long holiday. This is a most unsettling experience for any child, who must feel rejected travelling from pillar to post. It usually also means a lack of continuity in development, a loss of skills achieved, lack of continuity of work begun at school and no support from local services which will not know the child.

Where these schools are some distance from home, there is a danger that the local services forget them. There is no follow-up locally in the child's progress and no plans made for his return. In many cases this has caused a crisis when the child is only weeks away from leaving school. The other danger comes from within the family who have learned to live without the child for perhaps many years. The child's return may bring a crisis of reacceptance and organization within the family, or perhaps a total nonacceptance of his return. The children attending vocational training courses may be disappointed to discover there is no opportunity for them to use their new skills on their return home. Indeed, the only place available to them may be at the local day centre or social education centre where they become involved in a much broader curriculum.

In essence, what is needed is a co-ordinated service between the boarding school and the child's home to make the best use of his newly acquired and hard-earned skills.

## ALTERNATIVE PARENTS

Foster parents provide a much-needed service. For many children, the opportunity to live in a warm loving home meets a basic need and provides an environment in which to grow and develop their potential. Every effort to find suitable foster parents for these children must be made. It is important to find the right parents for each child, and not just a family because it is a family. However, foster care is not the answer for every child. Others perhaps more damaged by life's experiences will need the 'space' of a less emotionally demanding environment and may never settle with foster parents. Alternatives should be available for these children.

Foster care is currently the most sought-after residential care for children for both respite and substitute family care. This section will concentrate on the long-term aspects of foster care.

In at least one local authority, foster care is encompassed in the philosophy that every child has a right to a family. Consequently, this authority (and some others) are closing most of their children's homes and placing all children needing residential care with foster parents. What happens if the fostering breaks down or, even worse, repeatedly breaks down? Are there then no other alternatives for the child? When one alternative is pursued with such intensity it must create an anxiety about the arrival of yet another fashion of child care. Even though it is admirable for some, individuals can be lost in pursuit of a principle.

Indeed, it is sad to learn the story of Alfred, a severely handicapped boy aged nine who is overactive and destructive, but loved by his family. Currently, he lives five days a week in a children's home and returns to his parents most weekends. They brace themselves for this, stripping their home of all that is breakable and devoting all their time to his care. This has worked well for some years. The family has been presented with an ultimatum by the local authority that either they have him home full time or he will go into foster care for adoption, with or without their consent. What distress and despair this has caused everyone.

Mothers of now adults who have Down's Syndrome have related how 20 years ago when their children were very young, pressure was put on them both medically and socially, to place their child in an institution for the mentally subnormal. This was the best thing and, indeed, the *only* thing to do for the child because he had Down's Syndrome. Many complied reluctantly. We do not seem to have come much further on if we are now insisting on foster care for children *because* they are children.

Foster care undoubtedly should give children the opportunity for the nearest experience to growing up in their natural family. However, life is never as simple as that. There are many things to be taken into consideration for foster care to work successfully. That we do not always get it right is borne out by figures released over recent years where the breakdown of fostering arrangements has been as high as 50 per cent. Optimists will say that the other 50 per cent are presumably working well. Let us consider for a moment the people involved in a fostering arrangement.

## The child

Inevitably, there will be many variations because children are individuals and should be recognized as being people with particular needs. Each child will have his own culture or subcultural background. What is his age and ability to understand or express his feelings? What is his life experience so far and his perception of it? What is the range of his handicap? What is his relationship with his natural family and will contact be maintained? Is it desirable to maintain it? Will he be listened to? Even the most profoundly handicapped children have feelings. They deserve the dignity of having a variety of choices available.

## Natural parents

The attitude of the natural parents will be governed by the circumstances leading to the need for alternative residential care for their child. Often foster parents come from different social backgrounds and value systems and it is important to match foster parents with the expectations and experiences of the child. Parents have anxieties about their child being shuttled about by changing circumstances or by the prospect of a succession of foster parents. They may well feel guilty that another family can cope while they cannot, and this produces an awkwardness or aggressiveness with the foster parents, or they may stop visiting altogether. There is always a major difficulty in cases where the wishes of the parents conflict with the needs of the child.

## Foster parents

What do we need to know about foster parents? What are we and they looking for? It is not so very long ago that a prospective foster family was deemed substandard (as regards cleanliness and accommodation) for a nonhandicapped child but acceptable for a handicapped one. What is the expectation of the foster parents? What is their knowledge of the individual needs of the child, and what these will mean to the family as a whole?

Many authorities run teaching and support groups to alleviate these problems before the child is placed and afterwards. But still there are children like David, a boy with a mental handicap who was placed with an intellectually gifted family of academic background. The parents and natural children are gifted achievers and David will always be last, and outstandingly so where the expectation is an intellectual achievement. One wonders what perception David has of himself.

What will be the attitude of the foster parents to the natural parents? There are many cases of conflict, of resentment – a silent accusation for some and for those who work together as a team, as we have seen in the Link schemes (see 'Taking a break', page 225). Some foster parents will resent interference and criticism, sometimes rightly so.

Foster families need the same professional support as natural parents. They will need access to and guidance from CMHTs, links with self-help groups such as MENCAP, Contact a Family and so on, and also short-term care.

This section will not conclude with a list that, once followed, will provide perfect foster parents for each child. Children are individuals. It is incredibly difficult to find the right family for a particular child and ensure ongoing success. Some of the most carefully planned arrangements have not worked. Others look nonstarters on paper but work amazingly well. There is no doubt that fostering may provide a necessary and preferred alternative for some families, but other children will require a different placement. Foster care should be provided as one of several options available to families, and never presented to the exclusion of any other.

# A HOME FROM HOME

'Community care' is the catch phrase of the moment. Hospitals are no longer accepting children for long-term admission. Placements for those children who need residential care are now sought in small homes in the community or in foster care. What is meant by community care? It is more than the acquisition of a house in a residential suburb. Considerable effort is needed if the residents of these homes are to be a part of the local community and not apart from it. What of life within these homes? Will we be able to offer a homely atmosphere with a quality of life worth having, or will they become mini-institutions with residents' needs coming second to those of the institution?

Another popular, and by now well-worn, word is 'normalization'. Everyone seems to agree that it is a good idea to have a normal lifestyle instead of a regulated institutional one. Government papers, reports and professionals all talk about giving those in residential care a normal home life and everyday opportunities. The recent *Home Life* report gave much consideration to the provision of space, privacy, dignity and safe care.[6] But this report was based on a study of the needs of the elderly. The 1984 Registered Homes Act, developed from the report, has been accepted as a basic requirement for all those in residential care, including the elderly, children, handicapped and so on.[7] This has produced both confusion and differing standards by local authorities in their interpretation of the Act. It is ironic, then, that the legislation designed to improve the quality of life for people in residential care makes normal homelife nearly impossible.

Under the Act, all homes with four or more residents must be registered with the local authority. In creating homes for children who are handicapped, one is confronted with a veritable bevy of legislation which drops like a lead weight on preparations, flattening both aspirations and enthusiasm at a stroke.

The registering officer for the local authority will require single rooms of specified sizes with a wash handbasin in each room. The actual specifications vary between local authorities, as do the number of double rooms accepted; none, however, accept multiple occupancy rooms. How many ordinary families are able to provide single rooms with wash handbasins for their children? Children have different needs for privacy from those of the elderly, and some can be very frightened in a room on their own. Registration also requires notice boards in the corridors showing liability insurance, visiting hours, fire notices and the registration certificate. There should be an office for confidential visits, a call bell or indicator beside each bed and in toilets and bathrooms, and a satisfactory report from both the environmental health officer and the fire officer.

The environmental health officer will require such things as protective clothing for those working in the kitchen (aprons are not always acceptable), separate staff toilets (will this mean different standards?) and stainless steel cupboards in the kitchen. One officer has been heard to say in at least one home recently that 'the handicapped should *not* be in the kitchen as they obstruct the employees'.

The fire prevention officer has his own ideas on safety, and may require blanket cupboards to be locked (limiting the independence of the children), smoke detectors, emergency lighting, signed fire exits (can the residents read?), fire-retardant curtains, furniture and bedding, and fire doors that are often impossible to open from a wheelchair.

It is difficult to imagine how to create a 'home' under the weight of all this bureaucracy. Given that it is just possible to steer a course through these regulations and survive, what other factors need to be taken into account when setting up a home?

## Locality

Hopefully, one priority will be to situate the home(s) within an area where the families to be served are able to visit without having to travel miles and miles to do so. Other members of the family will also be able to visit and other local friendships maintained. The community team, who will already know the child, can keep a supportive link not only with him but also with his family and the residential staff. Schooling could continue with little disruption, as could his development of independence in the community.

# Numbers

There can be no set rules about how many children should live together. Smaller units (four to six residents) will give more individual attention, but provision of short-term care becomes intrusive. Staffing can be a problem. Larger units (8 to 12) can be more flexible about offering short-term care without encroaching on the privacy of the resident children. Some would argue that larger units are perhaps economically more viable, especially for very dependent children. They need not be institutional. There is room for both types of facility. While children are individuals and have different needs, a variety of facilities is essential.

# Age range

There are many stories to be heard about where a handicapped child (or young teenager) has ended up on a geriatric ward as the only place available for care. Where we would all agree this is undesirable, it seems to have led to an overall anxiety about mixing children with adults. Growing up in a group with a mixed age range is the experience of most normal children in families. Few of them grow up without some older people around. Neither do they find themselves bound by rules about leaving home based on age. It is very sad to see a young school leaver moved on from where he has 'grown up' because he has reached the chronological age to do so. His bed is then filled so there can be little recourse to returning for a weekend as other youngsters might to their families. For some young people it will be appropriate to leave the home, but for others it will not.

# Abilities

Will it be possible to have a range of abilities within the home – some children being very dependent, others more able? The range will be dictated partly by the size (i.e. numbers) of the home. For many years people have been labelled and categorized according to their ability level, which has in many instances failed to meet their identified needs as people. A flexible environment geared to individual need will be able to cope with this.

Children of different cultural or ethnic backgrounds need special consideration. Some groups have provided specialist homes, e.g. the

Jewish community supports the Ravenswood Village in Berkshire to continue the religious heritage of their residents. The Ockenden Venture in Surrey provides a home for refugee children. Joyce Pearce, one of the founders of Ockenden, has said: 'It is of great importance for the development of an integrated person that as many continuing links with past experiences and relationships as possible should be preserved, i.e. contact with family, friends, ethnic group and culture.'

How will individual children be selected for any particular home? Certainly, there will have been a case conference or discussion where those present (parents, social worker, teachers, members of the community team and perhaps the child himself) will be able to discuss the need for appropriate residential care, the child's needs and personality, and whether there are any problems. These should be matched with facilities in the area. Hopefully, there will be several to choose from. The managers of the prospective home should be consulted to be sure of compatability with the other children and visits made before the child is admitted. Of course, it may be that he is well known from visits for respite care, in which case admission will be easier for everyone. The other resident children will need preparation for his arrival. A child should never be admitted to any home that has a vacancy just as a matter of convenience.

Schooling is a major part of every child's day. When he comes home he will need to feel someone is interested in his day, and will help with his reading book, or help collect pictures, or continue with his training programmes. Team work with the school is essential. It is easy to slip into attitudes of either 'we know him best' or 'we have the expertise, of course'. This does happen and strong feelings develop between school and home. Blinkered views may persist.

Links with the school need to be strong, open and constructive, always viewing the development of the whole child. It is always important to attend school functions such as plays, fêtes and parties, as well as case reviews. It is also important to invite the teachers home for either discussion or to join in some festive occasion.

A child should have the opportunity to develop individual interests, for example, within appropriate clubs and associations within the local community (Scouts, Gateway Clubs, swimming clubs and churches). Some older children may be able to undertake the Duke of Edinburgh Award. A number of quite severely handicapped young people have done this with great triumph. Some youngsters may just like to go to the local cinema. For those with a physical handicap, this presents some problems. According to regulations governing cinemas, wheelchairs are not allowed in. A handicapped child would need to sit in an ordinary seat and take his wheelchair out into the foyer. Difficult if you can't walk! It does mean that if they go at all, they cannot go alone. It also means that though the aisles may be clear in case of a fire, the child will be confined to his seat.

The temptation, especially with a small group, is to do most things together. It is certainly a saving on staff time and on transport, but reduces the individuality and independence of the child, and often 'labels' the group, i.e. 'Here come the home's kids'. Where there are problems of transport, often the clubs themselves can help or transport can be shared.

Similarly, where it is easier to have a hairdresser come in one day and cut everyone's hair, it is of more benefit to the child to arrange an appointment at the local hairdressing salon, or call at the local barber, in ones and twos while out shopping. Many local dentists will take the children onto their patient lists and there is no need to go through hospital appointments.

Participation in ordinary 'chores' at home and shopping is another normal experience necessary in the general development of children. It is much easier to shop in bulk (and often cheaper) where there is a group of people living together. Many homes hold a 'cash and carry' card, or have weekly deliveries of perishables. Some allowances can be made, however, for local shopping expeditions where children can help.

## STAFF

Staff managing children's homes in the community need to be skilled and flexible. Over recent years there has been a dramatic and necessary improvement in working hours and conditions for those working in residential establishments, both for nurses and for social workers. While this is to be applauded, such changes can also bring with them lack of continuity with the children and a fragmenting of the work, leading to lack of job satisfaction and, finally, disenchantment with residential care. For the children, it can mean constantly changing staff and, at worst, restrict the quality of their lives. For example, children at one home have been unable to attend a particular club because it coincided with a change to night staff, and transport (escort) would only be possible if evening staff stayed on for another half hour. The attitude of 'We can't go to the park today because I am off at four and we won't be back in time', should be avoided at all costs. Sadly, it is not unusual. What perception does this give the child of himself? Who are the staff working for anyway? It is possible with a flexible approach, thought and some initiative to resolve these problems, but it is dependent on a team spirit and enthusiasm within the home; it cannot be imposed from without. It is also dependent on a child-centred attitude to life in the home.

The other end of the scale means that staff are simply worn out. Subjected to very long hours, the continual physical and emotional demands of children, the enormity of the job and feelings of lack of support, staff become unable to give any more of themselves and become 'burnt out'. Somewhere, there needs to be a middle path between these two.

Staff have needs too, especially when managing very difficult children. Time needs to be available, perhaps while the children are at school, for supportive discussion between the staff about what they are doing and the life of the home. Other professional help, such as from the district handicap teams should be readily available. The opportunity to attend day courses outside the home will also help in skills development. Time spent by staff members making local contacts and keeping up links with schools or parents will also make a valuable contribution to the life of the home as well as help individual children.

It is helpful if the GP for the house takes an interest and makes regular visits. But with a busy surgery, the GP may only manage to see the children when they are ill. The health visitor may be more available for supportive visits and advice.

What of the child's progress or lack of it in the home? Are regular reviews held where all those relevant to his care can be involved? The progress of the whole child can be assessed and a programme planned to tackle problem areas. It is important that all those working with the child are working together and know what they are setting about to help the child achieve.

Residential children's homes can make a very positive contribution to the development and integration of children. For too long, children's homes have been seen as a last resort, with low expectations of improvement and some stigma. With this unprofessional view and little positive input, these attitudes can be self-perpetuating. Residential children's homes should be seen as a first option and a very positive experience for some children.

# CONCLUSION

This chapter has looked at provision of residential care for children both in a family setting and in children's homes. The variety of services needed to give adequate provision for children who have a handicap, recognizing their individual needs, has been described. Sadly, the reality rarely meets the ideal. Regional and even local services provide a patchy, often fragmented, service. Facilities are few and far between. The danger here is that these facilities will be used inappropriately, especially where the cash flow dictates placement will be within local provision.

Co-ordination between the NHS, social services and the voluntary sector has been poor. Families have found themselves in the middle of disputes over criteria for admission, funding and differing support services. It is heartening to see the determined efforts in many areas to work together and present a more integrated service.

# REFERENCES

1. Exley, H. (1984) *What It's Like to be Me*, Exley Publications.
2. DHSS (1970) *The Chronically Sick and Disabled Persons Act*, HMSO, London.
3. Department of Education and Science (1981) *The Education Act – An Act to Make Provision in Respect of Children with Special Needs*, Chapter 60, HMSO, London.
4. DHSS (1976) *Fit for the Future – The Court Report*, Vol. 1, Cmnd 6684, HMSO, London.
5. The Family Fund of the Joseph Rowntree Memorial Trust, PO Box 50, York YO3 6RB.
6. DHSS (1984) *Home Life – A Code of Practice for Residential Care*, Report of a Working Party sponsored by the DHSS and the Centre for Policy on Ageing (Chairman Kina, Lady Avebury), Centre for Policy on Ageing, London.
7. DHSS (1984) *The Registered Homes Act*, Chapter 23, HMSO, London.

# USEFUL ADDRESSES

1. Contact A Family, 16 Strutton Ground, Victoria, London W1.
2. The Down's Children Association, 12–13 Clapham Common Southside, Clapham, London SW4.
2a. Kith and Kids, 61 Grosvenor Road, London SW5 2HP (Human Horizons Series, Collins).
3. The Junior Gateway Club, c/o The National Federation of Gateway Clubs, MENCAP, 123 Golden Lane, London EC1Y 0RT.
4. The Ockenden Venture, Guildford Road, Woking, Surrey.
5. Ravenswood Village Foundation, Nine Mile Ride, Crowthorne, Berkshire.
6. Royal Society for Mentally Handicapped Children and Adults (MENCAP), 123 Golden Lane, London EC1Y 0RT.

7. The Society for Autistic Children, 1a Golders Green, London NW11.
8. The Spastics Society, 15 Park Crescent, London W1.

# 10. A Dignified Life for the Older Person with Mental Handicap

*Marion Cornick*

## INTRODUCTION

We live in a society which does not value either elderly people or those with mental handicaps. Older and ageing people with mental handicaps have not been recognized as a special group until recently. This chapter looks at some of the problems of ageing, attitudes to ageing, and the special needs of this newly identified group. Several ways of meeting accommodation needs are considered, and some practical ideas are offered to fill unstimulated lives, and enhance the lifestyle with valued and meaningful activities.

## AN OVERVIEW

The change in the demographic pattern of mentally handicapped people over the last 20 years has resulted in them living so much longer. The proportion of mentally handicapped people growing up into adult and later life is steadily increasing. This is going to present a problem for the services in every country of quite frightening magnitude in the next two decades.[1]

In Britain today, elderly people suffer as an undervalued and often devalued group. To enhance the quality of life of all elderly people requires all the energies of pressure groups such as Age Concern. If the needs of this group are not yet met or recognized by society, how much greater are the needs of the elderly person with a mental handicap who suffers the 'double jeopardy' of old age and mental handicap?[2] One commentator has spoken of our unpreparedness to meet the needs of this newly identified and growing group.[3] It was suggested that special consideration should be given to all those people with mental handicaps over the age of 40 years, as their needs are going to be particularly great. The group as a whole exists in increasing numbers because of improvements in health care and medical knowledge. Previously, most of the group would not have lived into old age, and many of those who did survive would have spent their lives in long-stay hospitals where their individual needs were generally not met. Many elderly people with mental handicap are at present living at home. However, increasingly they survive their parents and their parents' ability to cope. They may well need a substitute house, and living accommodation is a major concern for this group.

Of those in hospitals and other kinds of residential care, many may be only moderately handicapped but have been institutionalized in hospitals for so long that their skills are not appropriate for community living.

## SOCIETY'S RESPONSE TO AGEING

In society, problems associated with old age such as physical disabilities, forgetfulness, slowing down and even retirement itself, are regarded as deviant, and the elderly are devalued. Our society also rewards intellectual high achievers, and dependence is viewed as scrounging and laziness.

It is always sad to watch people deteriorate as they grow old, to see loss of independence and inability, and even lack of respect and neglect by families.

It is therefore important to consider the needs of this group, develop a policy and ensure that local authorities and government departments become committed to quality care for all ageing and elderly people. Consideration should be given to the fact that they are 'people first'. In the light of our society's neglect of aged people without handicap, it is important to take a strong line and to promote the idea of high quality services. A service which does not meet needs or requirements cannot be a quality service. Perhaps services for elderly people with mental handicap can become the model for care of all elderly people. Usually services for those with a mental handicap are the last to be considered and follow progress rather than herald it.

## PRESENT PROVISION

In 1979 the Jay report quoted: 'We hope that more and more elderly people who are mentally handicapped will have recourse to normal provisions and services.'[4] In response to this and in the light of poor and limited services, MENCAP issued a paper to inform parents and professionals of their rights, needs and of the services to which the elderly are entitled.[5] The minimum standards it advocates are for a high standard of care and nothing less than is suitable for ordinary living. Several large long-stay institutions approached informally in 1986 and 1987 admitted that they make no special provision for the elderly. Some even confessed to wards full of very elderly people who have waited, or wasted, all their lives in institutions and still just sit all day every day in hospital without any programme of stimulation.

## CHALLENGES OF THIS EMERGING GROUP

The two important issues seem to be about: the identification of needs as this group emerges; and ways these needs can be met. In the light of these we can plan to offer a quality of service which is life-enhancing. Quality of care and quality of life together will assist these older people to lead their 'retired' lives with dignity, with opportunities for personal choice and with involvement in the community. There is a potential for continued development and growth throughout life and it is never too late to allow people personal control and power over their own lives. However small the amount of personal control, it should be respected.

Apart from the ageing process which affects and limits all older people, there are influences such as the attitude of society, the needs of the carer and the family, income, mobility and opportunities for developing relationships which offer ongoing personal growth.

## 'NORMALIZATION' AND THE ELDERLY PERSON WITH MENTAL HANDICAP

The normalization principle means making available to all mentally handicapped people patterns of life and conditions of everyday living which are as close as possible to the regular circumstances and ways of life of society.[6] (See also Chapter 2.)

The juxtaposition of retarded and nonretarded elderly people can do little to enhance the image of the retarded ones, but could do much to impair the image of the nonretarded ones.[7]

'Social role valorization' considers it is not enough to give people dignity and respect by taking out the 'dehumanizing' features in their lives.[8] It is important to make positive efforts in all services to be sure people have real opportunities for choice, for expression of individuality and for positive personal relationships.

As we get older our social expectations, opportunities and experience of self, change. The rhythms of our day, week and year change as increasing age brings higher expectations for responsible behaviour. People with mental handicap have difficulty in responding to such change in much the same way as they have difficulty in learning new ideas and skills. Carers should develop strategies to support them through these stages of development and to encourage them to leave dolls, toys, and childish activities behind. This is particularly the case when considering the lifestyle of ageing people. Many will have been deprived all their lives of age-appropriate opportunities. There is a continuing need to encourage many and varied experiences so that people can make choices which give dignity. This principle of normalization has implications when considering services for elderly people, and provides a useful framework for exploring and developing practical ideas to meet their needs and the needs of other similarly devalued groups.

## IDENTIFYING NEEDS

Older and ageing people with mental handicap have often had a lifetime of experiences of being controlled, managed, misunderstood, ignored and dominated.[9,10,11,12] Frequently, people with a mental handicap have been denied choice even about such everyday needs as clothes and food. Therefore, it seems important to ask these people about their needs and the kind of life they look forward to in retirement. A series of interviews with 25 ageing people with mental handicap revealed the following needs in priority order:[13]

- The need for more money.
- The need for a close friend; for someone with whom to share personal problems; and the needs for special and intimate relationships.
- The need for more opportunities for outings and recreation.

- The need for more understanding of death, dying, bereavement and loss, for opportunities for reminiscence and for help with spiritual matters.
- The need for literacy classes, readable books and improved communication skills. These need to be met in more interesting day centres.
- The need for meaningful employment.
- The need for advice on health and fitness, including nutrition, and sexuality.
- The need for autonomy and independence (supported by key workers if necessary).
- The need for special help in times of stress and worry, particularly about changes and relocation.
- The need for assurances over privacy and confidentiality.

In addition to the needs actually expressed by ageing and elderly people with mental handicaps, there are other areas of concern to be identified. A list of needs has been compiled that are common to all ageing people.[14] If we are committed to normalization, these needs become the needs of elderly people with mental handicap.

## To render some socially useful service

The author of this list of needs suggests that all older people have a need to render some socially useful service. Certainly this is not a concept often considered in the field of mental handicap, and yet in the light of the concept of social role valorization,[7] there is a need for elderly people with mental handicap to feel a sense of dignity; to be valued members of this group; to express needs; to be actively useful and involved in the community. Advocates and facilitators should be responsive to this need and creative in developing useful, locally based opportunities.

## To be considered part of the community

Writers in the USA[7,15,16,17] and in Great Britain[3,18,19,20] suggest there should be facilities in the community for people with mental handicap to use. One such writer suggests that there should be an active involvement in the life of the neighbourhood and the wider community.[19] He advocates the development of local social networks. Access to leisure facilities, community programmes and opportunities to mix with people of their own age in the normal statutory and voluntary services for the elderly, are other ideas suggested.

## To occupy leisure time in satisfying ways

The use of adult-appropriate materials and equipment has been recommended for leisure use in line with encouragement to give access to a normal lifestyle.[7] One researcher has found that the elderly people enjoyed doing the kind of things that most elderly people do, such as knitting, sewing, rugmaking, watching TV, listening to music or the radio, gardening and reading books and magazines.[12] Most of them attended social clubs for the elderly or Gateway Clubs for people with mental handicaps. It was noted that although these elderly people make use of community facilities such as pubs, churches, clubs and cafés, few have established any reciprocal social relationships among nonhandicapped members of the community since moving into the project outside of the long-stay hospital. Another worker suggests that caregivers should actively encourage daily opportunities for a variety of leisure activities;[15] yet another emphasizes the need to encourage people to join in.[21]

Attending functions does not ensure integration or participation, as people may maintain 'observer-status', lacking the confidence to join in and make contact with others. A need has been suggested for a variety of provision both specifically for mentally handicapped and in the community.[22] There should be alternatives to daily attendance at an ATC, which reflect age-related interests and individual stimulation.[3,9]

## To enjoy normal companionships

Loneliness and being isolated and separated from family and friends are hazards encountered by all elderly people, and the need for all older people to enjoy companionship has been emphasized.[14] Other workers are aware of the additional needs of the elderly person with mental handicap to maintain friendships.[2] People in this group will have had difficulty making relationships and it is therefore important that friendships are recognized and supported. One concern is the 'affectionate attachments' are respected and that when there is separation by death or relocation, counselling and help are available.[11] The need to grieve has been given little attention in the field of mental handicap and many people have had to continue with their normal daily activities following the news of the death of parents or family.[11]

MENCAP has published a series of papers to inform parents of their rights and the services to which they are entitled.[5] They remind us that it is important to recognize that people who are mentally handicapped are 'people first'. They have individual needs and may have additional special needs. MENCAP recommends that a 'named person' should be appointed to give particular attention to counselling in the event of bereavement. MENCAP also advises that those who are moved residentially need to be cared for sensitively, particularly if they move into hostels following the loss of parents. All their relationships and companions may have disappeared overnight. Their feelings, likes and dislikes should be acknowledged and their wishes ascertained sympathetically and with sensitivity. The support of an advocate from the local MENCAP society should be considered if there are no living relatives, and particular care should be taken to avoid loneliness.

## For recognition as an individual

The MENCAP paper[5] goes on to recommend an annual review for every adult with a mental handicap. The people themselves should participate in this review. Many workers have stressed the need to avoid labelling people as people with mental handicap, as this encourages group identity rather than personal recognition.[7,17,20,22] The idea of age-appropriateness and the concept of 'the eternal child' has also been focused upon.[17] An acknowledgement of a personal identity developed throughout life and a recognition for its individuality seem to be the most important concepts.

## For opportunities for self-expression

Elderly people with mental handicap need age-appropriate activities and lifestyle, with scope for independent action and free choice. The need for a key worker is supported by the Campaign for the Mentally Handicapped (CMH)[10] and MENCAP[5] so that individuals have an opportunity to express their feelings and needs to someone they trust and know well. Personal possessions, opportunities for self-advocacy, and making choices enables people to lead fulfilled lives which reflect their individual character and personality. Many have strongly supported measures to give an enhanced ordinary life to include particularly choice, decision-making, self-advocacy and being valued.[7,11,17,22,23]

## For health protection and care

All generic services should be available to this group, with particular attention to chiropody, dentistry, orthopaedics and the services of the local GP. Over and above this kind of service, it is important to recognize that ageing people with mental handicaps often have additional physical handicaps which cause increasing concern with age. In particular, the profoundly and multiply handicapped who now live longer lives and will certainly require additional medical support.[15] It is important to be aware of ageing processes and to adopt specific strategies to preserve physical well-being, such as exercise, diet and activity.

## For suitable mental stimulation

Mental stimulation for the ordinary retired person is of considerable importance for those who have had active professional lives followed abruptly by retirement.[14] Many elderly people with mental handicap will have had very unstimulating lives, but one study showed that this group does respond to mental stimulation and can indeed go on learning.[18] It has been recommended that day activities and opportunities for learning should ensure 'increasing competence in life-skills'.[19] Preparation-for-retirement classes have been successful in some areas. One pre-retirement course has started up under the auspices of the Workers' Educational Association in Salisbury.[24] The organizer's conclusions are that, 'although stimulation is possible, and interest can be aroused, and involvement can be encouraged, the greatest needs are for support, for direction and for security'.

A worthwhile job and further education have been suggested in spite of the person being elderly,[16] and this concept is certainly reflected in the needs expressed by the group themselves when interviewed. Attendance at clubs, day centres, ATCs and specific attention to aesthetic needs are mentioned by other workers.[3,5,10,25] The needs have been summed up by saying that most people with mental handicap will have spent their lives on poor programmes, which have offered no challenge, and usually only for short periods.[7] 'Utter inactivity' will have been their usual experience. Retirement will officially give 'such disgraceful practices legitimacy'.

Again, activity is recommended, as is enhancement of skills and a 'positive image both in their own eyes and in the view of others that comes with being a productive contributive worker'. There are no guidelines produced for such a programme and such centres that do exist seem to be pioneering projects still in their infancy.

## For living arrangements

An increasing number of people with mental handicaps now live in ordinary houses in the community. Some area health authorities have adopted a policy to close their long-stay hospitals quickly. Other authorities are being more cautious. At present, these people live in a variety of residential settings including, a home with their own family, a foster family, their own home, hostels, group homes and hospital. Elderly people with mental handicap have not generally been the priority for community placement, but some projects have specifically included the elderly. One particular study of 19 older people provides an example of an evaluation of Bath District Health Authority's 'Ordinary Life Project' (OLP) for elderly people with a mental handicap.[18]

The project was set up in 1980 in accordance with the principle of normalization.[26] By October 1984, 19 elderly people had been moved into six ordinary houses in the community. This successful project depends on ensuring that the support provided by volunteers enables and facilitates the people to adapt to their new life, and to continue growth towards maximum independence. The OLP is based on the main principles documented in the King's Fund Paper *An Ordinary Life*,[27] which says that people who have a mental handicap have the same human value as anyone else and so the same human rights. They should also be free to live like others in the community. This is both a right and a need, and services must recognize the individuality of people with a mental handicap.

> The logical conclusion of these principles is that however profoundly handicapped a person is, however old, and whatever length of time they have spent in an institution, their rights and needs remain the same.[18]

The least restrictive alternative to an institution is the basic right and need. The environment should be homely, warm, secure, non-institutional, small, local, ordinary, non-segregated and support should ensure a quality of life which reflects the rhythms and patterns usual in any ordinary home.

# For family relationships

Ordinary living should reflect family life. If it is possible, accommodation should be in the family neighbourhood so that normal family relationships may be maintained. A 'family style context for life' has been advocated[23] and others too emphasize the need to maintain family relationships.[3,18] Group homes should be organized for family living and care should be taken to avoid rigid routines and the problem of transience of caregivers. Families caring for their own family member need practical and family support if the situation is not to become too difficult. This is important as the parents themselves will be elderly when their mentally handicapped offspring are ageing. Friendships with companions who are not likely to be moved to alternative accommodation should be encouraged, particularly when there are likely to be family bereavements and the loss of parents.

# For spiritual satisfaction

A dignified death and an opportunity to mourn are seen as essential, [11,23] particularly the problems people with a mental handicap have had when, in large institutions, the opportunity to grieve has not been permitted and the deaths of parents and friends have been ignored. Support is important when parents die and counselling should enable the handicapped son or daughter to talk about the death and the feelings they have, and to recognize that their response may be different from another person's: 'Grief is normal, and due consideration must be given to mentally handicapped people who are grieving.'[11]

Attendance at church, if chosen, should be facilitated, and caregivers should recognize the need for engagement in religious activities. CAMR in its survey suggests church-going as part of its citizen-advocacy programme.[28] The religious needs of the group are not generally met by the community and may well be positively neglected. One writer has commented on the barriers that further handicap religious involvement by people with mental handicap,[16] including lack of understanding by clergy, and the feelings of powerlessness of handicapped people when they find the building, the attitudes and the communication threatening. Social prejudice encourages an attitude of 'doing for' rather than 'sharing with'. One recommendation is to 'adopt a zero rejection policy' and exclude no one from the congregation.[16] The clergy, by being part of a generic community group and institution, can wield tremendous influence locally so that handicapped people may become valued members.

# HOW ARE NEEDS CURRENTLY BEING MET?

The 'normalization' lobby, the work of CMH and the development of locally based CMHTs are certainly having their effect on the lives of people with mental handicaps generally. However, specific provision for the elderly is still difficult to find. Lack of finance and limited budgets do not help in planning provision and services.

## Adult training centres/social education centres

Many ATCs are undergoing dramatic change in keeping with normalization; but few can provide a service for the elderly which is designed to enhance life and responds to the needs suggested by the group themselves. Elderly people may continue to attend full-time centres before retirement without any change of routine or preparation for retirement. On the whole, ATCs now seem to offer more opportunities for choice and personal development, but changes often seem to be centred on young people. Some of these older people will have spent their entire adult life working in these cramped and dreary buildings unless we recognize their needs now and offer a stimulating experience.

## Long-stay hospitals

Two hospitals visited still have large, open wards where up to 30 residents spend most of their time. One hospital visited now has a special ward for the elderly where there is a television, video and new furniture and fittings. However, the elderly people there still live in large groups and spend their days in the same building, waiting as they have always waited. The kind of total inactivity noted by some[29] is still very evident today. Passivity, prolonged disengagement, no worthwhile activity and little interactions all contribute to a wasted life. For example, people only follow instructions to eat, to sit, to go to bed, and there is little attempt at 'client engagement' with people or materials, and little evidence of group activities. This kind of non-engaging environment does not lead to any kind of personal empowerment which depends on encouraging people to learn by exploring their environment.

Some hospitals are making major efforts to provide stimulating surroundings for their patients during their gradual closure, and are giving residents programmed preparation for an ordinary life after discharge. Some hospitals have developed particular education programmes to teach people self-help and independence skills. However, a hospital experience can never reflect true domesticity.

## An ordinary house

There are now numerous examples of elderly people living in ordinary houses in ordinary streets. Five or six people may live together in each home and probably have recently been discharged from health authority supervision. Four of the people in one such house had spent much of their lives in long-stay hospitals. Their house was situated in the locality of their birth. They all had their own rooms, tastefully furnished with good quality non-institutional furniture and decorations of their own choice. There was an *en suite* bathroom for the oldest retired lady. The group in one house was supported by 11 staff who worked in three shifts and covered sleeping-in at night. The residents managed their own post office accounts and paid their own share of the rent, overheads and food bill. The remainder was used for clothes, holidays and pocket money. Key workers helped residents to manage their accounts at the local post office.

The aim of these kind of projects is to provide as ordinary a life as possible with the minimum degree of support needed to maintain and encourage as much independence as possible. Within the household, the chores, the meals, shopping and gardening are all activities in which the residents can actively participate. After six months in one project there is some concern at the level of engagement throughout the day; it seems that additional 'day activities' may still be needed to maintain the programme, in addition to the individual outings and activities that they organize and choose with their key workers.

Projects such as these are often criticized for providing an isolated and isolating life outside the hospital away from leisure resources and lifetime friends. However, one lady in such a house recently had a birthday and staff were amazed at the number of local people who visited her that day, demonstrating that she had made her own friends in the neighbourhood during the six months she had lived there.

# A hostel in the community

Several of the people interviewed were residents in a local authority social services hostel. The hostel is purpose-built and caters for 25 people of all ages, who have rooms of their own or share with one other person. The hostel is a friendly, homely place in spite of its size, and the residents were most outgoing and relaxed. The staff were themselves very relaxed and had created an environment which allowed for a wide variety of tastes and activities without being over-structured or too organized and still maintaining a degree of domesticity. All the elderly residents interviewed, including three over 70, expressed a desire to stay there permanently and never to move. They all felt a strong bond of affection for the head of home and his wife, and all obviously felt that at last they belonged somewhere. Some said they had never felt so happy and well in all their lives.

Although this hostel would be classed as an institution because of its size, its large kitchen, its multi-purpose rooms and its office, it certainly met most of the needs of the people who lived there, probably largely due to the quality of staffing. The residents were able to chat confidently about their early lives, even describing harsh treatment in detail, hospitalization and rejection; but few pressing immediate needs were expressed by the five people interviewed by this author. They wished they had had a chance to be married, but enjoyed friendships now and led full, busy lives as far as health permitted, and enjoyed the active support of the staff.

# Ravenswood village

Ravenswood is a Jewish 'village' which caters for the needs of 170 people of all ages with severe mental handicaps. The village is largely organized into households of about 10 residents with care staff. There is one hostel for 25 residents and 10 residents live in flatlets with their own front-door keys. There are 21 people over the age of 40, and 12 people of 45 years of age scattered throughout the various kinds of accommodation. During 1985, the author was able to develop a club-type meeting for those over the age of 45 which they called '45+'. These people had had little experience of group work as they had previously attended a formal ATC, where the emphasis was on contract work, which they found boring and very repetitive.

The group sessions include opportunities to continue their education. They enjoy specific literacy sessions and associated skill-based learning activities. For example, handwriting, typing, coin-recognition and money management. They regret the earlier lack of this kind of education, but demonstrate that it is never too late to learn. Attention to domestic skills such as cookery, homemaking, repairs to clothing and self-help and self-care skills are also part of the curriculum.

In this group setting, health needs of a general kind can be discussed. Personal needs can be recognized and met as they arise. The chiropodist, community nurse, GP, optician and physiotherapist are all easily available to meet personal and individual needs.

The group expressed particular needs for volunteer personal friends who will write to them, visit, invite them out for tea and be especially important during inevitable separations from their own families as parents become very elderly and die.

A cultural adviser/volunteer co-ordinator has now been appointed by the organization to help meet these kinds of needs, particularly to link more observant Jewish residents with similar volunteer friends. Opportunities for reminiscence, personal counselling and meaningful employment have also been part of the service offered to the group. Nine out of the 12 now work for at least part of the week and are paid. Jobs range from laundry work to cleaning the synagogue and milk delivery. Ideas developed for these groups form part of the proposal for services needed for the group as a whole.

# WHAT KIND OF SERVICE SHOULD BE PROVIDED?

As workers we can't guarantee happiness for those with whom we work, or good health or agreeable company, or that birthdays will be remembered, or that Christmas wish lists will ever be read, or that families will continue to visit. But we ought to be able to guarantee the right to meaningful activity, the right to as much independence as possible, the right to participate in making choices that will affect our individual's life and the right to retire with dignity and respect.[30]

In the future, with the development of community-based programmes, support networks and less restrictive settings, there may well be fewer dependent people who have become victims of 'learned helplessness'.[31] However, regardless of the level of dependency throughout life, all adults come to old age and are affected by the biological, social and psychological aspects of the ageing process. Each person is affected as an individual and his/her needs are unique. The elderly person with mental handicap is unlikely to have developed the network of support gained through family life, a life at work and through living in a community.

## Physical needs

The basic physical needs of this group have generally been met, even if inappropriately, in terms of shelter, food and clothing. However, meeting physical needs alone is inadequate for any elderly person. The elderly person with mental handicap may never have enjoyed independence or personal fulfilment and it is, therefore, a particular duty that we as a society be prepared to support an enhanced lifestyle for the remaining years of an elderly person's life.

The need for a valued life, lived in an ordinary house, is considered in greater detail elsewhere in this book. Elderly people are no different in their need of this kind of accommodation in their own natural community, supported by a network of services, a key worker and friends.

However, there should be due consideration given to the need for appropriate adapted accommodation requirements as people become older. Architects and planners need to be aware that elderly people with mental handicaps will need buildings with ground floor accommodation and special individual design features. The occupational therapist should be used as an adviser when buildings are planned, and to contribute expertise and skills as needs change.

## Non-physical needs

A 'consumer-led' kind of service considering the individual needs of clients leads to personal empowerment and some control over the running of independent lives. Informed choice based on education, socialization, integration and wide experience, lead to a lifestyle chosen from a range of options. A support system including a multiprofessional staff network, adequate funding and an evaluation procedure are essential to ensure an adequate service.

In one writer's terms, only the initial stages of life, safety and security have been considered in the past in services available to people with mental handicap.[32] The development of a network of support which is underpinned by a commitment to a normal lifestyle should encourage independence, autonomy and personal dignity. The personal advocate or key worker becomes the crucial link in the network. The relationship with the key worker ensures that as personal needs are identified, they can be met by the appropriate professional link worker in the network. This group of people needs concrete support and actions, rather than philosophical theories with no practical basis if the local network is to lead to an enhanced, valued life.

The kinds of needs often expressed by the ageing do not necessarily reflect their age or the ageing process. Their immediate needs are largely the resources and facilities we in our society take for granted, but are areas of deprivation for them. The following are areas for particular consideration, however.

### Early onset of ageing

Presenile dementia (Alzheimer's syndrome) is often a problem for people with Down's Syndrome and symptoms may be evident as early as the age of 40. Symptoms may include dramatic behavioural changes, progressive deterioration of memory and cognition that culminates in a state very like profound retardation, signs of accelerated physical ageing and a rapid slowing down.

### Illness and injury

It is likely that elderly people with mental handicap will have a greater susceptibility to infection, and recovery will take longer than in early life. The prevention of further handicaps by attention to minor problems should be a major serious consideration. As life expectancy increases, the physical handicaps which often accompany mental handicap may well be accentuated. Added to the problems of normal physical ageing such as arthritis, there will be an increase in the primary health care service requirements.

### Bereavement and loss

Bereavement is a subject which is still taboo for most of society. Certainly in the field of mental handicap it is a subject which is only now beginning to receive attention as carers become increasingly aware of the feelings of people with mental handicap. Accounts have been written of people with mental handicap being denied the opportunity to know of the death of a parent, to grieve for parents or to discuss their feelings.[11] Thus guidelines have been produced for staff and those with mental handicap to explain the stages of grieving and the likely feelings.

The death of a parent often means the loss of a home, personal possessions, neighbourhood, friends and ATC when the son or daughter has a mental handicap. They may find themselves immediately in the care of the social services and away from their own house for the first time ever. They may be sent to a hostel or home miles away, whose routine they do not know and where they and their needs are not known. Careful counselling both at this time and in lifeskills workshops throughout their lives is essential to health and well being.

Local health education departments often have helpful resources. Experience has shown that euphemisms and indirect, complex use of language are unhelpful. The handicapped person needs to be afforded the dignity of grieving appropriately, including attendance at funerals and memorial services. Special keepsakes are also important.

Similarly, the dying person with a mental handicap is entitled to honest and sensitive counselling and support from carers, who should themselves be supported. Bereavement, grief, loss and mourning all need sensitive management to ensure awareness not only when there is a death but also when there is a loss such as staff leaving, others in the group moving, changes in routine, unexpected loss of possessions and even changes in plans for recreation. The problem of adjustment to change is further increased if an awareness of language level and comprehension is not understood by the counsellor. This kind of training, using a workshop counselling course, should be an established part of the curriculum for all adults with mental handicap, and is certainly an essential component of any pre-retirement course. Experienced speech therapists and occupational therapists may be helpful if such courses are planned.

### The use of reminiscence
One writer indicates that it is normal and necessary for everyone to reminisce.[33] Stress seems to be less of a problem to people who are able to recall the past; people also seem to approach old age with greater self-confidence and a strong concept of self if memories are encouraged. Memory of past events may be triggered by such things as smells, music, pictures, objects and by sharing in conversation.

Many elderly people with mental handicap have never been given the opportunity to share the past, which may include for them some painful memories. For some it is difficult to express feelings about these memories, because of limited language. However, the use of photographs, music, pictures, and family momentoes can enable them to share in their 'life review' and to feel a sense of identity.

Elderly people are as likely as anyone to become depressed, particularly if they have been moved without careful planning and preparation.

The problems associated with stress and depression may well be lessened if reminiscence is used as therapy.[34]

We tend to share special events with our families and collect momentoes in order to remember them. Photographs, newspaper cuttings and gifts act as 'pegs' so that we can bring order to our lives. Such momentoes are often seen as valueless in institutional life and so older people may not take treasured possessions from home to home. Photograph albums, boxes of letters and scrapbooks should be collected and developed as important aids for future use throughout a person's life.

Young staff may find the reminiscing of older people boring, and so limit the communication attempts by older people. A special group organized for people to share their memories and experiences encourages a positive attitude to the past and confirms that the memories are valued. Memories never before shared concerning feelings and emotions, a sense of rejection, sadness over wasted time and even joy over childhood games and holidays, are shared if the opportunity is planned. Initially, groups tend to share memories only of events, but when trust is established, feelings and emotions may also be explored. Collections of suitable items, including tape recordings and videos of events, can contribute to the experience.

# PRACTICAL IDEAS FOR ENHANCING THE DAY TIME SERVICE

In order to maintain the rhythm of the day, there is a need to develop focused purposeful activities in which elderly people may participate. These activities should be planned to meet needs in the following areas: recreational and social activities; employment (vocational or domestic opportunities); and stimulatory and habilitative tasks.

The daily programme should be structured, yet flexible enough to meet individual needs. It should aim to provide a productive leisure time and not merely another opportunity for passivity. The maintenance of existing skills, and particularly independence in self-care, should be priorities. Continued development of socialization skills and integration in the activities of the local community should ensure that the option of retirement does not mean the end of a planned programme.

Planned activities for the group may take place in rooms specially set aside in regular ATCs. These may be decorated and furnished to meet the needs of the group and develop a 'drop-in centre' atmosphere. Such an arrangement offers a permanent base in familiar surroundings, but local community centres, drop-in centres, clubs and domestic facilities may also offer the kind of resource needed. A 'homely' setting with a kitchen encourages the maintenance of domestic skills as well as social and independence skills training, in order to foster and maintain maximum independence. The setting that is the least restrictive is the goal so that freedom, choice, privacy and self-determination can be acknowledged.

For example, the Falmouth Day Centre is run in a youth club building leased for three days a week, in a relaxed atmosphere without pressure.[35] Volunteers and members enjoy a social time together, with activities such as sewing, knitting, painting, cooking, music, dancing, skittles, a football sweep and raffles.

The primary goals of day services for the elderly are to prevent regression due to inactivity, to enhance the quality of life, to minimize the effects of ageing, and to support participants as they develop new skills and also maintain the skills needed in their residential placement.

It is important to offer as integrated a service as possibie, with a whole range of activities on offer which reflect individual needs and interests. The following ideas should be considered in order to offer a complete service.

*Physical awareness.* Counselling in such topics as nutrition, ageing, sexuality, mobility, fitness and hygiene is important.

*Leisure and recreation opportunities.* These should be age-appropriate, individualized and supported. Participation, as well as being a spectator, in such sports as bowls, walking, swimming, dancing and snooker should be encouraged.

*Friendships.* Supported friendships with volunteers who are peers as well as friends in the group are recommended. Going out to tea is always a popular choice.

*Language and communication skills.* Continued support from speech therapists where needed is the ideal.

*Education.* This should include access to new and interesting areas of knowledge such as computers, local history, current affairs. Opportunities to maintain worthwhile, hard-learnt skills such as reading and letter writing.

*Group work skills.* Group discussions and group awareness activities.

*Training.* To develop and maintain self-help, domestic and independence skills.

*Art, craft and music.* Opportunities to go to concerts, exhibitions and demonstrations, as well as the development of personal skills using quality materials and instruction.

*Employment* – opportunities for real work, voluntary work and the encouragement of a sense of worth and usefulness, both inside the group and outside.

*Age-appropriate activities* including knitting, gardening, sewing, typing and photography, which help maintain manual dexterity, are creative and, while active, are not pressured.

*Opportunities for relaxation* including time for just sitting, reflecting, perhaps chatting; with an awareness that relaxation is not to be confused with lack of service.

A relaxed day which includes a variety of interests to stimulate body, mind and spirit, and which reflects the requests of the individuals and the group, will ensure that all participants are engaged in meaningful and valued activities. With creative and sensitive leadership, weary, sedentary, bored people will soon become an active demanding group.

## CONCLUSIONS

Professional interest in older and ageing people with mental handicaps is slowly increasing. Although this is a relatively small group of people, it is estimated that there will be a significant increase in those requiring services as they begin to live longer due to medical advances.

The needs will be to: identify emerging problems; consider needs; and develop programmes and services to meet individual requirements.

It is important to recognize that this present generation of ageing and elderly people have had limited opportunities for personal growth and development. Their experiences have been restricted by social influences outside their control which have segregated and isolated them so that they have mostly become institutionalized. Therefore, the needs of this group will be significantly different from those of the next generation of elderly people, who will probably have had experience of living outside of such restrictive environments. Passivity, prolonged disengagement, no worthwhile activity and little interaction all contribute to a wasted life. Some of the needs expressed can only be met by lobbying governments and supporting pressure groups; others can be met by implementing practical schemes which are structured, but recognize the need for choice and variety.

This chapter aims to increase awareness of the needs of the elderly person with mental handicap. Age is no excuse for lack of service to meet individual needs.

# REFERENCES

1. Solly, K. (1978) What about the retarded adult? MENCAP Easter Conference.
2. Thomae, I. and Fryers, T. (1982) *Ageing and Mental Handicap – a position paper*, International League of Societies for Persons with Mental Handicap (ILSMH), Brussels.
3. Heron, A. (1984) *The Older Person in the Adult Training Centre*, MENCAP (report of conference).
4. DHSS (1979) *Report of the Committee of Inquiry into Mental Handicap, Nursing and Care* (Jay Report), HMSO, London.
5. MENCAP (1985) *Stamina Paper No. 6 – Elderly People with Mental Handicap*, MENCAP, London.
6. Wolfensberger, W. (1980) The definition of normalization: update, problems, disagreements and misunderstandings, in Flynn, R.J. and Nitsch, K.E. (eds.), *Normalisation, Social Integration and Community Services*, Baltimore University Park Press.
7. Wolfensberger, W. (1985) An overview of social role valorization and some reflections on elderly mentally retarded persons, in Janicki, M. and Wisniewski, A. (eds.) *Ageing and Developmental Disabilities*, Brookes, Baltimore.
8. Wolfensberger, W. (1982) Social role valorization: A proposed new term for the principle of normalization, *Journal of Mental Retardation*, Vol. 21, pp. 234–9.
9. Wynn-Jones, A. (1984) The elderly person with mental handicap, *Mental Handicap*, Vol. 12, pp. 31–2.
10. CMH (1981) *Living for the Present*, CMH, London.
11. Oswin, M. (1981) *Bereavement and Mentally Handicapped People*, King's Fund Centre, London.
12. Fairbrother, P. (1986) Mencap's minimum standards for the elderly mentally handicapped people, MENCAP Easter Conference.
13. Cornick, M. (1987) *Meeting the Needs of the Elderly Person with Mental Handicap*. Unpublished dissertation, University of Southampton.

14. Tibbitts, C. (1979) Can we invalidate negative stereotypes of ageing? *The Gerontologist*, Vol. 19, pp. 10–20.
15. Thurman, E. (1986) Maintaining dignity in later years, in Summers, J.A. (ed.) *The Right to Grow Up,* Brookes, Baltimore.
16. Summers, J.A. (1986) *The Right to Grow Up,* Brookes, Baltimore.
17. Janicki and Wisniewski, H. (eds.) (1985) *Ageing and Developmental Disabilities – Issues and Approaches,* Brookes, Baltimore.
18. Faire, C. (1986) It's never too late, an evaluation of Bath District Health Authority's *Ordinary Life* project for elderly people with a mental handicap, MENCAP Easter Conference.
19. Fryers, T. (1986) Providing for the needs of ageing mentally handicapped people, MENCAP Easter Conference.
20. Wertheimer, A. (1987) *Images of Possibility,* CMH, London.
21. Atkinson, D. (1982) *With Time to Spare: the Leisure Pursuits of People with a Mental Handicap,* Somerset Social Services Department.
22. Hogg, J. (1986) Ageing People with Mental Handicap – what does the future hold? MENCAP Easter Conference.
23. Fryers, T. (1984) *The Epidemiology of Severe Intellectual Impairment – The Dynamics of Prevalence*, Academic Press, London.
24. Haines, C. (1986) Preparation for retirement: Workers Educational Association pre-retirement course, MENCAP Easter Conference.
25. Wynn-Jones, A. (1986) Elderly people with mental handicap. MENCAP Easter Conference.
26. Wolfensberger, W. (1972) *The Principle of Normalization in Human Services,* Toronto National Institute of Mental Retardation.
27. King's Fund Centre (1980) *An Ordinary Life*, King's Fund, London.
28. CAMR (1982) Ageing and people with mental handicap, *Mental Retardation,* Vol. 32, No. 3, pp. 28–30.
29. Wynn-Jones, A. (1974) Challenge of the aged resident, *Challenges of Mental Retardation,* MENCAP, London.
30. Panitch, M. (1983) Mental retardation and ageing, *Canada's Mental Health,* Vol. 31, No. 3, pp. 6–10.
31. De Villis, R.F. (1977) Learned helplessness in institutions, *Mental Retardation*, Vol. 15, pp. 10–13.
32. Maslow, A.H. (1968) *Towards a Psychology of Being,* Van Nostrand, New York.
33. Lewis, C.N. (1971) Reminiscing and self-concept in old age, *Journal of Gerontology,* Vol. 26, pp. 21–7.
34. Mitchell, A. (1986) The importance of reminiscence to elderly people who are mentally handicapped, MENCAP Easter Conference.
35. Carr, P. (1986) The Falmouth MENCAP Day Centre, MENCAP Easter Conference.

# Section Three: Managing Small Houses in the Community

# 11. Operational Aspects of Managing Small Houses – The Bolton Experience

*Paul Taylor and Owen Cooper*

## INTRODUCTION

This is the moment of truth. The ideological parcel has been passed from hand to fully participatory hand. The mostly harmonious music of shared philosophy, vision and policy has stopped. It is time to open the parcel and see what is inside. Will it be the booby prize, a back ward with its own back yard? Or might it contain those elements, beloved of advertisers (who know so well our subliminal aspirations), which turn a house into a home?

The answer now lies in our own hands. It all depends on what we do. Operating a network of small, staffed houses is an intensely practical activity. The material in this chapter is about what, when it comes down to it, you actually *do*. It is not a recipe, except one for disaster, if lifted wholesale. The views put forward are based on the contributors' experience of operating the Bolton Neighbourhood Network Scheme. This is a 'care in the community' pilot project which, at the time of writing, has provided an ordinary life in Bolton for 50 former longstay mental handicap hospital residents, over a two-year period.[1] But we have not stopped developing. Nor have we stopped learning. And we learn most of all from our consumers. What follows, then, is what we have learned so far. By the time you read this chapter, some, perhaps most, of what we do may have changed. We have to be practical though, so on with the practice issues.

This chapter is divided into eight sections. The first four are about the operational aspects of implementing a service from scratch. They are in chronological sequence, namely: preparing the ground; meeting the people; people moving; and living together.

The fifth and sixth sections are about more general issues, namely, rules for radical staff, and costs. The last two sections summarize the present position, and try to see into the future.

The authors can take little credit for anything in this chapter which may prove helpful. That is a product of the interaction between a small (and often terrifying) army of committed and talented staff, enlightened policymakers and, most importantly, our consumers. The sins of omission, however, are ours alone.

# PREPARING THE GROUND

## Who is it for?

Once committed to a dispersed housing scheme, the first step, if it has not already been taken, is to decide and/or discover who will be its potential users and what characteristics they have which may influence planning. Whether the people being considered are currently resident in the community or in hospital or in other institutions, it is advisable at this stage to obtain some information about the whole group. In most instances, it will not be sensible to approach directly potential consumers or their families, as this is likely to provoke false hopes or (more likely) groundless anxieties. The questions you need to ask at this stage include:

- How many people in total are there?
- What is the age structure of the group?
- How many people need ground floor or level access accommodation?
- How many of those also need a ground floor or level access bathroom and bedroom?
- How many of these need housing which is to wheelchair standards?
- How many people will need staff to be with them throughout the day?
- How many need staff available at night?
- How many need waking night staff?

All these questions are aimed at deciding how many houses will be needed and of what sort. This may sound like the wrong way to start, but in fact identifying housing will often be the longest part of the timescale.

There is little purpose, and some harm, in starting work with individuals, only to discover that there is no suitably adapted housing available, that such housing will have to be built and it will take four years.

Scanning for this kind of information is, however, fraught with difficulty. Even when it is available, it is likely to be inaccurate or otherwise misleading. Our own experience would lead us to treat with great suspicion, if not rank disbelief, information that, for example, 25 per cent of a hospital's population of residents were in Wessex categories 1/2 (more able). Even if such an assertion is found to be literally true, it is likely to be a poor indicator of what is needed in an ordinary life model. It is likely to ignore the fact that people do not need staff support all the time because the highly artificial environment (e.g. the absence of traffic) of the hospital itself renders this unnecessary; or that people who are quite mobile in hospital are so because there are no stairs to negotiate. We have found it useful to use our own physiotherapist and occupational therapist to get more relevant information on mobility and support needs. However, the following assumptions can be safely made:

- Far more people than the evidence at first suggests will need level access accommodation.
- Virtually everybody will need (at least at first) 24-hour support.
- Hardly anybody will need waking night staff.

It is not safe to assume that support needs will decrease over time as people attain greater levels of independence. In global terms, any such effect is likely to be offset by increasing dependence consequent upon the ageing process.

## Getting commitment to housing

Armed with information about housing need, the next approach should be made to a housing agency. Whether this is a local authority housing department or a housing association, the questions that need to be asked are:

- Can you meet this housing need?
- If so, over what timescale can you meet it?
- If not, can you meet part of it?
- If not, do you envisage that you will be able to meet it as part of your future development?

- If so, when?
- If not, would a capital injection help?
- What priority will you give to any commitment of housing?

The significance of the capital injection question is that it is clear that a move to an ordinary life model will have capital implications. Small schemes may be able to develop in the margins of housing development, but moving to a full-scale community care model means building more houses, and spending money to adapt houses. It is useful to know that health authorities are now empowered to make capital contributions direct to housing associations.[2] Although there are exceptions (for example, from opposite ends of the spectrum, areas of inner urban decay and areas where house and land prices are excessively high), a combination of political will and hard cash can resolve most problems of housing availability. The absence of either is the equivalent of being at the top of a very long snake in a game of snakes and ladders.

## Agreeing the model

Once commitment in principle to the provision of bricks and mortar has been given, agreement needs to be reached on the legal basis on which people will occupy the housing. A range of options are available and the most appropriate scheme should be chosen to meet the needs of individuals.

## Seizing the time

Having established the availability of housing and the model of housing provision, a timescale of housing availability should be drawn up. At this stage it is assumed that no specific housing has been identified. Discussions with the housing agency should be undertaken to determine what housing is available immediately or within months. It is highly desirable that a range of housing should be considered, to allow choice. The housing (or plans, if new-build, or converted property) should be viewed, as should the neighbourhood. It is helpful to have a checklist to determine the general suitability. The following factors are relevant.

- Indicates suitability: neighbourhood is valued, in demand; property is in good condition, well maintained; surrounding properties are in good condition, well maintained; streets, gardens are generally tidy; close to shops, services, public transport; mixed residential area; property does not stand out from other properties; property is domestic in character.

- Indicates unsuitability: neighbourhood is devalued, e.g. area of urban decay, 'hard to let' estate, property in poor state of repair; surrounding properties in poor state of repair; streets and gardens are full of refuse, abandoned cars etc; isolated, shops, services and public transport remote; adjacent to hospital, hostel, prison, abattoir etc; property stands out from surroundings, e.g. lone Victorian detached house in a terraced street; property is institutional in character or by past history, e.g. used to be a children's home, homeless persons' hostel etc.

This checklist should be used with a measure of common sense. The real world cannot be rebuilt to conform to our aspirations, and some measure of compromise may be necessary. Nevertheless, the checklist can be used to keep such compromises to a minimum.

Having identified a number of properties which will be available within the foreseeable future, and which are appropriate, the housing agency should be asked to 'reserve' those properties for the potential consumers. It may be necessary to have the facility to cover the cost of rent during the 'reservation period'. Financial constraints (as well as the moral issue about contributing to homelessness) may restrict the number of properties which can be so 'reserved'.

## Breaking into the circle

The next stage is to re-examine the potential consumers in the light of the 'reserved' properties. This stage may well induce the greatest sense of queasiness among purists. We are well aware that there will be those who will argue that this is putting the cart before the horse. We maintain that if an ordinary life model of service is actually, practically to be provided (rather than just talked about), the following points must be taken into account:

- Without housing, there is no service.
- A great deal of housing will need to be provided.
- Providing housing is a long process.
- Wholly appropriate housing will be hard to come by.
- Raising people's expectations too far ahead of time (much more than

six months) is productive of anxiety and frustration.
- The process described so far is a gradual reconciliation by closer and closer approximations, of housing available with housing need.
- The issue at question should not be who gets the service, but when they get it.
- It is necessary to break into the circle somewhere.
- This is the place to do it.

A subgroup of the target group is selected, who, on the available evidence, might be appropriately matched to the housing available. At this point, direct work with consumers begins. This aspect of the process will be dealt with in the second section. For the present, we will restrict ourselves to the housing-related aspects of the process.

## Making adjustments

A detailed investigation of housing needs of the identified subgroup can now be made. A comparison can be made of these needs and the housing identified as presently available. The likely outcomes of that comparison are as follows:

- For some of the group, the identified housing will meet the need.
- For some of the group the housing will meet the need given minor adaptations (e.g. provision of ramp, stair rail, shower). In this case, steps should be taken to ensure that such adaptations can take place.
- For some of the group the housing will not meet the need, or will do so only given major adaptation (e.g. ground floor extension, complete refit to wheelchair standards); in this case, a statement of the housing need should be made to the housing agency, so that they may either make alternative provision which meets the need or undertake adaptations to the same effect. In these circumstances it will be necessary to provide the housing agency with an architect's brief, specifying precisely what is required. Close cooperation between the project leader, occupational therapist, physiotherapist, housing agency and architect is necessary at this stage.

## Getting approval

Whenever major adaptation or new-build property is contemplated, the vexed question of planning permission is raised. This is not usually a problem where consumers are themselves the tenants of an existing dwelling house (even though they may need significant staff support to obtain benefit from that tenancy), but, under present regulations, will need planning permission if there is a change of use (albeit technical) from 'dwelling house' to 'hostel'. In the case of new-build or major adaptation, however, planning permission is always needed. The problem about this is that it entails a process of public consultation which, especially if insensitively handled, may be undesirable in that it draws unnecessary attention to the housing in question, and may serve as a focus of uninformed public opposition. The relevant questions to be asked are: How wide does the consultation have to be? Are the characteristics of the occupants relevant to the new development/change of use?

In our experience, unless adaptations will have a significant impact on the wider community (which is rarely the case), then immediate neighbours only need to be consulted. In the case of new developments, it is desirable if the housing selected is part of an overall development of general-let accommodation, so that consultation takes place about the generality of the development.

The question of relevance of the characteristics of the users will normally only be relevant if the housing is designated as a 'hostel'. There is, however, wide variation in local interpretation of the regulations, and, as a rule of thumb, it is preferable where planning permission will be needed, to involve the relevant people at an early stage in the planning process rather than to encounter them as immovable obstacles at a later stage. The relevant people include: the local authority planning officer; the housing department (whether or not the providing agency); local authority architects; local authority engineers; the environmental health officer (in some circumstances); the fire officer; and elected members, especially the councillors in whose constituency the housing is planned, and members of the relevant service committees.

Avoidance of this sort of consultation, while no doubt based on the most enlightened of motives, is likely to be interpreted as furtiveness, riding rough-shod over the population, or infringement of the public right to information. By observing these guidelines we have had no public opposition to planning applications, and no informal resistance from local communities. We believe, however, that this is largely attributable to two other consultative mechanisms, outside the statutory requirements, which we have employed. These are detailed below.

## Public participation exercise

From the time that we were aware that we would be undertaking a major resettlement programme, it was apparent that it would not be reasonable or practically achievable to do so in secret. It was therefore decided, at the very earliest stages, to undertake a series of three full day public participation seminars, to promote a positive image of the scheme and of people with a mental handicap, to seek to correct popular misconceptions and to enlist the positive support of a whole range of community leaders. This exercise took place in May and June of 1984, well in advance of any identification of specific consumers or housing. This timing enabled a forum for the expression of fears and even outright opposition, without this being focused on particular people or particular neighbourhoods. The exercise was sponsored and co-ordinated by the community health council, and took the following form:

- One-day seminar for elected and appointed members of the local authority, the health authority and the community health council.
- One-day seminar for parents/relatives of people with a mental handicap, and representatives of relevant local voluntary organizations.
- One-day seminar for invited members of the public who had expressed particular interest or who represented communities of interest which might be influential in the public acceptance of the project.
- The preparation and publication of information leaflets and information packs which were widely disseminated.
- The establishment, as a consequence of the public participation exercise, of a group of interested parties, who would continue to meet on a regular basis, hosted by the community health council, to maintain a level of awareness of the development of the project, to give feedback about public reactions, and to input proposals for improvement.
- This has led to a current research project, also sponsored by the community health council, on consumer satisfaction with the service.

The emphasis of the seminars varied, but typically included: the context of mental handicap services; presentation of the project; presentation of direct experience by staff/consumers of similar projects; a significant proportion of time devoted to group discussions, eliciting, recording and eventually publishing the issues/problems/opportunities raised.[3]

## Member consultation

As a matter of course, elected and appointed members of the local authority have formally been given detailed updates of the progress of the project. At a less formal level, however, direct consultation with elected members is an important element in securing public acceptance. Whenever a group of consumers has been identified in association with a particular house, a letter is sent to the relevant ward councillors informing them of this. The letter includes very brief details of the consumers concerned (with their consent), and invites comment from the ward councillors, as local experts, as to any unanticipated pitfalls or unidentified opportunities in the neighbourhood. The letter also offers the opportunity for future discussion which may be required. This has produced a very positive response. Local councillors undertake a valuable role in subtly educating grassroots opinion and, because of the consultation involved, are likely to engage any potential local opposition at source. Even more positively, they can offer information about local community networks, both formal and informal, which can be approached to facilitate the fullest positive integration of consumers into the neighbourhood.

## Getting going

We have concentrated so far on one end of the process – the preparation of the community and the organization of housing. All of this is essential, and has to be undertaken in advance. But it is a means to an end only. It is all subsidiary to the direct work with consumers, the establishment for them of real and meaningful choices. It is the essential and detailed work of preparing the ground so that the work undertaken with consumers is constructive, and, for them and the staff who work with them, a positive and exciting experience. In the following section we examine that direct work.

## MEETING THE PEOPLE (AND THEIR NEEDS)

This section sets out a process we have evolved for getting acquainted with potential consumers: working with them and their carers and relatives, and, by a gradual and experiential process, identifying their needs in an ordinary life model, ensuring that those needs can be met, and giving them the maximum opportunity to sample, test and choose their own living arrangements. The process relates directly to our own experience of resettlement from long-stay hospitals, but should prove sufficiently flexible to be adapted to other circumstances.

It might be argued that resettlement from hospitals is in many respects the most complex form of establishing a dispersed housing model. If starting from a community base, for example, some of the components of the process can simply be omitted (e.g. work with ward staff, elements of the community introduction exercise). The process assumes an established multidisciplinary project team, headed by a project leader. At this stage in the process the project leader has overall responsibility for the consumer group. As the process develops, this responsibility is devolved to individual key workers. In our service the project leader is usually a social worker or community mental handicap nurse, but there are no compelling reasons why other staff should not undertake this role. In addition to the project leader, the team will consist, as a minimum, of an assistant officer-in-charge (in our case the first-line manager of the residential element of the service), who will have prime responsibility for ensuring that the practical and organizational arrangements are in place in the community, and a number of direct care staff, who will be the most significant people in terms of contact time with consumers, and will continue to work with them after resettlement, thereby providing continuity.

To a considerable extent the process runs in parallel to that described in 'Preparing the Ground' (p. 268), broken down into the following subsections: identification; work with hospital staff; work with relatives; grouping; community introduction (part one); resettlement meeting; community introduction (part two). These stages are set out in more detail below:

# Identification

- Twenty people are identified by each project team. This is coordinated by the project leader in accordance with the policies of the hospital in question. The assistant officer-in-charge of the project team is also closely involved in this part of the process.
- An initial profile on all 20 people is established.
- Preliminary information about housing needs is communicated to the housing department.
- Preliminary information about relatives is obtained. It is helpful at this stage to identify those members of hospital staff who are most likely to have contact with and influence with relatives.
- Wherever possible, a member of hospital staff on each ward is identified as a link person for each project.

- By agreement with ward staff a project information/message book is available on each ward.
- Individual profiles are developed on the basis of a minimum of direct contact with each of the 20 consumers of the project, information from relatives and other professionals.
- A list of the project team's consumers is communicated to relevant additional health service staff (i.e. physiotherapist, speech therapist, etc.)
- Project leaders ensure that no more than one project team is dealing with any one hospital ward.

## Work with hospital staff

- In respect of individual consumers, the project leader acts as the principal link with ward staff, other hospital staff and a nominated member of the hospital resettlement team. Liaison at the broader or policy level is undertaken by the scheme co-ordinator in consultation with project leaders.
- The project leader and assistant officer-in-charge determine a programme and timetable of consumer and ward contact. This programme includes delegation of specific responsibilities and where possible is developed in consultation with a link member of ward staff. Where this is not possible the completed programme and timetable is made available to ward staff.
- The project leader and direct care staff each have particular responsibility for two or three clients.
- The programme of consumer contact includes one-to-one staff/client interaction, preferably away from a hospital situation. The duration of contact is brought up gradually, e.g. building from a 10-minute contact on or away from the ward, to short trips out to include a variety of experiences as a 'getting-to-know you' exercise. The period over which this steadily increasing contact takes place should not exceed four to six weeks.

## Work with relatives

- A social worker has prime responsibility for contact with relatives.
- Contact with relatives is maintained at a minimum level of six-weekly visits and, in addition, a visit in advance of each distinct stage of the resettlement process.

- Group work with relatives is made available at the discretion of the social worker.
- Relatives are encouraged to view the resettlement process as one of partnership with the project.
- Where such partnership arrangements prove unfruitful, social workers continue active work with the family over an extended period of time: until a move becomes inevitable due to external pressures; or a judgement is made that not to make a move would be damaging to the client.

## Grouping

The grouping exercise does vary from time to time and between hospitals. Nevertheless, the purposes of a grouping exercise remain constant, as follows:

- To gain information on existing or potential relationships between consumers (e.g. animosities, friendships, etc).
- The assessment of the likelihood and desirability of effecting a home placement.
- The observation of people in a non-institutional environment.
- The recording of information about interaction, relationships and personalities.

## Community introduction (part one)

The objectives of this part of the process are to enable consumers to become acquainted/reacquainted with the community in general; and to have the opportunity to sample a range of community facilities and services which may be available to them on discharge. The process is as follows:

- The project leader co-ordinates a group plan.
- In constructing the group plan the project leader takes into account all information currently to hand, especially information derived from the grouping exercise.
- Accommodation in the community for this part of the grouping exercise is established.
- The range of services and facilities to be sampled is likely to involve the following people: relatives; home carers; education support tutors;

rural training scheme staff; mainstream community resource providers; volunteers.

This part of the exercise involves at least seven full days in the community, inclusive of an experience of remaining in the community over the weekend. This varies from group to group and a decision about the apportionment of time is made by the project team.

Because the number of consumers involved in a community introduction exercise is fewer than those involved in the earlier grouping exercise, it is important to ensure that those consumers from the larger group not involved in the community introduction exercise are not left without a point of contact. Project team members therefore ensure that such contacts with hospital-based residents are maintained during the process of the community introduction.

The community introduction exercise should be recorded using the following: individual records including currently operational assessments; a visual record, e.g. photographs and where appropriate video tape material. (The project maintains its own visual record of the community introduction process but a copy should also be retained by consumers for future use as a record of significant life events.)

## Resettlement meeting

Preparation for the resettlement meeting is undertaken by the project leader who co-ordinates information from all other individuals who have been involved in the process, and determines attendance at the meeting. The content of the meeting includes the following elements:

- Report from the grouping exercise, especially about significant relationships.
- Views of relatives.
- Information about mobility.
- Information about attitude to resettlement.
- Discussion of accommodation needs of individuals.
- Discussion of education, occupational and leisure requirements.
- Discussion of how hospitals/ward staff can help facilitate decisions taken.
- Discussion of who will be involved in the discharge procedure.
- The working through of a discharge check list.
- Discussion on the appropriateness and mechanisms for maintaining links with the hospital following discharge.

# Community introduction (part two)

The purpose of this phase of the community introduction exercise is to begin to involve consumers in some detail with the specific services, contacts and accommodation which they will be taking up on discharge from hospital. The pattern of this phase of the community introduction exercise will be determined largely by the resettlement meeting decisions. The project leader is responsible for co-ordinating group aspects of this phase of the process, while the worker allocated to the individual at the meeting is responsible for monitoring the individual's response to the community introduction exercise.

The process is as follows: ideally, the exercise takes place in the four to six weeks before the agreed date of discharge; accommodation is ideally in the identified housing to which consumers will move; tenancies are taken up and benefits applied for; furniture and so on is purchased and installed; relatives and ward staff are invited to actively participate in the process; informal introduction to neighbours. It is the responsibility of the project leader at this stage to communicate all decisions and events to the link member of ward staff and to relatives. As with the earlier part of the community introduction exercise, it is important to maintain links with those clients from the larger group still remaining in hospital.

# PEOPLE MOVING

All this activity has taken place before any selected house has been tenanted. Much, indeed, has been left unstated. Whole volumes could (and no doubt will) be written about the intricacies of the welfare benefits arrangements, the delicate work needed with relatives, the complex and often ambivalent relationships with hospital staff and the sensitivity required in the grouping exercise. All of this, however, seems positively leisurely when compared to the flurry of activity which surrounds the move itself.

# LIVING TOGETHER

## Benefits

All of our clients depend for their income on DHSS benefits. It is therefore important that staff have sufficient information and skill to ensure that consumers are in receipt of the appropriate benefits and can liaise with the DHSS so that these are paid promptly and regularly. We arranged for a series of lectures by a local expert who explained the rules regarding entitlement, joint tenancies and special requirements payments.

The major source of income is likely to be Severe Disablement Allowance, topped up by Supplementary Benefit at the long-term rate. (In the event of a consumer being unable to sign in receipt of benefit, the assistant officer-in-charge is the nominated appointee.) Many consumers are granted weekly additions to their Supplementary Benefit for extra heating and washing. The consumers, who all are tenants of either local authority houses or housing association houses, receive Housing Benefit and rate rebate which covers their housing costs.

Applications are made for consumers for Attendance Allowance. This is a particularly valuable benefit as it is nontaxable and does not count as an income resource for Supplementary Benefit purposes (except when payment is made at the Residential Care Rate). Mobility Allowance has similar advantages, although the consumer has to fit the criteria of being physically unable or virtually unable to walk to receive it.

The cost of buying furniture and large items of household equipment is not covered by Supplementary Benefit scale rates. The consumers, however, fall within the category of people eligible for a single payment to help them set up home. This payment is not generous, currently averaging around £800 to £1,000 per household, in which to carpet a whole house, provide all the necessary furniture, household and kitchen appliances, and all the miscellaneous items like curtains, bedding, pots, pans and so on. We have had to top this up by approximately £2,000 per household to ensure that the physical environment is at least comfortable.

## Budgets and bills

All clients are personally involved in the cashing of their benefits at the local post office. The cashed benefits are brought back to the house, where the client can sit down with a staff member and review how much goes into the household account, how much goes into housekeeping, how much to hold for personal spending money and how much to put away into their savings account.

The household account, into which the members of the household contribute an agreed weekly amount, covers all repairs, TV licence, household insurance, and any collective purchases. The consumers also contribute an agreed weekly amount from their benefits into the house-keeping kitty, which covers all the food and daily household items. Each house decides for itself how much is paid into these two communal funds. The housekeeping kitty is supplemented by £52 per month, from the project's budget, to cover the cost of providing meals for the support staff. This is seen as a justifiable expense, as not only should the consumers not have to pay for staff meals, but nor should staff, who receive no meal breaks, and have an important function to play at meal times with regards to role-modelling, implementing applicable training programmes, and generally creating a 'home-like' atmosphere by their every action.

The entire food purchasing process abounds with learning opportunities. Identification of shopping needs by checking the cupboards; product choice; use of money; community presence. One or two larger shopping trips per week is the norm, supplemented by local shopping, as is the case with most households.

The one bill which the project takes primary responsibility for is the telephone bill. Telephones are seen as an essential item from the staff point of view, whereas many consumers might not see a telephone as a priority. Installation and rental is paid for by the project. The consumers are only responsible for the calls they make, and the project pays rental and the remainder of the charge as the majority of the calls are work-related.

## Holidays

Having looked at how the basic costs involved in three or four clients living together are met, we will now turn to the more exotic topic of holidays. Holidays are a focal point in clients' lives, as for the majority of the population.

To try to demonstrate that life exists outside of Weston-Super-Mare, holiday brochures fill the house as soon as Christmas decorations come down. Widening horizons is a gradual process, and whisking consumers halfway around the world, after 40 years of holidaying in Blackpool, might not be in their best interests. The feathers in one's cap might well be imaginary!

Clients pay their own way for holidays, from their savings made for that purpose, enabling selection from a wide range of holidays and enabling top-up cost for staff support to be covered. The project's budget includes an allowance for each household to allow for the cost of staff support, and staff receive the normal out-of-pocket expenses and benefits applicable to local authority employees.

## Daily life

Holidays end all too soon, so on with daily life. A critical analysis of social education centres (SECs) is not the aim of the next few paragraphs but, needless to say, the provision of an individual needs model and the use of SECs are not easily reconciled.

Consumers participate in activities and interests congruent with their position of being nonemployed or of retirement age. Adult education classes within colleges and community centres are popular, as are shopping trips to town, involvement in local events, over-60s luncheon clubs, pottering around at home or in the garden, or just sitting back and relaxing. In addition, both special and integrated sessions are provided within different community centres and sports centres, e.g. hydrotherapy, drama and movement, relaxation.

A major issue arising from the provision of an individual needs model is transport. The use of public transport has the advantage of community presence, but this sometimes has to be weighed against the counterproductive issue of spending half the day on the buses.

Where many direct care staff do not own cars, and staffing levels of one member of staff on at a time are the norm, the question as to whether the transport of clients in staffs' cars is the way forward is often answered by necessity or expediency. The further question as to whether this is an acceptable solution or not is therefore moot.

Developing local amenities and facilities so that transport is less crucial, combined with independent travel training, and use of taxis for the more awkward journeys or for clients unable to travel independently on public transport, seem more appropriate solutions.

## Conflict resolution

Finally, a few words on conflict resolution. Arrangements and disputes are a normal aspect of 'domestic life', and few people would value an immediate pacifier or 'judge' to appear each time some form of conflict in the home arose. Accordingly, clients will have moments where letting off steam or venting anger/frustration is appropriate and healthy.

Ongoing and unresolved conflict is not usually healthy or productive and therefore different methods may need to be tried, depending on the situation and the consumers involved, e.g. discussion over dinner, use of the tenants' meeting, simply sitting down together, with or without a staff member, and talking it through, or making a 'liveable' agreement. The style of staff intervention is probably the most significant determinant in resolving client conflict, and the next section will look at how support is provided to staff, so that unsupervised, nonprofessional staff are equipped to carry out their responsibilities.

# RULES FOR RADICAL STAFF

## Different ball-game

A significant aspect of staffing within a dispersed housing model is the responsibility given to 'nonprofessional' staff. Responsibilities like medication administration and the handling of consumer finances have been, historically, the exclusive domain of senior staff, whether they be officers in the social services or qualified nurses in the health authority. It has always been possible to pass on problem-solving and decision-making to the senior staff member on duty. In our dispersed housing model, there is usually only one member of staff in a house, and therefore these responsibilities, to a great extent, are carried by unqualified care staff. A 24-hour radio-pager is carried by the assistant officers-in-charge to provide necessary support, whether that be advice or actual physical presence.

A clear set of procedures combined with sufficient staff training, can ensure that specific responsibilities are carried out successfully by care staff. The assistant officers-in-charge, by rota, and through the radio-pager facility, provide the necessary back-up for the unpredictable and for emergencies.

A new model of service provision implies a new way of thinking and a new way of relating to clients. They are tenants of their own homes, not clients in a social services or health authority establishment, and staff are employed to provide the necessary support to this arrangement. There is of necessity a very different relationship between staff and client, where the service is provided in the client's own home. The staff induction, which starts with a three-week block and continues with eight weeks of day release, gives equal emphasis to understanding philosophies, principles, the role of support staff, the development of a dignified or appropriate approach to consumers and to skill acquisition.

Many care staff come with little or no experience, but that is not seen as a problem at all, especially if prior experience consists of years of inappropriate interaction. We have looked for people with a sound set of values, beliefs and attitudes in general; these are a firmer foundation on which to develop quality staff than having to undo years of inappropriate experience. The selection process is two-fold; we have a group interview as well as individual interviews. For the group interview we use the Escata normalization exercises called Lifestyles, which looks at peoples' attitudes and values.[4] This has proved to be a highly successful method of reducing the likelihood of appointing people whose main asset is a well-developed interview technique.

The induction and subsequent day-release module consists of the following main areas:

- Presenting the key concepts and principles involved in working with people with learning difficulties.
- Teaching of skills, e.g. the Bereweeke skill teaching programme,[5] aspects of basic physical care, basic counselling, first aid course.
- Consideration of the roles of different staff, with particular emphasis on the diversity of the role of direct care staff and the magnitude of the responsibilities in that role. Emphasis is given to the high standards and quality of support expected of staff. People are monitored to be aware of the significant role they play.
- Operational policies and procedures are presented. The key is to get the right balance so that one is not replicating an institutional model in the community, yet providing sufficient support and direction so that staff have clear parameters in which to operate. Form filling is kept to a minimum as the job is all about work with the clients and is not meant to be an apprenticeship for employment in the civil service.

## Who goes where?

Following induction, the next eight weeks are spent gaining experience in different houses as part of an assessment of where staff will be most effective. Staff are subsequently assigned to a 'core' house and a secondary house. In theory, 75 per cent of a staff member's time is spent working in their core house, and 25 per cent in the secondary house. The three major benefits of operating in this way are seen as: staff development through exposure to wider group of clients, to more ideas and to more styles of working; in times of staff sickness, annual leave or staff shortage, clients are supported by known staff; the working world extends beyond one building.

The assignment of staff to houses is a medium-term arrangement, as flexibility is essential in responding to changing client need. Staff assignments can therefore change where a particular input is felt to be more beneficial elsewhere. This is particularly true as the number of houses increases and a balance of experienced staff and new staff in the new houses is needed.

## Communication

Isolation is an inevitable consequence of a predominantly single-staffed, dispersed housing model. Communication which is essential in any environment, becomes absolutely crucial. A range of measures contributes to this and all play their part:

- Contact at the consumer's house or at other community locations. Contact can range from general discussion to more formal role-modelling.
- Meetings, which are often the bane of social services employees, take on a vital co-ordinating function. Staff house meetings serve to disseminate information from 'the office', to involve all staff in the decision-making process, to encourage the discussion of ideas, and to build a team spirit to promote a collective and consistent approach to work with consumers. House staff meetings take place every two weeks, usually in 'the office', but never at the client's house, as it is a home, not an office;
- Network-wide meetings take place monthly and look at the wider issues. Contact will include outside speakers, mini-in-service training, videos, small group discussions and information sharing. Social contact at the meeting and over lunch after the meeting for isolated staff is seen as a significant benefit.
- Membership of working parties. Involvement in development and change is an important factor in promoting ownership and a sense of collective responsibilities.

Two other means of communication that have proved to be successful have been written ones, namely *Rota News* and *Ivory Tower News*.

## Rota News
This is a 'journal' that comes out with the four-weekly rotas. What started out as a one-page attachment to the rotas to disseminate specific information, rapidly developed into an 'alternative' newsletter. *Rota News* is a mixture of straight information, tongue-in-cheek articles, mischievous items, articles by the readers, thought-provoking articles and philosophical statements. It is proving to be an effective way of maintaining a culture. A staff team of 42, but a circulation of 65 within Bolton speaks for itself!

## Ivory Tower News
The sister journal of *Rota News* is *Ivory Tower News*, of which there have been only three editions so far. *Ivory Tower News* has dealt with those decisions, along with detailed explanation, which are made by the management team, once consultation has taken place. One edition was devoted exclusively to the allocation of staff to houses when we were about to expand from three houses to six.

The final means of communication is the informal type. Popping in and out of the office is encouraged, and a 'social club' organizes evenings out. While there is nothing unusual or special about this, it has proved another area worth putting energy into.

## Quality assurance/monitoring

Even given the most rigorous philosophy and the soundest set of principles in the world, people are judged by what happens in practice. In contrast to the USA, where one could be forgiven for thinking that there are more people involved in monitoring than actually doing, this is an underdeveloped area in this country.

The individual programme planning (IPP) process is used to co-ordinate input from many disciplines in order to identify areas of need for an individual client and assigns responsibility for the meeting of those needs. A client co-ordinator is appointed for each consumer, who has the responsibility of ensuring that decisions made at an IPP meeting are carried out and monitored.

On a more informal level, all staff have a responsibility, as part of a team, to ensure that quality services are provided. The assistant officer-in-charge, as the 'co-ordinator' of input into a particular house, is the focal point for ensuring that the less tangible areas like 'homelike atmosphere' and appropriate staff interaction with the consumers exist. An objective measure of quality of services, or adequate performance indicators, are few and far between. This is a significant area of development for service providers. Standards could all too easily slip gradually and unconsciously, in the absence of a more objective measure of quality.

# COSTS

## Staff costs

### Who are the staff?
The project is multidisciplinary and staff-intensive, and will include staff of different grades to meet the needs of the client group.

### Staffing structure
An officer-in-charge is responsible for a network of 50 clients, 10 of whom are in home placements. For each network there are five assistant officers-in-charge. For each house there is a neighbourhood care worker (grade 3). The basic grade for neighbourhood care workers is grade 2, with new entrants starting on grade 1 for 12 months. Each network has one or two specifically allocated social workers and community mental handicap nurses. Other staff provide a service across the two networks of 50.

### Cover needed
Virtually all households require 24-hour staff cover, with a staff member sleeping in. Where one member of staff on duty at any given time is sufficient, this works out at four whole time equivalent neighbourhood care workers per household. Where two members of staff are needed on duty at most times, the equivalent figure is 7.5 neighbourhood care workers.

### Interaction with day provision
Initially, we made some rather rash assumptions about the availability of day services offsetting the costs of staffing the houses. These assumptions proved to be ill-founded. If any such assumptions are to be made, the

following conditions must be met: day services will be either compulsory or so popular that everybody wants to attend them; nobody will need any additional support in getting to, or making use of, the services; all members of a household will attend on a totally predictable basis; nobody will ever be ill; day services will not close for holidays, Bank Holidays, etc.

With the wisdom of hindsight, the chances of meeting any – let alone all – of the above conditions were always rather slim. However, the most significant factor is that, given a choice, most people take up day services on a selective and part-time basis, and need support to do so. This is not to deny the necessity to make provision for daytime activities. Indeed, it is essential to do so. But the costs of those services must be seen as essentially additional to, and not alternatives to, the staffing levels.

**Alternative models**
Alternative models of service provision are described throughout this book. Variations in costs are largely a consequence of variations of that model. The most significant variation used locally is that of home placements. In this model the majority of the costs are borne by social security payments to consumers. This is a valuable model of service provision, but is still in its infancy. We therefore aim to provide this form of service to approximately 20 per cent of consumers pending further evaluation.

## Other costs

These involve: office accommodation; capital costs; operational costs; staff expenses; training costs.

## Financial forecasting

Financial forecasting is notoriously unreliable. Our own experience has conformed to the general rule that everything takes longer, costs more and is more difficult than anticipated. We started from a basis which assumed that the costs of providing a service in the community could be contained within the average costs of maintaining a consumer in a long-stay hospital. This has proved a false assumption. On our current estimates, the average costs are likely to be some 30 per cent higher than hospital costs, and this is before we take account of the higher levels of benefit which are being claimed. This realization has been painful but necessary.

The task of forecasting has not been made easier by the fact that externally imposed assumptions about resource availability and necessary rate of progress have constantly changed. We have now programmed all the financial variables into a computerized spreadsheet, so that we can respond almost instantaneously to requests to rework timescales, recalculate costs given different assumptions and so on. Unfortunately, the computer cannot yet be induced into undertaking the necessary thinking which ensures that the pattern of service provision is the right one!

## SUMMARY

In this chapter we have set out a model which we have designed, and which has further evolved out of experience, for managing the transition to dispersed ordinary housing within community by clients, many of whom have spent decades living in long-stay mental handicap hospitals.

We do not presume to imply that this is the only model for the management of dispersed housing. Indeed, another approach to achieving much the same objectives is set out in Chapter 8.

The model we have described is, however, one which works for us locally, and while there will unquestionably be a proliferation of local solutions, we believe we have identified some of the important issues to be addressed in the success or failure of any model of provision. We are conscious of having skated over most of the areas we have described. We will now risk skating on even thinner ice by trying to summarize some of the more important lessons we have learned.

### Get ready

We have learned to ensure that we know enough about our consumers to secure for them the right sort of housing. In so doing, we have learned enough about housing to be clear about the different models of housing provision which can be considered. We ourselves have expressed a preference for a mixture of tenancies and home placements. We have given our reasons for this preference. However, we are not dogmatic about this. Others will find other solutions, and we will experiment with other mechanisms ourselves.

We have learned that large-scale social change cannot occur in secret.

We believe we have found an acceptable balance between the need to gain the confidence and support of the public and public authorities, and the need to safeguard the privacy of the consumer.

## Get to know people

We have learned to have a healthy disrespect for assessment instruments, classifications and categories. There is no substitute for actually getting to know people, on a one-to-one basis and in group situations, in a context which is comfortable for them, yet as similar as is possible to the situation to which they might be expected to move. Our most accurate assessment form is a blank sheet of paper to be completed with an open mind.

## Get organized

We have learned to be organized about moving. Checklists may be wholly inappropriate when applied to people, but for effective action they are *indispensable*.

## Get together

We have learned that the practicalities of living together in ordinary housing demands no particular arrangements. The experience is neither wonderful nor dreadful: it's . . . well . . . it's – ordinary.

## Get your head straight

We have learned, though, that what does need special attention is the attitudes of staff supporting ordinary housing. They need to be always mindful that they are providing a service in other people's homes. They need to maintain high standards, while often isolated. To do this they need: sound philosophies; a supportive and enabling culture; in-service training; co-ordination; monitoring and feedback arrangements.

## Get money

We have learned more about budgetary control, cash-flow, unit costs and other financial matters than we ever wished to. Go forth and do likewise, or you will end up underfunded or overspent.

## AFTERWORD

This chapter has been heavy on mechanisms and light on philosophy. Such has been our intention. It is important to be clear about the 'how' of what we do – but not at the expense of forgetting why we are doing it in the first place.

Why, then, this emphasis on ordinary housing supported, in the main, by 'ordinary' people? The answer is that the most damaging aspect of institutional practice is that it delimits and impoverishes the network of social relationships available to people – and that network of relationships is the very mechanism by and through which we all grow and develop.

In a dispersed, community-based system, on the other hand, the encounter between staff member and consumer is a social one. It is likely that the staff member is already integrated, by a multiplicity of relationships into the community. That integration can be extended to include and be shared with the client. Thus, the important aspect of the relationship between staff member and client is its human rather than professional nature (though professionals have their place as well – and a need to know it). If we can accept the implicit mutuality of a human-to-human encounter, then the activity of deepening and extending social networks is not only advantageous to clients – in the end we are all enriched.

## REFERENCES

1. DHSS (1983) *Care in the Community and Joint Finance,* HC(83)6/LAC(83)5, HMSO, London.
2. DHSS (1983) *The Health and Social Services and Social Security Adjudications Act*, HMSO, London.
3. Bolton Community Health Council (1985) *Bolton Neighbourhood Network Scheme – Public Participation Paper.*
4. Brown and Alcoe (1985) *Lifestyles*, Escata Publications, Kent.

5. Felce, D., Jenkins, J., Dell, D. *et al.* (1983) *The Bereweeke Skill Teaching System,* NFER-Nelson, Oxford.

# FURTHER READING

DHSS (1948) *The National Assistance Act,* Section 49, HMSO, London.
DHSS (1984) *The Registered Homes Act*, Chapter 23, HMSO, London.

# 12. Managing Services to Assure Quality

*David Sines*

## INTRODUCTION

The development of comprehensive services for people with mental handicaps will require the support of responsive and flexible management systems which facilitate the realization of the aims of local service delivery. This chapter explores some of the core components of flexible management systems and in particular considers the importance of quality assurance in human services.

The chapter deliberately avoids reference to uni-agency or uni-disciplinary management systems or processes, but presents those aspects of management which are common to all services in the community where individually designed services are in practice.

## WHY MANAGE HUMAN SERVICES?

The very suggestion that local services require management may appear to some to conflict with the ethos of consumer-led services. Few would disagree that complex social organizations require clearly defined management systems and processes, and the same is true for smaller, local services. There is a great deal of confusion about management and what it stands to represent, but quite simply, in human services, it is about the process of organizing human and physical resources and identifying the ground rules within which individuals may operate on the basis of their own motivation, experience and training towards the realization of a common goal or aim for their clients.

There have been numerous attempts at defining the most appropriate style of management for an organization and an equally prestigious array of suggestions for improving individual performance. No one theory has proven to be applicable to all settings and no one approach or management style universally successful. Rowden demonstrates this in his description of management style:[1]

> Typical management, therefore, is an unreal concept. Management in all its forms is a question of individual style, running from the extreme autocrat at one end of the scale to the extreme democrat at the other end, with a host of variable styles in between . . . The question of what is right or wrong is a matter of individual judgement. What one can say, however, is that all managers should understand quite clearly what they are doing and why they are doing it. To manage blindly with little or no insight into what one's actions, is, to say the least, a risky approach to take.

Management style should ensure, however, that the views and opinions of service users and staff are acknowledged and that resources are distributed in response to identified consumer need. Complex, bureaucratic structures have no place at the level of local service delivery, although they may be represented at senior management level. Hence the NHS, the local authority and other agencies may 'control' the overall pattern of service delivery in this country for people with mental handicaps, but there is clear evidence to demonstrate that a revolution in management practice is taking place within these organizations to delegate decision-making and resource management to local staff who are 'in touch' with consumer needs and demand.

The introduction of general management in the NHS has, for example, encouraged the devolution of service management to local practitioners who receive relative freedom to determine the way in which resources should be allocated within the overall framework of an agreed service strategy and budget. The local authority has promoted opportunities for 'patch' management and consumer involvement in the delivery and practice of social services, and the expansion of the voluntary and private sector in the care of people with mental handicaps has broken the franchise that statutory authorities held on this client group. Consumerism, efficiency, accountability and cost-effectiveness have all become catch words of this decade and with them have come new opportunities for a radical revision of how services are managed.

Perhaps one of the most important reasons for clearly defined management structures at such an important time of change is to ensure that consistent standards and policies are provided for consumers and staff across the service and between agencies. It is true to say that as services disperse from central hospital sites that this becomes all the more important. Imagine, for example, the problems that would arise if each component of a local services was left to determine its own philosophies and approaches without reference or account to an agreed strategy or monitoring agency. The result would probably be chaotic, providing individuals with the opportunity to plan and deliver services based on an interpretation of their own value base and interest. Successes would undoubtedly occur in some areas by careful and purposeful design, in others by default, and in some progress may be unrecognizable.

All services require some form of defined management structure within which services may be held to account for their common practices and outcomes. By their design they must also preserve the individuality and autonomy demanded by local needs and they must not be restricted by outdated management methods and practices designed more appropriately for another era. The role of central management serves to:

- define a common service strategy/philosophy;
- set minimum standards for the service to achieve;
- identify a system of positive monitoring/quality assurance;
- define and facilitate access to skilled manpower resources;
- set and provide a realistic budget for the service; consult with consumers to ensure services are relevant and responsive;
- initiate and develop policies and procedures to enable staff to realize service aims and objectives;
- facilitate meaningful multi-agency teamwork in human services.

## DESIGNING A SHARED VISION

The prerequisite to any service must be a shared vision and strategy which is developed and accepted by all those concerned with the service. This acts as a cornerstone upon which all components of the service will be designed and built. The task is, in itself, complex and requires the time investment and commitment of managers, consumers and professionals, and may involve several meetings before an explicit statement of the service's core purpose, aims and objectives may be agreed upon.

In any locality there will be a range of similar and, in some cases, varied perceptions and ideas relating to the nature of a local service for people with mental handicaps. Agencies may be restricted in their vision by the existence of rigid planning procedures and processes, or constrained by present service models. Staff may not have been exposed to different models of service delivery, thus becoming resistant to change and feeling threatened by new employment practices. Consumers may differ in their needs and in the methods they may choose to meet them and, all in all, the development of a common philosophy will require tactful and thoughtful preparation.

The use of bureaucratic joint planning processes has often failed to accomplish this task, possibly because it is so removed from the needs of local consumers and professionals. The formal process may also have failed due to the lack of preparation given to contributors who may be unfamiliar with alternative models of care and who may be rigidly adhering to approaches with which they feel comfortable and familiar.

In some districts the process has started from the consumer end of the spectrum, through the promotion of local discussion groups, seminars, guest speakers and the lobbying of managers. Attitudinal change appears to be a prerequisite to the process of identifying a common agenda for service delivery, and consumers may be best placed to encourage a shift in attitude with their professional peers. This will also require the provision of opportunities for all people involved in the service to learn of other models and practices. There is certainly a wealth of published material available, other schemes to visit, people to consult and national advisory bodies willing to provide local services with information.

Perhaps the most effective way to develop a common approach is to develop a local planning team with representatives from all agencies, disciplines and organizations working in the locality with people with mental handicaps. Consumers and their families will certainly need to be involved and encouraged to contribute to discussions in a valued and informed way. Parents may make excellent chairpersons of such groups, thus facilitating an unbiased forum for debate between various service agency representatives.

Senior managers can do much to enable the success of such groups by encouraging local staff to attend and by sponsoring the promotion of joint teamwork as part of the agencies' primary task or objective. Hidden agendas will inevitably surface, and managers may feel threatened as traditional boundaries between professional/agency groups are challenged. Support will be required and opportunities provided for the resolution of potential conflicts as joint strategies are realized. Surprisingly, there is more common ground between different service staff and consumers than would otherwise have been expected, and additional advantages are certainly available as people begin to share their skills and to work together for a common objective.

The development of a shared vision or philosophy is therefore a primary management task from which a strategy may be developed which outlines the aims and objectives of local services, irrespective of traditional agency boundaries or structures. It is within this shared philosophy that the quality of service delivery may be judged and monitored and new services planned and implemented.

## A QUESTION OF QUALITY

Authorities have been monitoring the quality of their services in some form or another for many years but have traditionally been at a loss in their choice of meaningful variables against which to measure the effectiveness of these services. In some cases the measures used have been quantitive in nature, comparing the expenditure of one service to that of another in a similar structure and considering the proportion of budgets allocated to estate maintenance and catering as an indicator of quality. For others, quality was measured in an unstructured way by service managers and representatives from local consumer groups, who were often uninformed in respect of service philosophy and who based their appraisal on a combination of value judgements and personal experience.

Certainly, all senior staff are obliged to monitor the use of their authority's resources and to ensure that all monies spent are put to effective and efficient use. Checklists of standards have been produced by various authorities and by national bodies, such as the National Development Team's Checklist of standards.[2] Management audits were frequently used throughout the 1970s and the use of positive monitoring techniques was common to determine the quality of care in respect of physical resources and structures. All in all, the result was the beginning of a gradual recognition that a dynamic approach was needed to measuring the human component of care delivery in local services.

The concept of quality pervades every activity and all people involved in the service delivery must demonstrate a clear commitment to providing care of the highest possible standard. This is beneficial to the agency in terms of cost-efficiency and to the consumer who deserves nothing but the most effective service possible within the restrictions of the resources available at the time.

Most importantly, assuring quality does not demand the use of high technology or sophisticated skills or methodology. Instead it demands a new way of thinking, self-appraisal and awareness about what we are aiming to achieve and the process we adopt to realize our aims and objectives. Quality assurance is applicable to all people involved in the care of people with a mental handicap, whether it be in the provision of direct care or in provision of support services. It requires a reappraisal of the value systems we adopt and use each day and will involve consumers, their families and managers in having to adapt to new ways of working and evaluating services.

The concept of quality assurance programmes is a continuous and systematic process of the evaluation of agreed levels of care and service provision. Before we consider the process of quality assurance further it may help to consider some standard definitions:

- Quality: 'A degree or standard of excellence' (*Collins*).
- Standard: 'An accepted or approved example of something against which others are judged or measured . . . a principle of propriety, honesty and integrity; a level of excellence or quality; of recognized authority, competence or excellence' (*Collins*).
- Quality assurance: 'Comprising a management or clinical process to assure that patients or groups of patients receive an agreed upon level of care.'[3]
- Evaluation: 'A process involving frequent use of different kinds of techniques, including measurement but is broader in scope . . . an intellectual act.[4] It is a systematic process of determining the extent to which . . . objectives are achieved.'[5]

It is in every manager's interest to promote a good quality service and to attempt to provide a service which is high in outputs (rated in terms of consumer satisfaction) and low in its presentation of problems and complaints. In order to achieve this goal, the service requires a motivated workforce who are skilled, trained and committed to the achievement of the aims and objectives of the service. The needs of consumers and their families must be known and their views on the structure and effectiveness of the service sought and included in all evaluation programmes. Hence consumerism and market research should be integral components of any quality assurance programme. The local CMHT may be in good position to seek and represent the views of consumers and may provide a forum for their opinions. Another way to involve consumers is through the use of local consultation groups which are held as part of the agencies' formal communication structure. Perhaps a quarterly meeting of service staff, consumers, families and other interested people might be held in each locality, where an agenda for discussion and debate is shared and to which service managers participate. Local voluntary groups, the community health council and other consumer bodies should also be asked to contribute to the evaluation of local services in order that services might respond meaningfully to identified needs and priorities.

Management structures must also promote the ethos of quality assurance, and organizations should include statements regarding monitoring and quality control in each of their employee's job descriptions. Annual reviews of service performance plans and employee personal objectives will also include a specific statement relating to individual responsibility in this process. Staff will also need instruction in problem-solving skills and efficient management promotion schemes. Leadership style will need to facilitate and encourage the expression of the personal views of all those people involved in the service and their experiences and ideas rewarded by being listened to and included in service plans and evaluations. Above all, the aims and objectives of the service must be made explicit to all employees and service users and redefined and reinforced at strategic intervals in their career.

Positive evaluation will also require employees to develop self-appraisal techniques of self-evaluation. Self-support groups, discussion groups, peer review and counselling in respect of individual performance will help staff to acquire the confidence and presentation skills required to promote this process. Thus staff will be supported in developing their evaluative skills by a firm commitment to a training strategy designed to encourage staff to internalize the goals and objectives of the organization. Should this be achieved, then quality assurance programmes have a much greater chance of success and will ultimately become an integral part of the organization's ethos and culture.

We have already considered the importance of stating the explicit values and core purpose of the service, and managers must feel confident that their staff are aware and understand how to implement each of the goals in their everyday work. Once this has been done staff will be able to evaluate and judge their own performance against the value base adopted by the organization. Each employee also needs to know what is expected of his/her own role performance and individually designed job specifications should detail the tasks to be carried out within the person's proven sphere of competence. Once staff feel confident in their work, they should be encouraged to evaluate critically the work of the service agency, and develop their own objectives within the framework of the service philosophy. In this way the service is directed but also allows opportunities for creative autonomy and sharing in the decision-making process. It is through this dynamic exchange of values and experiences that services promote evolutionary change to the mutual advantage of a motivated and satisfied workforce and an equally appreciative and contented consumer group.

The evaluation of service delivery and consumer outcomes should be sponsored and encouraged by managers and individual staff members. The tools and methods employed to monitor the quality of individual services will depend upon the variables to measure and will normally be a combination of qualitative and quantitive methods. In some cases external monitoring groups may be used to provide an objective appraisal of the service and may employ structured questionnaires, consumer surveys and also applied research methods. The results of all aspects of service evaluation must be acted upon and used to redefine the aims and objectives of the service and, ultimately, should result in a more efficient and effective service for consumers. It will be the responsibility of service managers to ensure that regular reports of evaluation exercises are received and responded to, to encourage the maintenance of a quality culture. Thus the main components of this approach are: consumer/staff consultation; redefine aims and objectives; ongoing evaluation; implementation of local plans; managers agree strategic plans; statement of service principles and values; statement of joint agency principles.[6]

Service managers should judge their success in developing a quality culture when individual staff members contribute their own aims and objectives to the process. As an integral reinforcement, a more satisfied workforce should result which is motivated to work within the operational guidelines determined by the agency. Staff turnover should reduce, retention strategies should become more effective as job satisfaction increases and, as a consequence, the service will become more cost-effective and efficient.

In order to illustrate some of these key concepts further, the following models of quality assurance are presented.

## A SYSTEM OF QUALITY

The following project description is adapted from Russell[7] and based on the recognition that a system of values underpins the development of philosophies of care in services for people with mental handicaps. In any locality it would be foolish to assume that all people involved in the delivery of care start from the same value base and the absence of 'any coherent set of values in strategic plans' may be the cause for the failure to realize certain service philosophies and aims. Many services are currently undergoing a period of rapid service change and reorientation which will require a reappraisal of staff attitudes and service philosophy.

Three main stages have been identified as being involved in the formulation of service plans:[7]

● The need to think strategically.
● The need to build an appropriate culture for the organization.
● The need to identify the new tasks that have to be undertaken.

The same writer has quoted six skills which are necessary when preparing a new strategy for any high quality service: creative insight; sensitivity; vision; versatility; focus; patience.

Not all staff will have these skills and it may be helpful to appraise each person's skills through the introduction of staff development performance reviews and individually designed training programmes. The sum total of the strengths and needs of the organization, its staff and its consumers will provide a meaningful agenda for the construction of a strategic plan for the service.

The building of an appropriate culture for the service will require the identification of service philosophies and value systems. It has been assumed that organizations are a mix of different value systems and cultural influences/approaches.[7] Cultures which support the ethos of individually designed services require empathy, trust, informal decision-making, regular procedural review and depend on the involvement of all staff in the process of informed decision-making for their success. There will often be a shared value system which is reinforced by the practices of staff and managers which is designed to facilitate and sustain new value cultures.

Tasks need to be identified carefully as the value culture is translated into practice. One of the key tasks will be to evaluate the effectiveness of the service in achieving its aims and objectives. Detailed implementation plans will be required with specific statements regarding who will do what, when and with which resources. Evaluations should identify the accomplishments which clients have actually been enabled to achieve, and service deficits recorded.

The key component of this model is the introduction of a quality culture which is built and reinforced by managers, service users and the workforce. It is a dynamic model which disregards the outdated 'role model' which encouraged staff to resist change through blind allegiance to their professional groups. The successful implementation of a quality culture also depends on the management style adopted by the service and on the commitment of managers to service users.

This model has recognized the importance of determining the value base of all people involved in the service and has recommended the introduction of common aims and objectives as part of a process of managing change in human services. The realization of a quality culture among the workforce aims to ensure that all services are constantly evaluated in client performance terms.

# QUALITY ACTION GROUPS

The principles of a local service described in this book acknowledge the rights and responsibilities of consumers to have meaningful access to ordinary services and to receive a range of specialist support delivered by appropriately trained staff. Specifying the core purpose of the service provides staff and service users with clear expectations of the service and provides managers with the opportunity to set clear objectives against which to measure the quality of the service.

Five key accomplishments have been identified which look at the quality of human services in terms of the lives of the people served:[8]

- Community presence: people with mental handicap have the right to live and spend their time in the community, not segregated in residential, day or leisure facilities which keep them apart from other members of society.
- Relationships: living in the community is not enough. People with mental handicaps also need help and encouragement to mix with other nonhandicapped people in the course of their daily lives. We should not deny them opportunities to form valued relationships at home, at work or in education and in community leisure activities.
- Choice: an important feature of the quality of life is the degree of choice that people can exercise. This can apply to small, everyday matters like what to wear or eat, and to major life decisions like who to live with or where to work. People with mental handicap often have limited power to make choices and look after their own interests. A high quality service will give priority to enhancing the choices available to people and protecting their human rights generally.
- Competence: in order for people with mental handicap to live a full

and rewarding life in their local community, many will require help in learning new skills. This increase in competence should be directly relevant to people's life situations, helping them to develop relationships and achieve greater choice and independence.

● Respect: people with mental handicaps often have an undeserved bad reputation and are seen and treated as second-class citizens. Services can play an important part in helping people to be seen and treated with the same status as other valued members of the community.[9]

In any service there will be a number of people who have a direct interest in the impact the service has on them as individuals and on consumers. The quality action group model (see below) identifies these people as 'stakeholders' and may include: clients; families; service staff; service managers; service planners; professional specialists; politicians; the local community.

The aim is to involve stakeholders in the decisions affecting the service and in the monitoring of its achievements and accomplishments. Stakeholders may need some form of preparation before they feel confident to participate in quality action groups; service providers must ensure that opportunities are provided to ensure that all participants feel confident in the process. The use of self-advocacy groups may help people with mental handicaps to express their own views and the introduction of peer support may also encourage people to contribute meaningfully.

The first task of the group will be to identify the core purpose and accomplishments for the service. Accomplishments should be clearly defined and achievable and should contribute to increasing the status and rights of consumers.

The process is based on the assumption that services are individually designed to meet the needs of consumers. The use of life planning or individual programme planning systems (see Chapter 3) underpins this concept as a process for reviewing the needs of people with a mental handicap and for agreeing action to meet those needs. The quality action model suggests that the next natural stage in this process should be an individual programme planning system for a service, with reviews monitoring how well a service is meeting the identified needs of its consumers. The process also suggests ways of improving the quality of the service, and to ensure that these ideas are acted upon, requires the involvement, support and commitment of the service managers.

The quality action group process can be summarized as follows:[9]

● Form a quality action group to review quality in part or all of the service system.

- Define what quality is for your service. This should be in terms of the important ways in which the service sets out to affect the lives of its clients.
- Hold regular meetings to review the extent to which you are achieving quality, and agree goals for action to improve your service.
- Between meetings work on the goals you have set, and continue to monitor your achievement of quality.

The quality action group will need to define those aspects of the service that it wishes to consider and monitor. In many districts there will be at least two levels of service which can be identified for action. The first will be the local services which form the basic component parts of the overall service. The second will be the service management group itself which sets standards, aims and objectives for the agency and which has as part of its responsibility, the task of assuring quality in all parts of the service.

The role of the quality action group will also be to assist in the identification of service strengths and needs. Questions will be raised in respect of the services current ability to meet the needs of its consumers and staff, both in terms of its availability and accessibility. The groups will also need to decide on the means that they wish to adopt to measure the achievements of the service. Examples may include:

- Individual client records – opportunity plans, IPP reviews, records of community contacts and records of new skill acquisition.
- Participant observation–group members spending time with consumers in their environments in order to experience and evaluate the quality of their lives first hand.
- Central records of client activity and statistical information may provide opportunities to monitor the number of people using the service.
- Consumer views will also help to assess the impact the service has on its users. The views of self-advocacy, parent and voluntary groups may provide excellent indicators of how the service is perceived.
- House records and diaries may also provide a useful source of information. For example, in a local service in Winchester records are maintained for all household routines in which clients are engaged. Summaries of significant activities or events affecting the lives of service users will also provide valuable sources of information.
- External monitoring may complement the process further. Some authorities have engaged in the use of external monitoring teams who submit regular reports to management groups of their impressions of the service.

The result should be a co-ordinated approach to the use of a battery of evaluation techniques which provide the quality action groups with the information required to monitor the quality of the service. Managers will need to consider how they maintain the enthusiasm and momentum of such groups and will need to ensure that opportunities are provided for regular staff training for individuals to acquire new skills and knowledge in their quest for service improvement and evolution.

The advantages of this process are that service monitoring and evaluation are built into the service management structure and are not superimposed from external monitoring agencies. As such the process should be self-motivated and seek to improve the quality of the service to the mutual advantage of all stakeholders. Often the process of social change will need initial priming; the use of external facilitators may assist stakeholders in defining their role and function and may help in the identification of the core accomplishments the service is to adopt.

In summary, the quality action group approach provides many advantages to its stakeholders:

- Service users will have a clear view of what their services are aiming to accomplish with and for them.
- Staff will set their own goals within the framework of agreed service objectives and will collect data on their own performance. They will be involved in all stages of service planning and help to design and revise their own services.
- Managers will have clear descriptions of what the service has accomplished for the users. They will be 'in touch' with the service and will be able to describe the primary aims of the service and report on its accomplishments to their superiors.

The aims of the quality action group can be summarized as:

- It is user-orientated and measures the accomplishments of the service in terms of client outcomes and successes.
- It involves a positive and systematic approach to monitoring service quality (good practices can be seen and supported and less good ones can be identified and improved).
- The approach is action-orientated, providing stakeholders with opportunities to shape, improve and build on their successes.
- The system is designed to be absorbed within the day-to-day nature of the job which ensures the greater likelihood of its success.
- The data collected is sought from staff and consumers as part of their

everyday routines and is spontaneous and therefore more reliable.

## THE MESSAGE SO FAR

So far this chapter has considered the importance of identifying core accomplishments and statements relating to the core purpose of human services involved in the provision of care for people with mental handicaps. The approach described requires the development of a partnership between consumers, their families, professionals and service managers towards the joint realization of quality-based services.

Two specific approaches have been described which involve the generation of a 'quality culture' and the introduction of 'quality action groups' to identify and point the way forward to achieve agreed service goals and accomplishments. The use of specific tools to measure the quality of all components of the service have been combined to allow services to evaluate quality in terms of the affect they have on the expectations of their consumers. It is therefore a humanistic and dynamic approach which relies on the full involvement of its consumers and avoids domination by inflexible management structures and systems.

The discussion continues with a consideration of other dimensions of the quality assurance process.

## MAINTAINING A HIGH QUALITY SERVICE

In any description of quality assurance in human services, account must be taken of the quality of the workforce and environment in which care is provided. In the first instance, staff must be motivated enough to believe that it is necessary to enhance the quality of the service and that it is possible and desirable to improve one's own practice and contribution to the service. In order to achieve this fundamental stage, staff must be able to define their own role in the system and set standards against which to measure their own achievements.

Traditionally, this function has been provided by the various professional bodies who validate and train nurses and social workers. Employers also set standards of care and practice to which staff are expected to work. In individually designed services, the task of standardizing national curriculum planning teams is becoming more and more complex as local services demand greater flexibility in the role interpretations of their workforces. The message appears to be in the form of a slogan 'progress, partnership between professionals and deprofessionalism'. To build an effective workforce capable of working in the services described in this book requires clear definitions of what does and what does not constitute professional care and practice.

The importance of professional training and practice for people working in human services becomes all the more essential as agencies pool their expertise and skills in local practice. Joint training opportunities for staff from different agencies and structures will be required which respect the skill base and background of all contributors. Agreements will need to be reached on local service philosophies and approaches and the setting of joint standards to employ in the care process generated.

The setting of standards is in fact one of the prime responsibilities of all service agencies. It is through the exercise of this function that services can effectively discharge its other key functions of planning and resource allocation. Setting standards allows managers to achieve a better fit of resources to needs and, in particular, to channel resources to those areas identified by consumers and local service providers. If managers are to direct resources to areas of particular need then some attempt to define criteria of good services and to identify concomitant measures of excellence is essential.

Everyone involved in the service will have some idea of what they consider their service is trying to achieve. We have already seen how important it is to formulate a statement of service policy objectives capable of practical translation, into terms of who does what to whom, with what resources, and with what intended outcome. Performance standards, in this context, have two components: a statement of policy objectives for the service; and the identification of measures to assess achievements.

The approach to be adopted in setting standards is similar to that of the quality action group described above and will involve all stakeholders in the identification of specific areas of performance for which the group believes a significant improvement is required. For each problem area, a standard statement should be written which is: reasonable; understandable; useful; measurable; observable; and achievable.

The identification of standards for the different components of the service is perhaps a prerequisite for the monitoring of quality. Standards, for example, take account of the structural aspects of the service: items which are put into the service to enable it to function. This includes: equipment; buildings; staff members; staff skill mix; staff work routines.

Standards also take account of the processes involved: methods employed in the delivery of care; assessment procedures; appropriateness of intervention; evaluating levels of competence.

Standards must also be capable of evaluation and measurement in terms of client/service outcomes, measuring outcomes for consumers in terms of: personal achievements; personal status; level of comfort; level of independence; and level of control over their lives.

The setting of standards leads to more effective problem-solving techniques and encourages staff to develop positive approaches to improving the quality of their work. The specification of standards for different components of the service also provides managers with opportunities to initiate new staff into established routines, thus reducing margins of error, since staff should be clear of what is expected of them. The importance of maintaining consistency in the lives of people with mental handicaps will in fact be reinforced by this approach and will avoid any necessity to return to the archaic practice of 'rule books' and 'procedure manuals'. In the model described in this chapter, the system relies on the self-generation of standard statements and practices which will eventually become part of the service system.

Equally important is the need for the organization to develop the right mechanisms to integrate and transmit the information required to organize such a service. This will have implications for the way in which the service is managed and for the formal and informal communication systems used to share and pass on information and ideas within the agency. Weekly staff/house meetings may be one way of ensuring that information is shared and opportunities provided for staff and consumers to contribute to the setting of standards and monitoring their implementation and measurement.

In practice there have been many examples of local project design to evaluate service quality within services for people with mental handicaps. Some districts have developed statements of joint policies which are designed to identify standards for the whole service, and in particular to identify the role of each group of professionals working within it. Hence the role expectations of residential care staff is described and their performance measured against pre-set criteria. Similarly, the roles of specialist support staff are specified. One particular example of this approach is worthy of note; that is the development of a 'quality assurance strategy'/check list of standards developed by the South Lincolnshire Health Authority for its mental handicap services.[10]

The project co-ordinator for standards of care at the Royal College of Nursing has identified a model for quality assurance shown in Figure 12.1.[11]

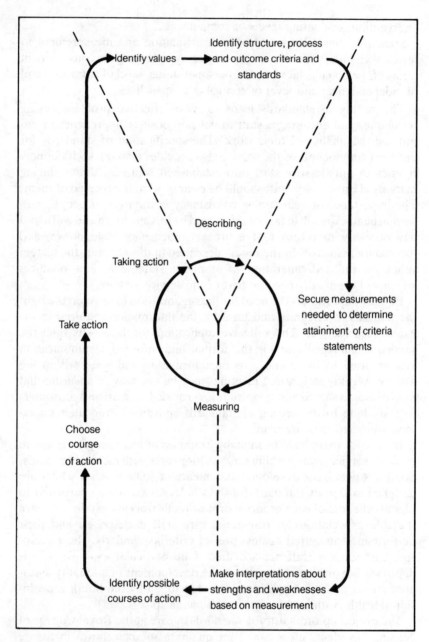

**Figure 12.1** Model for quality assurance

# MAINTAINING A HIGH QUALITY ENVIRONMENT

High quality care is not achieved in a vacuum. The whole process of care delivery is part of a complex interactive process between the needs of clients, the resources available and the values of the service. So far we have considered the value base of the service and systems which may be used to assure quality in human services. This section of the chapter considers the maintenance of quality of those aspects of the environment within which care is provided.

Within any organization there will exist a variety of policies and procedures designed to monitor the quality of the environment and the practices that take place within it. Examples are to be found of policies dictating the way in which the fabric of the building should be maintained and others relating to the quality of food preparation. Safety procedures also have their place in the 'handbook of good practice' and provide staff with advice on how to avoid accidents, fire and infection. How relevant are these procedures in the service model described in this book?

At a first glance many people would assume that they have no place in individual service design and that such procedures exist only to satisfy the needs of service bureaucrats who are intent on restricting the quality of life for consumers through their prescription of outdated rules and regulations. At the other end of the spectrum, many of these rules and regulations exist to ensure that high standards are maintained in all areas of service delivery; in fact, a compromise may be reached to ensure that managers and consumers reach agreement in how services are to be delivered without infringing their rights to live as ordinary people in ordinary environments.

Let us take, for example, the quality of catering provision in small houses in the community. In a four-bedroomed house staffed to meet the needs of people with severe learning difficulties, no less than 10 people may be involved in the preparation and cooking of meals. In a larger establishment two cooks may be involved, thus reducing the number of people involved in food handling. At the extreme, environmental health officers may insist that all staff attend food handling courses, that food is prepared in kitchens which appear to be more suited to a large institution rather than an ordinary house and that residents do not prepare their own food for fear of infection!

As a service manager, the author has realized that it is necessary to identify a procedure which specifies the minimum standards to be employed in ordinary houses in respect of food preparation. Such guidelines remind staff and residents of the importance of hygiene in the kitchen and insist that all people in the house receive one day's instruction in the correct techniques for food handling. Attention is needed for environmental hygiene, e.g. pets should not be fed in kitchens, clean towels should be available at all times, dustbin areas should be kept clean and a thorough cleaning of all kitchen areas should take place each week.

Such procedures should also emphasize the importance of variety and nutrition in the diet and should take account of good budget practice. The effect of these guidelines has been to provide a consistent standard throughout the service which has been accepted by the local environmental health officer as an official procedure for the service. As a consequence, many of the more restrictive practices prescribed by these officers in other parts of the organization have not been enforced in the mental handicap service.

Similarly, standards should be set for cleanliness in the domestic environment. In local services, care staff and residents will normally be involved in daily household chores. As such, the maintenance of consistent standards of cleanliness becomes increasingly difficult. However, the advice of local specialists and managers may assist local staff in formulating guidelines to ensure that a high quality of cleanliness is maintained in the service. Such guidelines may be translated into practice through the development of activity/opportunity plans for individual service users as part of their everyday contribution to the housekeeping tasks of their home. The result is obvious, with residents and staff taking pride in a home which enhances the acceptance and quality of life in the local neighbourhood.

Perhaps at this stage it should be emphasized that managers have a key role to play in ensuring that the imposition of restrictive practices and policies that reduce the 'ordinary nature of everyday experiences' for residents and staff are resisted. Policies should be written by local staff to restrict the number of official visitors to the house, and these should be agreed and accepted by service managers. This will ensure that residents are 'protected' from invasive visits from people who may not have been invited to the house. There will be occasions when visits from local officials, senior managers and people interested in developing similar services in their home area will be necessary. It would be impossible and indeed unacceptable to 'close' the house to all such people, but alternatives are possible. Managers may provide, for example, video presentations of some of the day-to-day features of the service; written material may also serve as an alternative to visits to the house. In this way, visitors may learn much of the nature of the service. For those occasions when people must visit the house, clear guidelines should be made available to ensure that certain parts of the house are restricted unless individual residents invite visitors to join them in seeing their home. Examples would be individual bedrooms.

Everyday maintenance of the fabric of the house will also need attention. For those properties which are managed by large or complex organizations, arrangements will normally be made to maintain the houses as part of the 'local estate'. Should this be so, then managers must be prepared to challenge some of the inappropriate practices usually employed by large estate departments. For example, large lorries or vans, emblazened with the 'logo' of the local authority or hospital will draw unnecessary attention to the status of the residents and, accordingly, inconspicuous vehicles should be used. Similarly, local staff must be able to break through the laboriously difficult process of receiving services when required rather than having to wait for prolonged periods while request forms filter through the system. In some services, local contractors are engaged to respond to maintenance needs; this provides staff with immediate access to a range of local tradesmen. This of course provides greater choice and selection of high quality services and, as a bonus, may prove to be financially competitive. Incidentally, it may also encourage integration within the community, as residents and their staff enter the consumer market as valued customers.

Quality assurance applies to all aspects of service delivery from the maintenance of a high quality living environment to the identification of standards which will affect the way in which people receive care and plan their lives. This chapter has considered the combination of qualitative measures of service accomplishments, e.g. the individual programme plan, the development of quality cultures, and the introduction of quality action groups and quantitative measures such as catering standards and maintenance strategies. There are other quantitative measures which may indicate the efficiency of human services.

## PERFORMANCE AND COST-EFFICIENCY

Perhaps one of the most familiar measures of service performance is the use of indicators. In the NHS for example, the use of performance indicators has become prolific. The purpose of performance indicators is to provide feedback on whether a particular service is or is not on course to its target. Before performance indicators can be of any use at all, the target to be measured must be clearly stated. In the NHS the indicators used tend to concentrate on the delivery of skilled expertise from specialists in relationship to need, rather than upon the provision of residential services alone. The indicators also aim to advise the DHSS of the extent to which resources are being directed towards joint agreed service aims and jointly planned service.

An indicator is a single measure which attempts to summarize a set of data, in the form of percentages, rates and ratios. For the mental handicap service these data sets may measure efficiency in terms of:

- availability of qualified nursing staff as a percentage of the workforce;
- number of children remaining in hospitals;
- number of day places available;
- amount of money spent on catering costs per resident per day;
- number of specialist staff available;
- number of occupied beds in any part of the service;
- average cost of the service per resident day.

One of the criticisms against performance indicators is that they have to rely on the return of check lists or questionnaires from local services on an annual basis. In some cases these may not be completed accurately and data has also been omitted from some returns. However, performance indicators may still prove to be a useful audit tool. They pose questions and do not boast or attempt to give answers but provide a starting point for investigative analysis. They do this by comparing the performance of one service against others in the region and in the country for each of the identified indicators. Averages are presented and each district 'scores' in rank order according to their own performance. Their functions can be summarized as: background, descriptive data for planning purposes; a monitoring tool; a means to identify serious service deficiencies or problems; and a register or point of contact to facilitate the dissemination of information relating to models of good practice elsewhere in the country.

The use of performance indicators is limited and should be used only as part of a wider battery of qualitative measures of local performance, such as those indicated above. They do serve to illustrate objectively certain trends in service provision, as the following examples may indicate:

- How much screening and assessment takes place within the locality?
- How far are services compatible with the declared policy aim?
- How far does the district engage in multidisciplinary teamwork?

- How far does the service support people in the community?
- Does the district have a comprehensive register to determine consumer need?
- How far is the district self-sufficient in service provision, or do consumers have to travel elsewhere to receive services?
- Are there adequate staffing levels available?
- Is there evidence of joint planning between agencies?
- To what extent is joint finance employed to develop services for people with mental handicaps?

Apart from the use of performance indicators, local services will also receive statements of performance from their managers in respect of cost-efficiency and performance. Each year statements are compiled and published in respect of the actual costs of providing residential services for people with mental handicaps. The outcome of these statements may have a significant effect on the pattern of subsequent service delivery which, in turn, may affect the quality of service provision.

The funding of public services varies widely between localities and agencies, and yet the real costs of maintaining a valued life in the community appear to escape full calculation. One research study published by the King's Fund Centre compared the costs and the quality of different residential services for people with a mental handicap.[12] It was found that the major resource used by all services was staff time, which accounted for approximately 80 per cent of total costs. It was also found that the cost of high quality service provision in small houses in the community costs more than hospital care and care in the private sector.

The report emphasizes that the true cost of services for people with mental handicaps should be measured in terms of client accomplishments and outcomes rather than simply in terms of cost-statements and unit size. These findings were also reported in a study of comparative revenue costs of nine different service models.[13] In this case it was found that larger community units were cheaper (25 beds) than small houses (8 beds) and mental handicap hospitals. The small houses were slightly more expensive than the hospitals, but the quality of care and lifestyle enjoyed by residents was far superior in the small houses. Both of these studies appear to suggest that small houses, although more expensive in respect of revenue costs, can provide a superior quality of care.

Managers would be wise to note that the cost of high quality services should not be the only consideration when planning new services in the community, as has been pointed out:[14]

Cost-effectiveness analysis should not be seen as having the power of veto but rather as providing one part of the information (in addition to political, social, medical and philosophical criteria) necessary to achieve a truly informed decision about using society's resources.

The whole question of cost-efficiency may appear to be in conflict with the principles of normalization described in this book. Certainly, managers who insist that 'voids' in bed numbers must be filled immediately despite interpersonal difficulties experienced by residents, and those who determine aspects of service quality in terms of cost-savings, may certainly support this hypothesis. However, there is little doubt that efficiency is a goal to which we should all aspire if scarce resources are to be put to their maximum advantage.

## BUDGET MANAGEMENT

There are very few people who could dispute the fact that one of the main excuses given for low performance or poor quality is the lack of sufficient financial resources. However, in the real world, there will never be enough money to meet the often conflicting demands of the organization to undertake all its tasks and responsibilities without some degree of compromise being made.

In most local services, budgets will be defined and delegated to the person in charge to manage, and it will require some considerable skill and ingenuity to budget to meet all household needs during a financial year. In order to assume responsibility for a budget, staff must be in a position to control expenditure and to set priorities in how the money is spent. Cumbersome accounting procedures will only mitigate against this principle and yet somehow arrangements must be made to protect the parent authority and consumers from the misuse of what may consist of extremely large sums of money. It is beyond the scope of this chapter to identify the policies and procedures that will satisfy the needs of the house, its residents and the visiting auditors, but there is no doubt that each house must determine its own financial guidelines which should be agreed by the managing authority. In general, however, the following principles should be reflected in any guidelines:

- They should allow flexible and immediate access to adequate sums of money to meet the needs of the house and its residents for at least one week at a time.

- They should not deny residents freedom of access to their own monies and should provide opportunities for local purchases from a variety of sources in the locality.
- They should be clearly written, including the minimum restrictions possible to protect the residents and authority from misuse.
- They should encourage the delegation of all budgetary control to the local service and should not impose unreasonable restrictions on expenditure which mitigate against local decision-making.

These guidelines are indeed fundamental but should be adopted to allow greater flexibility in the design, management and control of local budgets. After all, they will ultimately determine the extent to which resources will be purchased and allocated to the service.

Managers will be in the front line to account for how the authority's resources are spent and managed. An effective budgetary system is obviously one of the key aims of any service that is aiming to improve efficiency and to demonstrate that it provides 'value for money'. The questions that managers will be asking will reflect this and it will be up to budget managers to demonstrate that their resources are effectively managed and that any requests for increases are supported by statements of case which clearly identify the benefits that clients would receive in return.

Similarly, if savings are made within budgets, they must be justified and a case made for them to be redirected within the house budget for the benefit of service users. Managers must also determine the rules within which local staff may influence and redirect their budgets in terms of virement and expenditure limits. Certainly, the more flexibility that can be built into local guidelines, the greater will be the influence which managers will be able to delegate to consumers and local staff, who should determine their own priorities and purchases.

In most services, resources are allocated in response to identified service needs and will be influenced by changes in local circumstances and resident demands for improved services. The allocation of resources should be reviewed on an annual basis by local staff who, in turn, should advise managers of the changes required to effect service plans and objectives. Budget-setting exercises may provide many opportunities for managers and local staff to redefine the way in which finances are allocated and do not always require large increases in revenue. In fact, many services have proved that with efficient accounting procedures and expenditure practice, they can imaginatively create new opportunities for residents within their own budgets, for example:

- Using public transport instead of taxis for resident outings.
- Reviewing the use of medicines in the house through the use of reduced prescribing practices.
- Reviewing menus to use local, fresh produce instead of purchasing frozen foods.
- Exercising economies in heating bills.
- Replacing overtime with the use of flexible 'bank' staff in times of staff shortage.
- Using local contractors competitively for maintenance work in place of 'in-house' tradesmen.

These examples demonstrate economies of scale which do not reduce the quality of the service but enhance it. They represent nothing less than good housekeeping practice and cost-efficiency which, in turn, may facilitate the purchase of additional resources when required.

Managing finances and budgets in local services requires considerable initiative and skill and an informed management system that will facilitate and enable staff to make the maximum use of their resources without penalizing them for efficient budget practice. There is no doubt that this aspect of management will prove to test the patience and creativity of all staff, but when managed effectively it can present challenges that may prove to be both rewarding and satisfying for staff as they realize new opportunities for their clients.

Finally, it is perhaps necessary to include some reference to the role of senior managers in this process as services develop the principles of an ordinary life in the community. Certainly, pressures will be exerted on senior managers to trim budgets to the maximum and make efficiency savings wherever possible. It is always easier to sacrifice the principles or values of the service to achieve this objective than to resist persistent requests to save money. Take, for example, the manager who receives a request to purchase a specific piece of equipment for a resident and suggests that local staff should engage in fund-raising activities to pay for the appliance rather than use part of a specified budget. Is this not an erosion of the individual's right to a service, or does fund-raising enhance the person's status in the community?

This example has been chosen deliberately to illustrate the importance of upholding the basic principles of a valued lifestyle. In fact, services should specify detailed fund-raising procedures for their staff to provide them with guidance on how to receive and deal with requests from charitable bodies or from neighbours who make donations or gifts to individual service users. Of course, local purchasing power will be limited to the amount of funds available, and rigid guidelines may deny individuals the opportunity of enhancing the quality of their own lives. However, there is a considerable difference in accepting support on an individual basis, and compensating for services which should be funded from designated budgets.

Therefore, managers have a responsibility to uphold the values of the service. These will be reflected in the way in which finances are credited to the service. Poor maintenance, shabby clothes and unkept gardens will all reflect on the way in which the house and its residents are seen in the local neighbourhood, and will have a direct bearing on their status in the community. Therefore, local staff are not being a persistent nuisance when they request and insist that budgets reflect adequate finances to purchase support services and resources of a high quality. When they do so they are demanding, quite reasonably, that their managers respect their requests for the promotion of a valued lifestyle for their clients, in keeping with the philosophy of the service.

## THE MOST EXPENSIVE RESOURCE OF ALL!

Staff costs may reflect up to 80 per cent of the budget for any house in the community. No wonder that so much has been written and commented upon in respect of methods of staff selection and staff deployment practices. There are many examples of staffing models in community-based services for people with mental handicaps, ranging from houses employing only qualified nurses and social workers, to others with no staff support at all.

The only formula to apply when calculating staffing levels is to consider the actual needs of the clients themselves and to consider making staff appointments in response to the skills that will be required to enhance the quality of life for people living in the house and which will facilitate their integration in the community. In fact, staff should be selected in direct response to the identified needs of residents to ensure that an appropriate mix of skills is available.

This approach to staff selection is a great advancement on the previous practice adopted in many authorities where staff were deployed to specific client areas in response to dependency ratings and historical allocation systems. These systems became particularly cumbersome when manpower planning technology aimed to provide standard staffing formulae to all client groups as a means to assist service planning and budget forecasting. In fact, some of this data continues to provide direction to setting staffing levels in new services, but there is no substitute for the 'needs-led' formula suggested above.

Should this approach be accepted then the choice of selection becomes far more objective and is not constrained by agency allegiances to their own workforces. It provides some degree of competition for staff from different backgrounds to put their skills to the test in the selection process. In practice, qualified staff are still required to provide leadership, management and skilled support to people with mental handicaps in many services, although it should be acknowledged that not all people will need the benefit of qualified people to meet their everyday needs. Perhaps the most progressive and resourceful service will have a variety of skilled practitioners to call upon to meet the needs of their service users. Hence, nurses, social workers and a variety of specialist support staff may lead a mature workforce of appropriately trained care staff to meet the varied needs of their consumers.

Although it is difficult to prescribe the skill mix that will be required to staff any 'model' district service, there are some general principles to be applied when selecting and deploying staff:

- Staff should be accountable directly to the manager and consumers of the local service in which they work, and should not be moved between residential services.
- Clients should be involved in the selection of all new staff.
- All staff should receive regularly revised job specifications which identify the core elements of their work and the expected standards of their performance.
- Staff should be selected in respect of the skills they offer to meet consumer needs and not just as the result of any one specific qualification.
- All staff should receive individually designed induction programmes to prepare them for their work.
- All staff should receive regular reviews of their performance and appropriate training opportunities to enhance their skills and competences.
- Account should be taken to select staff in accordance with age and sex mix to complement the needs of consumers.
- Staff must demonstrate that they have the necessary interpersonal skills to work with others in teams and that they support the philosophy and value base of the service.
- Staff should be flexible in their approach to meet the changing needs of their client group and to contribute to the process of service change for the benefit of consumers.

- Staff should demonstrate that they have the appropriate life experience and maturity to meet the needs of others and should be sufficiently skilled and motivated to meet the needs demanded of them by their clients in all aspects of their daily lives.

Flexible deployment practices will be particularly important if services are to meet the needs of their consumers. For example, rigid shift patterns, fixed meal breaks and inflexible rules regarding overtime will serve only to reduce the provision of opportunities for service users and may also serve as a cause of immense frustration for staff. More appropriately, managers should design staff employment contracts to encourage maximum flexibility in working hours, which should be allocated in accordance with the needs of people living in the house. Naturally, due consideration must also be given to staff themselves, who will have their own lives to lead and who have a right to plan ahead to meet their own commitments. Taking this factor into account, there are many examples of good practice to demonstrate that flexible staffing patterns do in fact enhance the quality of the service and improve satisfaction for both consumers and their staff.

Managers must also take into account that local staff will need to ensure that adequate numbers of staff are available during the working week if individual opportunity plans and arranged activities are to be realized. All too often, inflexible allocation systems have forced services to work with extremely low staffing levels, and in dispersed services this would prove to be disastrous to the quality of life provided and the ability of senior staff to maintain adequate 'safety' levels of staff at any one time. Hence managers should delegate budget management for staff to a local level and allow managers to exercise their discretion in the allocation of overtime within pre-arranged budget limits.

The use of a 'bank' of local part-time staff to cover on a casual basis during periods of staff shortage may also prove to be both cost-effective and supportive to the establishment. The advantages are that local people will be encouraged to participate in the house and residents will not be subjected to a range of unfamiliar faces, which may often occur if managers are forced to use agency staff to cover unexpected staffing deficiencies.

The service will require a system of flexible budgeting and employment practices to support this approach. Employment policies will need to protect and support staff through the introduction of personal support, in-service training and personal counselling. In addition, clearly defined principles and procedures should be available to support staff in their everyday work, and access to statutory personnel policies to cover such instances such as official disputes, grievances, complaints and disciplinary matters must be available in the service.

# STAFF DEVELOPMENT, PERFORMANCE REVIEW AND PERSONAL SUPPORT

One of the key factors involved in the provision of a high quality service will be the maintenance of a highly skilled and motivated workforce. One of the aims of local services is that it will invest in its workforce to enhance the range of skills and competences available to its consumers. To achieve this aim, services must identify and implement comprehensive systems of staff development and performance review for each of its employees.

Strategies to improve the efficiency of any organization, whether it be a small house in the community or large commercial enterprise, will need to set precise performance objectives for each member of the workforce. The staff development and performance review system ensures that staff meet with their immediate manager at regular intervals (usually six-12-monthly) to discuss aspects of their personal performance and achievements against previously set targets which reflect the needs of people living in the house and of the organization. The central concept of this approach is a crucial part of the overall strategy of staff and management development, since it enables managers to set realistic targets for its staff in terms of achievable goals. It also identifies the development and training needs of its staff.

The principal aims of staff development performance reviews are: to enable each member of staff to receive periodic and systematic feedback upon their performance; and for managers, in reviewing strengths and needs with their staff, to set targets for the future and ensure that appropriate training and development is identified, prioritized and provided to enable staff to enhance their skills and contributions to their part of the overall service.

The benefits of such reviews to the manager are that they:

- Lead to a better sharing of the organization's and manager's expectations and requirements of each member of staff.
- Enable managers to be aware of the aspirations/needs of staff which can be developed or met as appropriate.
- Clarify the key areas/tasks upon which staff should concentrate and

determine how these relate to the performance of the service.

- Facilitate a clearer perception of staff needs/feelings which may be supported and developed.
- Lead to an agreement of plans for the next review period and identify that support staff will need to realize the aims of their development programme.
- Help staff to maintain their motivation towards improved/increased performance through recognition of personal strengths and successes, and to identify where enhanced performance is needed.
- Assist in fostering improved staff relationships and lead to a stronger, more cohesive team.

A critical feature of this approach is to measure staff performace in terms of quality and to set realistic and achievable targets for staff as part of the overall strategy adopted for the service. Certainly, staff development performance review systems should be adopted as an integral part of any management system and they are certainly not an optional extra! In fact, they complement the process of management performance which sets its targets in terms of performance objectives. Of course, this system lends itself well to the test of quality assurance outlined at the beginning of this chapter.

Staff will also require reinforcement from their everyday work and from the employing organization if they are to remain highly motivated and interested in contributing to the development of high quality services. To encourage this managers need to consider the following.

## Methods of participation

Broadly speaking, people working in small houses tend to be offered more opportunity to participate in the running of the house. This can range from such things as choice of menu and choice of shopping items, to specific named responsibilities for medicines, estate maintenance and direct care. Other forms of participation should include client and peer/staff selection, client intervention, service planning, review and evaluation.

## Communication structures

Opportunities should be provided to encourage staff to share ideas and to receive regular support and feedback from colleagues and managers. In most houses the main forum for communication will be the weekly staff meeting which provides an opportunity for client review, the passing of messages, in-service training and the resolution of interpersonal staff conflicts. Other systems of communication include access to new information, communication books, work books, handover periods, day and week planners, client records and opportunity plans. Other opportunities for a wider sharing of ideas may be provided through in-service training days, joint consultative meetings, and other occasions designed to bring staff members together to discuss service developments and future plans.

Access to training opportunities is also essential if a highly skilled workforce is to be maintained. Access to library facilities, study leave and visits to other services may also encourage and motivate staff. (Staff training is covered in greater detail in Chapter 14).

The development and nurturing of teamwork within the service will also help to motivate staff and provide them with support in their everyday lives. In dispersed services problems associated with isolation cannot be ignored and managers should provide opportunities to develop peer group support structures both within care teams and with wider community support networks. Access to occupational health services and to counsellors should also be negotiated in times of stress; after all, a proactive approach to supporting staff will prove to be a major determinant in retaining staff and maintaining high levels of staff performance and service quality (see Chapter 13).

## THE MANAGEMENT OF CHANGE

In any organization, new developments and practices will inevitably place demands on service users and their staff. Old practices will often be challenged in the light of new experiences and the old order will often appear to be inadequate to cope with the demands of new technology and social change. The realities of planning, initiating and implementing change will require sensitive management, and will present new services with a challenge that will test their theories and in many cases their patience.

Change, of course, affects staff as well as consumers. One can find examples of good and bad practice in the preparation change of both groups but, essentially, they require the same sensitive approach in adjusting to new practices and service systems. Any change in the way in which services are structured or in the way in which they function will influence the delivery of care in practice and, of course, the quality of care and intervention.[15] One suggestion has been that for change to occur, there must be a stimulus, and influential and powerful people in the organization must perceive the need for change.[15]

Change is therefore a constant element in any vital organization and there will be very few people in today's human services who will remain unaffected by the dynamic process of evolution. The catalyst for change should always be a reappraisal of what consumers require, not just in terms of professional excellence but also in terms of realizing their own status and value in society. Change is often sold in terms of what it will provide for the consumer, but experience is slowly proving the basic fact that incentives have to be provided for staff as well if they are to be committed to the change process. The question they will ask is, 'What's in it for me?'

Feeling change is therefore a prerequisite for all team members. In the first instance there will need to be a perceived need for change, and all stakeholders should share in the formulation of that vision and influence their peers locally to join them in a concerted effort to revise the system to the mutual benefit of all concerned. Change inflicted exernally has little success of being internalized by the workforce or their clients; change that is self-directed and sponsored by stakeholders will be far more attractive and successful. The following ingredients of change will need to be considered:

- Perceived need for change.
- Sharing a common vision.
- Sharing and enlisting support for the change and its process.
- Identifying effective communication networks.
- Informing and educating all stakeholders of the benefits of change.
- Involvement of all stakeholders in the process at all stages.
- Identifying opportunities for individual counselling for all stake-holders.
- Identifying the obstacles and potential problems.
- Identifying a realistic and sensitive time-scale for change.
- Sharing an implementation strategy supported by all involved.

This will require investment in staff teaching and training and will also involve staff from the local personnel department, who should be fully involved throughout the process. Staff representatives from various bodies should also be involved, and representatives from resident/

consumer groups must be encouraged to participate. As a precursor, opportunities to train stakeholders in the following skills may be required if they are to contribute equally to the change debate: teamwork; problem-solving; communication; how to present a case; how to assert oneself in groups; decision-making.

Access to training materials and resources will also be required and it may help for stakeholders to visit other areas where alternative models are in practice and learn of the benefits and difficulties that may be inherent if they were to be introduced locally. Change will therefore require an investment in people, their skills, their experience and their attitudes. Cultural needs and values will need to be explored and opportunities provided for the expression and resolution of minority views. Above all, people will need to feel involved, that there is really 'something in it for everyone', and that the new structure/system has been designed by them and builds on their own strengths as individuals towards the realization of new opportunities.

The process of change requires sensitive management and can succeed if all those involved are listened to as individuals, and are encouraged and supported to express their views, feelings and anxieties in a secure environment. A useful conclusion to this section follows:[16]

> Change can evoke stressful reactions . . . but it can also have a stimulating and dynamic effect which results in new ways of living and of seeing and understanding permanent truths.

# MANAGING AND DEVELOPING LOCAL SERVICES

The task of maintaining the momentum and motivation of people involved in the process of change and in the development of new services is certainly no easy task. It will require the commitment of a team of managers to steer new developments into practice. The introduction of 'service development teams' is one approach adopted by some agencies to undertake this task.

In any service there will be a need to review and monitor the quality of service provision to consumers. Similarly, there will be a need to guide and shape the design of new services. Service development teams, therefore, have an essential role to play in this process. Their key tasks are:

- Guiding the service.
- Providing leadership such that provides the most effective service within available resources.
- To ensure that at any time all people involved know where the service is going, how it is going to get there and what progress has been achieved in realizing its objectives.
- To monitor, develop and provide support to people in the service; to evaluate the quality of care and service delivery within defined and agreed parameters.
- Determining the equal distribution of service resources to consumers.
- Identifying methods to promote meaningful teamwork in the service and to make efficient use of all available resources.

The membership of these groups should be determined locally but, as a rule, should include representatives from all key agencies, disciplines and consumer representatives and service managers. Leadership of the group should be self-determined, but clear lines of accountability to senior managers should be defined to ensure that the necessary authority and status of the group is preserved. The group should agree on an agenda for action determined through consultation with each component of the service. Priorities should be identified and tasks allocated to service staff and consumers in order to monitor and evaluate the quality of service delivery and to develop new strategies to promote the implementation of service goals and objectives.

The autonomy of local services will also need to be preserved, and occasionally this may challenge the degree of control such groups exert on the service on behalf of senior managers. In order to overcome this, local services should develop team structures to encourage stakeholders to determine their own priorities and to present development bids within a framework of service principles accepted by the whole service and endorsed by the service development team. The benefits of this co-ordinated approach to the management and delivery of services will be:

- Consumers will realize a co-ordinated pattern of care.
- Unrealistic expectations will be removed.
- Services will plan and deliver efficient services within their budget.
- The community will be aware of what the service has to offer.
- Clients and local staff will be involved in shaping the pattern of their own services.
- Consumers and staff will be involved in the day-to-day decision-making process of the service.

- Services will be implemented and consolidated without disillusionment.
- All stakeholders will have a set of clearly determined needs and objectives and a shared agenda for action.
- All stakeholders will have a clearly defined management structure in terms of their own degree of autonomy, responsibility and accountability.

Perhaps one of the most important tasks of the group will be to bring all stakeholders together at least twice a year to share in the development and definition of the service's aims, objectives and 'vision'. It is from this shared value base that local agenda for action may be determined and agreed in performance terms through the setting of specific client-centred objectives. In order to facilitate a 'bottom up' approach to service development, each component of the service should identify a spokesperson or co-ordinator who will advise the service development team of their needs, priorities and accomplishments. It will be this person's role to set local objectives with their team and to identify the support and resources that will be required to realize them.

Service managers will need to determine clear structures for decision-making and identify the limits of each person's role in this process. Clear guidelines will need to be provided for the monitoring of the service and its accomplishments, and it will be the responsibility of the service development team to set standards for the service and to co-ordinate monitoring arrangements for each component in terms of: consumer satisfaction; value for money; an equal distribution of services and resources; and the efficiency of its staff, service structures, systems and practices.

The team will also need to ensure that local staff and consumers receive feedback regarding their performance and achievements, and adequate support, resources and training to fulfil the expectations of the service and of themselves. The actual support needed by each individual will depend on their particular needs at the time. These will change as they develop and circumstances alter. Many of these needs can only be met if managers are willing to listen and to provide meaningful support networks for their staff and consumers. Other forms of support will depend on the amount of professional and informal networks available and the individual's own skill and initiative in using these. Staff will also need to be rewarded for their successes and supported in their 'failures'; the degree of job satisfaction they receive from the job will be an essential element in determining the success of the organization.

There will be a need for good information, continuous dialogue, flexible thinking and meaningful evaluation of services. There will be questions to answer which may pose particularly difficult and, in some cases, contentious solutions, such as:

- How do we involve consumers in the planning and management of services?
- How do we involve representatives from other agencies in the joint planning and management of services?
- How do we improve communication between all stakeholders in the service and facilitate their involvement in decision-making processes?
- How do we overcome established professional practices and defensive attitudes in order to enable the emergence of a client-led service?
- How do we provide staff with adequate support structures to realize and carry out their jobs effectively and efficiently?
- How do we ensure an even and fair distribution of work between team members, some of whom may be part-time but equally important in sharing the vision and management of the service?

Opportunities must be provided for meaningful joint-service planning and for the appropriate allocation and sharing of resources including finance (e.g. joint finance and joint funding), skills and experience. Staff should be encouraged to participate in other services and to share their experiences in order to cross-fertilize new ideas and to improve on local practices. Senior managers should plan their services in response to local need and should ensure that their role is limited to determining the allocation of resources and checking that all local initiatives and schemes are in keeping with agreed strategic plans, rather than limiting the involvement and decision-making influence of stakeholders in determining their own services.

Comprehensive services are becoming increasingly complex in the way in which they can be managed effectively. More and more people are influencing the direction and delivery of services, but there must be a consistent strategy determined by central managers to set the pace and to facilitate the delivery of services wtihin an overall agreed framework. Within this framework there must be clearly defined management systems and lines of accountability. This will require the recognition that all efficiently, co-ordinated services will need leadership and a named service manager who will be responsible for the service and for its day-to-day operation. How this is realized will be decided upon locally, but it is essential that managers respond to local needs democratically while retaining the power of veto when local initiatives are unrealistic or 'out of tune' with the agreed service philosophy or strategy.

# DECISION-MAKING AND ACCOUNTABILITY

In any service there must be clear and published policies regarding decision-making processes and limits of individual decision-making. Such guidelines will determine the way in which services are delivered and managed and will identify the role of certain staff members and consumers in making decisions in how services are delivered and implemented.

In the first instance, all people will be expected to make decisions about their own work performance and activities. Professionals will also have to account within the terms and conditions of their own professional codes of practice; in addition, all employees will need to work in accordance with local conditions insisted upon by their employers. Managers will need to ensure that all staff members have the appropriate skills, knowledge and experience before they delegate certain responsibilities. They will also have to ensure that adequate resources are available to enable staff to carry out their tasks safely and without undue risk.

In human services, most decision-making will take place in groups made up of a variety of people from a variety of backgrounds and experiences. These groups will need to learn how to respect each other and to invite and accept views from all members, irrespective of their status or the number of hours they work each week. The multidisciplinary approach to decision-making which these conditions introduce calls for support from managers and flexibility from its members.

In some cases managers will disagree with local decisions; clear guidelines should be available to deal with such occasions. Usually it will be the responsibility of the service manager to intervene and mediate between different perceptions and expectations. Questions of power, status and the status quo will also arise, and all team members will have a responsibility to be aware of their own motives as well as those of others. (The team work approach is described in detail in Chapter 5).

Accountability is personal in the first instance but may become corporative when decisions are made and shared with others. The group decision-making process should involve all those people who are involved in the matter to be discussed. Minority views must be noted and an agreement made when consensus has been reached. All decisions should be recorded and made in accordance with the basic principle of accepting the outcome that is felt to be best for the person whom the decision will affect after considering all other alternatives.

It must also be accepted that all professionals are responsible for their own decisions when they affect clients. It is usually agreed that local managers will be responsible ultimately for all decisions made in the service, but only after all those people who have involvement with the service have been consulted. (It will be a matter for local debate to decide who will be consulted for different decisions.) In any comprehensive service, a multidisciplinary ethos will prevail, and the aim of specialist staff should be to support and to provide an objective opinion on client-related decisions.

It will be the responsibility of the team to identify any areas of potential risk that may be involved before accepting or agreeing on any course of action or decisions (see Chapter 3 for a description of risk-taking procedures). Decisions should be made following consideration of the person's life-needs and the impact that the decision would make on the person's quality of life. The benefits of this approach ensure that no one person is expected to determine important life decisions in isolation. However, there will be occasions when decisions may have to be made in an emergency, and procedures must be identified for such occasions that allow immediate intervention and subsequent review by the local team. This leads to a sharing of views and opinions, and support for agreed decisions when implemented.

In conclusion, services must identify clear decision-making guidelines for their staff and consumers. Managers must determine appropriate support and resources for staff when implementing their decisions if they are made in accordance with locally determined policies and procedures. Risk-taking may be a necessary consideration in the decision-making process and guidelines should be provided for all staff on how to make informed decisions and on how to calculate risks. Ultimately, all people in the service account to their clients for the quality of their decisions and interventions and, of course, to their managers and professional bodies. Finally, senior managers and professional heads must take full responsibility for all decisions made by their staff and must therefore be held to account for the consequences of their actions; central co-ordination, agreed policies and directive management is therefore required in addition to local decision-making processes.

## SUMMARY AND CONCLUSION

Quality will be based on an investment of skill development and knowledge acquisition for staff and consumers, with freedom to practise and live together within fair and acceptable resources. Political changes and pressures will always prevail, but it is essential that any changes in government or local policy or practice be introduced in a way which enhances the quality of service delivery and consumer satisfaction.

All agencies will need to identify the key stakeholders for each component of their service and introduce written policies and procedures which allow for the maximum degree of consumer and local involvement in their formulation and implementation. Sound and accepted systems to monitor the outcomes of the service will also be required. The measurement of quality will require the combination and use of a variety of qualitative and quantitative tools, ranging from measures of staff self-appraisal and quality action groups, to an analysis of performance data such as the number of complaints received in the service from consumers and cost statements identifying the relationship between consumer experience and financial investment.

The management of change will play an essential role in determining the success of new services, and the way in which change is managed and maintained will require the introduction of challenging and innovative management structures and support services. All people involved in the development of new services will require new information upon which to judge new services and to make informed choices regarding their involvement in shaping the pattern of their own services in the future. They will all need to be aware of their own motivations and stake in the service and, above all, their own strengths and needs. The management of 'self' will prove to be as essential as the management of the whole organization in terms of positive success and outcomes for consumers.

The approach to service management and development outlined in this chapter has been to identify various strategies which may be employed in the realization of client-led services. Operational managers will need to manage their services in accordance with the expressed needs of their consumers and local staff and within the resources available. Operational policies must be introduced and reviewed regularly, and operational guidelines provided for local managers which specify the limits and parameters of local decision-making and which outline the processes which determine the efficient management of the service.

What has been proposed in this chapter will not be a perfect fit for any one service, nor is this the intention. There will be gaps and there will be better ways of doing things. However, the principles outlined are sound and can be changed and developed to suit local need. All that is required to realize a valued service is initiative, interest, commitment and, of course, a management system that reinforces the value-base of the service in practice.

# REFERENCES

1. Rowden, R. (1984) *Managing Nursing,* Baillière Tindall, London, p. 13.
2. National Development Team for Mentally Handicapped People (1980) *Improving the Quality of Service for Mentally Handicapped People – A Checklist of Standards*, DHSS, London.
3. Donabedian, A. (1980) *The Definition of Quality and Approaches to its Assessment*, Health Administration Press, Ann Arbor, Michigan.
4. Rines, A.R. (1963) *Evaluating Student Progress in Learning the Practice of Nursing,* Teachers College Press,
5. Gronlund, N.E. (1971) *Measurement and Evaluation in Nursing*, Macmillan, London.
6. South West Thames Regional Health Authority (1987) *Consultation Document for Quality Assurance*, S.W. Thames RHA, 29 April.
7. Russell, O. (1986) Planning for quality, in *Getting Better all the Time? Issues and strategies for ensuring quality in community services for people with mental handicap*, Project Paper No. 66, King's Fund Centre, London, p. 55.
8. O'Brien, I., Poole, C. and Galloway, C. (1981) *Accomplishments in Residential Services: Improving the Effectiveness of Residential Service Workers in Washington's Developmental Service System,* Responsive Systems Associates, Atlanta, Georgia.
9. IDC (1986) *Pursuing Quality: How good are your local services for people with mental handicap?* Independent Development Council For People With Mental Handicap, London.
10. Davies, T. and Nash, D. (1987) *Quality Assurance – A strategy designed to evaluate and monitor services provided by the Mental Handicap Unit of the South Lincolnshire Health Authority*, South Lincolnshire Health Authority.
11. Kitson, A. (1986) Quality assurance, *Nursing Times,* 27 August, Vol 82, No. 35, pp. 28–34.
12. Davies, L. (1987) *Quality, Costs and 'An Ordinary Life'*, Project Paper No. 67, King's Fund Centre, London.
13. Felce, D. (1986) Accommodating adults with severe and profound mental handicaps: Comparative revenue costs, *Mental Handicap*, Vol. 14, September, pp. 104–107.
14. Davies (1987) in J.L. Appleby (ed.), Why doctors must grapple with health economics, *British Medical Journal*, Vol. 294, p. 326.
15. Cope, D. (1984) Changing health care organizations (Chapter 9), in Skevington (ed.), *Understanding Nurses*, John Wiley, London.
16. Owen, G.M. (1983) The stress of change, *Nursing Times*, Occasional Papers, Vol. 79, No. 4.

# Section Four: Caring for the Carers

# 13. Stress Caring and Counselling

*Roy Bailey*

## INTRODUCTION

This chapter has a number of aims. Its main one is to help residential care staff better understand stress in themselves and how it can affect the quality of care they provide to clients. By understanding in more detail the kinds of stress we experience, we can increase our awareness of ourselves as helpers. We will have started to care for helpers in caring as well as those who receive their care. However, to do this requires a better knowledge of our own stress and how we cope with it. Increasing our awareness provides a basis for: helping ourselves; being more responsible to those whom we care for; and being of greater help to our clients. To know ourselves in this way is an important stepping stone to more effective helping.

Another aim of the chapter is to show how carers in residential care can gain a practical knowledge of stress and what might be done to overcome and avoid it.

## STRESS

There are many definitions of stress.[1-6] The one used here is simple and easy to understand. Stress is regarded as any unpleasant and undesirable behaviours, emotions or physical complaints. But stress need not always be damaging. Some writers even suggest that stress is good for us.[7-12] In the main, however, most of the literature on stress sees it as something unwanted. Stress is something that interferes with our otherwise healthy transaction with the environment. It is this view of stress that is adopted here.[5,13] Essentially stress occurs when we appraise the demands in our environments as *exceeding* our coping resources.[6,14-17]

## STRESS AND CARING

There are now many studies showing that stress arises out of the demands of caring. The way professionals are expected to provide care to those in pain, the dying, the mentally handicapped and the maimed puts them in a vulnerable position where they are more likely to suffer from stress than the public at large.[5,6] Stress is more likely to occur in caring for others more than in other occupations.

It is now well-documented that coping with change can be very stressful. One author argues that change and the rate of change is a major cause of stress that occurs when moving from one culture to another.[18] It is the transition between the currently agreed and valued philosophies, behaviours and objectives, towards a future set of goals that raises difficulties for many people. It is likely that we will find similar difficulties occurring where real change has to be made from acceptable institutional values and practices and the provision of care towards the philosophies such as normalization.

This is highlighted particularly when a new philosophy is introduced into the service. For example, the Winchester Health Authority, whose policy for services for people with a mental handicap is based on a client-centred service, can bring about new stresses for carers. They have to implement policies which may stretch their own resources and those of the clients. In other words, the changes demanded can be stressful for carers.

Ironically, however, we often fail to recognize the signs of stress in ourselves and our colleagues. As time passes and it goes unchecked, a pronounced form of stress can occur called 'burnout'. Burnout is a particularly disabling form of stress. It is usually recognized when a previously committed carer loses his or her motivation, enthusiasm and commitment to caring. Fortunately, stress and professional burnout can be identified and something done about it. Consistent with this approach, this chapter is presented so that it can help the carer to:

● recognize those carers and staff suffering from stress;

- highlight the responsibilities of those in contact with sufferers of stress;
- map out methods for carers which can be used to assess and manage stress;
- change the culture of caring services in this country.

# SIGNS AND SYMPTOMS OF STRESS

## The casualties of caring

There is an army of carers. Carers in the health professions, the education services, and the social and welfare services. Families are also carers. However, professional or otherwise, they all have something in common. They are exposed to cirumstances in their lives which make demands for caring: caring for the disabled and the sick, the dying and the maimed, the acute and chronically ill, and the person with a mental handicap. All of this caring can 'cost' those who care and try to help clients and their relatives. The cost to the carer can be stated quite simply: 'Caring can be dangerous to your health'.[5,19,20]

Unfortunately, the casualties of caring usually suffer in silence, not wanting to draw attention to their own need for caring and coping support. Equally, they are likely to be unaware that they are suffering from stress.[3,5,6,13]

## Spotting the sufferer

The first task, then, is to be able to identify the troubled helper, the carer who is suffering from stress. This is easier said than done. A great deal of recent research has shown how doctors, nurses, social workers, physiotherapists, speech therapists, occupational therapists and care staff in small houses for people with a mental handicap, fail to recognize they are suffering from stress,[5] which can impair their own health and the quality of service they provide to their clients. What is a typical pattern for the casualties of caring? This is not something that can simply be specified for everyone. But there are often common features to those carers who are suffering from stress. The most common, perhaps, are that: they do not regard themselves as suffering from stress; they try to carry on caring for clients, despite suffering from stress themselves; and, finally, they do not usually seek help for their own problems until they are quite serious. All of this points to carers who suffer in silence and are not functioning well. The following case studies provide an insight into the 'carer' who is not functioning.

### Carol: Social worker specializing in residential care for people with a mental handicap

| | |
|---|---|
| Source of Stress: | Number of clients she has to see each day. |
| Stress experienced: | Fatigue/extreme tiredness; irritability/depression. |
| Coping adopted: | Talks to colleagues and smokes 65 cigarettes a day. |
| Outcomes: | Carol feels able to 'lay off' her stress to some extent with her colleagues. The smoking helps to calm her irritability. But she continues to feel the same each week. The source of stress remains. What else could she do? |

### David: Person in charge of group home

| | |
|---|---|
| Sources of stress: | The noise and particularly the screams of adults arguing. |
| Stress experienced: | Headaches, general feeling of increased tension and 'edginess'. |
| Coping adopted: | Shouts at colleagues. Appears very off-hand and dismissive of clients. Does not listen to clients' or colleagues' views anymore. |
| Outcomes: | Some relief for the general tension. But the headaches remain. And staff and clients prefer to avoid contact with David. Is this coping helpful? |

### Susan: Care staff member on training course

| | |
|---|---|
| Source of stress: | Lack of knowledge in understanding behaviour. |
| Stress experienced: | Anxiety and feelings of helplessness. |
| Coping adopted: | Started drinking before lectures and workshops to reduce anxiety. Went to seminars and attended education groups in behavioural psychology. |
| Outcomes: | Temporary reduced anxiety. But still problems remained of anxiety and lack of confidence to carry out work. Danger of alcohol dependency. |

# WHAT TO DO?

What do you do when you do not know that you are stressed and burning out? When care staff do not realize their situation they may tend to engage in what is termed 'palliative coping'. Palliative coping entails intentional or unintentional efforts by the individual to overcome or avoid stress.[14] However, these attempts at coping are palliative in the sense that they do not actually overcome stress.[3] They merely put it into 'cold storage'. It temporarily delays or blocks out the stress experienced. Palliative coping, then, is only of a short-term benefit to the troubled helper. For example, smoking may bring some relief from anxiety. Drinking alcohol is also a partial and transient escape from depression. Similarly, temporary relief from stress may be obtained by outbursts of rage or excessive eating.[3] However, none of these forms of palliative coping solve the troubled helpers' real problems. Indeed, palliative coping can have some serious long-term cumulative effects. For example, persistent smoking does not 'cure' anxiety, but can lead to smoking-related problems such as bronchitis and lung cancer. Likewise, excessive alcohol consumption can lead to physical complaints associated with the liver and uncontrollable antisocial behaviour.[21]

Clearly, not every care staff falls into these categories.[2] Nonetheless, there are stunning statistics which show doctors, nurses, social workers and carers in mental handicap services persistently smoke and drink alcohol.[5] There is a moral in this for all of us. Palliative coping – at least of the kinds mentioned here – is more likely to compound the stress experienced by carers. This is especially so if these forms of coping are adopted over long periods of time.[14,17,22]

Perhaps the unpalatable answer to the question 'What do you do when you don't know you are stressed-up and burning out?' is: 'You get worse if you're using palliative coping as a means of carrying on the job of helping clients.'[2,3]

Not every individual carer suffers from stress at work all of the time. This would be a distortion of the many challenging and satisfying aspects of practical caring. However, it is also clear that many people who are engaging in caring and helping others will experience at some time unwanted levels of emotional, mental and physical stress.[5]

# HELPING THE TROUBLED HELPER

There are three ways the troubled helper can be helped. First of all, colleagues can look out for signs of stress in each other. This means being more co-operative in the work we do and the way we see caring. Caring should be seen as not only caring for clients but also caring for each other. By doing this we can acknowledge that helping needs to be monitored periodically and at frequent intervals by examining the stress levels of carers working in small houses. Second, those in caring services can begin to recognize the limits of their own human resources in providing care.

This can be done by identifying stress in ourselves and regularly checking how this influences our work. In other words, we should be paying more attentioln to how we cope with the demands of caring,[3] and more especially, how it affects our helping. Finally, the residential organizations and mental handicap services that employ care workers should take a more active role in promoting their welfare. It has been argued elsewhere that strong support and a comprehensive counselling service should be made available to all employees engaged in health care.[1,2,5,13] Such a service could do much to care for the health and performance of carers as much as the clients in their service facility.

There is also clear evidence that helping professional carers to cope can reduce sickness absence at work.[4] Benefits like these can also mean good news for managers of social and health care systems and the services they provide to clients. Clearly, there are many good reasons for helping the troubled helper in residential care work. None the least of these being that they provide a basis for 'collective coping' with the stress arising out of the demands of caring for others.[5,23]

## Collective coping

Collective coping utilizes real or imagined supports in the environment which enable us to achieve adaptation and personal or shared objectives.[5,24] These can be based on informal or formal networks of social ʂupports, and help to mediate stress and promote personal and work goals.

The most obvious examples of informal networks for collective coping are those we can observe in everyday life, such as coffee and tea breaks, and party-going. These all serve as 'buffers' to the continuous demands of work.[23] These forms of collective coping offer opportunities for mutual moaning, gregarious gossiping and mutual ventilations of feelings about work and colleagues' attitudes. This form of informal collective coping enables emotions to be regulated and achieves one of the goals of coping – satisfactory adaptation.[5,6] Without it, work and professional goals are often hindered and, at worst, we fail to achieve work objectives. So moaning, gossiping and ventilating our feelings do serve a purpose. They help to express our emotions. When this is done we can 'get on with the job'.

However, mere discharge of feelings and reduced stress in itself are only part of collective coping. We also need to achieve work objectives; to do this, we need to be able to perform effective problem-solving and engage in appropriate actions to achieve specific goals.[25] More *formal* networks of social support often help to make these aspects of collective coping possible.[24]

A recent visit to California confirmed for the author how important and productive formal social support networks can be for client care workers.[3,26] An example of the staff support function provided by Stanford University Hospital is shown in Table 13.1.

The consultative facilities of the staff support service at Stanford University Hospital are available to all nurses. In the UK, St Thomas's Hospital, London, has made substantial progress towards a comprehensive counselling service, offering collective coping options to all staff in their health district. It would seem that St Thomas's model of a collective coping facility may be a blueprint for future developments in health care, social services and educational organizations. In short, organizations providing social support for their employees should provide facilities that aim to: reduce stress; improve their general health; and improve performance at work. This can only be good news for all care staff and the service organizations within which they work.

**Table 13.1  Staff support service**

| Goals | Facility functions |
|---|---|
| Promote and strengthen role performance | One-time consultations |
| Confidential counselling | Long-term consultations |
| Problem-solving proficiency | Individual options |
| Intra-interprofessional conflict resolution | Group support |
| Promoting and maintaining well-being | Seminars/workshops on stress, coping and burnout |

## What to look for

However, the first steps in helping care staff to cope with stress are to: know what signs to look for; and identify those suffering from undesirable levels of stress.

For example, how many of the signs of stress in the following check list are identifiable among care staff in small group homes? Previous field work on staff training and stress management courses at Castle Priory College, Wallingford, clearly confirm that stress is a pressing problem and of considerable concern to carers.[4,5,6]

### Are you under too much stress?
In the past six months:

Yes/No

1. Have you been drinking, smoking or eating more than usual? ..........
2. Do you have difficulty sleeping at night? ..........
3. Are you more 'touchy' and argumentative than normal? ..........
4. Do you have trouble with your boss? ..........
5. Have you or a loved one experienced a serious illness recently? ..........
6. Have you been recently divorced or separated? ..........
7. Has there been an increase in marital or family arguments? ..........
8. Have you been experiencing sexual difficulties? ..........
9. Has a close relative or friend died? ..........
10. Have you married recently or started living with someone? ..........
11. Has there been a pregnancy or birth in your family? ..........
12. Do you have financial problems? ..........
13. Have you been dismissed from work or become unemployed? ..........
14. Do you feel jumpy, on edge, flying off the handle at little things? ..........
15. Do you watch television more than three hours a day? ..........
16. Have you been in trouble recently with the law? ..........
17. Has there been an increase in the number of deadlines or hours you are working? ..........
18. Have you recently moved or changed the place where you live? ..........

19.  Do you have trouble with your in-laws?                         ..........
20.  Are you exposed to constant noise at home or at work?       ..........

## Warning – warning – warning

Long before the serious signs of stress become obvious there are a number of warning signals to look for which indicate stress. One suggestion is a common set of features to all stress problems, and research at the university of Prague revealed the following warning signs of stress in patients.[7] It became evident that each of the patients felt and looked ill, had a coated tongue, and complained of aches and pains in their joints. Other warning signals of stress were gastrointestinal disturbances with an accompanying loss of appetite. Skin rashes, inflamed tonsils and sometimes fever with depressed mood and mental confusion were also present. These warning signals are equally applicable to care staff working in residential care services for people with a mental handicap.[5]

# WHEN STRESS BECOMES A SERIOUS PROBLEM

Stress can become a serious problem. In some senses of the word, any form of stress is serious. Occasionally, stress can be helpful, but most of the time stress, if unattended, can lead to severe problems of human functioning. In other words, stress is a signal for coping. If coping, or some form of collective coping, is not available in the carer then stress is likely to undermine their general health, well-being, decision-making, performance efficiency, attitudes towards clients and commitment to service and caring objectives.

Clearly, these problems are of concern to all of those engaged in the provision of care. The concern is twofold. First, the clients with a handicap are often affected by stress and inability to cope with the demands made on their lives. Second, and particularly important, are the problems experienced by carers themselves. Care staff and other carers such as parents and volunteers can all have their health, well-being and performance impaired through stress. The message is clear. If it is ignored, stress becomes a serious problem. Stress will not go away.[5]

## Stress as the snapshot – burnout as the movie

It is also helpful to realize that stress is something which is evident at any one time and something which occurs over time. One is the *product* at any particular moment. The other is the *process* that seems to be taking place in any individual through time. The signs and symptoms of stress illustrated earlier are all 'snapshots' of stress at any one point of assessment. This should be remembered when we want to estimate our own level of stress or that of people with a mental handicap receiving care from health, education or social services.

Another reason for being aware that we are only taking a snapshot of stress is to remind us that we should also monitor and evaluate stress in carers and their handicapped clients over time. For stress and its manifestations can also change from moment to moment. It can become progressively more serious, leading to 'burnout', a pronounced state of stress which occurs over time and with long-term risks ultimately undermining the quality of caring activity.

Put in other terms, care staff can become unable to carry on caring. This may be so serious at times that it actually interferes with the helping activity, and has undesirable consequences for people who are handicapped.[1,27]

# STRESSCHECKING AND BURNOUT

A fundamental reason for stresschecking is to keep tabs on burnout. By regular stresschecking we can look out for any of the telltale signs of burnout, such as emotional stress, physical fatigue and an increase in behavioural signs such as excessive drinking and smoking.[5] We can help carers and their clients avoid running into more unnecessary stress. In doing so, we can use stresschecking as a method to prevent further deterioration in human functioning.

A clear message comes out of this approach to stress assessment. Do not wait until carers have unbearable stress problems. Instead, make a point of conducting stresschecks when they are as well as can be expected. This attack on stress will help to combat burnout, waste of human efficiency and alleviate poor work performance. In other words, you will be helping constructively to reduce the sometimes miserable conditions of caring. By combatting stress in this way, we begin to advance the idea of *health education*. Stresschecking should prove a productive and useful facility to our colleagues providing caring services. Further, regular stresschecking should be made available to care staff within a broader set of carer counselling services.[5,6,25] It has already been demonstrated to management that this can be a cost-effective development.[4]

## Stress and the burnout profile

What happens to carers who do not watch out for the warning signs of stress and the process of burnout? What happens to their view of themselves and the kinds of stress they experience? What is the price paid for failing to attend to the problem of stress and burnout? More simply, are stresschecking, stress management and care staff counselling facilities really necessary? A few selected stress-burnout profiles from the clinics and courses the author has run on stress, counselling, coping and burn-out, show how the price of neglecting care staff is high; sometimes so high, that carers and their human resources are reduced to ashes, inadequacy and apathy. Here is what some previously committed carers have to say about themselves.

### Stress-burnout profile 1
A manager from a community special care unit for people with a mental handicap expressed the way demands are made on her, and her experience of stress in this way:

> There are times when an avalanche of problems arise together. They all seem to bunch up and have to be dealt with very quickly. You're thinking, 'Which one will I try to solve first?' But there are always so many interruptions that I soon get 'heated' and irritable. No sooner is one problem out of the way – the next is demanding and pressing to be solved. I find I then build up a great deal of tension inside myself. I get headaches, and on occasion I shout when I shouldn't. I am finding it increasingly difficult to put a brave face on things. The trouble is, I don't have someone to turn to with my problems and difficulties. I have to face up to all the pressures in this kind of work. I get more and more 'worked up' so that I get more and more agitated. Sometimes I just can't cope with it any more.

### Stress-burnout profile 2
A residential care worker working with people who have a mental handicap reported:

> My colleagues and my residents depend on me too much. I used to love that part of the work. But now I think they drag me down to the point where I

am exhausted. Sometimes it is my own fault. I can't say 'No' to anyone who asks me for help. When I have tried I feel guilty at turning them down. All these demands drain my physical strength. Emotionally, I feel trapped inside myself. There seems no escape from it all. It's like being caught up in a perpetual treadmill.

# CARING FOR CARERS

There can now be little doubt left that caring for others is stressful.[2,5] The demands of caring present us with a clear challenge. What can be done to alleviate and prevent unwanted stress and burnout among carers? And in particular, what directions can we take in providing more appropriate training for care staff in residential homes for people with a mental handicap? Training in itself has been singularly insufficient to date to help care staff effectively manage stress. Furthermore, no satisfactory planning has been pursued or implemented in the UK whereby the care of carers is the cornerstone of service policies. We should begin to move vigorously towards a position that does include provision of care for carers as a priority for those in residential care services for people with a mental handicap. The first practical step in this new direction should be to provide options for stress management and stress counselling services for carers.[1,4,6]

## Options in stress management

### Helping yourself
By being able to see how life demands, stress and coping affect carers and their relationship to people with a mental handicap, we make a big step forwards in our philosophy and practice of caring. Why? Because it acknowledges that we cannot artificially exclude carers from the problems of providing care. It overcomes the compartmentalizing of care. For carers, it permits us to follow the path of what Wolfensberger has termed 'moral coherency'.[28] We have tended for too long to compartmentalize caring. One of the first things we can do is dismantle this and act on our recognition of stress problems among staff providing care in small group homes for people with a mental handicap.

This first development should be seen as a beginning. A first phase of a multi-phasic programme of care which encompasses caring for carers as a service priority. Self-help options for stress management should be part of this strategy.[4] Carers and cleints should be encouraged and supported to take a significant step forwards; a first step towards managing stress. We can begin generating realistic options for managing stress. Helping ourselves to stress management amounts to self-management. There are a number of stress management options that have been found to be of practical and immediate benefit for overcoming stress and managing performance more effectively. Organizing personal–work priorities is one distinct area where a start and an impact can be made.

### Organizing personal–work priorities

How often do you sit down and organize your day? Every day, once a month, every six months, never? When was the last time you sat down and decided what was important about your day's work; what was to be dealt with first, last, not at all? How much of your time is spent on nonproductive work activity which is irrelevant to your work goals and life tasks?

If you do not know the answers to these questions, the chances are you need to reorganize your work behaviour. In other words, you need to organize yourself. When you organize yourself and your work behaviour, you will also be managing stress more effectively.

Try this exercise:

- List all of the tasks that are before you today.
- Separate the relevant from the irrelevant (the irrelevant are those that can wait for another day or find the waste bin).
- Of the relevant tasks, rank them in order of importance.
- Now from this rank listing, select those tasks which can be done quickly, e.g. within five minutes, 15 minutes, 30 minutes etc.
- Next tick or checkmark those tasks which can be done by telephone, letter or meetings, or which require travel.
- Decide on the tasks to be done in order from this list.
- Now go to work.

# BENEFITS VERSUS COSTS OF PALLIATIVE COPING

We have seen how palliative coping has its limitations. Palliative coping can cost carers dearly. But it also has a set of short-term benefits to carers. Why? Because palliative coping allows us to employ a set of actions that

**Table 13.2  Palliative coping**

| Type | Benefits | Costs |
|------|----------|-------|
| **Smoking** | Short-term benefits Relaxation, Concentration | Long-term health costs (bronchitis, cancer etc) |
| **Alcohol consumption** | Relaxation | Alcoholism/dependency Altered personality/ aggressive/physical complaints/cirrhosis of the liver etc |
| **Absenteeism** | Relief from work demands and 'pressure' | Work tasks not completed; increasing 'pressure' from untackled work demands Tendency towards more stress and disorganization |
| **Denial** | Apparently not emotionally upset Carry on with work tasks | Longer term 'glueing-up' of emotions and efficiency; tendency to be closed-off as a person; the person becomes a machine |

temporarily provide relief from stress. Yet smoking, alcohol consumption, absenteeism and denying we have stress problems, are all surely undesirable forms of palliative coping. So what are the benefits of palliative coping?

Palliative coping provides a temporary time-out from the demands made on the carer who is suffering from stress.[5] Think of it like this: when we cannot find effective direct coping like problem-solving to overcome or reduce the source of stress, we often resort to palliative coping. This is not necessarily a 'no-win' form of coping. It means, however, understanding how palliative coping can be used and abused. In other words, we need to know the limits of palliative coping.

Palliative coping helps when we 'need some time to think the matter through'. When we want to relax. There is evidence that palliative coping, such as smoking, does help some people relax and even improve their concentration.[29] But the cost to physical health is increased. So the price to pay for smoking is an increase in problems of physical health. The benefits are temporary relief from a problem and increased concentration. Ironically, problems can arise from reduced smoking. It has been shown that when doctors led the way in health education by substantially cutting out smoking, they significantly reduced smoking-related illness and disease such as bronchitis and lung cancer. Unfortunately, research has also revealed that a corresponding staggering rise in alcoholism and cirrhosis of the liver among doctors took place in a similar period to their 'no smoking crusade'.[5] Clearly, palliative coping can bring some benefits in temporarily relieving stress but it can also induce more stress-related problems in its wake. It is one of the classical paradoxes of coping with stress (Table 13.2). A great deal depends on what form palliative coping takes, how long it is used for, and to what purpose.[4,6,17,22]

## An exercise in palliative coping

Try out this palliative coping exercise with colleagues or clients. They may be surprised at how it reveals to them the kinds of palliative coping they use, under what circumstances, and to what effect.

1. Describe what palliative coping is.
2. Ask for a report or get the person to write down under what circumstances they use palliative coping.
3. Detail what form the palliative coping takes (e.g. smoking, drinking, etc).
4. Record the benefits this brings for the carer(s) or client(s).
5. Now help them to identify the costs involved in using this form of palliative coping.
6. Explore the possibilities of changing their form of coping.
7. Get a detailed picture here also of the benefits and costs of changing their coping efforts to manage stress.
8. Find out if and when they are going to put alternative coping tactics into practice.
9. Arrange to review the use of palliative coping at some agreed date in the near future (e.g. within one month, two months, three months, etc).
10. Now write a report about the influence palliative coping is having on the health and stress levels of the individual and their performance.

# DENIAL – THE SPECIAL CASE

It is not unusual for carers and professional helpers to deny the stress they experience through work or their personal relationships. And this is often no bad thing.[22] If we never used denial, our contact with other human beings could become unbearable. For instance, we cannot like everyone we meet at work, through business or in our social relationships. So using denial can sometimes provide a healthy distancing effect;[30] and enough distance to carry on caring.[6] However, denial also means 'turning off' and 'tuning out' our true thoughts and feelings.[5] Too much denial can actually starve us of what we really think and feel about situations. When this happens we end the benefits gained from denial and begin to count the costs. As we become dependent on denial we become less reliant on ourselves to solve the problems of coping with stress. Managing stress solely using denial is 'quick-fix' coping. It works for a while but generates its own personal, professional and client-based problems. It is not that denial should not be used to come to terms with stress. Denial, as a form of palliative coping, is useful in some instances but only for a limited period of time.[31] Denial as a form of coping – some would say as a way of 'life' – leads to a dead-end for many carers and their clients. Denial cuts off psychological pain. But overused and becoming stuck with it, denial dulls human performance and personal effectiveness. Carers and people with a mental handicap should bear this clearly in mind when examining the specific coping styles they adopt in their efforts to overcome or avoid stress.

## Denial and counselling

Denial is not a disease. But continuing to use denial can prevent care staff and clients from seeking appropriate help for their problems. Tackling denial would seem to be a priority for carers with stress problems which threaten their health and performance. In other words, denial may temporarily stave off stress. But the costs may be greater – even to the point of carers putting their lives at risk.[13] For those carers who continue to deny the stress of caring, we need to remember that terrible warning: 'Caring can be dangerous to your health.'[5,19,20]

What hope is there for overcoming denial, facing up to stress and mourning our losses in life, as well as being joyful in our achievements? How are 'our people' to face up to stressful changes in their lives? The argument here is that the answer lies in *counselling*. Counselling has a vast literature and this chapter about stress and caring does not intend or claim to cover it.

However, it can be said that counselling often deals with people in their pain and their joy. It accepts people where they are. It makes few assumptions about wrong and right. Counselling is not moralizing or advice-giving.[32] It sees denial as just one part of a process of coping with life. Counselling is a process that can be facilitated by the counsellor to enable the client to establish desired goals and more effective living.[1,2,33,34] Counselling should enable care staff and people with a mental handicap to 'dig out their own resources' and live their lives more effectively.[32] When denial or any form of 'stuckness' occurs for carers or clients, they should be encouraged to seek assistance from their own counselling service and from competent counsellors skilled in dealing with human stress.[2,6] Handled sensitively and from an informed perspective, the stigma of stress should be removed from caring.

# RELAXATION TRAINING

Many of the stress-related problems reported by carers and indeed helping professionals can benefit from practising recognized relaxation training procedures.[5,35] Sometimes relaxation training can be combined with counselling to good effect. For instance, if a client is 'too tense to talk', a series of easily administered relaxation exercises can relax them enough to share their thoughts, feelings and what they are trying to do to cope with *their* situation.

# CARER AND 'CLIENT'

It will be clear from the ground covered so far that much of what concerns the carer can also be applied to helping clients. Clients can be helped to reorganize *their* work priorities. Clients can be helped to explore the kinds of palliative coping they use and what effects it has on their lives.

Care staff can also work with clients to tackle their unnecessary dependence on denial as a way of coping with stress. Working together through caring and counselling relationships, clients can acknowledge the pressure of everyday demands, or the loss of important people and dramatic changes of events in their lives, and begin the process of discovering more effective coping as basis for new lifestyles. Reorganizing personal priorities, practising systematic relaxation, participating in counselling and engaging collective coping through group support, are all management strategies that carers and clients can adopt to lead less stressful and more satisfying lives.

# COUNSELLING SERVICES – A FOUNDATION FOR FUTURE HELPING

With the assistance of, and participation in, counselling services, carers and clients should become more effective in discovering better ways to deal with their personal problems. Counselling services should make personal–work organization, stresschecking and stress management readily available to carers and their clients. However, counselling services for carers and clients must do much more than this. They should form the foundation for meeting the demands of *change* and closer carer–client–community relationships. For this to happen, care staff and their clients need to be supported in the pursuit of mutual helping and the realization of self-efficacy.[36]

Mutual helping means carers and clients being *more open with each other* over their sources of stress, their symptoms, the coping they use and the effect this has on their lives and those close to them. Counselling services are needed for carers and their clients to cope more productively with the transition from institution-based cultures to family-based living. Even more than this, though, counselling services need to be the foundation on which carers and clients can explore the nature of stress, their coping resources and how to put them to good effect in their everyday life.

Comprehensive counselling services of the kind advocated here may not yet be available to all care staff or people who are mentally handicapped. However, this is a weak argument for failing to develop counselling services that deal with the core of caring. The core of caring can be and often is stressful.[6] Though competence and performance are essentials for human functioning, it is the relationship that has the centre stage in caring. We may have lost sight of this important assumption in recent years. However, it is now time to highlight the importance of relationships for carers and clients alike. Counselling services which enable carers and clients to cope with significant demands in their lives and manage stress are servicing relationships. This is why counselling services should provide the cornerstone for combatting the often stressful consequences of caring. In establishing the provision of counselling services to carers and clients we will change the culture of caring.

# REFERENCES

1. Bailey, R. (1981) Counselling services for nurses – a forgotten responsibility, *Journal of the British Institute of Mental Handicap*, Vol. 9, pp. 45–7.
2. Bailey, R. (1982) Counselling services for nurses, *Journal of the British Association for Counselling*, Vol. 39, pp. 25–39.
3. Bailey, R. (1983) 'Stress and coping with the demands of caring'. Seminar, School of Nursing and School of Medicine, University of California, San Francisco.
4. Bailey, R. (1984) Autogenic regulation training and sickness absence amongst nurses in general training, *Journal of Advanced Nursing*, Vol. 9, pp. 581–8.
5. Bailey, R. (1985) *Coping with Stress in Caring*, Blackwell Scientific Publications, Oxford.
6. Bailey, R. (1986) *Systematic Relaxation*, Winslow Press, Bucks.
7. Selye, H. (1956) *The Stress of Life*, McGraw-Hill, New York.
8. Selye, H. (1974) *Stress Without Distress*, Lippnicott, London.
9. Selye, H. (1975) Confusion and controversy in the stress field, *Journal of Human Stress*, Vol. 1, pp. 37–44.
10. Selye, H. (1976) Forty years of stress research: Principal remaining problems and misconceptions, *Journal of the Canadian Medical Association*, Vol. 115, pp. 53–60.
11. Selye, H. (1979) The stress concept and some of its implications, in V. Hamilton and D.M. Warburton (eds.), *Human Stress and Cognition: An Information Processing Approach*, Wiley, New York.
12. Selye, H. (1980) Stress and a holistic view of health for the nursing profession, in K. Claus and J. Bailey (eds.), *Living with the Stress and Promoting Well-Being: A Handbook*, C.V. Mosby, St Louis.
13. Bailey, R. and Clarke, M. (in press) *Stress and Coping in Nursing Care*, Croom Helm, London.
14. Lazarus, R. (1966) *Psychological Stress and the Coping Process*, McGraw-Hill, New York.
15. Lazarus, R. (1971) The concept of stress and disease, in L. Levi (ed.), *Social Stress and Disease*, Vol. 1, pp. 53–60.
16. Lazarus, R. (1976) *Patterns of Adjustment*, McGraw-Hill, New York.
17. Lazarus, R. (1981) The stress and coping paradigm, in C. Eisdorfer, D. Cohen, A. Kleinman and P. Maxim (eds.), *Theoretical Bases for Psychopathology*, Spectrum, New York.
18. Toffler, A. (1973) *Future Shock*, Pan, London.
19. Murray-Parkes, C. (1978) Psychological aspects, in C.M. Saunders (ed.), *The Management of Terminal Disease*, Edward Arnold, London, pp. 44–64.
20. Murray-Parkes, C. (1983) *Bereavement: Studies of Grief in Adult Life*, Pelican, London.
21. Edwards, G. (1982) *The Treatment of Drinking Problems*, Grant McIntyre, London.
22. Lazarus, R. (1983) The costs and benefits of denial, in S. Breznitz (ed.), *The Denial of Stress*, International Universities Press, New York.
23. House, J.S. (1981) *Work Stress and Social Support*, Addison-Wesley, Reading, Massachusetts.

24. Caplan, G. and Killilea, M. (1976) *Support Systems and Mutual Help,* Grune & Stratton, New York.
25. Bailey, R. *Masterstress: A Professional Programme for Identifying and Managing Stress* (in preparation).
26. Baldwin, A. (1983) How nurses cope successfully with stress, Stanford Nursing Department Study, Stanford University Hospital, Stanford, California.
27. Oswin, M. (1978) *Children Living in Long-stay Hospital,* Spastics International, Lavenham Press, Suffolk.
28. McCloskey, R. (1986) Personal Communication, Castle Priory College, Oxon.
29. Eysenck, H. (1986) Nicotine's not all nasty, *The Best of Health,* Vol. 1, pp. 21–3.
30. Barton, D. (1977) The caregiver, in D. Barton (ed.), *Dying and Death. A Clinical Guide for Caregivers,* Williams, Baltimore.
31. Breznitz, S. (1983) (ed) *The Denial of Stress,* International Universities Press, New York.
32. Bailey, R. (in prep.) *People Skills: Counselling Through Facilitation Skills.*
33. Claus, K. and Bailey, J. (1980) *Living with Stress and Promoting Well-Being: A Handbook,* C.V. Mosby, St Louis.
34. Eisenberg, S. and Delaney, D. (1977) *The Counselling Process,* Rand McNally, Chicago.
35. Jacobson, E. (1938) *Progressive Relaxation,* University of Chicago Press.
36. Bandura, A. (1977) Self-efficacy: Toward a unifying theory of behavioral change, *Psychological Review,* Vol. 84, pp. 191–215.

# FURTHER READING

Cherniss, C. (1980) *Staff Burnout: Job Stress in the Human Services,* Sage, London.
Edelwich, J. and Brodsky, A. (1980) *Burn-out: Stages of Disillusionment in the Helping Professions,* Human Science Press, New York.
Freudenberger, H.J. (1975) The staff burn-out syndrome in alternative institutions, *Psychotherapy: Theory, Research and Practice,* Vol. 12, pp. 73–82.
Goldfried, M.R. (1977) The use of relaxation and cognitive re-labelling as coping skills, in R.B. Stuart (ed.), *Behavioral Self-Management: Strategies, Techniques and Outcome,* Bruner/Mazel, New York, pp. 82–116.
Goldfried, M.R. and Goldfried, A.P. (1975) Cognitive change methods, in F.H. Kenfer and A.P. Goldstein (eds.), *Helping People Change,* Pergamon, New York, pp. 89–116.
Holmes, T.H. and Rahe, R. (1967) The social readjustment rating scale, *Journal Psychosomatic Research,* Vol. 11, pp. 213–8.
Lazarus, R. and Launier, R. (1978) Stress-related transactions between person and environment, in L. Dervin and M. Lewis (eds.), *Perspectives in Interactional Psychology,* Plenum, New York, pp. 287–327.
McConnell, E. (1982) *Burnout in the Nursing Profession,* C.V. Mosby, St Louis.
Maslach, C. (1976) Burned-out, *Human Behaviour,* Vol. 5, pp. 16–22.

Maslach, C. (1982) Job burnout: How people cope, in E. McConnell (ed.), *Burnout in the Nursing Profession,* C.V. Mosby, St Louis.

Rosa, K. (1976) *Autogenic Training,* Victor Gollanz, London.

Volin, M. (1980) *The Quiet Hour,* Pelham, London.

# 14. Service Issues in the Training and Development of Staff

*Felicity Lefevre and Roy Bailey*

## INTRODUCTION

This chapter will consider: the assessment of staff training needs; induction; in-service training and continuing education; multi-agency training; multidisciplinary curriculum planning teams; matching training needs to personal and service objectives; service development team links; and staff performance and development reviews. Consideration is also given to how these issues are accommodated in a client-centred service and the difficulties that may arise.

## WHAT IS CURRENTLY HAPPENING?

When we look at what is happening in the services delivered to people with learning difficulties at present,[1] we find a conglomeration of models across a wide variety of both statutory and voluntary settings. The literature is sparse and scattered. Most of it comes from the United States. This seems to indicate that much of what has been researched and evaluated has been confined to large institutions where some pockets of good practice have emerged. There are some notable projects and evaluations of smaller residential units in this country but most of the community services are still developing.

This chapter focuses on issues of training and staff development in small residential units in the community. The place of the person with a learning difficulty (hitherto the mentally handicapped person) also raises significant questions for service philosophies, their organization and practice.

In the recent King's Fund conferences and publications on *Planning for People*[2,3] based on the principle of *An Ordinary Life*,[4] staff recruitment and training were issues which were widely debated. These conferences gave support to the notion that recruitment and training play a vital part in the new small homes for people with learning difficulties.

However, research has indicated that there can be particular problems in terms of job satisfaction and staff turnover. Some workers have claimed that 'personnel issues including recruitment, retainment and development of staff ranked highest as the most pressing problem' in a survey of 5,038 community homes in the United States.[5] Perhaps predictably, another worker has indicated that it might be easier to recruit staff if there was more adequate staff training, client training and support staff.[6]

Emphasizing a different point, we can also argue that those staff already in appointments are sometimes left to pick up methods of working with little or no in-service training. Some writers would argue that staff can become 'troubled helpers' as a result of insufficient relevant training and staff support.[7] It is not at all unreasonable to suggest that 'troubled helpers' can have deliterious effects on the client. Further research is needed to substantiate this hypothesis, but staff may need training in the skills of stress management.[8] Indeed, as we have already seen, recent research suggests increasing recognition of stress at work. Stress management training should help to alleviate some of the undesirable effects stress has on the well-being of staff and their work performance.

## WHY TRAINING AND TRAINING FOR WHAT?

When asking the question 'Why training?', it leads to consideration of 'Training for what?'. We could define this as the gap between where people are and where we want them to be. This implies that systematic strategies for training and development are required to fill that gap. First of all, however, we need to know what it is staff are training for so that appropriate programmes can be developed.

# Answering questions

Training is essentially an attempt to answer certain questions. Whether it is done in a whole package or elements, it is an attempted practical solution to a practical problem. However, these practical problems have to be conceptualized in a schema that helps us to answer questions such as: What is training? What are people required to train for? How is training evaluated? Is training enough?

A number of constructive attempts have already been made in this direction.[9] We could also argue that some training is better than no training at all, but this may be an irresponsible and unwarranted assumption. For if it is likened to 'a little knowledge is a dangerous thing', it can be argued that training of itself is not enough. There is certainly a mass of 'psychological' training achieving all sorts of things, but little of it is satisfactorily evaluated for its effectiveness. This training should not be discounted, but psychological approaches to staff training and development should also take into account the relationship between the individual learner *and* their environment. In other words, staff training and development from this viewpoint should be concerned with 'fitting' staff training to suit client needs and in differentially valued cultural contexts.

# Person-environment fit

Some writers have put forward a similar ecological analysis of staff training.[10,11] Put in simple terms, this can be said to mean a person–environment fit. If a cultural framework is used as a guide for staff training then an important criterion is met. Choices can be made about what training is required for any person and their present set of life circumstances.

Therefore, in adopting this perspective on training, staff training only makes sense when it is tied to a specific cultural context. This also suggests that we can decide what is valued and appropriate to learn. It arguably then helps us to decide what staff training is required to facilitate culturally valued behaviours. This approach would generate choices that are made for members of a particular culture. People with learning difficulties are part of this culture and these choices should be made available to them. This fits in nicely with the principles of normalization described by Wolfensberger and his colleagues.[12,13,14]

What has been written so far indicates that staff training is tied to a basic set of values. This is the service philosophy. For the purposes of this chapter we are making an assumption that the philosophy is based on the principles of normalization. Choice is inherent in these principles. The issue arising from this is one of advocacy and self-advocacy. Who makes the choices? What are the choices? How are the choices made?

## Who should have a say?

If we talk about a person-centred service then it follows that the service receivers should have a say or a choice in what is delivered to them. One writer has said: 'We are now living in the 1980s not the 1960s or 1970s and we want to see something new. Forget what's happened in the past, because you can't change the past but we can change the future.'[1] Training for staff will therefore produce a less effective service for the users unless we listen to them. We could claim that training should be demand-driven. But whose demands? Surely it has to be a balance between the ultimate service delivered and those needs of the supporters (staff) and the organization. It seems that this is possible only if the service organizations are flexible and creative in their management and structure.[9]

Another implication of this approach is that training is only one part of the practice and outcome of good service delivery. It would appear that research and recruitment also have large future roles to play in what happens before staff are selected for training and development. There is a need to be much more scientific in personnel selection to make training work. This means that job-fit is an important feature related to recruitment of staff. Staff need to be better matched or fitted to the job they are expected to do. Character as well as competence are prerequisites for any job performance.

Mismatches can take place in a number of ways. For example, a job advertisement not matching the philosophy of the service with principles of the employing organization; or, a job advertised setting out the organization's principles but selecting people who do not implement them. There needs to be informed psychological testing of prospective staff to supplement interviews. This should be based, among other things, on testing personality and values and attitudes of applicants for staff positions towards work with people who may have learning difficulties. Inappropriate selection of staff can lead to long-term problems in realizing the objectives of service organizations, and obstruct the effective application of service philosophies.[15,16]

Systematic psychological personnel selection will undoubtedly reduce the incongruence between service requirements and those staff who are trained to deliver service objectives. Incongruence between staff and any organization means difficulties in making change happen. Increasing incongruence in any changing service results in policies that simply will, in practice, not work.

One commentator in a recent television interview stated that the selection of staff was of vital importance to the success of his work at a school for very emotionally disturbed young people.[17] He was looking for people who were 'young, sensitive and flexible'. We see no reason to suppose that this same value should not apply to those supporting and facilitating the development of people with learning difficulties. The exception is the description 'young'; but certainly sensitive and flexible are attributes that we should be willing to select in potential staff for small group homes.

## Competence–performance fit

So far, therefore, we have postulated that there needs to be a match between the job environment and the staff person. Another type of match is what one can term the competence–performance fit. A person can be competent but not necessarily perform. Small group home staff also require a satisfactory supervision system to support competent performance of skills in which they have been trained. However, it is not always possible to monitor whether a competent person is performing well.[18,19]

If we accept these are important facets for recruitment and ongoing training and development, the primary purpose of the small group home must be to better equip staff to better understand the individual person and promote group living. The literature indicates there are enough competence models around. However, there is insufficient attention paid to organizing and providing staff support mechanisms. Even the most competent staff require, and rely on, others to carry out skilled work performances.[20]

Support for carers is referred to in Chapter 13. It follows that training forms a substantial part of this support. But other forms of support should be provided, such as regular supervision, monitoring of development and practice and staff meetings. All of this helps to better prepare staff to meet the demands of work.

# STAFF PREPARATION

There is evidence that training can increase staff morale and reduce staff turnover rates.[21,22] Research suggests that greater concern should be given to ensuring that prospective staff are well-oriented to the role that will be required of them. Training has an important part to play here. One writer has given an indication of this fact, and reports that there are very often assumptions made that new staff will learn both from on-the-job experience and some specific content areas through in-service training.[23] These assumptions are often not met and new staff have to 'learn to sink or swim with little or no assistance'.[22] This view lends additional support to the argument that it is recruitment, training and development that are essential to good service provision for people with learning difficulties.

Preparation of staff also means management involvement and commitment. Here, managers are likely to need support as well as providing supervision and helping their staff to develop. There are training implications here, too, for managers will need to acquire further skills in how to supervise and develop staff. Managers should be aware that training for the sake of training and responding in desperation to staff needs – just 'doing something' – will be a waste of everyone's energy, and is not an effective or efficient use of resources.[5]

## Managers as staff developers

What we have argued so far is a need for a continued development that involves even greater care in the recruitment and preparation of staff. There would seem to be more chance of success in these areas where a new community residential service is set up, especially where the service organization is committed to the idea of managers as staff developers.

We believe there can be a 'catch-22' situation, however, if insufficient attention is paid to selecting and recruiting staff to work in small residential settings. This raises the question of whether we should be looking for people with personal qualities that are suitable for this work, and for people who are 'trainable'. That is, people who are able to cope with personal change and, by implication, changes in the way the service may be delivered. This refers back to earlier comments about a more scientific method of staff selection and the flexibility of the person(s) subsequently appointed.

These comments presuppose that all members of staff, including managers, are in the first instance, new to the work. As this is highly unlikely and may even be undesirable, there will be a need for the re-training of many present staff.

This can take many forms but one method might be to target key people – i.e. the new managers of homes – and to train these people in the philosophy, values and practices of the new and preferred systems of providing care. A typical strategy would be to involve multidisciplinary conferences on the philosophy and policies and principles to be implemented. On the more practical side, conferences can be followed by workshops on formulating and applying particular training policies. More individualized work could follow on from this to help managers plan strategies for managing change. The key to making such training strategies achievable is a common commitment, vision and skill.[24] Without managerial and staff commitment to the service philosophy and its ensuing objectives, the quality of service delivered will fall short of its espoused excellence. Vision and skill are needed to deliver the service well and creatively.

If this is successful then managers will become more effective in their own practice and therefore better able to facilitate the development of their staff. This is by no means the only way to effective and efficient service provision, but it seems to us to provide a good basis for it and at the same time go some way towards maintaining good staff morale. It follows, therefore, that it is important for managers to acquire good supervision skills.

## Supervision and service strategy

There is growing evidence that supervision has a large part to play in maintaining effective staff behaviour and helping to develop behaviours required for good practice.[25] If it is possible, managers of new residential houses should have a sound knowledge of what they expect of their staff. Current and future employees will then have a realistic direction and become more accurately informed about the service performance expected of them.[26]

Clearly, sensitive supervision will have an important part to play in helping staff to maintain practice, to maintain competence and to maintain their service performance.[27] The whole point of supervision is to ensure performance effectiveness and high standards of service delivery. This is why it is important for management to have clear objectives for each member of staff. We regard this as important for a number of reasons:

- Supervision has to be linked with the service strategy.
- Supervision has to be linked with the previous points made about competence and performance.
- Supervision should ensure that staff acquire behaviours that lead to actual performance and the achievement of service objectives.

Supervision should also be a central part of a coherent service strategy related to the study days and any in-service training staff receive. It is important that members of staff are enabled to put their learning into practice. Supervision can also take place both on a formal and informal basis, planned or unplanned. But whichever form it takes it is essential that it does happen.[26]

Increasingly, managers will be the people who are training their staff to meet the individual needs of the people they are serving.[23] This also holds if advocacy and self-advocacy are to be treated with any seriousness. People's needs have to be met on an individual basis and the service itself will need to be flexible enough to allow for this. Similarly, flexibility should apply to each member of staff. They will have individual needs which may be best met through development by managers of small group homes.

# PHILOSOPHY OF CARE – THE CORNERSTONE FOR TRAINING STRATEGY AND POLICY

The first issue is that of identifying what training strategy we are using. Training strategies, whatever their complexion, should be based on a clear philosophy of care upon which any service to people with learning difficulties is based. Moreover, training strategy should be validated by applied research, and in some service organizations this is the case. For example, many organizations base their staff practices on the philosophy and principles of normalization.[28] When this has been established the philosophy of care can then be more easily translated into training policy and objectives. It is the training policy and objectives of the service organization that then must be pursued and put into operation in each unit.

However, complications can still arise out of apparently straightfor-ward training strategies and policies being pursued under the principled guise of normalization. For instance, it may be argued that staff training should be demand-driven. But driven by whom? The client? Ratepayers? The demands of the group with whom a person is living? Clearly, there are important distinctions to be made between philosophies of care, and what is to be included or left out of training strategies, which staff will operate the training policy and the place of the client in making choices to participate in such opportunities that are made available to them. Some authorities are only just beginning to set up community services in the form of small residential units, and these are questions they should be tackling with vigour, understanding and commitment.

# PERFORMANCE INDICATORS AND TRAINING

Performance indicators are another way of examining the efficacy of staff training. Evaluation can be made of the outcomes of training and their effects on service delivery. This is taking place in Buckinghamshire and will be conducted in one area of mental handicap.[29] Strategies for staff training and performance evaluation, however well-chosen, should also take into consideration the politics of mental handicap.[30] By this, we acknowledge that the training strategy or policy chosen is also heavily influenced by the beliefs of those running service organizations and in charge of small group homes.

Within such a scenario we therefore need to ask ourselves these questions. Are we operating a: rights-driven model, a staff-driven model, a consumer-driven model, or an organization-driven model?

## Rights-driven model

Are we developing training strategies that respect the protection of people's rights alone, without regard to social responsibilities, the wishes of the consumer and the wishes of the staff involved? To pursue this thinking to its conclusion may present too many difficulties for staff and service organization alike. The right to choose, a fundamental human right, may cause immense problems for staff members, mainly because of the way many services for people with learning difficulties are currently organized. Most people receiving services have not had the experience or opportunities of making wide-ranging choices. It seems to us in the present climate, that to adopt an exclusively rights-driven model, although laudable in its approach, would not be substantially supported by those working in the service and could lead to frustration, lack of job satisfaction, stress and poor service delivery; some of the very things staff training should aim to avoid. Yet, part of any training strategy operating from a human rights perspective must include staff work on how to offer, and enable clients to make, choices, safeguarding people's rights, helping them accept responsibility and how to take risks.

## Staff-driven model

What happens if a model is entirely produced and run to satisfy the needs of the service organization? Perhaps this is what has happened in some large institutions, as adaptation is necessary in order to survive within them and the regimes are often more supportive of staff than clients.[30] Perhaps this has happened more by default than design as many staff desire the freedom and autonomy to work creatively with people with learning difficulties. But this free-ranging role is often circumvented when only meeting the objectives of the service organization are paramount. Ironically, satisfying organizational priorities can deny staff and people with learning difficulties living in small group homes their individual human rights. Such an operation of training strategy and application of policy fails in practice to meet the needs of staff or the needs of the individual people living in the units. Service organizations that ignore the motivational needs of staff do so at their peril. Ignorance of this magnitude is detrimental to staff performance and by implication to the needs of clients.

## Consumer-driven model

If a consumer-driven approach were to be adopted then services as they are today would have to be radically altered. We are very keen to promote this idea as it seems to be a productive way forward if we are to serve people with learning difficulties in a better and effective way. One of the key problems here is that we only pay lip-service to this idea. On the one hand, service planners and deliverers state that the provision of services is designed and implemented to meet individual needs. On the other, the growing number of self-advocates with learning difficulties are denying this is always the case. People with learning difficulties or other problems need to be listened to, and be involved in planning either by self-representation or through citizen advocacy.[31] That is, by a representative or an individual person who has a learning difficulty, and who has no vested interest in the particular service organization offering services. People living in small residential units, and elsewhere, should be involved totally in what happens to them.

Naturally, if this were carried to its logical conclusion, it could well be that the service we end up with would be very different from that offered today. This is already happening and people with learning difficulties are being encouraged to participate in decision-making about the types of service they require, their wants and needs.[32,33,34] Of course, if this model is adopted then the implications for staff training take on a completely different perspective. It would probably be in response to actual needs, which may be so various as to even contradict any previously planned training strategy.

Admittedly, it may not always be easy to simply judge what is required for a person or group of persons with little or no verbal communication at their command. This taxes workers. Staff need to be creative and find ways, possibly through citizen advocacy, to interpret for, or with that person, the choices they wish to make and perform in their lifestyle. One way of doing this is to measure to what extent that person's lifestyle matches up to the opportunities available to the more privileged members of the community in which they are living.[35,36] Too often, we 'make do' and people with learning difficulties receive a second-class service. This is not to say that any one person is to blame for this situation; it has arisen for historical, political and sociological reasons. Fortunately, self-advocates are beginning to speak up and various 'People First' movements in the UK need encouragement to enable their voices to be heard. Service planners and developers need to listen and produce staffed services which are capable of providing relevant opportunities to meet 'consumer demands'. For example, at a recent self-advocacy conference, one person spoke up and asked for some sex education. This request had been turned down in the past but the larger group acknowledged her need and it was followed up.

It would be ideal to have a totally consumer-driven model, but this may not be a realistic possibility in the small residential community units. One reason for this could be that staff needs might be largely ignored. People with learning difficulties may well require social supports for some time. However, with this scenario consideration also has to be given to the staff helpers involved.

## Organization-driven model

If we consider what might happen in a staff-driven model the results may have a parity with those of an organizational model. The service to people with learning difficulties is not only about personal development of staff at the expense of the former. If staff needs were considered to the exclusion of the consumer then the service delivered to the client might be irrelevant. It would be a staffed service operating solely to satisfy the morale and well-being of staff. For example, if a group of staff suddenly decided they would operate a service in a custodial role and for them this meant easier management, then a reversion to a previous, less-valued service could occur. Training strategy and policy would become meaningless for those with learning difficulties and who wished to advocate alternative positions. Clearly, there are limitations to any training strategy or policy.

Of necessity, we have to arrive at a balance between principles and practice that takes into consideration the complexities of philosophy, training strategy, policy and its operation. Because of these complexities, at first sight, the task of assessing staff training needs appears to be insurmountable. This, in part, might account for the lack of any coherent national staff training strategies, as needs are constantly changing. Schemas have to be flexible to accommodate the changing demands of staff training.

## IDENTIFYING STAFF TRAINING NEEDS

Training strategies can be identified by establishing an acceptable fit between staff training and development needs and client needs. This produces a programme fit; a programme for people. The difficulty is that not only is each client an individual, but also each member of staff is an individual. Each person has individual needs to be met in order to produce an individual service for each person who receives the service. Of course, there will be commonly identified training needs and these will be referred to when the core curriculum is examined.

Another issue to be considered is development and training for what? So far the arguments in this chapter lead to the conclusion that training could be said to be a process of socialization within a particular culture.[37] What will be developed, therefore, from a training strategy and identified or assessed needs, will be programmes for people.

So how can we identify what staff training and development needs are?

In the first instance, this will depend on the kinds of past experience staff bring to the job. It is not necessarily dependent on whether people have qualifications or not. Having a qualification does not necessarily equate with competence or performance. The training received by staff may not be relevant to what is currently required for effective service delivery. Prioritizing needs is also crucial. Whether it is the expectation that all members of staff will have precisely the same training or whether it is more important for some than for others should be the decision of the manager. For example, if groupwork has been identified as a core element for training and all members of staff feel they need this skill, should they all be trained as groupworkers or would better use of human resources be made by having some people more proficient in these skills than others?

At some time during the planning stage of a service and the formulation of service objectives, translated into operational policies, it becomes important to list the tasks involved, and the staff skills required to fulfil these tasks will need to be implemented as part of the training strategy.

The assumption is made that these skills are those that staff will require and are those that should be performed. It is clear that staff require training for specific tasks but the benefit of this training to the client needs to be assessed. This is often a missing variable in research studies. Not enough time, so far, has been spent on evaluating benefits for clients. Training is often carried out and remains unevaluated except at end of training course level. Other studies indicate that where observation takes place to evaluate performance, staff performance levels do increase but subsequently decrease once observers have left.[25] On the whole, researchers do not carry out follow-up evaluations to assess the 'client' impact of training. Managers could be involved with researchers on a more long-term evaluation of the impact of staff training, and its short and longer term consequences.

Once the skills required by staff have been identified, it becomes a simpler task to identify staff training needs. At least, this seems to be the case if we accept that we can identify training needs through staff performance and development reviews. Examples have been given of what might happen if there is insufficient training or staff may not be sure of the performances expected of them.[38] It is also stated that it is often 'staff with the least initial training who have least access to subsequent training'.[38]

It is not unreasonable, therefore, to suggest that inexperienced and new members of staff should receive a great deal of training during the initial phases of their employment. This precept applies equally well to people with previous experience but who are unaccustomed to the new culture of care and are inexperienced in management procedures. When the process has begun and the outcomes have been identified through a sensible and flexible training strategy, then identification of staff training needs follows a more coherent pattern. Assessment of these needs can be made during supervision sessions, based on observation of practice and self-assessment; during staff meetings; and through a staff performance and development review system. The benefits of a system such as this will be considered later.

# Induction training

The initial phase of staff training is usually described as induction and forms the basis of the future service provided by staff to the people living in the house. It is very important that this initial training is well planned, well co-ordinated, implemented and evaluated. Good induction training, however, applies to all new staff; methods of enabling new staff to receive basic but essential information could be seen as one of the responsibilities of the manager. Training departments can also offer core courses in collaboration with colleges, as in the case of many social services departments. These help to fulfil the need for new staff to acquire knowledge, skills and attitudes received by other members of staff during an induction period.

One of the first considerations is who will plan the induction. This may be the multidisciplinary team, the training officer, the officer-in-charge or a combination of all three. Once the person(s) have been identified, it will be necessary to decide the duration of the induction course. Six to eight weeks have been recommended,[2] but the Winchester Health Authority, for example, decided that a two- to three-week initial induction period would be satisfactory. One reason that the course should not be too long is that the motivation and enthusiasm to start work can be drained by too much introduction to the work. Another way the duration of an induction course can be decided is by the scope of its objectives. Some new members of staff can judge the transmission of too much information in a course as 'confusing'. Also, skills which were demonstrated by trainers during the course may be forgotten and the benefits of the training may be wasted. It is one thing to try and assimilate information and another to practise it.

Therefore, careful consideration needs to be given to the purpose of the initial training package and as to how this will be followed up afterwards. Much will depend on the person(s) planning it. Our own preference for this initial training is to base it on values and attitudes, normalization, team-building and working towards ways of implementing the service operational policy. Understanding their staff roles and responsibilities and seeking out local resources may also form part of an induction. Coming to terms with our own values and attitudes early in the induction programme helps us to discover what it is like to receive services if we are disabled and devalued. All of this provides a realistic foundation from which to build a client-based service. If the purpose of the service is to help people with learning difficulties re-integrate into the community, then initially at least, staff will need to have some understanding of what this means to them, to the organization and mostly to the client.

The content of training should be focused on achieving these objectives. There may be times when this has to be flexible because the group of staff receiving the training may have different expectations which may be realistic to try and meet. It is also important during the initial training period, wherever possible, to include the people who will be living in the house. There are different paths to involvement; for example, when planning the day, the menus, and being able to find local resources. These should be fairly straightforward to organize and mean instant involvement for the person with a learning difficulty. It is also important that staff have time for themselves: to assimilate what they have learned; to begin building a team; and to get to know each other.

Another way of involving staff with residents is taken from a recent induction in Buckinghamshire Social Services. This took the form of a 'getting to know you' day. Each member of staff had to spend the day receiving the same services as a resident. In fact, they had to shadow the resident as it proved impossible to organize a more integrated day. During the ensuing discussion the following day and the evaluation of the course, it was found that this day had had a great impact on each member of staff. They saw the person in a different light and had much more understanding of what it is like to receive the same services being offered to people with learning difficulties. Some of the feedback helped to produce ideas for change. The 'getting to know you' idea is not new and has arisen from the work of others.[39] It can be thoroughly recommended as being of great value during any induction period.

Most of the staff skills needed to work with the people living in the house can be acquired and accommodated, perhaps even more successfully, once the house is in operation. This is particularly true if staff are given some information on coping with change. Transition is a difficult time for everyone and information on loss and bereavement is most helpful.[40] The experience gained after conducting several staff inductions in the Winchester Health Authority and Buckinghamshire Social Services seem to confirm this view.

## Content for induction training

We put forward a subjective list of contents for induction training as we perceive them, based on our own experience and discussions with colleagues and other professionals. This list is by no means conclusive, exhaustive or in order of priority, but it has been used to good effect in the past:

1. Introduction.
2. Getting to know the residents: life from their perspective.
3. Normalization: brief introduction using, for example, 'Lifestyles', and including some exercises on rights, choices, vicious circles, risk-taking and power.[41]
4. Introduction to the organization, service principles, operational policy or guidelines for practice.
5. Resource-finding exercise in the community.
6. Advocacy and self-advocacy.
7. Team-building.
8. Roles, tasks and responsibilities clarification.
9. Planning the day (with residents involvement).
10. Loss and bereavement including transition and adjusting to change.
11. Supervision.
12. The role of the key worker.
13. Communication, including listening and giving feedback.
14. Personal relationships and sexuality.
15. Working with families: an overview involving parents.
16. Working with other professionals: an overview using the multidisciplinary team (N.B. This can take place during the introduction so that the idea of a complete team can take place from the first day).
17. Budgeting.
18. Menu-planning with resident involvement.
19. Visits to relevant establishments.
20. Recording and administrative procedures.
21. Evaluation and future training needs.

The content is fairly comprehensive but as one of the objectives of an induction should be to orient staff to their job, then this type of introduction is very important. The other objective of substantial importance is teamwork – both within the unit and with others involved with the people living in the house. The theme of teamwork ought to be continuous throughout the course. Teamwork is central to the successful running of a house. It is essential that sound groundwork is laid for later effective teamwork to take place. Staff must learn to support one another, to trust, to be open and to confront one another. If this is unsuccessful, then the service delivered to the clients will be impaired. The whole team needs to be able to understand what the objectives are for individual people living in the house, what it is like to be that person and to help that person to be seen as a valued and accepted member of society. The whole staff team also needs to understand what the group needs are and to learn how to balance individual needs with group needs. This latter concern could also form part of an in-service training package.

## In-service training

It will be necessary to put in more training fairly quickly after an induction of this sort, which is largely attitudinal, informative and ideological. However, these needs have to be identified. This is particularly true as far as assessment, understanding behaviour and teaching new skills are concerned. Also, members of staff will need information on how to implement individual programme plans with the resident for whom they are the key worker. At some time during this second stage of the training strategy staff may need some refresher work on their perceptions of people with learning difficulties. This may be especially true if the people living in the house are presenting challenging behaviours.[42,43]

Staff may need training in how to cope with some of the stresses of the work. This can take the form of stress management programmes, and information about how stress can affect staff as individuals.[44,45] Staff need to see that there may be good reasons for apparently undesirable behaviours. This is particularly true if these occurrences coincide with moving into 'a new house'. It is not simply living in a new house that can be a problem. The loss of friends can lead to a period of mourning and readjustment. In these instances, care and understanding are essential. More specifically, happenings in the immediate vicinity can induce fear and phobias for the previously 'protected' handicapped person. Fear of dogs, cats, birds and other animals can lead to a broad spectrum of 'problem behaviours'.

Staff need to be able to differentiate perceptions of troubled persons from 'trouble-makers'. Desensitizing phobias should be the goal in these cases – not removal of privileges or home comforts. Staff themselves can begin to learn that behaviours often clearly and directly express how the individual feels about what is happening around them.[7,46] It can be a stressful time all round and people with learning difficulties need help to manage stressful situations. Meanwhile staff members may also need more help in how to offer 'their' people choices and to be able to accept the decisions they make.

This discussion leads us to state that ongoing development and training for staff should fit in with a client perspective of individual needs, so that the content of continuing education should include appropriate further knowledge and skill development. For example, if one person living in the house is unable to communicate using words then it would seem sensible for all members of staff to be trained in using an alternative form of communication. The converse suggests that there is no point in all members of staff learning an alternative communication style if all people living in the house can communicate adequately with words. So once again, it is important to prioritize staff training needs according to the needs of the individual.

Ongoing training should not just be about attending courses. Structured visits to other places of service delivery to people with learning difficulties, meeting peers at seminars and conferences, multidisciplinary workshops and distance learning, may well meet specific learning needs and be of great value.[47] This type of learning should not be confined to managers of homes, but other members of staff also should have opportunities to take part and be prepared to report back their views and findings to the whole team.

## Core curriculum

It is difficult to be overly specific about continuing education and in-service training and development. This position, however, makes sense and is justifiable. Being overly prescriptive would not fit in with the precepts of matching client, staff and organization needs. These are variables which are constantly changing. However, one writer has suggested a fairly comprehensive list of skills needed by staff working under the following headings: working with clients; working with professionals; working with families; management and organizational skills; skills in learning and acquiring information.[9]

These headings appear to form the basis of any core curriculum, but much thought needs to be given as to how the skills decided upon might be taught and in what order. There is a life-time of learning that could be decided upon under these headings and, hopefully, the client is not dependent upon an outcome while waiting for staff to be trained. Staff are working with people and if they have a good grounding in how to assess and teach people new skills with the right attitudes, motivation and creativity, then this should go some way towards solving this vast training problem. Most of the skills included in any core curriculum will be those that are offered on basic training courses, some of which take three years of full-time study to complete. So some pruning to essential skills is called for.

There is also a basic assumption that there are enough people around to carry out the training, and who are sufficiently acculturated to the radical changes that have taken place in the last few years. This may not always be true, especially as individual authorities have developed their own forms of training and time spans for meeting service objectives. Although patterns of training across the country may vary, one common way forward is to carry out continuous staff development and training in a multidisciplinary way. This has been argued for very strongly by some,[9] and it certainly seems to be a common way forward for providing more co-ordinated services to clients with learning difficulties.

It follows, therefore, that any core curriculum cannot be prescribed by a single individual and that consultation needs to take place on a fairly wide basis. This means, too, that nonprofessionals and professionals should work much more closely with each other.

It might be agreed by those in an educating role that there are certain basic skills that are essential to any member of staff working in small residential units. But as each unit will form its own culture, it might be that any amount of training will not alter staff performance. The social environment needs to be taken into consideration when designing any training programme.[11] Some of the basic skills are essential to developing relationships, but these need to be taught with due regard and consideration given to the context in which they will be used.

A case can be put forward for including in the core curriculum not only training for positive attitudes, motivation, creativity, and skills for developing relationships, but also skills which will help people with learning difficulties to become self-advocates. This would be particularly true if the service were based on the principle that the consumers should eventually be running their own services. It gives an alternative starting base. Another area in which staff need considerable help is developing skills to 'sell' other people.[48] This is particularly true for those members of staff helping people with learning difficulties to find employment.

Although training should be client-driven, trainers and planners will still make many decisions about what should be included in any training programme for clients. If, in an ideal world we were able to change all attitudes towards people with learning difficulties, then client training programmes would have a very different content. However, we are working with a situation that is not ideal and there are important basic skills that need to be learned.

# MULTIDISCIPLINARY CURRICULUM PLANNING TEAMS

In order to develop a less biased curriculum, training strategies and programmes can also be planned by a multidisciplinary team. This is the method currently used by the Winchester Health Authority. Teams should also consist of people who are directly involved in the client's lifestyle. Perhaps, 'multidisciplinary' may be a misnomer since this implies only professionals are involved in team decisions and actions. Other people need to be represented as well as professionals on any curriculum planning team so that outcomes reflect consumer involvement.

It may be that making space for the client's voice is a threatening and less efficient process both for consumers and professionals alike. However, there is no reason why someone who is receiving a service should not have a say in the way staff behave towards them. It may also make for more job satisfaction among staff to find they are not constantly struggling to implement ideas that are resisted by the very people they are trying to help.

Regarding reduced efficiency, we would be trading this off against greater relevance and effectiveness; surely the dream of every service manager.[49] Once it is accepted that there will be consumer representation on the curriculum planning team, the team can then work with other people such as a community nurse, a social worker, a psychologist, an officer-in-charge, a planner, a training officer, another therapist and a parent. It is important that these representatives have intimate knowledge of their clients so that a relevant curriculum can be devised *together* to meet these current needs. These teams will need to have clear terms of reference and to meet regularly. Meetings could comfortably be co-ordinated by the appropriate staff training officer as part of that role. Teams should also be able to discuss other issues such as new training methods and materials and new developments – acting as sources of information for each other so that training may be updated constantly. The team may also have the responsibility of monitoring what training takes place and could be used with some effectiveness for evaluating benefits. Another function of the team will be to report to the service development team their findings and recommendations for improvements in the service delivered to people with learning difficulties. This should enable planners to implement ideas that are pertinent to clients' needs. However, this also raises the complex question of how we match staff training to personal and service objectives.

## Staff performance and development review

One way of providing an answer to the above question is to implement a formal system of staff performance and development review (SPDR). This system should not replace staff supervision but should supplement it. If the service objectives have been clearly laid out with their inherent tasks and skills, it should be possible to measure how well these have been achieved by individual members of staff and to measure how well they are performing. Each member of staff should also have an opportunity to talk about their personal development and training goals. The gap that occurs between meeting the criteria to practise skills and complete tasks could then be filled by relevant training and development.

So how could it work? SPDR is another phrase for staff appraisal. Without a system such as this it becomes impossible to see where training and development is needed for each person. Time is set aside annually (or more often as agreed) for a discussion between a manager and a member of staff about the latter's performance and development. There should be a precise agenda and the staff person receiving the review should hear nothing that is really new during this time. Good and bad practice should have been talked about when it actually happened so it is not the disciplinary interview so many staff fear. It could be described both as a time for reflection and looking forward. The discussion can be recorded and agreed and signed by both manager and staff member. A separate section of the SPDR can also be completed regarding future training needs and subsequently forwarded to the training department.

Several benefits of the SPDR are immediately obvious. First, each member of staff has a defined time to discuss their own individual needs. This helps them to feel they are being listened to, valued and supported. Support of this kind should be continued throughout working life within a broader system of staff supervision. Second, it enables managers to see where the gaps are between staff performance and client needs. Third, it enables a training department to acquire an overall picture of what staff learning needs there are, and forms the foundation for future staff development programmes.

There is another spin-off from using a system such as this. It can be seen as an individual programme plan for each member of staff. Managers should enable their staff to see the benefits of this and how it was achieved. They can then point out how this method could be used for people with learning difficulties – involving them all the way in the planning of their own individual training and development. It is another method of realizing how important it is to involve people in the planning of their own lifestyles.

The SPDR system enables managers to feedback to planners information which can be used for future service developments. Staff development officers should also commit themselves to liaising closely with the service development team. They are the link personnel between the service planners, managers and the field operation of the service.

## MULTI-AGENCY TRAINING

Multi-agency training is not a new concept but the practical application of it is still in its infancy. The Jay report recommended that there should be a shared model of training that involved staff working in both the health service and local authorities.[50] Much has been written about this and we do not propose to elaborate further here. With a few exceptions, we still seem to be a long way from common interdisciplinary basic training. There is, however, progress in this area. For instance, some health authorities such as the Isle of Wight and Winchester, second staff to the Certificate in Social Service (CSS). A recent draft report prepared by the English National Board and the Central Council for Education and Training in Social Work (CCETSW) has also proposed some alternative models to bring joint training nearer.[51]

On the post-basic side there is also optimism. The All Wales Strategy has meant that a post-qualifying joint training course has been implemented successfully for qualified staff from both health and social service settings. It is likely that a similar course will take place in Hampshire. It is essential that staff train together if they are to share a common care culture and support people with learning difficulties more effectively.

There are other avenues which should be explored such as CSS mentioned above and the In-Service Course in Social Care. This is a pre-qualifying generic course. The Winchester Health Authority has seconded some staff to this course but it is not generally used by health authorities. Most of the CCETSW validated courses are supported by social services staff and staff from voluntary agencies.

In northern Scotland there is currently a project underway based on the Co-operation in Training Initiative.[52] The project provides a programme of separate and shared training opportunities for the nursing and social work professions at the qualifying and post-qualifying level.[53] Some more local in-service courses could be shared by both statutory and voluntary organizations. This can be made possible through good liaison between different training departments. It has practical benefits for staff members who can share experiences, discuss practices and exchange views and ideas.

Another way of promoting this idea is to involve the CMHT.[54] Using the team as a base from which shared training evolves means that health and social services can work together. This should enable the idea of joint or shared training to be dispersed throughout each district health authority.

Yet another way forward in joint training is to make more use of colleges of education. For example, in Buckinghamshire the college of higher education has appointed a tutor with particular responsibility for mental handicap, as part of the Oxford Regional Health Authority's 'Care in the Community' initiative. One function of the post holder will be to liaise between health and social services to enable them to undertake more shared staff training in the colleges. An advantage of employing a person with this purpose lies in the challenge of obviating biases towards either nursing or social work and promoting a shared vision and purpose among staff in training.

There are also opportunities for shared learning through the use of distance learning packages. For example, the recent Open University package 'Patterns for Living' lends itself both to individual work and to the use of group discussions which can involve staff from different agencies.[55]

The Independent Development Council recommended exchanges between staff from different agencies.[56] The benefits include helping personnel acquire new knowledge and develop better working relationships between groups of staff with different backgrounds.

It is clear, then, that the current training (CSS/RNMH) needs examination to identify what must happen to closer align the curriculum to meet the service objectives for people with learning difficulties within society. The arguments and the issues that we have made for staff in training will also apply to those who lead and manage the service.

However shared training is approached, it is vital to the development of services for people with learning difficulties that students and staff share the same culture of caring. Supervision and training should act as catalysts for genuine collaboration between staff and services.

## CONCLUSIONS AND IMPLICATIONS

It seems to be clear from many types of research that staff training is not an answer to all problems concerned with supporting people with learning difficulties.[9] However, it does have an important part to play along with other recognized practices, including behavioural psychology, and clear organizational and personal supports. Staff training can be effective only when philosophies, policies and personnel systems in service organization are understood and accepted, and staff have the commitment to make them work.

In this area, recruitment using psychological tests and selection methodologies would seem to be a significant issue in future staff training. Staff selection needs to be improved. This will undoubtedly increase the pool of trainable staff and our confidence in achieving service objectives.

Role clarity has a major influence on morale.[37] This can be facilitated through staff development. Roles, priorities and goals should be clarified at every level in the health and local authorities. As Bailey observed in Chapter 13, role ambiguity can lead to stress for people working in small units. Discussions are needed to clarify these problems so that staff have some idea of where they are going and what is expected of them. Training will be futile if some of the above problems are not resolved.

With the advent of more self-advocacy and citizen advocacy, role clarity becomes even more important. As people with learning difficulties demand different services, so will staff have to learn new ways of responding to these demands. All of this suggests a major transition in attitudes, behaviour and service practices. During this time staff in small homes will need a clear service structure within which to work. If not, they may feel unsupported and hastily provide pseudo solutions to real problems. We have been made acutely aware of this point:[32]

> Each type of advocacy has its use. There is no one model. But we have to be careful because advocacy could become a symbol of spurious unity. It could lead us to pretend that conflicts have been solved when they have not.

Moreover, regular and systematic evaluation needs to be carried out to look into the effectiveness of staff training in the longer as well as in the short-term:[56]

> There is considerable evidence that the benefits of in-service training may have only a limited effectiveness and that the effects may be short-lived. Consideration needs to be given as to how the benefits of training can become more long-term. Continuing staff support may be one way of ensuring that the benefits of training are maintained.

A word of caution seems necessary: just as we should not be role-bound, so we should not become training-bound. We should treat people as people. We should avoid becoming bound up with inherited training and methods cycles from the past. To achieve this we should continue to develop a genuine person-based approach to staff training. The first step is to find out what people with learning difficulties want to do and learn. The advocacy movement provides one way forward.

Yet the balance to be achieved between staff training and user needs is a fine one. Efficient staff training is likely to be ineffective training if the service organization cannot 'deliver' the services required by the consumer population.

## POSTSCRIPT

Since the completion of this chapter, the Disabled Persons (Services, Consultation and Representation) Act 1986 has become law (see Chapter 2).[57] Already some sections of the Act have been implemented. It forms the basis for a significant and strategic development, and a service based on advocacy and on valid consumer priorities. The implications for staff training are too numerous to detail here. However, a summarized reading of the Act suggests the first point of departure is to acquire information from consumers about what sort of service they want.[58] It is hoped the client advocacy movement will play a central part in providing authorized representatives for those people with learning difficulties. The training required by advocates and indeed by staff are what we would broadly term 'client consultation skills' – the skills needed to support clients in identifying and making decisions and participating in shaping future service provision.

# REFERENCES

1. Bourlet, G. (1987) in Hersov J. and Cooper D. (eds.) *We Can Change the Future. Self-Advocacy for People with Learning Difficulties: A Staff Training Resource*, National Bureau for Handicapped Students, London.
2. Ward, L. (1984) Planning for People. Developing a Local Service for People with Mental Handicap: 1. Recruiting and Training Staff, Project Paper No. 47, King's Fund Centre, London.
3. Ward, L. and Wilkinson, J. (eds.) (1985) *Training for Change, Staff Training for An Ordinary Life*, King's Fund Centre, London.
4. King's Fund Centre (1982) *An Ordinary Life. Comprehensive Locally Based Residential Services for Mentally Handicapped People*, Project Paper No. 24, King's Fund Centre, London.
5. Bruininks, R.H., Kudla, M.J., Wieck, C.A. *et al.* (1980) Management problems in community residential facilities, *Mental Retardation*, June, pp. 125–30.
6. Humm-Delgardo, D. (1979) Opinions of community residence staff about their work responsibilities, *Mental Retardation*, October, pp. 50–1.
7. Bailey, R., Matthews, F. and Leckie, C. (1986) Feelings – The way ahead in mental handicap, *Mental Handicap*, Vol. 14, No. 2, pp. 65–7.
8. Bailey, R. (1987a) *Coping with Stress in Caring* (2nd edit.), Blackwell Scientific Publications, Oxford.
9. Hogg, R. and Mittler, P. (eds.) (1987) *Staff Training in Mental Handicap*, Croom-Helm, London.
10. Landesman-Dwyer, S., Sackett, G.P. and Kleinman, J. S. (1980) Relationships of size to resident and staff behavior in small community residences, *American Journal of Mental Deficiency*, Vol. 85, No. 1, pp. 6–17.
11. Landesman-Dwyer, S. and Knowles, M. (1987) Ecological analysis of staff training in residential settings, in R. Hogg and P. Mittler (eds.), *Staff Training in Mental Handicap*, Croom Helm, London.
12. Bank-Mikkelsen, N.E. (1980) Denmark, in R.J. Flynn and K.E. Nitsch (eds.), *Normalization, Social Integration and Community Services*, University Park Press, Baltimore.
13. Nirjfe, B. (1980) The Normalization Principle, in R.J. Flynn and K.E. Nitsch (eds.), *Normalization, Social Integration and Community Services*, University Park Press, Baltimore.
14. Wolfensberger, W. (1980) A brief overview of the principle of normalization, in R.J. Flynn and K.E. Nitsch, *Normalization, Social Integration and Community Services*, University Park Press, Baltimore.
15. Bailey, R. (1987b) *Consulting for Change and Making it Happen*. In Press.
16. Dubin, R. (1976) *The Handbook of Work Organization and Society*, Rand McNally, Chicago.
17. Bettleheim, B. (1987) BBC2 Television interview, February 3.
18. Bailey, R. (1974) *What Are We Doing When We Describe Things?* unpublished MA thesis, University of Dundee.
19. Greene, J. (1972) *Psycholinguistics: Chomsky and Psychology*, Penguin, London.
20. Cartwright, D. and Zander, A. (1970) *Group Dynamics: Research and Theory*, Tavistock Publications, London.

21. Lakin, K.C., Bruininks, R.H., Hill, B.K. *et al.* (1982) Turnover of direct care staff in a national sample of residential facilities for mentally retarded people, *American Journal of Mental Deficiency*, Vol. 87, No. 1, pp. 64–72.
22. Pritchard, C. (1985) Maintaining morale through staff development and training, *Social Work Monographs,* Norwich.
23. Ebert, R.S. (1979) A training program for community residence staff, *Mental Retardation*, October, pp. 257–9.
24. Mansell, J. and Porterfield, J. (1986) *Staffing and Staff Training for a Residential Service*, Talking Point No. 4, CMH London.
25. Ivancic, M.T., Reid, D.H., Iwata, B.A. *et al.* (1981) Evaluating a supervision program for developing and maintaining therapeutic staff-resident interactions during institutional care routines, *Journal of Applied Behavior Analysis*, Vol. 14, No. 1, pp. 95–107.
26. Schiers, W., Giffort, D. and Furticamp, E. (1980) Recruitment source and job survival for direct care staff, *Mental Retardation*, December, pp. 285–7.
27. Jones, I. (1979) Sensitive supervision, *Community Care*, 1 November, pp. 25–6.
28. Wolfensberger, W. and Tullman, S.A. (1983) Brief outline of the principle of normalization, *Rehabilitation Psychology*, Vol. 27, pp. 131–45.
29. Harper, J. (1987) Personal communication, Independent Consultant, NHS Training Authority.
30. Ryan, J. and Thomas, F. (1980) *The Politics of Mental Handicap,* Penguin, London.
31. Forrest, A. (1986) *Citizen Advocacy: Including the Excluded,* Sheffield Advocacy Project.
32. Berry, D. (1987) Power to the plea. Society tomorrow, *The Guardian*, 4 Marcy, p. 13.
33. Hersov, J. and Cooper, D. (1987) *We Can Change the Future. Self-Advocacy for People with Learning Difficulties. A Staff Training Resource,* National Bureau for Handicapped Students, London.
34. Williams, P. and Shoultz, B. (1982) *We Can Speak for Ourselves,* Souvenir Press, London.
35. Flynn, R.J. and Nitsch, K.E. (1980) *Normalization, Social Integration and Community Service,* University Park Press, Baltimore.
36. Tyne, A. (1981) *Staffing and Supporting a Residential Service*, CMH, London.
37. Berger, P.L. and Luckman, T. (1968) *The Social Construction of Reality*, Penguin, London.
38. Firth, H. and Myers, M. (1985) Supporting staff in community services, *Mental Handicap*, Vol. 13, September, pp. 100–102.
39. Brost, M.M. and Johnson, T.Z. (1982) *Getting to Know You*, c/o Wisconsin Coalition for Advocacy, 2 West Mifflin Street, Madison, Wisconsin 53702.
40. King's Fund (1981) *The Right to Grieve*; *A Leaflet to help mentally handicapped people who are bereaved,* King's Fund Centre, London.
41. Brown, H. and Alcoe, J. (1984) *Lifestyles for People with Mental Handicaps: A Staff Training Exercise Based on Normalisation Principles,* ESCATA, Brighton, Sussex.
42. Holden, P. (1987) Personal communication, District Psychologist, East Suffolk Health Authority, St Clement's Hospital, Ipswich.

43. Maher, P. (1986) Ensuring Quality in Services for People with Challenging Behaviours, in L. Ward (ed.), Getting Better All the Time? Issues and strategies for ensuring quality in community services for people with mental handicap, Project Paper No. 66, King's Fund Centre, London.
44. Bailey, R. (1985) Autogenic Regulation Training (ART), Time and the Emotion-Physical Stress of Student Nurses in General Training, unpublished PhD thesis, University of Hull.
45. Sines, D. (1985) Personal communication, Director of Nursing Services, Winchester Health Authority.
46. Eckman, P. and Friesen, W.V. (1976) Measuring facial movements, *Environmental Psychology and Non-Verbal Behavior*, Vol. 1, No. 1, pp. 56–75.
47. Duberley, J. (1985) Continuing education – whose responsibility? *The Professional Nurse*, October, pp. 4–6.
48. Setchfield, A. (1987) Personal communication, Manager, Castlefield Centre, Cardiff.
49. Drucker, P. (1979) *Management*, Pan Books, London.
50. DHSS (1979) Report of the Committee of Enquiry into Mental Handicap Nursing and Care (Chairman, Mrs Peggy Jay), CMND 7468–I, HMSO, London.
51. English National Board and Central Council for Education and Training in Social Work (1987) *Cooperation in Qualifying and Post-Qualifying Training Mental Handicap Report of the ENB/CCETSW Joint Working Group*, draft report.
52. GNC/CCETSW (1982) *Co-operation in Training. Part 1 – Qualifying Training. Report of the Joint Working Group on Training for Staff Working With Mentally Handicapped People*, GNC, London.
53. Osborne, A. and Wakeling, C. (1985) Co-operation in training, *Senior Nurse*, Vol. 6, December, pp. 21–3.
54. National Development Group for the Mentally Handicapped (1976) *Mental Handicap: Planning Together*, DHSS, London.
55. Open University (1986) *Patterns for Living*, OUP, Milton Keynes.
56. Independent Development Council for People with Mental Handicap (1984) *Next Steps, An independent review of progress, problems and priorities in the development of services for people with mental handicap*, IDC, London.
57. DHSS (1986) *The Disabled Persons (Services, Consultation and Representation) Act*, Chapter 33, HMSO, London.
58. Brandon, A. and Brandon, D. (1987) *Consumers as Colleagues*, MIND, London.

# Conclusion
# Towards Comprehensive Services for People with Mental Handicaps
*David Sines*

The development of comprehensive services for people with mental handicaps will involve considerable effort and an investment in innovative thought and attitude change. Services will not develop of their own volition and the search for new solutions will require dynamic leadership, charisma and above all confidence in futuristic perspectives and service models.

There is no greater advocate for service change than the consumers themselves, and it is from them that we should take the lead in approaching the future with renewed enthusiasm. To date, many people with mental handicaps have proved that they are able to adapt to life in the community given the necessary encouragement and support to do so meaningfully. Many have demonstrated their ability to integrate within naturally occurring neighbourhood networks, and have gratefully appreciated being able to make choices from a range of opportunities which are enriched beyond the 'walls of the old institution'. Some continue to choose to spend their leisure time and working lives with others with similar needs, but many at least have the opportunity to make choices in designing their lives and in determining how to spend them.

People are beginning to recognize that the concept of 'community care' requires more than 'lip-service' to facilitate its success, and there are many examples of the emergence of a true neighbourhood ethos developing to involve people with mental handicaps in the daily life of the local community. Some have attempted to superimpose a 'community-based culture' on existing networks and have provided specialist support services which have ignored or failed to integrate with those facilities which exist for others. One measure of the success of community care will be the extent to which people are accepted within their neighbourhoods and the only way that this may be achieved is by exposing each other to local services and sharing in the life of the local community.

People need to believe they are valued and that they are contributing to the life of their community. True, some may choose to distance themselves from this reciprocal process, and for them a choice must be provided, but for most people, to belong and to be accepted by neighbours will be an understandable requirement. To achieve this, people with mental handicaps will require the support of their families, carers and society. The need to enlist their support presents a major problem for many services.

A programme of public education is required to enable people to understand and to become involved in the establishment and assimilation of people with mental handicaps within local neighbourhoods and friendship groups. Consumers must not be passive in this process and should be encouraged to design and manufacture their own 'acceptance programmes', since their greatest asset will be themselves and the opportunity to demonstrate their own personalities and contributions to their neighbours. There is no doubt, however, that without a deliberate and co-ordinated preparation programme the process of valued integration will be harder to achieve.

The move to the community represents a major life change for many people and for their carers. People adapt slowly to change and in many cases there has been obvious initial resistance. Questions have been raised in respect of the advantages of 'community care' and the 'degree of risk' to which people are exposed. All life changes entail an element of calculated risk, and this is no less the case for people with mental handicaps, their families and carers. Sensitive preparation is required for all people anticipating changes in their lives; care in the community programmes should ensure that an individually designed preparation programme is provided for each person involved in the change.

All services should be designed to meet the needs of the proposed client group. Consequently, there may be as many solutions as there are needs and standardized 'packages' may not be the most appropriate way to design services. A range of services should be made available to facilitate choice and to enable the development of individual service design. The basis for matching individual needs to services should be the 'individual programme planning' or 'life planning system' which should take account of the views and opinions of as many people as possible (who are identified as being significant in the person's life). Obviously, not all needs will be met within available resources, but comprehensive services should ensure that they are identified and should aim to provide appropriate services which approximate as closely as possible to identified action plans. Any process should allow consumers to make their own choices and should not limit opportunities by the nature of the service system used.

Staff must also be considered in the community care equation and will need to approach new challenges with confidence. They will require individually designed development plans which identify their skills and needs and which are matched by an intensive investment in staff training programmes. Community care will present a range of new opportunities for some staff who may have practised for many years in very different environments and with limited resources. The philosophy of care may also be different and will require a readjustment or change in attitude for some people before they can undertake the responsibilities of their new role in the community. Such challenges may be faced with optimism, and experience has proven that the majority of staff are only too willing to embark on 'transition courses' and to adapt their skills within a new framework of care practice.

Some staff may feel particularly concerned to leave their familiar surroundings, and managers must accept that some people may not wish to join the majority in the 'community'. For those that feel unable to make the adjustment (for whatever reason), acknowledgement of their choice and personal interests must be made. Others may find the move stressful or threatening, and may require support during the initial stages of transition. This may be particularly true for staff who transfer between agencies and have to adjust to very different conditions of service. Individual training packages and counselling services should be available to people who require them, provided by managers who have had the foresight to invest in an appropriately skilled and highly motivated workforce.

The move to the community will also challenge traditional working patterns and professional boundaries for all staff. Previous allegiance to a unidisciplinary approach to care will be replaced by a multi-agency ethos built on the premiss of responding to the identified needs of the client group. Inevitably, this will have a major change on staff education programmes; the emergence of shared training, related to local needs and validated by national training bodies, will be required to service the demands of a comprehensive, community-based service. Evidence has already been seen regarding the opportunities available to staff in adopting such an approach and, rather than restricting career advancement, a range of new and exciting challenges are being facilitated for more adventurous staff members.

## SUMMARY OF RECOMMENDATIONS

This book has presented a charter of basic rights and opportunities for people with mental handicaps in the community and has identified the main components of a comprehensive service for them and their families:

- People with mental handicaps should have the same basic rights, human value and where possible the same responsibilities as other members of society.
- People with mental handicaps should have access to an appropriate individual programme planning system and should have a 'named person' of their choice to assist them in the realization of the aims and objectives of their life plan.
- All local services should accept that the provision of additional responsibilities in the community may also entail calculated risks, and provide local policies and guidance to all staff and others involved in the project.
- A policy of positive discrimination should be endorsed for people with mental handicaps in the community and should be accompanied by a comprehensive programme of public education and community awareness.
- People with mental handicaps should continue to have unrestricted access to a range of specialist skills to assist them in realizing their maximum potential in the community.
- Existing services should acknowledge that they have a moral and professional responsibility to invest appropriately in the provision of training and development programmes for staff aiming to work in evolving services in the community.
- Staff working with people with mental handicaps should be encouraged to share their skills and to 'train' together wherever possible for the ultimate benefit of people with mental handicaps and their families.
- People with mental handicaps, their families and significant others should be involved in the design of future services and consulted regularly at all stages of the planning process.
- The concept of a multidisciplinary and multi-agency teamwork

approach should be adopted for all community-based services for people with mental handicaps.

- The development of a spectrum approach to the provision of residential services for people with mental handicaps should be emphasized, thus maximizing the range of opportunities and choice available to them.
- All staff working in community-based services should work within specifically identified and agreed standards of performance which are monitored regularly by service managers.
- For those people who cannot easily articulate their needs, someone should be provided to represent them and their interests.
- Normal services should be used wherever possible to promote a feeling of 'community presence'; specialized services should only be provided where absolutely necessary and should be as unobtrusive as possible.
- Maximum co-ordination of services should be aimed for within the provision of local service design.
- Opportunities should be provided for people with mental handicaps to engage in a range of valued daily activities (including work) and these should be provided in such a way as to enhance their integration in the community.
- Encourage access to a wide range of integrated, recreational and leisure activities for people with mental handicaps in the community.
- Children with mental handicaps should have access to a range of services provided for all children in the community and should not be discriminated against in respect of their educational or residential needs.
- Elderly people with mental handicaps should receive services which respect their age and position in society and should expect appropriate support to live with dignity in a manner to which they have become accustomed.
- People with mental handicaps should receive adequate finances to live as independently as they choose and should not be restricted in their range of choices and opportunities by inflexible and devalued award systems.
- Opportunities should be provided for people with mental handicaps to 'make and choose' their own friends and to engage in meaningful interpersonal relationships and thereby enrich their lives.
- Planning procedures should be revised so that small, community-based projects can be established without prejudice and rejection of the incoming dwellers.
- Foster with a range of local and government departments access to a

wide range of community-based housing schemes to provide people with mental handicaps with additional and unrestricted housing opportunities.

## TOWARDS THE FUTURE

People will raise many objections and identify obstacles whenever care in the community projects are recommended. Some will challenge its premiss and others will pay 'lip-service' to its development. However, there is an enormous difference between acknowledging a new philosophy and realizing it in practice. This book has presented several examples of how this transition can be made and has challenged traditional views and opinions on behalf of people with mental handicaps, their families and their carers. Most of the projects described started locally with a group of consumers and professionals seizing the opportunity to reshape the pattern of service delivery for people with mental handicaps. Every person involved in the care of this client group has a responsibility and active part to play in realizing more appropriate services within the heart of local communities and neighbourhoods.

This is where community begins, and people with mental handicaps are already demonstrating the valued contribution they have to offer to their neighbours and friends as valued members of society. Some people remain unconvinced that this is the most appropriate way forward; what is required is a concerted effort to widen their horizons towards greater acceptance of the basic principles of community care. To accompany this there must also be the reassurance that new services will be closely monitored and evaluated in respect of service quality and client accomplishments, and must be appropriately financed.

In conclusion:

- All services must be client-led and individually designed.
- All services must be flexible in design and adaptable to local needs and circumstances.
- All services must be· dynamic, continually changing in response to developments in client needs/local resource patterns.
- Services must also facilitate changes in attitudes and practice in order to maintain those principles identified in the maintenance of 'an ordinary lifestyle'.

The importance of the process of social change and the part each person has to play in its manufacture, pace and design cannot be underestimated, and this book ends with a quotation from Trevor Clay, General Secretary of the Royal College of Nursing, which encapsulates this theme:[1]

> For economic and social reasons, society is beginning to examine the way it provides health and social services to its people, how much it can afford and what role the professions should play. That timetable is much shorter than many seem to realize and unless we can enter the debate with the two essential ingredients I have described – a clear view of our own ideology and a knowledge of what the consumers want – then we will risk having change imposed upon us.

# REFERENCES

1. Clay, T. (1986) Unity for change? Katherine Raven Lecture, June 1985, Royal College of Nursing, London, *The Journal of Advanced Nursing*, Vol. 11, pp. 21–33.

# Index